STATISTICS IN THE LAW OF EVIDENCE

This book evaluates the role played by statistical evidence in litigation. Despite the increasing prevalence of statistical evidence in modern litigation, how such evidence should be admitted and used by courts is often inconsistent and widely criticised. Accepting that statistical evidence can lead to more accurate decisions, the book proposes criteria that could allow courts to decide that statistical evidence is good for fact-finding.

The many and varied scholarly debates regarding statistical evidence have by and large avoided judicial attention. Unlike previous works, this book contextualises those debates in the language and practice of evidence law, focusing principally on Australia, as well as the UK and the USA.

It does so by identifying that the controversy around statistical evidence follows the three-tiered statistical syllogism underlying statistical inference: first, whether statistical evidence is capable of establishing an association between phenomena in a state of nature; second, inferring that phenomena to an individual from the general association; and third, whether statistical evidence can be sufficient for proof of contested facts. Objections are said to arise at each level of this syllogism and, by mapping these objections onto evidence law, the book argues that a pathway for the judicial evaluation of statistical evidence can be constructed.

Statistics in the Law of Evidence

Nicholas Lennings

• HART •
OXFORD • LONDON • NEW YORK • NEW DELHI • SYDNEY

HART PUBLISHING

Bloomsbury Publishing Plc

Kemp House, Chawley Park, Cumnor Hill, Oxford, OX2 9PH, UK

1385 Broadway, New York, NY 10018, USA

29 Earlsfort Terrace, Dublin 2, Ireland

HART PUBLISHING, the Hart/Stag logo, BLOOMSBURY and the Diana logo are trademarks of Bloomsbury Publishing Plc

First published in Great Britain 2024

A catalogue record for this book is available from the British Library.

A catalogue record for this book is available from the Library of Congress.

Library of Congress Control Number: 2024940201

ISBN: HB: 978-1-50995-733-0
ePDF: 978-1-50995-735-4
ePub: 978-1-50995-734-7

Typeset by Compuscript Ltd, Shannon

FOREWORD

Statistical analysis in the forensic legal context usually involves the analysis of surveys, observational studies or experiments to draw cause and effect inferences. There are various litigation scenarios where this interface between the scientific and legal methods can manifest itself. So, for example, epidemiology may be used to infer a cause and effect relationship between exposure to a chemical, dust or radiation and a subsequent disease or injury. Event studies may be used in shareholder class actions to infer the materiality and price effects of the non-disclosure of allegedly material information to the market. Multiple linear regression analysis may be used in price fixing collusion cases in order to identify whether a price change in the posited cartel period is referable to the existence or implementation of the asserted collusion. Generally, there are unbounded possibilities for the utilisation of statistical evidence in civil and criminal cases.

The present work by Dr Lennings is a fine contribution to this field. He has engaged in a detailed analysis of how statistics can be and should be used in evidence. And in his discussion he has nicely blended theoretical concepts with the practical aspects and problems of such use, but without descending into too much specialised statistical theory or context-specific quantitative tools.

The author provides a comprehensive treatment of various dimensions to the use of statistics, including distinguishing between their use in dealing with general causation as compared with the question of specific causation involving inferences tailored to or available to be drawn in an individual case.

The author also discusses various contentious topics, including whether there should be a reliability threshold for the admissibility of expert evidence, particularly in jury cases. Of course, in judge-only cases any reliability difficulties can comfortably be addressed as a question of weight rather than admissibility. There is also some reference to the use of Bayes' theorem, although there are serious forensic problems in its application even accepting that its underlying tenets have intuitive appeal. There is also the question of whether it should only be used to update one's belief system, rather than as an objective measure of the probability of a hypothesis.

The author also rightly recognises that statistical evidence may be only one aspect of different qualitative and quantitative expert and lay evidence that may need to be synthesised by the trier of fact in assessing causation.

This excellent work is thorough in its treatment of its topic. I well recommend this text to legal practitioners and judges who have to grapple with using and analysing statistical evidence. Further, legal academics working or interested in this field will find the author's insights to be very informative.

Justice Jonathan Beach

PREFACE

Quite some time ago now, while dealing with copious amounts of expert evidence, I had what I thought was an original idea: the reliance by experts on statistical evidence is no different to coincidence reasoning. If so, why is it that experts are (usually) entitled without objection to rely on such evidence, especially in circumstances where reliance on such studies may be problematic?

It would turn out that this idea was neither original nor especially well formed. But it sparked an interest that has carried me all the way to this book, a decade later.

My goal for this book was to explain how scholarly theories about statistical evidence can be relevant to the practice of law. From the beginning of modern scholarship on this topic there has been a clear divergence between the practical manner by which statistics are dealt with in court and what academics have to say on the topic. That divergence is only becoming more and more apparent. What I hope I have achieved in this book is a reconciliation of those two streams of thought such that the relevance of academic theories about statistical evidence can be contextualised into objections to and arguments for the admissibility and use of statistical evidence in court.

ACKNOWLEDGEMENTS

This book started life in earnest as my doctoral dissertation at Oxford. I am forever grateful for the patient and wise counsel of my supervisor, Professor Roderick Bagshaw. The time and effort that he invested in me was substantial, and the project would not have been possible without him.

The majority of the thesis and the book was completed after I had returned to full time practice as a solicitor at Quinn Emanuel in Sydney. I cannot say that this was especially conducive to the timely completion of either form of the project. But my time at QE did provoke a number of important questions that I think contributed positively to the book.

It has been a pleasure to work with the team at Hart. I am especially grateful to Kate Whetter, who was instrumental in bringing the book to publication. I would also like to thank Verity Stuart and Ceri Warner for their guidance through the publication and copyediting process.

No person is an island. Outside of the professional context, I have benefited greatly from the love and support of my family. I must profusely thank my parents for reviewing more drafts of this work in all its forms than any sane person ever should. Their feedback throughout the thesis and book phases of this project have been invaluable. My wife and children, Alexander, Henrik and Andersen, have been on this journey with me throughout the writing of this book. I am forever grateful for their patience and their love.

CONTENTS

ABBREVIATIONS

ALM	acral lentigious melanoma
APA	American Psychological Association
BME	Black and Minority Ethnic
CSA	Core Skills Assessment
FCA	Federal Court of Australia
FCAFC	Full Court of the Federal Court of Australia
HCA	High Court of Australia
LR	likelihood ratio
NSE	naked statistical evidence
NSWCA	New South Wales Court of Appeal
QCCS	Superior Court of Quebec
RAB	reasonable apprehension of bias
RCT	randomised controlled trials
RMP	random match probability
RR	relative risk
SIDS	sudden infant death syndrome
UKSC	UK Supreme Court

TABLE OF CASES

AUSTRALIAN CASES

CANADIAN CASES

UNITED KINGDOM CASES

UNITED STATES CASES

TABLE OF STATUTES AND OTHER LEGAL DOCUMENTS

Introduction

A plaintiff[1] (*p*) alleges that her injury (Y) was caused by the negligent conduct of a tortfeasor (*t*) who released a contaminant (X). The causal pathway between X and Y cannot be shown by direct evidence alone. So how is the fact-finder to accept that X caused Y because *p* displays Y after exposure to X? Mere co-occurrence is not sufficient by itself; *t* has a strong argument that the co-existence of X and Y is nothing more than coincidence or the product of the fallacy '*post hoc ergo propter hoc*'. Other things (Z) for which *t* is not responsible may have caused Y. Lacking any direct evidence of causation, *p* must turn to statistical inference; by reason of the fact that a causal propensity between X-like contaminants and Y-like injuries has been shown in a sample (*n*), and that sample was representative of a population (*N*) to which *p* arguably belongs, statistical evidence from *n* may be probative evidence that X caused Y in *p*.

Statistical evidence has proven to be a controversial feature of fact-finding in common law jurisdictions for decades, both in practice and scholarship. The degree of this controversy is surprising, given the widespread use of statistical evidence in other professional disciplines. Statistics is a branch of knowledge that seeks to make sense of relationships like that of X and Y. One observation of X and Y in proximity is unlikely to be sufficient for a causal finding.[2] The more times X is observed in conjunction with Y increases the likelihood that there is some non-coincidental association between X and Y. The sciences provide the platform for studying relationships between variables in an organised manner. Statistics are the tools scientists use to demonstrate that their hypotheses are robust. In this example, epidemiology (the study of disease in humans) utilises regression analyses to test, over the long run, the association of occurrences of X and Y in *n*. From there, one may infer from the finding of an association in *n* to an association between X and Y in *N*, in turn forming the basis for an inference of a causal relationship between X and Y under certain conditions.

[1] 'Plaintiff' is widely used to denote 'claimant' in many Australian and US courts, and is adopted as the standard term in this book.

[2] cf S Steel, *Proof of Causation in Tort Law* (Cambridge, Cambridge University Press, 2015) 75. Steel argues that causation could be inferred from a single or small number of events. The conditions suggested by Steel, such as biological plausibility, are revealing. Biological plausibility would only arise where there existed sufficient prior knowledge about the variables (or something like those variables) to give them biological plausibility. A fast-acting poison would need few reported instances of its effect before causation of death in subsequent cases could be inferred. This still requires some prior knowledge.

Legal scholarship continues to identify statistical evidence and probabilistic reasoning as a problematic, or potentially problematic, feature of legal fact-finding. Some claim the judges are reluctant to make findings on statistical evidence, especially 'naked statistical evidence'.[3] Others point to the fact that judges make decisions based on statistical evidence all the time.[4] This literature is so numerous and so diverse that it has taken on hydra-like characteristics. The problem for this literature, at least in terms of its relevance to the law of evidence, is that the tenor of the arguments underlying it for the most part does not match the reality of civil or criminal litigation. It is undeniable that statistical evidence is commonly, and increasingly, relied on by judges (and juries) for fact-finding, including in novel ways. It is also true that there are numerous authorities across common law jurisdictions that can only be explained by a reluctance on behalf of judges to accept the utility of statistical evidence. In one particularly striking example from Australia, a judge referred to the adage 'lies, damned lies and statistics' as an 'aphorism' in the context of evaluating certain statistical evidence.[5] It may be that these comments can be explained as 'scattered remarks' taken out of context.[6] Even so, there remains at the core of the common law approach to fact-finding a resistance to statistical and probabilistic evidence, at least where other specific evidence may be adduced. It rises from canonical statements, repeated throughout common law jurisdictions, to the effect that

> when the law requires the proof of any fact, the tribunal must feel an actual persuasion of its occurrence or existence before it can be found. It cannot be found as a result of a mere mechanical comparison of probabilities independently of any belief in its reality.[7]

This implicates statistical evidence in particular, because it is expressed as numerical probability that is derived from circumstances that are usually independent of the facts in dispute.

In evaluating statistical evidence, this book starts from the proposition that statistics can be epistemologically sound for fact-finding. Enoch and Fisher explain that

> good statistical evidence actually promotes accuracy. Because statistical evidence, in the cases we've been focusing on, is probabilistically good, over the long run, excluding statistical evidence is bound to lead to less accuracy (just like other cases of ignoring genuinely probative evidence). Why should we be willing to pay this price?[8]

[3] See, amongst many others, L Levanon, *Evidence, Respect and Truth: Knowledge and Justice in Legal Trials* (Oxford, Hart, 2022) 15.

[4] AJ Allen and CK Smiciklas, 'The Law's Aversion to Naked Statistics and Other Mistakes' (2022) 28 *Legal Theory* 179, 181–182.

[5] *Eastlings Pty Ltd v Calidu Import Export Pty Ltd (No 2)* [2021] NSWSC 316, [487].

[6] Although, not necessarily just from old cases: cf Allen and Smiciklas (n 4) 182.

[7] *Briginshaw v Briginshaw* (1938) 60 CLR 336, 361 (Dixon J).

[8] D Enoch and T Fisher, 'Sense and "Sensitivity": Epistemic and Instrumental Approaches to Statistical Evidence' (2015) 67 *Stanford Law Review* 557, 579.

Putting to one side whether judges are willing to pay the price suggested by Enoch and Fisher, if it is assumed that good statistical evidence is good for fact-finding, the obvious question is how a court ascertains that statistical evidence is good. The problem Enoch and Fisher do not confront, and indeed the literature tends to avoid, is that even if statistics are epistemologically sound, courts lack a method to evaluate and accept that statistical evidence is 'good' for fact-finding. If a court is unable to distinguish between good and bad statistical evidence in addressing the factual controversy that the statistics are adduced to prove, it is moot whether the statistics are epistemologically sound. The problem of bad statistical evidence (or, as Allen and Smiciklas have called it, 'lousy' evidence)[9] does explain a great number of the practical problems associated with the admission and use of statistical evidence – particularly where that evidence is complex and novel.[10] The reference to the aphorism in *Eastlings Pty Ltd v Calidu Import Export Pty Ltd (No 2)* appears to derive from a complaint directed to the reliability and utility of the evidence in that fact-finding context, rather than necessarily a complaint about statistics as a discipline.[11] Further, scientific or epistemological explanations divorced from the legal process for why statistical evidence is 'good' are not sufficient in the legal fact-finding context. If the purpose of evidence and laws regulating the admission of evidence are to promote accuracy[12] and allocate the risk of error in an acceptable manner,[13] courts have to be able to assess the extent to which statistics can facilitate those goals. The challenge is how to do that in circumstances where judges and juries often have limited knowledge of statistical techniques and may be suspicious of what can meaningfully be shown using statistical evidence. If the debate is to have any utility for the law itself, it has to be couched in the processes and rules of the law of evidence.

The question that this book confronts is how courts are supposed to make the assessment of whether statistical evidence is good or not. In doing so, it seeks to identify a practicable method, by reference to evidence law, of analysing statistical evidence that can explain how the common objections to statistical evidence in litigation can be understood and allow for an assessment of why and how good statistical evidence surmounts those objections.

Underlying this inquiry is a vast interdisciplinary scholarly literature spanning decades concerning the use of statistics in fact-finding. It is curious that relatively tiny fractions of this literature feature in judicial reasons. There are a number of reasons why this might be the case. The first is that there may be a divide between how practitioners and the academy approach evidence law. Whereas practitioners

[9] Allen and Smiciklas (n 4) 182.

[10] There are many examples, but a recent attempt to rely on novel statistical evidence came unstuck in *Dwyer v Volkswagen Group Australia Pty Ltd t/as Volkswagen Australia* [2021] NSWSC 715.

[11] cf *Eastlings* (n 5) [487].

[12] *R v War Pensions Entitlement Appeal Tribunal* (1933) 50 CLR 228, 256 (Evatt J).

[13] MS Pardo, 'The Nature and Purpose of Evidence Theory' (2013) 66 *Vanderbilt Law Review* 547, 559.

focus on the practicalities of litigation, the 'New Evidence Scholarship' that has come to dominate discussions about statistical evidence at least, tends to focus on incorporating interdisciplinary and increasingly complex theories of fact-finding and evidence. Courts and practitioners are (rightly or wrongly) not generally concerned by the intricacies of epistemological and philosophical debates about the nature of probabilistic reasoning and statistical inference.[14] Following the seminal Boston Symposium in 1986 regarding the use of statistics in law, Professor Twining noted that of all the luminaries that attended that symposium (which ultimately became a decisive turning point in the literature on the use of formal mathematical methods in legal scholarship), few, if any, were specialist litigators.[15] That comment proved to be a prescient observation for the subsequent decades of scholarship that has been mostly ignored in judicial reasons about statistical evidence.

Second, judicial officers may pay little attention to statistical evidence scholarship because of the nature of legal decision-making. Courts can create precedents regarding the use of evidence in legal proceedings. Even so, the features that make statistical evidence objectionable are often factual and context dependent. Not only does this mean that any precedent created by the decision is of limited practical utility in developing a coherent jurisprudence, but judicial authors themselves attempt to caveat the applicability of their reasons to future decisions because of these individual circumstances. In *Sienkiewicz v Greif*, the UK Supreme Court (UKSC) considered appeals from decisions utilising epidemiological evidence in proof of causation of the claimant's mesothelioma. The UKSC was taken to US literature on statistical evidence that had been informed by vast experience with epidemiological evidence arising from mass tort litigation and class actions. Whereas that material may have been of some benefit to the UKSC, especially given the subsequent criticism of *Sienkiewicz* by legal scholars on how the majority reasoned with statistical evidence,[16] the UKSC largely disregarded the scholarship.[17]

Third, the literature identifies the key objections to the use of statistical evidence as epistemological, moral or normative.[18] But these are not objections that correspond directly with how statistical evidence is used, or objected to, in fact-finding. An 'epistemic' objection to statistical evidence could, as this work will show, be an objection to the relevance, admissibility, weight or capacity for proof of that

[14] W Twining, 'Narrative and Generalization: Argumentation about Questions of Fact' (1999) 40 *South Texas Law Review* 351, 352. A discussion of the divergent approach to evidence law theorising can be found in Allen and Smiciklas (n 4) 180–81.

[15] W Twining, 'The Boston Symposium: A comment' (1986) *Boston University Law Review* 391, 393.

[16] Generally, C McIvor, 'Debunking some Judicial Myths about Epidemiology and its Relevance to UK Tort Law' (2013) 21 *Medical Law Reports* 553, 576–77.

[17] See *Sienkiewicz v Greif* [2011] 2 AC 229 (UKSC) [194].

[18] A Pundik, 'Statistical Evidence and Individual Litigants: a Reconsideration of Wasserman's Arguments from Autonomy' (2008) 12 *International Journal of Evidence & Proof* 303, 306; Enoch and Fisher (n 8).

evidence. The literature rarely seeks to categorise its analysis by reference to these terms. Indeed, many scholars have complained, across a variety of domains, that the legal scholarship regarding statistical evidence oscillates between questions of admissibility and sufficiency without regard to the disparate principles that apply to either. The most recent battleground where these allegations are made is in the debates regarding whether the objections to statistical evidence, and naked statistical evidence in particular, are better explained by the epistemological concepts of safety or sensitivity.[19] Johnson King's complaint in this respect – whilst quite valid – is somewhat undermined by the fact that her own discussion of admissibility does not engage with any evidence law at all, and rather consigns her definition of such rules as a 'motley crew serving diverse purposes'.[20] Unless those objections can be put into a form that is capable of engaging with the law of evidence, there is little chance that actors within the law will pay much regard to them.[21]

Instead of seeking to add to the literature on statistical evidence in the terms of how the debate is usually expressed, this book attempts to strike a different perspective by focusing on how statistical evidence ought to be viewed by evidence law and fact-finding as performed by courts. One challenge in undertaking that exercise is the jurisdictional specificity of evidence law. The principles that underpin the discussion in this book are generally similar across the common law world. But there is little utility in trying to formulate a theory of evidence law objections to statistical evidence in a vacuum of actual evidence law. Historically, the bulk of the literature on this topic has focused on the law of the United States of America, with some discussion among scholars from the United Kingdom. This book instead uses the law of Australia as the fulcrum for its discussion, to broaden the scope of the discussion beyond the US and the UK. Where appropriate, it has sought to identify comparative principles from the US and UK to understand how objections to evidence law may be dealt across the common law world and, therefore, expose fundamental principles to the common law approach to evidence.[22]

The task is also complicated by the fact that statistical evidence can be used in a wide variety of contexts, and each of these contexts raise separate evidentiary, procedural and substantive considerations. This fact and context dependency are why courts have rightly refused to create a 'catch-all' rule for statistical evidence.[23] How statistical evidence is used influences the type of fact-finding objections that can be taken to it.

At its core, statistical evidence is useful insofar as it identifies the nature and degree of associations between variables of interest. The ultimate goal of identifying such association is to establish causal relationships between variables.

[19] eg ZA Johnson King, 'Sensitivity, Safety and Admissibility' (2022) 200 *Synthese* 1, 3.
[20] ibid.
[21] See also Allen and Smiciklas (n 4) 185.
[22] cf P Roberts, 'Theorising Evidence Law' (2023) 43 *OJLS* 629, 646–47.
[23] See *Tyson Foods v Bouaphakeo* 577 US 442, 459–60 (2016).

When statistical evidence is adduced as evidence of causation, the following syllogism typically applies:

> X caused Y in *n*.
>
> *n* is representative of *N*, such that *n* identifies a causal effect in a state of nature (that is, in the population *N*).
>
> *p* is a member of or sufficiently similar to *N*, such that *N* informs some fact about *p*.
>
> X caused Y in *p*.

When this syllogism is imported into fact-finding, three broad categories of objection arise. Levels one and two of the syllogism give rise to objections to the 'effect' asserted by the statistical evidence: that is, the fact-finder's belief that there exists a causal propensity between certain variables in a state of nature. Level three of the syllogism gives rise to objections to inferring the effect identified by the statistical evidence from the population to an individual or individuals. Level four gives rise to objections to the ability of statistical evidence to prove causal associations.

Understanding and resolving these objections is one pathway by which the law can assess whether statistical evidence is 'good' for fact-finding. Accordingly, this book is structured around how objections to each level of the syllogism have been expressed, and put in their proper context, how each of those objections may be better understood and resolved. Chapter one (Statistics in Adjudicative Fact-finding) introduces the key concepts that explain and contextualise how the objections are said to arise.

The first two levels of the syllogism concern whether the association between the variables of interest and the strength of that association (effect size) reported in the statistical evidence itself is real. Given that statistical evidence is almost always adduced in support of expert evidence, there is a high degree of interaction between general factual causation and expert opinion.

The approach to general factual causation in Australian courts is clouded. In the US, courts accept that there are two distinct stages to the causal inquiry: 'general causation' (whether an agent can cause an outcome) and 'specific causation' (whether the agent caused the outcome in this case).[24] Australian courts, by contrast, contend that only specific causation is 'relevant' to fact-finding.[25] Nevertheless, at least logically, if a court is to make a decision about specific causation, it must first accept that general causation is possible where the evidence being relied on to prove specific causation is in the nature of general causation. So as to avoid confusion with terminology employed in tort law, the term 'general factual causation' is used here to describe the step of proving the existence of an effect in *N*. The court must accept that the statistical evidence is capable of demonstrating the contended causal proposition and does so with sufficient reliability. The real

[24] eg *Merrell Dow Pharmaceuticals v Havner* 953 SW2d 706, 714–15 (1997).
[25] *Seltsam v McGuiness* (2000) 49 NSWLR 262 (NSWCA) [22].

challenge to general factual causation is distinguishing between objections to the admissibility of the evidence or its weight.

Chapter two (Admitting Evidence of General Factual Causation) addresses and evaluates how the reliability of evidence proving general factual causation is, or ought to be, evaluated. Chapter three (Statistical Proof of General Factual Causation) contends that artificially maintaining different standards of 'causation' between the law and science has led to a misunderstanding on the standard of evidence necessary to prove general factual causation by statistical evidence.

The third level of the syllogism involves inferring from an effect observed in a particular reference class, being *N*, represented by *n* in the statistical evidence, to *p*. Inferring from statistics to present facts, referred to in this book as a generalisation or individualisation,[26] has preoccupied legal scholarship and caused consternation in judicial decisions over how to cross the inferential gap from the studied population to the individual.

At its most strident this objection suggests that statistical evidence is of 'no value' to the present case.[27] In *McTear v Imperial Tobacco*, Lord Nimmo Smith stated:

> [6.180] … It is consistent with the above views and gives extensive reasons for concluding that epidemiological data cannot be used to draw conclusions about the cause of disease in any individual … epidemiological evidence cannot be used to make statements about individual causation. The information provided in observational epidemiology is generally such that it can neither confirm nor refute a causal relationship, particularly when the exposure in question is not specifically associated with a certain condition (ie the exposure is always associated with the condition, and vice versa). Epidemiology cannot provide information on the likelihood that an exposure produced an individual's condition. The population attributable risk is a measure for populations only and does not imply a likelihood of disease occurrence within an individual, contingent upon that individual's exposure …
>
> [9.10] … Epidemiology cannot be used to establish causation in any individual case, and the use of statistics applicable to the general population to determine the likelihood of causation in an individual is fallacious. Given that there are possible causes of lung cancer other than cigarette smoking, and given that lung cancer can occur in a nonsmoker, it is not possible to determine in any individual case whether but for an individual's cigarette smoking he probably would not have contracted lung cancer.[28]

[26] The term individualisation has been used widely in the literature to denote inferences of this kind: see, eg, KN Kotsglou, 'The Specific Evidence Rule: Reference Classes – Individuals – Personal Autonomy' (2023) 4 *Quaestio facti – International Journal on Evidential Legal Reasoning* 1. It is not intended by the use of this term to pick up the debates regarding any rule for the individualisation of forensic science evidence, which concerns a different, but related, problem: see, eg, DH Kaye, 'Probability, individualization, and uniqueness in forensic science evidence-listening to the academies' (2010) 75 *Brooklyn Law Review* 1163; JJ Koehler and MJ Saks, 'Individualization claims in forensic science: Still unwarranted' (2010) 75 *Brooklyn Law Review* 1187, 1191.

[27] eg RW Wright, 'Causation, Responsibility, Risk, Probability, Naked Statistics, and Proof: Pruning the Bramble Bush by Clarifying the Concepts' (1988) 73 *Iowa Law Review* 1001, 1052.

[28] *McTear v Imperial Tobacco* [2005] CSOH 69.

This objection can be found in various forms and is articulated to varying degrees in both judicial decisions and scholarship. Expressed in that way, the objection to the individualisation of statistical evidence is fundamentally flawed both in logic and in law. Gatekeepers and fact-finders should approach the individualisation of statistical evidence with some caution, but caution predicated on a principled and consistent approach.

Chapter four (Individualising Inferences from Statistical Evidence) seeks to demonstrate that there is in fact an identifiable epistemic 'objection' to individualisations and generalisations from statistical evidence. Generalisations are a part of all evidence. Cohen suggests, rightly, that commonsense fact-finding itself is based on the belief of the fact-finder that the present asserted facts most closely follow their own view of what likely occurred by reference to generalisations held and applied by the fact-finder.[29] These generalisations are then in turn used to form individualising inferences from those general categories to particular events. Statistical evidence presents an additional individualisation challenge, and therefore an additional layer of epistemic objection, by reason of the inferential structure of statistical evidence. Crossing the inferential gap between *N* (inferred from *n*) and *p* necessarily requires a 'leap of faith' by the fact-finder in asserting that there is a sufficiently proximate relationship between *p* and *N*.

Recognising the existence of the individualisation objection then leads to the first stage of how to resolve that objection. Individualisation objections are far from unique to statistical evidence. Most prominently, similar fact evidence also requires inferences of a kind similar, and sometimes identical, to statistical evidence,[30] by drawing on the fact of events outside of the immediate circumstances to prove the existence of those circumstances. Chapter five (Statistics and Similar Facts) demonstrates the inferential similarity between similar fact and statistical evidence, and the common basis for the relevance of both. By understanding that statistical evidence is relevant to facts-in-issue about *p* in much the same way as similar fact evidence and by appreciating the standard of relevance that ought to be applied in admitting statistical evidence, this book seeks to evaluate how courts have approached and articulated objections to statistical evidence, and how the individualisation objection to statistical evidence should be determined.

Understanding statistical evidence as relevant to facts-in-issue like similar fact evidence leads to the next stage of how courts should evaluate statistical evidence that is relevant to *p*. Ordinarily, gatekeepers do not have any say in what weight fact-finders should give to evidence. The law does not interfere with the process of weighing, other than to say that weight ought to accord with the fact-finder's commonsense. But, much like similar fact evidence, once statistical evidence is admitted, there is a risk that the weighing exercise could miscarry by reason of the

[29] LJ Cohen, *The Probable and the Provable* (Oxford, Clarendon Press, 1977) ch 18.

[30] See discussion in *BDS17 v Minister for Immigration and Border Protection* [2018] FCA 1683, [41]–[42]; *R v Villalon* [2014] NSWSC 725, [8], [22]. See also Allen and Smiciklas (n 4) 200 ff; Levanon (n 3) 123 ff.

prejudicial effect of statistical evidence. Prejudice in fact-finding is the erroneous attribution of weight to evidence over and above what it can reasonably support. Chapter six (Prejudicial Statistical Evidence) considers how statistical evidence might be prejudicial to the fact-finding process, and how the law ought to weigh the probative value of statistical evidence against this potentially prejudicial effect in deciding to admit that evidence.

Level four of the syllogism requires accepting that the causal effect observed in *n* is true for *p*. Legal scholarship has been preoccupied with whether statistical evidence can by itself (referred to as 'naked statistical evidence') be sufficient for proof. The 'proof paradoxes' are used to demonstrate that statistical evidence cannot appropriately fulfil either the civil or criminal standards of proof. Chapter seven (Objective Probabilities and Naked Statistical Evidence) engages with this debate. It demonstrates how the standard of proof operates in practice and argues that naked statistical evidence does not fall foul of the civil standard, at least under the artificially controlled conditions of the proof paradox. But outside those artificial conditions, there are more factors that need to be taken into account if statistical evidence is to be accepted as proof that *p* has experienced the effect observed in *n*.

More typically, statistical evidence forms part of a factual matrix of proof. There is widespread (albeit not universal) agreement that statistical evidence can be an important link in the chain of proof of facts-in-issue.[31] Uncertainty lies in how to understand *n*'s contribution to the probability of *p* experiencing the same effect in light of all the evidence. One means of doing so is utilising formal (or mathematical) methods of computation. This is not a question about statistical evidence per se, but rather how evidence, whether statistical evidence or not, is analysed using mathematical or statistical techniques. These approaches are believed to challenge the commonsense approach to fact-finding. Chapter eight (Statistical Analysis of Evidence) briefly introduces what the law has said about mathematical approaches to fact-finding and the core debates surrounding their use.

[31] eg LH Tribe, 'Trial by Mathematics: Precision and Ritual in the Legal Process' (1971) 84 *Harvard Law Review* 1329, 1350; *Seltsam* (n 25) [98].

1

Statistics in Adjudicative Fact-Finding

Introduction

Before embarking on an analysis of the objections to statistical evidence, this book identifies the basic principles and concepts underpinning that discussion. These include, first, the distinction between legislative and adjudicative fact-finding and the operation of evidence law in respect of the latter; second, what facts are statistical evidence commonly adduced to prove in adjudicative litigation; third, an explanation of the rules of expert evidence that govern the use of statistical evidence by expert witnesses; and fourth, the difference (if any) between expert evidence that relies on pre-existing statistical evidence and expert evidence relying on litigation-generated statistical evidence.

I. Fact-Finding and the Law of Evidence

Fact-finding is, for the most part, governed by rules encapsulated by evidence law. Evidence law is an invention of the common law, increasingly subsumed by statute throughout common law jurisdictions, to regulate the use of evidence in fact-finding. But it does not apply to all circumstances where statistics might be used to 'find' facts. The law distinguishes between 'adjudicative' facts that comprise relevant facts-in-issue to proceedings between litigants and so-called 'legislative facts' that are 'beyond the interests of the parties' and assist the court in formulating the 'content of law and policy and to exercise its discretion or judgment in determining what course of action to take'.[1] Courts can use the concept of legislative facts (including the doctrine of judicial notice) to admit and consider statistical evidence in a variety of contexts.[2] Perhaps the most famous use of this doctrine occurred in *Brown v Board of Education of Topeka*, where the US Supreme Court stipulated that because social psychological research had demonstrated poor outcomes associated with distinguishing between social groups, the policy of forced racial segregation of educational facilities ought to be abolished.[3]

[1] JD Heydon, *Cross on Evidence*, 14th edn (Chatswood, LexisNexis, 2023) 3005; M Hodge, *Phipson on Evidence*, 20th edn (London, Sweet & Maxwell, 2021) 3-01–3-03.

[2] *Woods v Multi-Sport Holdings* (2002) 208 CLR 460, [63]–[69].

[3] *Brown v Board of Education of Topeka* 347 US 483, 494 (1954).

Australian and UK courts have been prepared to inform themselves of a variety of social and scientific phenomena by way of judicial notice of legislative facts.[4] In *Woods v Multi-Sport Holdings*, McHugh J relied on statistics demonstrating the scope of accidents and injuries in the general population and their cost to the taxpayer in raising the standard of care for the owner of an indoor cricket centre,[5] who was accused of negligence in not providing helmets to players to prevent eye injuries. According to McHugh J, the statistics demonstrated, without the need for proof or direct application to the facts of that case, that adhering to industry practice in not providing a helmet was no defence and breached the standard of care in circumstances where 'the risk of injury is high, the effect of injury likely to be serious and the cost of eliminating the risk of the injury small'.[6]

Legislative fact-finding and judicial notice exist to facilitate trials and avoid the need for proof of every last factual detail. Such facts are not meant to directly touch on matters in dispute between the parties and are not subject to the rules of evidence that apply in adjudicative fact-finding;[7] they are 'notorious' and part of 'general public knowledge'.[8] Whether statistics are ever sufficiently 'notorious' and appropriately admitted as the basis for legislative facts is a complicated and controversial question.[9] Their use in public and constitutional law contexts has been questioned, in no small part due to the absence of argument and witnesses to properly explain them in context.[10] Indeed, whether the concept of legislative facts should exist at all has been the subject of controversy for some time.[11] But this work does not extend to that debate.

Evidence is admitted and processed in adjudicative fact-finding by way of a fourfold process: relevance, admissibility, weight and proof. How these tasks are allocated, and to whom, depends on the mode of trial. Where a jury is empanelled, the presiding judge acts as 'gatekeeper' and determines relevance and admissibility. The jury sits as 'fact-finder', deciding the weight of the evidence and ultimately whether the facts are proved by the evidence. Understanding these principles, and how they may interact with statistical evidence, is important. Gatekeeping and fact-finding are fundamentally different, and too often scholarly debates around statistical evidence elide these distinctions.[12] If these debates are to be useful in understanding how the law does or should approach statistical evidence, these concepts must be taken into account.

[4] Heydon (n 1) 3005.
[5] *Woods* (n 2) [64]–[71].
[6] ibid [73].
[7] ibid [64]–[65].
[8] *Stenhouse v Coleman* (1944) 69 CLR 457, 469 (Dixon J).
[9] *Woods* (n 2) [163]–[169].
[10] See P Yowell, *Constitutional Rights and Constitutional Design: Moral and Empirical Reasoning in Judicial Review* (Oxford, Hart, 2018) 69–71.
[11] eg, J Monahan and L Walker, 'Social Science Research in Law: A New Paradigm' (1988) 43 *American Psychologist* 465.
[12] See ZA Johnson King, 'Sensitivity, Safety and Admissibility' (2022) 200 *Synthese* 1, 6–8.

In the US, jury trials are a constitutional right, and remain the primary mode of trial. Elsewhere, common law jurisdictions are increasingly reducing the scope of jury trials. In Australia and the UK, jury trials are largely reserved for serious criminal offences and defamation proceedings, with few exceptions. Where judges sit without a jury, and assume both roles, the distinction between gatekeeper and fact-finder becomes strained. One reason for maintaining a distinction is to prevent the fact-finder from becoming infected by irrelevant or inadmissible evidence and then inappropriately relying on that evidence in fact-finding. When the offices of gatekeeper and fact-finder are merged, distinguishing between those offices appears artificial and yet remains fundamental to the common law trial. Fact-finders will hear evidence that is otherwise inadmissible. A great degree of trust is placed in the judiciary that inadmissible evidence will not infect their decision.[13] For the most part, however, the rationale of divided labour is maintained when a judge sits without a jury. The judge will either make a preliminary finding as gatekeeper that the impugned evidence is inadmissible at the start of a trial in a preliminary hearing or following a voir dire, or they will hear the evidence contingent upon making a finding of admissibility in their reasons for a decision. As such, there remains some utility in referring to the separate functions of gatekeeper and fact-finder, even though the rationale for keeping them separate is eroded in the judge-alone trial.

A. Relevance

Under Australian law, relevance is defined by s 55 of the Uniform Evidence Law (UEL) as 'if [the fact] were accepted, [the evidence] could rationally affect (directly or indirectly) the assessment of the probability of the existence of a fact-in-issue in the proceeding'. The UK and US adopt functionally similar definitions of relevance.[14] Only evidence that is relevant to the facts-in-issue – that is, the facts that are in dispute in the proceeding – is admissible. Logically, there are degrees of relevance; evidence can be anywhere between negligibly to overwhelmingly relevant to the existence of a fact.[15] At law, however, relevance is binary; evidence is relevant or it is not, and it will be relevant irrespective of its degree of relevance as long as it has *some* bearing on the existence of a fact-in-issue.[16] The degree

[13] Whether that trust is justified is a matter for debate outside the ambit of this work: see R Munday, 'Case Management, Similar Fact Evidence in Civil Cases, and a Divided Law of Evidence' (2006) 10 *International Journal of Evidence & Proof* 81, 96–97.

[14] See US Federal Rules of Evidence (FRE) r 401 and *DPP v Kilbourne* [1973] AC 729 (HL) 756 (Lord Simon).

[15] See S Haack, 'Correlation and Causation' in M Martin-Casals and D Papayannis (eds), *Uncertain Causation in Tort Law* (Cambridge, Cambridge University Press, 2015) 6.

[16] *IMM v The Queen* (2016) 257 CLR 300, [40]–[41], [43]. This standard is equally applied in the UK (see *Kilbourne* (n 14) 756C–F (Lord Simon)) and the US (FRE r 403; *US v Pugliese* 153 F2d 497, 500 (2dCir, 1945) (Hand J)).

of relevance is the 'weight' or 'probative value' of the evidence. Whereas assessing relevance is the responsibility of the gatekeeper (and supposedly a question of law), weight resides with the fact-finder. Gatekeepers must exclude evidence that is irrelevant and has no probative value and must admit evidence that is relevant unless otherwise inadmissible.

Given the consequences of irrelevance, the standard of relevance is set deliberately low.[17] 'If it were accepted' requires that relevance assessments occur when the evidence is 'taken at its highest' and assumed to be true.[18] Gatekeepers cannot take into account the reliability or credibility of the source of the evidence, or the possibility of error,[19] unless the evidence is so spurious, or so unbelievable, that even when it is taken at its highest, the fact is so improbable that it could not be true.[20] Outside these limited circumstances, the mere fact that evidence appears unlikely to meet the standard of proof does not make that evidence irrelevant.[21]

One of the more confusing questions around relevance is the nature of relevance at law. Gleeson CJ in *Smith v The Queen* expounded that relevance is *not* a discretionary exercise.[22] An erroneous determination of relevance is, as such, an error of law. But the standard of relevance is 'rationality'; evidence is relevant if, as a matter of 'logic' and 'commonsense', the fact-finder believes it to be relevant.[23] This is akin to how questions of fact are resolved. After all, relevance is simply the existence of probative value irrespective of its degree. This creates a problem for the review of relevance. Usually, factual findings cannot be overturned on appeal for mere disagreement; there must be an error in the process of fact-finding.[24] If relevance is simply a matter of commonsense and rationality, if an appellate court were to conclude that a trial judge was wrong as to relevance, that would suggest the trial judge's decision was irrational and contrary to common sense; a striking finding for any appellate court to make of the court below.

In practice, relevance controversies are often mere differences of opinion. Whether evidence has the 'capacity' to prove a fact is typically a matter of degree, even though the outcome is purportedly binary.[25] This is consistent with the view that commonsense (and to some extent, rationality itself) are individual and

[17] R Eggleston, *Evidence, Proof and Probability*, 2nd edn (London, Weidenfeld and Nicolson, 1983) 83; *IMM* (n 16) [40].

[18] *IMM* (n 16) [44].

[19] ibid 313, 323–24; for a rejection of this position, see G Edmond, 'Icarus and the Evidence Act: Section 137, Probative Value and taking Forensic Science Evidence "at its highest"' (2017) 41 *Melbourne University Law Review* 106, 124ff.

[20] eg, *IMM* (n 16) [39]; *Dasreef v Hawchar* (2011) 243 CLR 588, [90]; cf *Commissioner for Government Transport v Adamcik* (1961) 106 CLR 292, 303.

[21] See *Chamberlain v The Queen* (1984) 153 CLR 521, 627.

[22] *Smith v The Queen* (2001) 206 CLR 650, [6].

[23] See JD Heydon, 'Is the Weight of Evidence Material to its Admissibility?' (2014) 26 *Current Issues in Criminal Justice* 219, 224.

[24] See *Fox v Percy* (2003) 214 CLR 118, [65].

[25] *Piddington v Bennett* (1940) 63 CLR 533, 559 (Evatt J).

subjective concepts.[26] The dividing line between difference of opinion and legal error is blurred; and as will be shown, this poses a special problem for the relevance of statistical evidence. Although not the accepted standard of assessment and review of relevance, it would be more appropriate (and accurate as a matter of principle) to consider relevance as 'an evaluative decision of a subjective nature, regarding an issue upon which reasonable minds may differ'.[27] The basis of review of subjective, evaluative standards of this type is materially the same as for a discretionary decision.[28]

B. Admissibility

Gatekeepers can also exclude relevant evidence that is otherwise inadmissible at law. Relevant evidence is typically inadmissible for a variety of normative considerations that correspond with the twin goals of evidence law: increasing accuracy and allocating error.[29] Inadmissibility rules can be divided into three tranches: discretionary procedural exclusions, for example where the evidence would be unduly costly or wasteful; discretionary and non-discretionary exclusion for prejudice; and the 'exclusionary rules of evidence' that apply to specific types and uses of evidence. One such rule concerns hearsay evidence, or previous representations made out of court.[30] Hearsay is excluded not because it is irrelevant, but from the historical view that evidence which cannot be tested directly in court should not be admitted. Likewise, otherwise relevant opinions of witnesses are inadmissible because it is for the fact-finder to draw conclusions and for witnesses to report what they perceived.[31] There are general exceptions to these rules. Expert evidence is admissible as an exception to the opinion rule because it informs on areas outside common knowledge and experience.[32] It is not proposed to canvass each basis for the inadmissibility of evidence here. Those relevant to this book will be referred to and defined where necessary.

C. Weight

Weight (or the degree of probative value of evidence) is a question of fact for fact-finders. Gatekeepers should not instruct fact-finders on the weight to be given

[26] P Roberts, *Roberts & Zuckerman's Criminal Evidence*, 3rd edn (Oxford, Oxford University Press, 2022) 158–60.

[27] *Ghosh v NineMSN* (2015) 90 NSWLR 595 (NSWCA) [37], concerning the nature of determining abuses of process.

[28] *R v Zhang* (2005) 158 A Crim R 504, [141].

[29] MS Pardo, 'The Nature and Purpose of Evidence Theory' (2013) 66 *Vanderbilt Law Review* 547, 559.

[30] UEL s 59.

[31] UEL ss 76, 78.

[32] *Velevski v The Queen* [2002] 187 ALR 233, [82]; UEL s 79.

to evidence.[33] Fact-finders use their own internal schemas and knowledge to assess the weight of evidence and are not bound by legal rules. The only exception to that principle is where the evidence assumes (or could assume) more importance than it warrants. Such evidence is considered prejudicial and may be excluded ex ante,[34] or a decision may be considered unsafe ex post.[35]

There are at least two widely recognised stages to the assessment of weight. First, the fact-finder's belief that the evidence is reliable, referred to here as 'credit weight'. Second, the degree to which the evidence affects the assessment of the probability of a fact-in-issue, or 'fact weight'. For example, if a witness A gives evidence about topic B, the believability of A's evidence about B is credit weight. The degree to which A's evidence makes B more or less probable is fact weight. These two forms of weight are synergistic – the degree of belief in the reliability of the evidence may impact the overall assessment of weight to the fact-in-issue and vice versa. As this work will demonstrate, the difference between credit weight and fact weight has posed significant problems for statistical evidence, especially where the two become enmeshed in the opinion of expert witnesses. Overreliance on the fact-finder's impressions of credit weight can overbear the fact weight the evidence ought to have been given.

Legal scholarship has also identified a third form of weight. Whereas fact weight and credit weight refer to the fact-finder's belief in the truth of B, so-called 'Keynesian' weight refers to the degree to which the evidence offers a 'complete picture' of B.[36] Keynesian weight purports to measure the 'flimsiness' of the evidence in explaining the fact to be inferred from it. There has been relatively little discussion about Keynesian weight in judicial decisions. And yet, it is apparent that Keynesian weight is a metric that judges use to assess the 'reasonableness' of a fact-finder's decision,[37] or whether the evidence provides an appropriate basis for fact-finding,[38] even if that terminology is not employed. Understanding Keynesian weight helps explain some of the objections taken to statistical evidence, especially concerning objections to so-called 'objective probabilities'.

D. Proof

Proof at law is the point by which fact-finders accept that the fact is considered 'true' for that fact-finding exercise.[39] Proof of adjudicative facts is essential to a

[33] D Nance, 'The Weights of Evidence' (2008) 5 *Episteme* 267, 270.

[34] *Festa v The Queen* (2001) 208 CLR 593, [14].

[35] *M v The Queen* (1994) 181 CLR 487, 494–95.

[36] DA Nance, *The Burdens of Proof* (Cambridge, Cambridge University Press, 2016) 9.

[37] Where evidence is capable of supporting inferences that may lead to opposing outcomes, a fact found on that evidence may be subject to review for the reasonableness of the conclusion. In *Chamberlain* (n 21) 600, Brennan J noted '[a]n appellate court will give more anxious consideration to a verdict of guilty where the basis of primary fact is thin and the room for inference is large'.

[38] *Amaca v Hannell* (2007) 34 WAR 109 (WASCA) [382] (Steytler P and McLure JA).

[39] *Mallett v McMonagle* [1970] AC 166, 176 (Lord Diplock).

legal process that aims to reconstruct past or predict future events. Regulating the concept of proof are, first, the burdens of proof and, second, the standards of proof.

1. *Burdens of Proof*

Parties possess a 'burden' to prove the facts they assert.[40] Failing to meet the burden means that the fact is not established. Usually, the burden is reposed on the plaintiff such that a defendant in civil proceedings can 'put a plaintiff to proof'. But where a defendant asserts a fact or defence, the burden is on the defendant to make good that fact.[41] The burden extends both to proof of individual facts as well as to the elements of the cause of action as a whole. If a plaintiff asserts that their doctor was negligent, the plaintiff has to prove that the doctor's actions fell short of the standard of care. The plaintiff must prove each of the facts that comprise the breach, for example, failing to appropriately suture a wound,[42] as well as the element of breach of duty of care itself from the aggregate of those facts.[43] Importantly for probabilistic proof, there is no overriding duty to prove the cause of action as a whole, such that facts relevant to one element of the action can feature in the probabilistic calculus of another element. If a plaintiff can prove breach of duty, but falls short on causation, the plaintiff cannot rely on a clear breach to remedy the plaintiff's failure to establish cause (save and except where doctrines of substantive law intervene, such as *res ipsa loquitur*). All elements in a cause of action are essential, and need be proven.

2. *Standards of Proof*

Facts are proven to the requisite 'standard' of proof. The standard of proof is the law's attempt to cope with the absence of certainty in retrospective and prospective fact-finding. The fact-finder will almost never witness the event in question (and even direct observation may be insufficient for certainty). It is an impossible expectation that fact-finders would need to believe that the event occurred with 'certainty'. Recognising this limitation, the law sets the 'standards of proof' at a threshold less than certainty, but which are adjusted depending on the nature of the proceedings.

The criminal standard of proof for the prosecution to satisfy is if the fact-finder accepts that the facts are established 'beyond a reasonable doubt'.[44] This

[40] *Potts v Miller* (1940) 64 CLR 282, [299].

[41] I Dennis, *The Law of Evidence*, 7th edn (London, Sweet & Maxwell, 2020) 488.

[42] *Chamberlain* (n 21) 538, endorsing a passage from *Moss v Baines* [1974] WAR 7 (WASCFC) 11 that 'every fact necessary to be proved to sustain proof beyond reasonable doubt of every element of the offence charged must itself be proved beyond reasonable doubt'.

[43] See CR Williams, 'Burdens and Standards in Civil Litigation' (2003) 25 *Sydney Law Review* 165, referring to the 'legal burden'.

[44] *Miller v Minister of Pensions* [1947] 2 All ER 372, 373.

standard is deliberately exacting, purportedly reflecting the greater stakes of the criminal law in denying an individual their freedom and Blackstone's famous observation that it is better that 10 guilty men go free than one innocent be convicted.[45]

The standard for civil disputes is significantly lower; facts are 'proven' if the fact-finder believes they are true 'on balance of probabilities' or 'by preponderance of the evidence'.[46] These statements interrogate the fact-finder's belief that the fact is more likely to have occurred than not.[47] This belief is not purely subjective, but an epistemic and rational belief,[48] mirroring the ideals of Keynes' concept of probability as a logical construct of rational belief.[49] The civil standard is expressly not an objective standard. Reasonable minds can, and are permitted, to disagree on when a fact has met the standard of proof.[50]

3. *Truth and Certainty*

If a fact satisfies the standard of proof, it is 'proven'. Even if there is a lingering doubt, the fact is treated as the truth and becomes 'certain'.[51] Fact-finding as such is binary. Even though standards of proof can be expressed numerically, the true (albeit, mathematically obtuse) representation of the civil standard is that facts are either found ($>.5 = 1$), or they are not ($\leq .5 = 0$).[52] When the probabilities are equal, the cause of action has still failed because the burden 'more probable than not' is not satisfied.[53]

There is no room in that lexicon for uncertainty or for degrees of belief once the standard is satisfied about an event that has occurred. To say that a fact is proven to the standard of proof is, theoretically, to make a statement about the fact, not the belief in the fact. What happened in the past has happened. It would be nonsensical for factual reconstruction to suggest that a past event exists in a

[45] W Blackstone, *Commentaries on the Laws of England* (Oxford, Clarendon, 1765–1769) 352.

[46] *Miller* (n 44) 374; see also M Redmayne, 'Standards of Proof in Civil Litigation' (1999) 62 *MLR* 167, 168.

[47] *Briginshaw v Briginshaw* (1938) 60 CLR 336, 361; *Davies v Taylor* [1974] AC 207, 220.

[48] *Jones v Dunkel* (1959) 101 CLR 298, 304–05. This concept is expanded on in ch 7, section II.B.

[49] See JM Keynes, *A Treatise of Probability* (1921) 4.

[50] *Fox* (n 24) [16] (regarding a finding of the court below). See also LH Tribe, 'Trial by Mathematics: Precision and Ritual in the Legal Process' (1971) 84 *Harvard Law Review* 1329.

[51] *Mallett* (n 39) 176F (Lord Diplock), cited with approval in *Malec v JC Hutton* (1990) 169 CLR 638, 639–40 (Brennan and Dawson JJ), [643] (Deane, Gaudron and McHugh JJ). For US evidence law, see C Nesson, 'The Evidence or the Event? On Judicial Proof and the Acceptability of Verdicts' (1985) 98 *Harvard Law Review* 1357, 1386.

[52] *Dingley v Chief Constable Strathclyde Police* [1998] SC 548, 603 (Lord Prosser); cf LR Jaffe, 'Of Probativity and Probability: Statistics, Scientific Evidence, and the Calculus of Chance at Trial' (1985) 46 *University of Pittsburgh Law* Review 925, 934; B Robertson and GA Vignaux, 'Probability – The Logic of the Law' (1993) 13 *OJLS* 457, 468–69.

[53] *West v Government Insurance Office of NSW* (1981)148 CLR 62, 68.

state of uncertainty. Belief in the past can be uncertain (and can remain so even after the fact is 'proven'), but not the event itself, which either occurred or not.[54] This conferral of certainty (represented by a probability of 1)[55] does not mean that the fact is objectively and absolutely 'true'. It means is that the law treats the fact as true irrespective of any remaining subjective doubt.[56]

Exactly when certainty is conferred is a matter of some controversy. A fact need not be certain on its face.[57] Nor are facts found sequentially, divorced from other facts in the case:

> With any chain of circumstantial evidence, the chances of error in the conclusion arise first from the chances of error in each fact or consideration forming the steps and second from the chance of error in reasoning to the conclusion from the whole of those facts and considerations. It is therefore wrong to take each fact or consideration separately, to assess the possibilities of error in finding it is established and then if you think it should be found afterwards to treat it as a certainty and pass to the next fact or consideration and so on to the conclusion. The possibilities of error at all points must be combined and assessed together.[58]

Some care must be taken in interpreting Dixon J's statement. It cannot be correct that the law accepts that circumstantial facts can be considered untrue, but nevertheless a necessary condition for the truth of a fact that is proven. Facts that are relied on must be proven by admissible evidence.[59] But the sequence in which this occurs is not linear.[60] Courts can look at the corpus of the evidence in determining what is proved.

Manufacturing certainty from uncertain propositions is necessary to give effect to the 'once and for all' touchstone of judicial dispute resolution. Even though the conferral of 'certainty' is a legal rather than logical artefact, it is an essential part of the fact-finding process. Courts must be able to 'reduce to legal certainty questions to which no other conclusive answer can be given'[61] because their task is to decide questions of 'legal significance' to a dispute that must be resolved.[62] Proven facts are labelled as truth between the parties even if they are possibly false. If uncertainty were allowed to coexist with factual findings there would be room for doubt and for challenge to judicial decisions that might give rise to never-ending litigation.

[54] *Hotson v East Berkshire Area Health Authority* [1987] AC 750, 757 (Lord Donaldson MR); D Gillies, *Philosophical Theories of Probability* (Oxford, Routledge, 2000) 117, 130.

[55] cf B Robertson and GA Vignaux, 'Inferring Beyond Reasonable Doubt' (1991) 11 *OJLS* 431, 434.

[56] *Commonwealth v Amann Aviation* (1991) 174 CLR 64, 124.

[57] *Belhaven and Stenton Peerage* (1875) 1 App Cas 278, 279. See also R Schmalbeck, 'The Trouble with Statistical Evidence' (1986) 49 *Law and Contemporary Problems* 221, 235.

[58] *Morrison v Jenkins* [1949] 80 CLR 626, 644 (Dixon J); see also Robertson and Vignaux, 'Inferring' (n 55) 436.

[59] *Ramsay v Watson* (1961) 108 CLR 642, 649.

[60] S Gageler, 'Evidence and Truth' (2017) 13 *The Judicial Review* 249, 254.

[61] *Bank of NSW v Commonwealth* (1948) 76 CLR 1, 340 (Dixon J).

[62] *Tabet v Gett* (2010) 240 CLR 537, [113].

II. The Role and Purpose of Statistical Evidence

There are a myriad of types and uses of statistical evidence in fact-finding. Although by no means a complete accounting of how statistical evidence interacts with the law, there are at least three categories of evidence that are commonly employed in legal proceedings and which are the subject of debate in the literature. These include background probabilities, forensic evidence and empirical statistical evidence used to prove causation.

Background probabilities (or 'base rates') refer to the frequency with which an event or characteristic occurs in a given population. Evidence of background probabilities can be adduced in legal proceedings in a variety of forms and for a multitude of reasons.[63] For example, one may seek to adduce evidence of how frequently a judge finds against a particular party in order to infer that the judge is biased against that party.[64] Background probabilities have been the basis of a number of controversial legal decisions. These legal decisions have in turn given rise to the concept of 'naked statistical evidence' that continues to be vociferously debated in the literature. As chapter seven argues, however, there are critical differences between naked statistical evidence as it is typically, and highly artificially, defined and other evidence of background probabilities. Even so, there will be a significant risk of error where background probabilities are adduced to prove causation because by definition such evidence obtains its probative value from the coincidence of the magnitude of the event occurring without necessarily exploring the causal mechanism underlying that coincidence. By contrast, such evidence may be commonly used in support of non-causal factual propositions without significant controversy. For example, in *Rogers v Whitaker*,[65] the plaintiff adduced evidence of the probability that the procedure would cause her bilateral blindness in support of the proposition that the medical practitioner negligently failed to warn her of that risk. The inference to be drawn from the background probability was that the risk was a material risk inherent in the treatment and that the medical practitioner had breached their duty of care by failing to bring that risk to the plaintiff's attention.[66]

Forensic evidence is commonly adduced in criminal and civil proceedings to link a person with an event or place. Defining what constitutes forensic evidence can be challenging, as the term forensic evidence can be construed to mean the deployment of any scientific evidence in a court. What forensic evidence usually denotes is a scientific test on some material that can link that material to a person. DNA is perhaps the most well-known form of forensic evidence.[67] Unlike statistical evidence adduced to prove causation, forensic evidence follows a different syllogistic pathway. Even so, the inference that the fact-finder is asked to draw is

[63] JJ Koehler, 'When do Courts Think Base Rate Statistics are Relevant?' (2002) 42 *Jurimetrics* 373.
[64] See *ALA15 v Minister for Immigration and Border Protection* [2016] FCAFC 30.
[65] *Rogers v Whitaker* (1992) 175 CLR 479, 482.
[66] ibid 490 (Mason CJ, Brennan, Dawson, Toohey and McHugh JJ).
[67] DNA evidence is described in detail in ch 4, section IV.A.

that the person has a relationship with a particular person, event or place by reason of a causal association with a sample. That is, the match between the fingerprint of the accused (A) and the fingerprint at the crime scene can only be explained by the fact that A's fingerprint is unique, or is so unlikely to be replicated by anyone else, that the chances of the fingerprint being left by someone other than A are infinitesimal, and therefore the only reason why A's fingerprint was at the crime scene was because A caused it to be there. The fact-finder is being asked to infer that the fingerprint was left by A by reason of the incredible improbability that there another individual could be responsible for that fingerprint.

Empirical statistical evidence used to prove causation can take many forms utilising a variety of statistical methodologies. Epidemiology, which is the premise of the example given in the Introduction to this book, is one common form of statistical evidence that is widely written about in the statistical evidence literature. But there are many others. What draws these analyses together is the goal to explain an association between variables leading, over time and after repetition, to an inference that one variable causes, is involved in the causation of, or is commonly associated with, another variable. For example, regression analyses in the form of econometric 'event studies' can be used to show that misrepresentations by the offerors of securities are associated with market movements in price on the disclosure of correct information.[68] An event study purports to measure the degree of 'abnormal' movement in the price of a security following corrective information being released to the market, relative to the expected movement of the share price given that security's previous trading history as well as the trading histories of similar securities.[69] Whereas epidemiology is used to establish whether the impugned contaminant caused the alleged injury, event studies can serve a dual purpose. First, they can be used to demonstrate 'causation of loss', that is, the release of information to the market was statistically associated with and thereby caused the fall in the price of the security in the absence of (and as such, controlling for) any other explanation.[70] Price corrections are taken to be the 'true value' of the security but for the misleading conduct. A fact-finder could then infer that had the release of information occurred earlier in time (in compliance with the offeror's continuous disclosure obligations),[71] a similar fall in price would have been experienced. A statistically significant fall in the security's price is evidence of 'indirect causation' insofar as it is assumed that had a purchaser known of that information at the time of the purchase, they would have either not have purchased or paid less for the security.[72]

[68] *TPT Patrol v Myer Holdings* [2019] FCA 1747, [740] (describing an econometric 'event study').

[69] ibid [662]–[663].

[70] This inference is predicated on the 'efficient market hypothesis' that the price of the security 'reflects all publicly available information' about that security: ibid [667], [669]–[772].

[71] Corporations Act 2001 (Cth) s 674, picking up r 3.1 of the ASX Listing Rules.

[72] *Myer* (n 68) [1659]. Similar causal theories exist for US securities class actions: see *Basic Inc v Levinson* 485 US 224, 243–44 (1988) and *Halliburton Co v Erica P John Fund Inc* 573 US 258, 279 (2014).

Second, event analyses also serve an additional function in quantifying what the lesser price would have been. The theory of loss for the holder of securities in such cases is typically described as the difference between the purchase price of the security and its 'true' or 'real' value, calculated at 'what would have been a fair price to have paid for the [product] in the circumstances of the [product] *at the time of the purchase*'.[73] As event studies measure the extent to which the price movement of the share was 'abnormal', the quantification of the loss suffered by the security holder is the effect size of the event study.

Similar econometric studies can be applied to other products. For example, if a manufacturer or seller of a product is found to have engaged in misleading and deceptive conduct in the sale of that product, purchasers who relied on that conduct may seek to recover the loss in value of the product under the same theory of loss. One could try to establish both causation of loss and quantification by asking the purchaser questions such as 'did you rely on the information in making the purchase' and 'what would you have paid for the product had you known the information was false at the time of purchase'. Such evidence is often considered unreliable and self-serving, or indeed may even be inadmissible for some causes of action.[74] Or, one could try to achieve the same effect by tendering the same evidence from numerous purchasers in a similar position. But even assuming away reliability and admissibility concerns, calling a large number of witnesses is impractical.[75] This impracticality could in part be overcome by using a simple survey to collect a large number of views. A mere aggregation of responses is, however, rightly considered to be weak. Repetition of an association is not, by itself, enough to conclude that a true association exists.[76] Statistical measures and methods are essential if the plaintiff wants to present robust evidence that can be extrapolated beyond the surveyed few to the wider population.

What statistics adduced in this way permit above and beyond any other technique is control; the ability to exclude or at least test for other potential causes of the factor (Y), which in this scenario is the inflated value. One cannot conclude that it was the misrepresentation (the 'independent variable' or 'IV') that caused the inflated value (the 'dependent variable' or 'DV') unless the evidence is capable of explaining away any other potential causes of inflated value (referred to as either extraneous or confounding variables). Alternately, price may not be affected by misrepresentations alone, but by a collection of factors relating to the product, the market and the purchaser. Statistical design and analysis allow researchers to 'control' for extraneous or confounding variables, or variables that influence the impact of the IV, known as 'covariates'.

[73] *Potts* (n 40) 297; *Peek v Derry* (1887) 37 ChD 541, 593.

[74] Such as in negligence proceedings in New South Wales: Civil Liability Act 2002 (NSW) s 5D(3)(b).

[75] eg, *Arnotts v TPC* (1990) 24 FCR 313, 361, citing *Zippo Manufacturing v Rogers Imports* 216 FSupp 670, 683–84 (SDNY, 1963).

[76] See A Bradford Hill, 'The Environment and Disease: Association or Causation?' (1965) 58 *Proceedings of Royal Society of Medicine* 295; LJ Cohen, *The Implications of Induction* (Yorkshire, Methuen, 1970) 116.

In most empirical research, it is impossible to survey every member of a population (*N*). Statistical inference relies on extrapolating conclusions about *N* from a sample (*n*). For *n* to be a useful measure of *N*, it must be 'representative', that is, possess all or close to all of the varied characteristics of *N* proportionately.[77] A representative *n* provides much greater control over extraneous or confounding variables because if *n* is truly representative, and an association between misrepresentations and price are shown, it is less likely that the cause of the change in price was the result of some extraneous or confounding feature of *n*. Returning to the example outlined in chapter one, consider the individual (*p*)[78] who alleges that her injury (Y) was caused by the release of a contaminant (X), but other factors (Z) are also present. If Z is randomly distributed in the population (and has no true relationship to X), a sufficiently large and representative *n* will display Z in proportion to its presence in *N* with no changed association in *n*, thereby controlling for any effect Z has on the incidence of Y.

Empirical evidence can be observational or experimental. An observational study simply records what exists in a state of nature. In the proof of value, event analyses are observational; they record and analyse the incidence of changes in prices following the release of information to the market. Likewise, a study of whether a disease is caused by a contaminant will usually be observational. In a manner similar to assessing value by reference to event analysis, epidemiological studies track the incidence of disease in a defined population; the event being the coincidence of the hypothesised cause and the disease. By observing how diseases develop, and in proximity to different hypothesised causes, epidemiologists can infer that, because the contaminant is seen in conjunction with the disease and controlling for other potential causes, there is an association between the contaminant and the disease.

Proof of value could also be achieved by way of 'experimental evidence'. That is, instead of passively observing the incidence of the IV and DV, the researcher could actively manipulate the IV to observe how the DV responds. This occurs by the researcher creating (at least) two distinct levels of the IV; the experiment group, that is presented with the corrective information, and the control group, that is not. In empirical economics, these are referred to as 'conjoint analyses', and have been a regular feature of production litigation in the US,[79] and are becoming so in Australia.[80] If an effect on price is obtained in the experiment group and not in the control group, one may infer that the corrective information was the cause of the price decline.

[77] T Lash and others, *Modern Epidemiology* 4th edn (Philadelphia, Wolters Klewer Health, 2021) 390.

[78] The term '*p*' is used in this book to denote both the individual and, especially in later chapters, an event associated with that individual.

[79] R Befurt, N MacMenamin and AP Mohammad, 'Use of Conjoint Analysis in Litigation' in JE Gersen and JH Steckel (eds), *The Cambridge Handbook of Marketing and the Law* (Cambridge, Cambridge University Press, 2023) 10.3.

[80] *Williams v Toyota Motor Corporation Australia Limited* [2022] FCA 344, [360] ff (intermediate appeal dismissed ([2023] FCAFC 50), appeal to the High Court of Australia (HCA) pending).

Experimental designs allow for tighter controls of potentially extraneous or confounding variables because researchers can exercise greater control over the information that is given to the participants. They also permit the study of events that are yet to occur in the real world, or where there is too much background noise to appropriately assess the link between two variables, X and Y. For example, where there is incomplete disclosure of the corrective information, it would be difficult, if not impossible, to observe an impact on price by observational studies, because 'knowledge' could differ in *n*, and would confound any results. Experimental designs can also be conducted using true (or close to true) random samples, which in turn increases the probability that *n* will be representative of *N*.[81]

Medical researchers also use experimental designs. Testing the efficacy of pharmaceutical products usually occurs by way of randomised controlled trials (RCT), whereby participants with a certain disease are split into two groups; the experimental group is given the drug, and the control group is given a placebo. By measuring the effect of the drug on the progress of the disease in the experimental group, and comparing the outcome with the control group, the RCT allows researchers to infer that it is the drug, and not some other extraneous or confounding variable, causing the change in condition.

Regression (and statistical techniques generally) measures both the fact of association between variables and its magnitude, referred to as 'correlation'. For those using statistics, including lawyers, the ultimate aim is to extrapolate a causal relationship between variables from this correlation. Causation in this context is being used to describe a factual causal relationship between variables that exists in the natural world, independently of any legal or policy based considerations.[82] That is, simplistically, X causes Y if X preceded[83] and contributed to the existence of Y.[84] Save for within tightly controlled laboratory settings, empirical studies, statistical associations and correlations do not by themselves identify causal relationships. No matter how well designed a study, a researcher cannot entirely exclude the possibility of a confounding variable by statistical means alone. Moreover, statistical associations can be demonstrated even where the associations between variables, when viewed rationally, are entirely spurious. Human judgement is needed to identify the association between X and Y as causal.[85] That judgement is usually facilitated in legal proceedings by way of expert opinion.

[81] Lash and others (n 77) 486–487.

[82] The definition of causation at law is considered further in ch 3, but otherwise reflects and is informed by Stapleton's formulation of causation as 'factual' causation, that cause at law is causation in a state of nature and not otherwise altered by reference to legal or normative considerations: J Stapleton, 'Choosing what we Mean by Causation in the Law' (2008) 73 *Missouri Law Review* 433, 441–43, 458.

[83] S Haack, *Evidence Matters* (Cambridge, Cambridge University Press, 2014) 71.

[84] J Stapleton, 'Reflections on Common Sense Causation in Australia' in S Degeling, J Edelman and J Goudkamp (eds), *Torts in Commercial Law* (London, Thomson Reuters, 2011) 341.

[85] Haack (n 83) 186, referring to the Bradford Hill criteria.

III. Expert Evidence

Save for certain niche circumstances, facts about *p* derived from evidence drawn from *n* are previous representations made out of court intended to prove the truth of the fact asserted by that representation (that X caused Y in *n* and therefore in *p*). Used for that purpose, and adduced directly into the proceedings, statistical evidence is hearsay. Unless otherwise exempted, hearsay evidence is inadmissible.[86] Whereas the force of the common law hearsay rule has been watered down in most jurisdictions (where it exists at all),[87] prima facie, statistical evidence has been and likely would be inadmissible by itself.

Hearsay objections to statistical evidence are overcome by the common law exception applied to such evidence relied on by an expert.[88] It would be fanciful to tender complex statistical evidence in court and expect the decision-maker to grasp not only the statistical analyses but the place of that study in the surrounding literature.[89] Rules of evidence notwithstanding, for the most part, statistical evidence will or should always be accompanied by some form of expert distillation.[90] Because statistical evidence is admitted in this way, it is typically subordinated to and obscured by the expert opinion that it supports. This appears to have led to a perverse logic to the hierarchy of evidence; when weighing expert opinion based on rigorous statistical analysis against expert evidence based on observation or anecdote, the latter is often preferred. For example, in the context of exploring the use of survey evidence in intellectual property litigation, Huang, Weatherall and Webster observe that plaintiffs tend to rely on anecdotal evidence over and above statistical evidence based on surveys that are more likely to be representative.[91]

Notwithstanding the increasing presence and importance of statistical evidence in litigation,[92] practitioners[93] and scholars have identified for some time that courts appear to prefer anecdotal or direct evidence to statistical evidence.[94]

[86] UEL s 59.

[87] eg, the hearsay rule no longer applies to civil proceedings for English law: Civil Evidence Act 1995 (UK) s 1(1).

[88] *Dasreef* (n 20) [69], citing *R v Abadom* [1983] 1 WLR 126 (CA) 129D–E.

[89] *Parker v BHP Billiton* [2011] SADC 104, [552].

[90] *Aytugrul v The Queen* (2012) 247 CLR 170, [68].

[91] V Huang, K Weatherall and E Webster, 'The Use of Survey Evidence in Australian Trade Mark and Passing Off Cases' in A Kenyon, M Richardson and WL Ng-Loy (eds), *The Law of Reputation and Brands in the Asia Pacific* (Cambridge, Cambridge University Press, 2012) 182.

[92] I Freckelton, *Expert Evidence*, 7th edn (Sydney, Thomson Reuters, 2023) 1071; P Roberts, *Roberts & Zuckerman's Criminal Evidence*, 3rd edn (Oxford, Oxford University Press, 2022) 577–80; E Magnusson, 'Statistical Proof of Causation' in I Freckelton and D Mendelson (eds), *Causation in Law and Medicine* (Oxford, Routledge, 2002) 401.

[93] See, eg, a useful extra-judicial summary by Branson J articulating, precisely, the concerns of Australian judges and practitioners about the use of statistical evidence in litigation: AHRC, *An Age of Uncertainty: Inquiry into the treatment of individuals suspected of people smuggling offences who say that they are children* (2012) appendix 5.

[94] eg, C Beaton-Wells, *Proof of Antitrust Markets in Australia* (Alexandria, Federation Press, 2003) ch 6; E Beecher-Monas, *Evaluating Scientific Evidence* (Cambridge, Cambridge University Press, 2007) ch 4.

In *Seltsam v McGuiness*,[95] the plaintiff contended that he contracted liver cancer as a result of asbestos inhalation. The trial judge found in favour of the plaintiff on the basis of, amongst other evidence, epidemiological evidence showing a weak association between asbestos fibres and liver cancer. Regarding the causative propensities of asbestos for liver cancer, Davies AJA stated:

> To my mind, the evidence given by the employers' medical experts is the more persuasive. Dr Burns and Dr Nankivell considered that, as it is likely that the development of renal cell cancer has many causes, then asbestos, which is known to cause cancer elsewhere in the body, was probably a cause of Mr McGuiness' cancer. That is clearly a tenable view. However, I am persuaded that the weight of the medical evidence is against it. *I am also influenced by the fact that there is no evidence from any medical expert that he or she has encountered in the course of his or her practice, a case or cases of renal cell cancer which he or she has attributed to asbestos.* Anecdotal evidence to that effect, such as one encounters in other areas of medico-legal disputes, is absent, notwithstanding the long history of the mining and use of asbestos in Australia.[96]

It is striking that Davies AJA appears to have put substantial weight on the absence of anecdotal evidence, from a handful of medical practitioners, alongside rigorous epidemiological evidence.[97] This is especially so when there is substantial evidence to suggest that clinical judgements are poorer than statistical conclusions drawn from actuarial evidence.[98]

Preferences of this kind (whether real or imagined) play an important role in influencing the development of the law. If practitioners perceive that judges are less likely to give weight to one form of evidence over another, they will tend to prefer the evidence that is more likely to be accepted. One would expect that a court's preference for types of evidence will depend on the circumstances of the fact to be proven. Eyewitness evidence that an accused swung a cricket bat at a victim would be logically more probative of the fact that 'the accused hit the victim with a cricket bat' than rigorous statistical evidence showing the people like the accused tend to hit others with cricket bats more frequently than the general population do. Likewise, DNA evidence has become increasingly important as evidence tending to identify an accused. For the fact 'did the accused touch the murder weapon at around the time of the murder', 'good' DNA evidence from that knife

Such a preference would be consistent with the seminal findings of Tversky and Kahneman that fact-finders tend to prefer evidence of observation to base rates, even if the base rate evidence is probabilistically more accurate than the observation: see A Tversky and D Kahneman, 'Causal Schemas in Judgments under Uncertainty' in D Kahneman, P Slovic and A Tversky (eds), *Judgment under Uncertainty: Heuristics and Biases* (Cambridge, Cambridge University Press, 1982).

[95] *Seltsam v McGuiness* (2000) 49 NSWLR 262 (NSWCA) [22].

[96] ibid [281] (emphasis added).

[97] Similar conclusions were expressed in *Novartis Grimsby v Cookson* [2007] EWCA Civ 1261, [74] where the 'personalised' probabilities offered by a clinical specialist were preferred to the probabilities ascertainable from epidemiological evidence: see C McIvor, 'Debunking some Judicial Myths about Epidemiology and its Relevance to UK Tort Law' (2013) 21 *Medical Law Review* 553, 576–77.

[98] See FF Schauer, *Profiles, Probabilities and Stereotypes* (Cambridge Mass, Harvard University Press, 2003) 96–97.

is likely to be stronger than a witness' observation that the accused was holding a similar looking knife.

Context, and perhaps even personal preference, must play a significant role in the view formed by the court about the weight of that evidence.[99] The limited empirical evidence that does exist, emanating from the US, focuses on the capacity of judges to process statistical evidence rather than whether there is a distinct preference.[100] Koehler previously identified certain conditions, in US proceedings, where courts construed statistical evidence presented as base rates as irrelevant.[101] In many instances, that was likely due to the perceived weakness of the statistical evidence to explain the circumstances of the individual in question.[102] As Koehler suggests, this perception of weakness is more likely due to some policy concern apart from the actual potential probative value of the evidence,[103] and may reflect a judicial preference for anecdotal evidence over statistical evidence.

What is intriguing about evidentiary preferences is a potential differentiation in the way scientists and lawyers approach the hierarchy of evidence. In the medical sciences, evidence is often described as fitting within a loosely structured pyramid where the top is occupied by meta-analysis,[104] followed by RCT, and then observational studies. Case reports, or individual recounts of events, are at the lowest rung.[105] By contrast, the law appears to prefer evidence of direct observation over statistical analysis, reversing the scientists' hierarchy of evidence. This may, in part, explain the longstanding angst expressed within judicial reasons and debate in evidence scholarship over the usefulness of statistical evidence in fact-finding. The effect of this angst is that when statistical evidence is adduced by way of expert evidence, very often the underlying basis for that opinion is obscured in favour of the perceived credibility of the expert giving the evidence independently of the empirical bases of their opinion.[106] Of course, that preference will

[99] Preferences for non-statistical evidence are not universal: cf *Sims v MacLennan* [2015] EWHC 2739 [74] (an expert's clinical experience may be sufficient in a clinical setting but not for legal causation).

[100] eg C Guthrie, JJ Rachlinksi and AJ Wistrich, 'Inside the Judicial Mind' (2001) 86 *Cornell Law Review* 777.

[101] Koehler (n 63) pt III.

[102] For an Australian example, see *Merck Sharp & Dohme v Peterson* (2011) 196 FCR 145 (FCAFC) [113].

[103] Koehler (n 63) 385.

[104] AB Haidich, 'Meta-analysis in Medical Research' (2010) 14 *Hippokratia* 29.

[105] MH Murad and others, 'New Evidence Pyramid' (2016) 21 *Evidence Based Medicine* 125.

[106] See G Edmond, 'Re-assessing Reliability' in P Roberts and M Stockdale (eds), *Forensic Science Evidence and Expert Witness Testimony* (Cheltenham, Elgar 2018) 72, 75, 90. This difference between the opinion and the evidence underlying it roughly comports with Brewer's dichotomy of the difference between believing a proposition or a person: S Brewer, 'Scientific Expert Testimony and Intellectual Due Process' (1998) 107 *Yale Law Journal* 1535, 1583. Brewer refers at length to HLA Hart's account of epistemic deference that

> [t]o be an authority on some subject matter a man must in fact have some superior knowledge, intelligence, or wisdom which makes it reasonable to believe that what he says on that subject is more likely to be true than the results reached by others through their independent investigations, so that it is reasonable for them to accept the authoritative statement without such independent investigation or evaluation of his reasoning.

be influenced by the fact that the law is usually concerned with resolving disputes about individuals whereas science seeks to identify causal trends in populations. In Dawid, Faigman and Feinberg's terms, this is the difference between the 'causes of effects' and the 'effects of causes', respectively.[107] The opinion may be more salient to the decision-maker because it is the vehicle by which the effects of causes are translated to causes of effects.

Ironically, perhaps, it is this very same phenomenon that leads to overt criticism of expert evidence in curial litigation. Experts are called to provide opinions on matters that are expressly outside the knowledge of the ordinary person or judge. It is no surprise that one principal complaint against expert evidence is that it can be confusing and difficult to understand. There are, however, more serious systemic allegations against expert evidence. The academy and practitioners have long expressed concerns about the so-called 'hired guns' providing biased opinions for their instructors that may not necessarily assist a court in finding the truth,[108] as well as experts willing to testify on matters that have been described as 'junk' science,[109] or from disciplines that have been inadequately tested for their validity.[110] Courts too have expressed some scepticism towards expert evidence despite its extensive use in civil and criminal litigation, often due to concerns over the independence and reliability of the evidence to be given.[111] So, at once, courts are sceptical of being too involved in the underlying data of an expert's opinion but are also sceptical that the opinion is sufficiently tied to the source of the expert's expertise.

In the US, courts are required to consider the 'scientific validity' of scientific evidence to justify its admission.[112] Reliability is expressly a criterion for admissibility and is assessed through a procedural pre-trial stage commonly called a '*Daubert* motion', after the leading case interpreting rule 702 of the Federal Rules of Evidence.[113] The approach in the UK appears to be somewhere between the US

There is some rational force to this account of expertise (or even Brewer's augmented approach at 1588). But that presupposes that the expert's expertise and basis for the opinion has been adequately exposed. A fact-finder must form an actual belief in the truth of a fact by 'deciding the matter for themselves using their own commonsense': *Murphy v The Queen* (1989) 167 CLR 94, 131 (Dawson J). Independent investigation of at least the underlying basis of the expert's opinion is therefore essential. The underlying rationale of this book is that statistical evidence presents the best means by which an expert's expertise and basis for their opinion can be tested.

[107] AP Dawid, DL Faigman and SE Feinberg, 'Fitting Science into Legal Contexts: Assessing Effects of Causes or Causes of Effects?' (2014) 43 *Sociological Methods Research* 359.

[108] ML Livingstone, 'Have we Fired the "Hired Gun"?' (2008) 18 *Journal of Judicial Administration* 39, 40.

[109] DE Bernstein, 'Junk Science in the United States and the Commonwealth' (1996) 21 *Yale Journal of International Law* 123, 125.

[110] G Edmond, 'What Lawyers Should Know about the Forensic "Sciences"' (2015) 36 *Adelaide Law Review* 33, 79.

[111] eg *ASIC v Drake (No 2)* (2016) 340 ALR 75 (FCA) [370]–[381].

[112] DE Bernstein, 'The Misbegotten Judicial Resistance to the Daubert Revolution' (2013) 89 *Notre Dame Law Review* 27, 31ff.

[113] *Daubert v Merrell Dow Pharmaceuticals* 43 F3d 1311 (9dCir, 1995). See further ch 2, section II.

and Australia. The common law provides that expert evidence must have 'sufficient reliability' under English law to be admissible.[114] This principle is said to have arisen from the common law and applies generally to English courts. Unlike the more unified approach taken by the UEL, there are distinct legislative and practice instruments that provide additional guidance in criminal proceedings.[115] Further, how one is to assess sufficient reliability in either jurisdiction is far from clear.[116]

There is expressly no such corresponding principle under Australia's approach to expert evidence.[117] In keeping with Australia's approach to relevance, it may be possible to have manifestly unreliable expert evidence excluded on relevance grounds if the evidence is so bad it does not contribute in any way to the probability of the existence of a fact in issue. Relatedly, if the source of the expertise is so unreliable that it might be said that there was no relevant expertise on which the expert based their opinion, that may also justify the non-admission of the expert evidence. Outside of these extremes however, Australian law does not regulate the admission of expert evidence by reason of its reliability.

The gravamen of this book is that expert evidence is at its most useful when it is based on sound empirical evidence generated within, and according to the conventions of, the expert's field. Presently, failing to identify the existence of that basis is a ground for inadmissibility under Australian law.[118] Failing to adequately explain how the opinion relies on the empirical evidence, or the perceived unreliability of the empirical evidence, are bases for undermining the weight of that evidence. However, courts approach the evaluation of underlying material inconsistently. Focusing on the underlying material and not just the opinion per se is a more robust way of analysing the admissibility and weight of expert evidence. The opinion is, or should be, a conduit for explaining the underlying evidence and its applicability to the instant case. Approached in this way, the court would be better placed to assess where the opinion departs from accepted evidence, and to form its own view as to the existence of the facts-in-issue by reference to the available empirical evidence.

IV. Scientific and Litigation-generated Statistical Evidence

Experts who present their opinions based on statistical evidence to courts usually do so by reference to scientific literature that has been prepared independently of

[114] *R v Dlugosz* [2013] EWCA Crim 2, [11].

[115] See discussion in Dennis (n 41) 897.

[116] ibid 899; cf T Ward, 'Explaining and trusting expert evidence: What is a "sufficiently reliable scientific basis"?' (2020) 24 *International Journal of Evidence & Proof* 233, 234.

[117] *R v Tang* (2006) 65 NSWLR 681, 712 [137].

[118] *Dasreef* (n 20) [42].

the litigation ('scientific statistical evidence'). An expert may refer to such evidence in their reports and infer from those studies to the circumstances in the present case. Sometimes the precise proposition that is necessary for the resolution of a legal proceeding has not been addressed in the scientific literature.[119] In that situation, the expert has two options. The expert may infer from existing scientific statistical evidence that is similar, but not the same, as the proposition to be established. For example, if the goal is to prove that a particular share would have decreased in value by reason of a piece of information, one might adduce evidence of similar shares (or groups of shares) being downgraded by the release of similar information. The difficulty with that approach is that it increases the perception of the risk of error, and makes it more difficult for a fact-finder (or gatekeeper) to assess statistical evidence as 'good' due to the differences between the scientific statistical evidence and the instant case. The degree of difference between an effect evidenced by a 'reference class' and the instant case is called the 'inferential gap', and, as chapters four to six explain, the existence of the gap is the primary reason for the concerns expressed about statistical evidence.

The second option is for experts to conduct studies themselves ('litigation-generated statistical evidence'). One of the more famous, albeit infrequently used, examples of litigation-generated statistical evidence is the use of science panels in US litigation.[120] Australia does not have the same science panel mechanism as the US. It may be possible to replicate a science panel using the various civil procedure rules to appoint a either a referee or court-appointed experts. The advantage of court-appointed experts and referees are that such processes may reduce the chances that party alignment by experts will impact their independence, and they will allow the parties to have equal input in instructing the experts. But such court-appointed processes can be extraordinarily expensive and time-consuming. Outside of high-value class actions it is difficult to conceive of circumstances where these procedures are appropriate. Certainly, they have not replaced the traditional model of party-adduced expert evidence in any significant way.

An example of party-adduced litigation-generated statistical evidence are event studies of the kind discussed earlier in this chapter. Although not without controversy of their own, event studies are simple in the context of litigation-generated statistical evidence because the method underlying such regressions are well-known, have few moving parts, and the data necessary to conduct such analyses, being daily share price movements and, usually, the published contemporaneous opinions of market analysts, are readily available. By contrast, litigation-generated statistical evidence used to prove effects in people and products can be far more challenging. In *Re ConAgra Foods*, the defendant company was alleged to have engaged in misleading conduct by marketing its brand of cooking oil as '100%

[119] E Beecher-Monas, 'Lost in Translation: Statistical Inference in Court' (2014) 46 *Arizona State Law Journal* 1057, 1073.

[120] LL Hooper, JS Cecil and TE Willging, 'Assessing Causation in Breast Implant Litigation: The Role of Science Panels' (2001) 64 *Law and Contemporary Problems* 139.

natural' when the oil was in fact made from genetically modified organisms.[121] Consumers contended that there was inherent additional value from the marketing of the product as 100% natural, which they paid for and did not receive. To prove this allegation, they relied on a 'hedonic regression' to determine the value placed on the 100% natural label compared to products that did not contain that label, and a conjoint analysis that measured the stated preferences of participants in the value assigned to the 100% natural label.[122] While the statistical analysis underlying this study is similar to an event study, being in the nature of a regression analysis, what causes it to be more difficult in the litigation context is the need to design and implement an experiment and data collection exercise that is specific to the questions in issue in the litigation.

One might find scientific statistical evidence in economic literature about the value of labelling, but the specificity of the fact-in-issue reduces the probative value of that evidence in proving those facts. Conducting the study for the litigation ensures the narrowest possible gap between the reference class and the effect to be established. Doing so comes with attendant risks. Even in the US, where litigation-generated statistical evidence is fairly common,[123] courts have drawn a distinction in reliability between scientific and litigation-generated statistical evidence. In *Daubert v Merrell Dow Pharmaceuticals* (on remand from the Supreme Court of the United States), Kozinski J stated:

> One very significant fact to be considered [in determining admissibility] is whether the experts are proposed to testify about matters growing naturally and directly out of research that they have conducted independent of the litigation, or whether they have developed the opinions expressly for the purposes of testifying. That an expert testifies for money does not necessarily cast doubt on the reliability of his testimony, as few experts appear in court merely as an eleemosynary gesture. But in determining whether proposed expert testimony amounts to good science, we may not ignore the fact that a scientist's normal workplace is the lab or the field, not the courtroom or the lawyer's office.
>
> That an expert testifies based on research he has conducted independent of the litigation provides important, objective proof that the research comports with the dictate of good science. For one thing, experts whose findings flow from existing research are less likely to have been biased toward a particular conclusion by the promise of remuneration …[124]

A general proposition that litigation-generated statistical evidence is less reliable than scientific statistical evidence is misconceived. In the first instance, all statistical and empirical evidence is, by its nature, subject to risk of falsification and error. For example, the design, and therefore outcomes, of scientific statistical evidence can be influenced (consciously or unconscionably) by professional

[121] *Re ConAgra Foods* 90 F Supp 3d 919 (CDCal, 2015).
[122] ibid 944–45.
[123] *Sanchez-Knutson v Ford* 310 FRD 529, 538 (SDFla, 2015) and cases cited therein.
[124] *Daubert v Merrell Dow Pharmaceuticals* 43 F3d 1311, 1317 (9dCir, 1995).

rivalries, entrenched beliefs and mistakes. There are more serious problems still that can pervade empirical research. Academic misconduct and the falsification of empirical work is a prominent problem for empirical research, especially in light of the now well-documented pressures on academics to 'publish or perish'.[125] Notwithstanding the checks and balances that are inherent to the scientific technique and the relative transparency of the publication process, and putting any deliberate misconduct to one side, human frailties still play a significant role in the decisions that are made by researchers and can easily infect the design and implementation of empirical research. Of course, litigation-generated statistical evidence is subject to a theoretically superadded risk that, in addition to the usual risks associated with empirical research, it is being prepared for the purpose of litigation, often at the request of a partisan party, and that could be a factor influencing the researcher. Unless the court appoints the researcher to conduct the study (paid for equally by both parties), a risk of party-aligned partisanship will remain.

For common law countries like Australia and the UK that insist on the independence of expert evidence, there is an inherent fallacy in specially tarring experts, and litigation-generated statistical evidence, with the 'hired gun' label. Experts, especially professional experts, must be aware of the obligations that are owed to the court in preparing the evidence. Such obligations are not a panacea for the problem of bias in expert evidence, however. Alleging that an expert has deliberately sought to mislead a court by introducing false or confected evidence is extremely serious. It is a matter that can be tested in cross-examination. Given its serious nature, it would be inappropriate for there to be any general principle discounting the utility of litigation-generated statistical evidence. Further, such evidence may be the most appropriate in the circumstances. Using research based on the parameters set by the litigation allows for evidence that measures as precisely as possible the causal proposition in issue. Survey evidence, for example, is utilised in Australia and the US to demonstrate the existence of markets, or whether consumers can be confused by the similarity between goods,[126] and can be 'uniquely suited' to proving such facts by reason of that specificity.[127]

A more pressing concern with litigation-generated statistical evidence is the real difficulty in designing a study for the purpose of litigation that can survive the scrutiny of the litigious process. Whenever statistical evidence is being specifically adduced for litigation (scientific or litigation-generated statistical evidence) it can be subject to intense scrutiny, including with respect to its design and methodology. Litigation-generated statistical evidence is particularly susceptible to this scrutiny. First, in any experiment there are numerous integers that comprise the experiment. If any one of these integers fail to meet expectations or are insufficiently explained

[125] I Freckelton, *Scholarly Misconduct: Law, Regulation, and Practice* (Oxford, Oxford University Press, 2016) 21ff.

[126] See discussion in *Arnotts* (n 75) 358.

[127] *Saliba v State* 475 NE2d 1181, 1185 (IndCrtApp, 1985).

the study may be significantly undermined or even disregarded.[128] These risks have led judges to treat litigation-generated statistical evidence with substantial caution due to its costly nature and risk of the study being impugned.[129] Further, whereas the authors of scientific statistical evidence are not generally called for cross-examination, experts who conduct litigation-generated statistical evidence can be robustly cross-examined on methodological and design decisions. Second, either because of any one of those factors, or for other reasons, there is a real risk that the expert will be accused (fairly or unfairly) of partisan conduct because of the decisions that need to be made in the preparation of the evidence and the high degree of interactivity that requires with the lawyers conducting the litigation. For these reasons, whilst such evidence may be the most statistically 'useful' evidence in that it can narrow the extent of any inferential gap between the evidence and the effect in issue, the difficulty and expense in preparing the evidence has tended to limit its use in common law litigation.

Litigation-generated statistical evidence has been used more widely in class actions. As noted above, it is often used in US proceedings involving employment and discrimination disputes, and product liability litigation, among others. As the UK does not have a general class action regime, litigation-generated statistical evidence is rarely deployed in that context. One example of where it has been used is in discrimination cases, where there have been attempts to prove that certain employment policies are discriminatory.[130] The Australian approach to litigation-generated statistical evidence is still in its infancy. Whereas Australia has had a class action regime since 1992, outside of event studies in securities class actions, such evidence is rarely introduced. The most common form of such evidence, especially where it involves human decision-making, is 'survey evidence'. As survey evidence is comprised of numerous out-of-court statements, Australian courts admit survey evidence either as an adjunct to expert opinion,[131] like scientific statistical evidence, or on discretionary grounds to minimise the procedural concerns and attendant costs associated with calling hundreds, and potentially thousands, of individual witnesses.[132]

The Australian approach to survey evidence provides a useful window into the problems that can be experienced by litigation-generated statistical evidence. Survey evidence is admissible, conditional 'upon proof that it has been satisfactorily conducted using relevant and unambiguous questions'.[133] The reason for this distinction in the admissibility test between scientific and litigation-generated statistical evidence (where both may equally rely on surveys) is not immediately clear. Both are forms of hearsay evidence containing out-of-court statements

[128] eg *Dwyer v Volkswagen Group Australia Pty Ltd* [2021] NSWSC 715, [238]–[252].
[129] These concerns are clearly articulated in the Federal Court's *Survey Evidence Practice Note* (GPN-SURV) (2016) at [2.1].
[130] *Essop v Home Office* [2017] WLR 1343 (UKSC).
[131] *Ritz Hotel v Charles of the Ritz* (1988) 15 NSWLR 158, 178–80.
[132] *Arnotts* (n 75) 360.
[133] ibid 361.

asserted to prove a fact-in-issue subject to an exception. Both tend to be admissible by way and in support of expert opinion. Both likely rely on statistical analysis that 'can confirm that to a specified degree of probability and subject to a specified error rate, the result can be projected to the whole or a defined section of the population'.[134]

It seems likely that the justification for distinguishing between scientific and litigation-generated statistical evidence is procedural, including the recognition that the latter is often costly and hard fought.[135] Perhaps because of these practical concerns, in a departure from the usual approach to evidence, *Arnotts v TPC* set down criteria for the evaluation of survey evidence based on those of the Handbook of Recommended Procedures for Trial in Protracted Cases, adopted by the US Judicial Conference in 1960.[136] Those criteria were summarised in *Greynell Investments v Hunter Douglas*,[137] and later adopted by the Federal Court's Survey Evidence Practice Note (GPN-SURV); the only such practice note in operation in Australia. The decision in *Arnotts* and the terms of the GPN-SURV are curious because they purport to set out both criteria for admissibility and how that evidence is weighed.[138]

The rationale underlying the distinction between scientific and litigation-generated statistical evidence is poor. Each should be scrutinised using the same factors. Expert evidence has been, and continues to be, an area of great expense and procedural manoeuvring in most forms of litigation. The fact that Australian courts are increasingly concerned with the quality of expert evidence puts into sharp focus the need to pay more attention to the quality of that evidence, including the statistical evidence underlying it. The existence of admissibility and weight criteria in the *Survey Evidence Practice Note* lends credence to the view adopted by this book: that statistical evidence should also be admitted and weighed by reference to standardised common factors.

Conclusion

One of the chief complaints made against the statistical evidence in law literature is the level of abstraction at which it is directed. It is, respectfully, correct that

[134] ibid 361, quoting *Sterling Pharmaceuticals v Johnson & Johnson* (1990) AIPC 90-686 (FCA) [81].
[135] GPN-SURV (n 129) [2.2].
[136] *Arnotts* (n 75) 359. Those criteria include that 'a proffered poll was conducted in accordance with accepted principles of survey research … the proper universe was examined, that a representative sample was drawn from that universe, and that the mode of questioning the interviewees was correct … the persons conducting the survey were recognised experts; the data gathered was accurately reported; the sample design, the questionnaire and the interviewing were in accordance with generally accepted standards of objective procedure and statistics in the field of such surveys; the sample design and the interviews were conducted independently of the attorneys; and the interviewers, trained in this field, had no knowledge of the litigation or the purposes for which the survey was to be used'.
[137] *Greynell Investments v Hunter Douglas* (1979) 4 TPR 173 (FCA).
[138] *Arnotts* (n 75) 364; GPN-SURV (n 129) [2.4].

any discussion about the role of statistical evidence in legal proceedings has to be premised on how the law will, or ought, to treat such evidence. That in turn requires identifying a particular law of evidence on which to anchor the discussion. This chapter has identified the underlying evidentiary concepts that inform the balance of the discussion in this book, focusing on the law of Australia, and drawing on principles from the US and UK to demonstrate commonalities and comparisons between common law jurisdictions.

2

Admitting Evidence of General Factual Causation

Introduction

Proof of facts from statistical evidence requires some acceptance by the fact-finder that the causal or associative relationship between variables posited by that evidence is probably true. Statistical evidence seeks to proffer a window into a causative or associative relationship between variables in a state of nature. In US parlance, this is referred to as 'general causation'. Australian law disavows 'general causation' as a necessary element in a cause of action.[1] As a factual proposition, however, a fact-finder's belief in general causation is a necessary step in causal inferences from statistical evidence. Otherwise, the chain of reasoning falls afoul of a 'canon of logic, rather than of law, that one cannot prove a fact by a chain of reasoning which assumes the truth of that fact';[2] the fact, in this case, being the capacity for a causal relationship between the variables of interest.

Impugning general factual causation gives rise to two clear evidentiary objections to statistical evidence. First, that the statistical evidence does not reliably[3] demonstrate that a variable (X) caused or is associated with a variable (Y) in a sample (n), or that n is representative of a population (N). In statistical terms, the generic concept of reliability (as the law understands it) can be described as the 'robustness' of the statistics. Although the reliability of statistical evidence is often put in doubt, under the Australian approach to evidence law, reliability generally is assessed by the fact-finder in determining the weight of evidence and plays no part in the calculus of admissibility.[4] This is a surprising position given the angst

[1] *Seltsam v McGuiness* (2000) 49 NSWLR 262 (NSWCA) [22].

[2] *Sutton v The Queen* (1984) 152 CLR 528, 552; see also *Perry v The Queen* (1982) 150 CLR 580, 612. In *Shepherd v The Queen* (1990) 170 CLR 573, Dawson J stated at 581 that 'intermediate facts' that were a 'necessary basis for the ultimate inference' ought to be established to the standard of proof. General factual causation is an intermediate fact that, it follows, must be proven to the standard of proof, and by admissible evidence. See further HW Smith, 'Components of Proof in Legal Proceedings' (1942) 51 *Yale Law Journal* 537, 561.

[3] The term reliability here refers to reliability in the legal sense, that the evidence may not in fact be an epistemically good basis to find the fact it is adduced to prove. Statistical reliability is a different concept: section II.C.1 below.

[4] *R v Tang* (2006) 65 NSWLR 681, 712; M Kumar, 'Admissibility of Expert Evidence: Proving the Basis for an Expert's Opinion' (2011) 33 *Sydney Law Review* 427, 430; JD Heydon, 'Is the Weight

directed towards statistical evidence in the literature and by the courts, and is now out of step with Canada and the US, and increasingly with the UK.[5]

Second, general causal associations that one can infer from statistical evidence are different to causal propositions in law, such that the former is inappropriate for the latter. These objections arise from the (true) statement that correlation does not equal causation but have been subverted in legal discourse by a failure to understand how statistical evidence and causation interact.

The effect of these objections, if successful, suggests that the statistical evidence falls short of the first two levels of the statistical syllogism. The purpose of this chapter is to evaluate the conditions by which statistical evidence ought to fail this crucial step, and the evidentiary mechanisms that should be used in assessing general factual causation. The jurisdictional focus is the law of Australia. However, given the uncertain footing of how reliability is to be assessed under English law, the principles that are discussed have some bearing on the approach that could be taken in England and Wales. Section I evaluates the justification for the position that statistical evidence should not be subject to a reliability test as a matter of admissibility. Section II proposes a test of reliability objections to the admissibility of statistical evidence.

I. Reliability and Admissibility

Statistical evidence reported in an academic journal or report and then relied upon in court is an out-of-court statement and prima facie hearsay. Likewise, data underlying statistical analyses collected from human respondents are hearsay.[6] Such evidence is rarely excluded on hearsay grounds, however. First, gatekeepers may have a legislative discretion to ignore the operation of the hearsay rule.[7] Second, as regards the statements of participants about themselves, courts may consider such underlying statements to be 'a contemporaneous representation about the person's health, feelings, sensations, intention, knowledge or state of mind',[8] and admissible as an exception to the hearsay rule.[9] Third, and most typically, statistical evidence, whether relying on data drawn from previous representations or otherwise, is admissible as an exception to the hearsay rule when relied on by an expert witness.[10]

of Evidence Material to its Admissibility?' (2014) 26 *Current Issues in Criminal Justice* 219, 224); I Freckelton, *Expert Evidence*, 7th edn (Sydney, Thomson Reuters, 2023) 1089–90.

[5] Freckelton, *Expert Evidence* (n 4).

[6] *Arnotts v TPC* (1990) 24 FCR 313, 360.

[7] ibid.

[8] *Ritz Hotel v Charles of the Ritz* (1988) 15 NSWLR 158 (NSWSC) 178D.

[9] UEL s 66A.

[10] *Dasreef v Hawchar* (2011) 243 CLR 588, [69], Heydon J characterised the exception as the ability of experts to 'give evidence of hearsay matters which go to demonstrate their expertise'. That construction of the rule is too narrow. The exception equally applies where the expert is inferring the existence

When statistical evidence is admitted in this way, no consideration is given to its robustness as evidence of general factual causation. The exception to this position is that statistical evidence can be irrelevant if it has no capacity whatsoever to be probative of facts-in-issue; X could not have caused or been associated with Y in *n* because the study itself was so poorly implemented that it said nothing at all, or that any conclusion about *n* is not, in any way, capable of being evidence of *N*.[11] This latter conclusion would usually only arise if the variables were spuriously correlated, insofar as the results showing an association are in fact entirely incorrect.[12] As relevance is assessed with the evidence taken at its highest, demonstrating that the statistics are completely worthless is a necessarily high burden and, in the ordinary course, one would expect practitioners to self-exclude such evidence from the corpus of evidence. Moreover, as will be considered below, because experts rarely engage with the underlying reliability of their evidence as a function of admissibility, gatekeepers are unlikely to engage with the reliability of the statistical evidence so as to conclude that the statistical evidence was, in fact, spurious and irrelevant.

Likewise, one could object to the degree of the probative value the statistical evidence possesses. Such an objection would only result in exclusion under particular conditions, such as demonstrating that adducing the evidence would be a waste of time and cost relative to its probative value.[13] Objections to weight are more typically expressed as a function of whether the fact should be found or not and are left to commonsense devices of the fact-finder.

Hearsay objections to statistical evidence are objections to the form of the evidence. Even when an objection is brought against the statistical evidence by reason of its probative value being outweighed by its prejudicial effect, a gatekeeper does not take into account the 'reliability' of the expert opinion, nor the statistical evidence the opinion relies on.[14] The substance of the evidence, including its robustness, is not considered for admissibility. Leaving the robustness of statistical evidence to fact-finders alone, especially for statistical evidence in which lay fact-finders have likely had no formal training, is unsatisfactory. And if statistical

of general factual causation as part of their opinion: see *R v Abadom* [1983] 1 WLR 126 (CA) 131F (Kerr LJ); R Pattenden, 'Expert Opinion Evidence based on Hearsay' (1982) *Criminal Law Review* 85, 87.

[11] *Dasreef* (n 10) 622; *IMM v The Queen* (2016) 257 CLR 300, [39]; *R v Shamouil* (2006) 66 NSWLR 228, [56].

[12] One famous example of spurious statistics is the apparent association between divorce rates in Maine and the US consumption of margarine: see T Vigen, *Spurious Correlations* (Sydney, Hachette, 2015).

[13] UEL s 135. Similar powers exist in the UK in both the civil (Civil Procedure Rules r 32.1) and criminal jurisdictions (eg Police and Criminal Evidence Act 1984 s 78 or at common law).

[14] *IMM* (n 11) [54], and consideration in G Edmond, 'Re-assessing Reliability' in P Roberts and M Stockdale (eds), *Forensic Science Evidence and Expert Witness Testimony* (Cheltenham, Elgar, 2018) 97. A similar approach is taken under English law even though a standard of 'sufficient reliability' is in place: see M Redmayne, *Expert Evidence and Criminal Justice* (Oxford, Oxford University Press, 2001) chs 5 and 6.

evidence (or an opinion based on statistical evidence) is admissible without the need to explain that evidence, experts and lawyers have no incentive to ensure that the opinion has sufficient depth of analysis of the underlying material to make that evaluative exercise possible. It would be beneficial for an evaluative test of statistical evidence to be established both to regulate the admissibility of statistical evidence and to provide a guide to the evaluation of the weight of statistical evidence.

A. The Importance of Reliability

Within evidence scholarship, there exists a debate over whether evidence should be reviewed for reliability as part of its admissibility. This debate is especially important for expert evidence and the statistical evidence that underlies it. Edmond is a major proponent of the view that expert evidence ought to be subject to a review for its reliability prior to its admissibility.[15] His principal focus is on the review of 'forensic evidence' in the context of criminal proceedings, but the principles that he discusses are apt for statistical evidence more broadly. Edmond defines the reliability of forensic evidence as 'validation studies, indicative error rates, uncertainties and limitations, and empirically-warranted forms of expression',[16] each of which would be measured by statistical analyses. Statistical evidence is, in effect, one measure of reliability of expert evidence.

Insufficient attention is paid to the reliability of statistical evidence both when that evidence is admitted and when it is being weighed. This is of particular concern where it is not unusual for experts to refer to empirical research in their opinions without demonstrating the reliability of that evidence. Gatekeepers rarely, if ever, scrutinise that evidence for its reliability as a part of its admissibility, and, Edmond argues, nor do fact-finders, who appear to focus on the expert opinion itself, rather than the underlying indicia of that opinion.[17] As Edmond observes:

> Forensic science evidence is frequently evaluated in conditions where challenges focus on the credibility ... of individual forensic practitioners ... and other issues less important than knowing whether the [forensic] procedures actually work, how well and under what conditions.[18]

Failing to consider the reliability of expert evidence, and the statistical evidence on which it relies, as a function of admissibility means that the reliability of the

[15] See also C Maxwell, 'Preventing Miscarriages of Justice: The Reliability of Forensic Evidence and the Role of the Trial Judge as Gatekeeper' (2019) 93 *Australian Law Journal* 642; I Freckelton and others, *Expert Evidence and Criminal Jury Trials* (Oxford, Oxford University Press, 2016) ch 2.

[16] G Edmond, 'Against Oracular Pronouncement: A Reply to Heydon' (2015) 36 *Adelaide Law Review* 173, 173.

[17] See G Edmond and D Mercer, 'Keeping "Junk" History, Philosophy and Sociology of Science out of the Courtroom' (1997) 20 *University of New South Wales Law Journal* 48, 59.

[18] *Edmond*, 'Re-assessing' (n 14) 90.

evidence is only scrutinised if it is put in issue. Leaving the parties to their own devices is dangerous. The parties themselves may not understand, or have limited incentives or resources to challenge the underlying bases for the expert opinion.[19] Cross-examination or evidence in reply is a poor substitute for rigorous standards of review, especially when it comes to encouraging how statistical evidence is to be understood.[20] Overall, very few civil or criminal proceedings ever result in a full hearing of the facts, reducing opportunities for testing evidence in individual cases and institutional learning about statistical evidence. Leaving the burden of disproving the reliability of the statistical evidence with the opposing party is inappropriate in those circumstances.[21]

Edmond gives a number of reasons why it is important to scrutinise forensic scientific evidence as a matter of reliability, rather than leaving the assessment exclusively to the fact-finder as a matter of weight. Chief among those is that many of the forensic scientific techniques relied on in criminal trials have never been validated and there is a substantial history of techniques, including statistical techniques, having been invalidated after wrongful convictions were quashed.[22] This work suggests that the review of statistical evidence is even more fundamental than weeding out 'unreliable' or 'junk' evidence. Rather, it is about informing gatekeepers and fact-finders about how statistical evidence works and how fact-finders should approach the task of weighing that evidence in the proof of general factual causation and ultimately specific causation.

Much of the scholarship about defective expert evidence concerns the criminal trial where judge and jury play distinct functions. A key focus was the ability of a lay jury to appropriately understand complex scientific evidence and assess its reliability based on the evidence given by the witness and in their report. Common law courts typically give a great deal of deference to jurors, and, in most cases, refuse to withhold relevant evidence simply because it is complex or potentially confusing unless there is some identifiable risk.[23] But in light of the reduced prevalence of jury trials outside the US, one might argue that the need for a reliability review of statistical evidence is limited to criminal proceedings where a jury is empanelled.

At least where statistical evidence is relied on, such an argument fails to appreciate the difficulties faced by judges in interpreting statistical evidence, and the

[19] G Edmond, 'Icarus and the Evidence Act: Section 137, Probative Value and Taking Forensic Science Evidence "at its Highest"' (2017) 41 *Melbourne University Law Review* 106, 140, 143.

[20] G Edmond, 'What Lawyers Should Know about the Forensic "Sciences"' (2015) 36 *Adelaide Law Review* 33, 86.

[21] SJ Odgers and JT Richardson, 'Keeping Bad Science out of the Courtroom' (1995) 18 *University of New South Wales Law Journal* 108, 128.

[22] Edmond, 'Icarus' (n 19) 127.

[23] See discussion in *GK* (2001) 53 NSWLR 317 (NSWCCA) [29]–[31]. See also Freckelton, *Expert Evidence* (n 4) 1074, noting that 'scientific evidence' can be potentially prejudicial when such evidence is '[d]ressed up in scientific language which the jury does not easily understand … this evidence is apt to be accepted by the jury as being virtually infallible and as having more weight that it deserves', quoting *DD* 2000 SCC 43, [53].

widespread use (whether overt or tacit) of empirical evidence in civil proceedings to justify the conclusions of experts. Gatekeepers have no framework for assessing the reliability of statistical evidence relied on by expert witnesses. Outside of narrow fields such as epidemiology or econometrics where statistics are the crux of the opinion, experts often gloss over the extent to which statistical techniques are relied on. By evaluating statistical evidence for reliability as part of its admissibility, experts will be required to put forward an explanation of the reliability of the statistical evidence underlying their opinions. Such an explanation allows decision-makers to properly evaluate the reliability of the statistical evidence for themselves, with the benefit of that experts' opinion on reliability. That, in turn, would filter through to the exercise of evaluating the weight of the evidence either because the judge could direct the jury on the indicia of the reliability of the evidence, by reference to a cogent and considered judicial theory of reliability, or because the dual gatekeeper and fact-finding function would overlap. As the indicia of admissibility are equally relevant to the assessment of the weight of the statistical evidence, using an admissibility framework for assessing statistical evidence would allow a fact-finder to employ that same framework in considering the probative value of the statistical evidence in the proof of general factual causation.

Against this proposition that reliability ought to be taken into account is a form of evidentiary formalism. As the common law has not traditionally required gatekeepers to review reliability in making admissibility decisions, and more recent statutory codifications of those common rules have not explicitly changed that status quo, there is, it is argued, no basis for gatekeepers to perform such a review.[24] If this contention extends to statistical evidence that is adduced (and, as noted below, there are good reasons for why it does not), it is problematic. Outside the purely formalistic argument,[25] there are three major substantive and procedural reasons against a reliability review for the admissibility of statistical evidence.

1. *Usurping the Fact-finder*

Allowing gatekeepers to evaluate reliability, it is argued, may transgress on the functions of the fact-finder. The weight of evidence is exclusively in the province of the fact-finder. Reliability is a feature of the weight of the evidence that a gatekeeper is not supposed to consider when making decisions about the admissibility of evidence.[26]

Aside from historical significance, there are pragmatic reasons for this rule. Principally among them is that decisions about the weight of evidence are not made in a vacuum but by reference to all of the evidence in a proceeding.[27] Almost

[24] Heydon (n 4) 230.
[25] Which itself can be multifaceted, but ultimately beside the point for present purposes: ibid 235ff.
[26] *Wendo v The Queen* (1963) 109 CLR 559, 562; *R v XY* (2013) 84 NSWLR 363, 400, 405.
[27] *R v Adams* [1996] 2 Cr App R 467, 481.

all admissibility decisions are going to be made prior to the reception of all of the evidence. As such, admissibility usually does not take into account the real probative value of that evidence because it cannot do so by reference to all of the adduced evidence. Assessing probative value prior to the admission of all evidence in the proceeding is technically impossible and counts against a preliminary assessment of the weight of evidence in which reliability is an integral factor.

In the premises, a distinction can be drawn between jury and judge-alone trials. For a judge-alone trial, this argument no longer carries any real value. Judges sit contemporaneously as fact-finder and gatekeeper, and can make their decisions about the admissibility of the evidence after all the evidence is received. Although it is possible that a reliability review could be conducted prior to a full hearing on the evidence, by way of voir dire, there is no reason why it has to occur in that way, and any procedural differences between reliability being reviewed as part of admissibility or weight are negligible to non-existent.

For case management decisions – where the case management judge is separate from the trial judge – and jury trials this procedural hurdle is more significant. To decide on the reliability of the evidence prior to the conclusion of the full hearing does necessarily involve some assessment of the probative value of the evidence, or at least the capacity of the evidence to have that probative value.[28] That requires either assuming the existence of certain facts (and how they will be accepted by the fact-finder), or acknowledging that the assessment is being made in an artificial vacuum. This concern cannot be entirely explained away. Instead, what has to be considered is how to best balance the risks to the fact-finding scheme in the context of a particular case. A judge does not have to exclude evidence. It may be that the judge forms the view that the evidence is admissible because of its potential significance. If that is the case, in circumstances where there remains a concern about the evidence, the judge may issue a direction or warning in respect of it.[29]

There are two reasons why a judge may nevertheless exclude the evidence for insufficient reliability. First, as Edmond notes, '[t]here is no judicial usurpation if the jury cannot be placed in a position conducive to the evaluation of opinion evidence'.[30] It can hardly be contended that it is appropriate to allow jurors to consider bad evidence potentially prejudicing and at least unnecessarily extending the trial. Second, what this chapter considers is the use of statistical evidence to prove general factual causation. If the evidence offers some support for general factual causation, it is properly admissible, and may then form the basis of an inference to specific causation. But aside from establishing a theory of objections to evidence adduced to prove general factual causation, it is not clear how additional evidence might come out that is relevant to this decision during the trial. Expert

[28] *DSJ v The Queen; NS v The Queen* (2012) 215 A Crim R 349.

[29] For an analysis in respect of the effectiveness of such warnings or directions, see G Edmond and others, 'A Warning about Judicial Directions and Warnings' (2023) 44 *Adelaide Law Review* 194.

[30] Edmond, 'Icarus' (n 19) 135.

reports for all parties should be tendered in advance of the trial. Perhaps some evidence could be extracted on cross-examination that could change the nature of the theory of general factual causation or could cast further light on the statistical evidence. Requiring the parties to establish the reliability of their evidence should, however, turn the attention of the experts to that issue in advance, making their opinions on the reliability of the evidence underlying their opinion clear from the outset.

2. *Cost and Procedural Hurdles*

Heydon argues that a gatekeeper reliability review would increase the cost and duration of litigation by increasing interlocutory disputes and otherwise undermine the distinction between gatekeeper and fact-finder.[31] Duplication also results from charging the gatekeeper and fact-finder to sequentially adjudge reliability, especially where the gatekeeper's conclusion may be that no decision can be made pending the receipt of further evidence.

In the first instance, it is not clear that an additional procedural motion on evidence would increase costs. Scholarship regarding the *Daubert* procedure in the US, involving a preliminary hearing on the reliability of expert evidence, has not identified significant increases in costs as a major detriment of the concept.[32] Where a hearing does go to trial, the addition of a further procedural step would logically increase costs. But very few cases actually reach a full trial. Bringing forward an assessment of the reliability of the evidence, or at least having a common framework to scrutinise that evidence, would allow the parties to better understand the relative strengths of their expert evidence, and, logically, better enable an early settlement or plea.[33] That in turn would decrease the costs associated with unmeritorious litigation propped up by poor expert evidence, or less dramatically, fact-finding concerns about the robustness of statistical evidence. Such approaches may even shorten or avoid hearings by allowing the parties to better evaluate their respective positions.

This work does not propose, however, that a separate hearing of reliability is necessary in non-jury trial cases. Its central tenet is that engaging in a reliability review for admissibility will lead to the development of a framework by which statistical evidence can be assessed. That framework can then be applied either by the parties during the life of the litigation or by the judge at trial after receiving the evidence. In the vast majority of cases, including many criminal cases, a bifurcated approach to this reliability assessment is unnecessary.

[31] Heydon (n 4) 236.

[32] Indeed, quite the opposite. Some scholars imply that *Daubert* motions may decrease costs: MD Green and J Sanders, 'In Defense of Sufficiency' (2014) 23 *Widener Law Journal* 663, 664.

[33] Maxwell P, extra-judicially, noted that orders for the production of a pre-trial joint expert report (some of which concerning the reliability of the forensic evidence) saved the 'time and expense and trauma' of the trial: Maxwell (n 15) 654.

Alternately, where there is a sufficient basis for doing so, a party could seek to have a preliminary determination on the expert evidence. Whereas Heydon contends that the use of a voir dire is problematic because it may 'swamp' the main trial process, there is clearly a balancing act to be struck. Using an additional procedure will necessarily bring forward some aspects of the case prior to a hearing of all the evidence. That is consistent with procedural rules requiring the parties to put forward their evidence well in advance of any hearing. That is not to discount the possibility that new and different facts will emerge after the forensic process of cross-examination. But for the purpose of understanding whether statistical evidence can reliably prove general factual causation based on existing evidence, that review could be conducted on the basis of assumptions that will be proven in evidence – or, if one party disputes those assumptions, evidence can be called in reply. If that is to result in additional expense (and it is not clear that either in the individual case, or in the long run, it will), then that expense may be justified where the reliability of the statistics employed is to be improved, and courts and lawyers will become better versed in how to appropriately use statistical evidence. The alternative is for that evidence, and those defects, to come out in the trial process before the fact-finder, after the ability for any rectification is long past.

3. *Inappropriate Forum*

Another objection against a reliability review of expert evidence comes from the view that the law is an inappropriate place to put science on trial.[34] Structurally, common law fact-finding is dependent on what evidence the parties produce. If insufficient work is done to interrogate the scientific field from which the evidence is drawn, there is a risk that insufficient information about that field will be put into evidence.[35]

Legal decisions are made expressly to resolve disputes. The consequence of a legal decision is that the facts found are 'true' notwithstanding any remaining uncertainty.[36] Decisions are made 'once and for all' between the parties to ensure finality in the judicial process. Later advancements in knowledge would not ordinarily justify a re-opening of spent proceedings to further agitate evidentiary matters.[37] Scientific research, by contrast, is subject to ongoing renewal and effort. A conclusion that X causes Y at time 1 does not in any way inhibit or devalue the later conclusion that X does not cause Y at time 2. These two different perspectives clash when it comes to finding the existence of events that occur in a state of nature at a particular point in time.[38] Sometimes, the results of an attempt by

[34] *Daubert v Merrell Dow Pharmaceuticals* 509 US 579, 600–01 (1993) (Rehnquist CJ) (in dissent). See also I Freckelton, *The Trial of the Expert* (Oxford, Oxford University Press, 1987) 163.

[35] *Commissioner for Government Transport v Adamcik* (1961) 106 CLR 292, 298.

[36] *Mallett v McMonagle* [1970] AC 166, 176.

[37] *Daubert* (n 34) 596–97.

[38] cf L Brilmayer and L Kornhauser, 'Quantitative Methods and Legal Decisions' (1978) 46 *University of Chicago Law Review* 116, 126.

the legal system to determine the truth of a causal relationship prior to sufficient research being done can lead to troubling results. The US breast implant litigation is an oft-cited example, where billions of dollars in damages were paid, and regulatory bans imposed, for the purported link between breast implants and autoimmune diseases that was subsequently found by research to be false.[39] To exemplify the problem, more recent evidence appears to suggest that women with breast implants are more likely to develop autoimmune diseases than women without breast implants.[40]

Epistemic risks of these types cannot be entirely avoided, and nor is there a panacea for the fundamental difficulty in fact-finding for all time against prevailing uncertainty. Nature rarely provides simple causal explanations. How human beings understand causal relationships evolves as more evidence is collected. There are practical steps that can be taken to offset some of these risks. In the breast implant litigation, for example, one judge ordered the formation of a science panel to comment on the state of the evidence linking breast implants to autoimmune disease. Those findings were then used in subsequent litigation to reject scientific evidence of general factual causation.[41] In a perfect world, these panels would be commonplace, albeit they too are not immune from the evolution of knowledge. But who should bear the cost of these panels? For most litigation the cost would be prohibitive. The hard reality is that the law must make these determinations based on the evidence before the court. Legal systems cannot adopt a wait and see approach, and nor can they (usually) require the parties to undertake further testing or research, or convene a science panel, on a difficult causal pathway. Against these practical limitations is the simple fact that failing to find that causation exists has the same legal consequence as 'X does not cause Y'. The inquiry that must be undertaken by the fact-finder is not 'does X cause Y' as an absolute matter but has the plaintiff discharged the burden of proof in the present case as to the causal association between X and Y? Of course, creating such a fiction cannot avoid overlapping with what the fact-finder actually perceives to have occurred – and nor should it. The standard of proof reflects the subjective belief of the fact-finder. If a fact-finder fails to believe in the truth of the causal association, the fact cannot be found. The standard that should be applied is nonetheless one that is bound to the evidence in the proceeding at hand, and not on hypothetical evidence that may or may not exist outside of the proceeding. To say that the law should not, or is not equipped to, perform a review of the scientific basis of evidence relied on in court, even where that is directed at a gatekeeper review of the evidence, is ultimately a concession that the fact-finding process will abdicate its responsibility to consider

[39] *Re Breast Implant Litigation* 11 FSupp2d 1217 (DColo, 1998), and discussion in J Hersch, 'Breast Implants: Regulation, Litigation, and Science' in WK Viscusi (ed), *Regulation Through Litigation* (2002) 160.

[40] CJ Coroneos and others, 'US FDA Breast Implant Postapproval Studies' (2019) 269 *Annals of Surgery* 30.

[41] See comments in LL Hooper, JS Cecil and TE Willging, 'Assessing Causation in Breast Implant Litigation: The Role of Science Panels' (2001) 64 *Law and Contemporary Problems* 139.

and weight all of the evidence. Since the fact-finder must decide on the facts in any event, the gatekeeper is in no worse position than the fact-finder to review the underlying scientific basis of the evidence.

The law does not ordinarily set parameters for how evidence should be weighted, and instead the review of such evidence is left to the 'commonsense' of the fact-finders. Unless the opposing party takes explicit issue with the statistical evidence, and seeks to adduce evidence in reply, the basis for the expert opinion may never be properly interrogated. If there is no requirement that the underlying basis of an opinion be interrogated for its admissibility, then there is no incentive to put that basis forward. The opinion rule only ever encourages experts and lawyers to put forward the connection between the opinion and the body of knowledge from which it is drawn with bare references to the literature and limited or no evaluation of that literature. This means that fact-finders are poorly equipped to make a determination about the reliability of the evidence. Imposing a reliability standard for admissibility would ensure that an obligation is imposed on the party tendering the evidence to ensure that it can be appropriately weighted. Otherwise, the law is conferring an evidentiary advantage (or potential disadvantage where the evidence is not properly understood) to parties adducing statistical evidence by failing to properly evaluate that evidence.

B. A Mechanism for Assessing the Reliability of Statistical Evidence

How might courts consider the reliability of statistical evidence given the prevailing view that reliability does not feature as part of the admissibility of evidence? This book walks a path between two opposing views. On the one hand, it argues that there is a need to consider reliability for admissibility, both to prevent poor evidence being admitted and to guide the process of fact-finding. On the other, it accepts the legal formalistic approach that it is difficult to perform a genuine and complete reliability review prior to the admission of the evidence. That is not to defend the formalistic approach per se; rather, when statistical evidence is relied on directly by experts, there is sufficient scope under the existing approach to require an assessment of the reliability of that evidence as a necessary indicator of its relevance and admissibility in support of an expert opinion, or, when it is submitted that its potential probative value is outweighed by its prejudicial effect.

1. The Existing Interpretation

Statistical evidence of general factual causation has two major components. First, superficially, the fact and degree of the association between X and Y in *n*. Second, the extent to which that association in *n* identifies an effect in *N*. If the evidence is not capable of showing the existence of an association between X and Y, it is irrelevant, as it has no capacity to prove general factual causation. Otherwise, it is relevant for that purpose. Likewise, if the statistical evidence is so unreliable that it would be considered dangerous to rely on any conclusions it purports to show, or where those conclusions are likely to be spurious, it will be irrelevant.

Once relevance is established, the task of deciding the degree of association to accept in the proof of general factual causation, and the reliability and validity of the statistical evidence in doing so, is commonly left exclusively to the fact-finder. Instead of reviewing the expert opinion for its reliability in deciding whether to admit it,[42] the evidence (and any underlying statistics) is admissible as long as the expert has specialised knowledge based on training, study or experience, and their opinion is based on that knowledge.[43] Specialised knowledge only means that the body of knowledge is 'sufficiently organised or recognised to be accepted as a reliable body of knowledge or experience'.[44] In the oft-cited words of Spigelman CJ in *Tang*, the 'focus of attention must be on the words "specialised knowledge", and not on the introduction of an extraneous idea such as reliability'.[45] As a result, statistical evidence that is admitted in support of an expert opinion, but is itself admissible as evidence in the proof of general factual causation as an exception to the rule against hearsay,[46] is admitted without any effective scrutiny or standards.

Even though an expert must '[fully] expose the reasoning relied on … [and that] examining the substance of an opinion cannot be carried out without knowing the essential integers underlying it' for their opinion to be admissible,[47] this rule does not appear to extend to reliability; it is limited to only whether a basis for the opinion exists at all.[48]

It is also the case, however, that if the evidence is admissible and yet based on little more than the *ipse dixit* of the expert, the weight of that evidence is negatively affected.[49]

Nor can there be a proper review of statistical evidence under rules excluding expert opinion if the probative value of that opinion outweighs its prejudicial effect. Using prejudice as a means of excluding statistical evidence of general factual causation (as opposed to specific causation) is a blunt and, in its current formulation, largely inappropriate, instrument. Chapter six demonstrates that prejudice in the sense employed by evidence law arises from individualising the evidence drawn from a reference class. Further, under Australian law, balancing prejudice and probative value is not undertaken on a full fact-finding assessment of the evidence. The probative value of the evidence is assessed 'at its highest'.[50] There has

[42] JD Heydon, 'Evidence of Forensic Scientific Opinion and the Rules for Admissibility' (2015) 36 *Adelaide Law Review* 101, 103.

[43] UEL s 79.

[44] *HG v The Queen* (1999) 197 CLR 414, 428 (Gaudron J).

[45] *Tang* (n 4) 712.

[46] *Dasreef* (n 10) 632.

[47] *Makita v Sprowles* (2001) 52 NSWLR 705 (NSWCA) [71].

[48] *Dasreef* (n 10) [42].

[49] *Davie v Magistrates of Edinburgh* (1953) SC 34, 40. Similar concerns arose in *Adamcik* (n 35) 303.

[50] *IMM* (n 11) [49]–[54]; *R v Bauer* (2018) 266 CLR 56, [69].

been historically a great deal of controversy over what is meant by the term 'at its highest'. Courts in NSW and Victoria were split on this issue. For the NSW Court of Criminal Appeal, 'at its highest' did not permit considerations of the reliability of the evidence.[51] The Victorian Court of Appeal by contrast expressly permitted reliability to be evaluated as an essential element in assessing what probative value the jury would give to the evidence.[52] First in *IMM v The Queen*, and then in *R v Bauer*, the High Court of Australia (HCA) grappled with this conflicting authority.[53] In *IMM*, a majority held that reliability could not feature in the assessment of probative value for the purpose of determining its prejudicial effect, unless the evidence was so unreliable its relevance was rendered void.[54] *Bauer* unanimously confirmed this interpretation of the process of the assessment of probative value.[55] If the focus of the inquiry is only on the opinion, assessing the probative value of the opinion will not require a court to scrutinise the underlying evidence as long the court could be satisfied that the basis for that opinion is rational. The consequence of that view is that potentially unreliable expert evidence can be admitted as long as the opinion is not completely contrary to scientific or learned discipline and the expert is apparently qualified to give that evidence.

2. *A Revised Approach*

Edmond has proposed that the current exception to the opinion rule is sufficient to enable the review of expert evidence for reliability.[56] He suggests, at least in the context of s 137 of the Uniform Evidence Law (UEL), that in order to appropriately assess 'probative value' at its highest, it is impossible to do so without regard to the underlying reliability of the expert opinion:

> In order to determine the probative value of an opinion based on specialised knowledge we need to know whether the procedure does what it is supposed to do, how well, and in what conditions.[57]

Edmond further suggests that there is at least tacit recognition of this in the High Court's reasons despite its finding that reliability cannot be considered.[58] This work largely agrees with Edmond's view. But it need not go that far when it comes to statistical evidence that has been referred to by an expert.

Where an expert does rely on statistical evidence, the basis rule requires the expert (or, alternatively, the party adducing the expert evidence) to identify the basis for each causal proposition, including identifying and putting before the

[51] *Shamouil* (n 11) [61].
[52] *Dupas v The Queen* (2012) 40 VR 182, [162].
[53] *IMM* (n 11); *Bauer* (n 50).
[54] *IMM* (n 11) [51]–[52].
[55] *Bauer* (n 50) [69].
[56] See Edmond, 'Icarus' (n 19) 135ff.
[57] ibid 122.
[58] ibid 120.

judge the statistical evidence in support of that proposition. Once the statistical evidence is explicitly referred to, that explicit reference results in the statistical conclusion becoming evidence of a fact-in-issue,[59] therefore needing to be relevant and otherwise admissible. The assessment of relevance is taken 'at its highest'. But the difference between statistical evidence and expert opinion is plainer at this juncture. Much like similar fact evidence, where much of this controversy about the reliability review of evidence for its admissibility arises, expert evidence can be reviewed in such a way as to only superficially consider what it is capable of supporting. If an expert opines that X caused Y, it is possible to blind oneself to the strength and cogency of the underlying material in support of that simple statement. The opinion rule, or rules regarding exclusion of evidence for prejudice, only require a court to evaluate the opinion itself, even if it rests on the *ipse dixit* of the expert.

By contrast, the conventional reporting of statistics is different. Statistical evidence will ordinarily state the basis on which an effect between variables is shown, including by reference to the strength of the effect between the variables,[60] the known type I and type II error rates,[61] the validity[62] and reliability of the measures used in the statistical evidence,[63] and the power of the statistical analysis.[64] That is, the means to review the reliability of the statistical evidence are expressly stated in the statistical evidence. For the assessment of the capacity of statistical evidence to have some probative value necessarily requires an appreciation of the robustness of the statistical evidence. It follows that taking statistical evidence at its highest still requires the gatekeeper to evaluate the causal pathway purportedly supported by the statistical evidence in light of its robustness.

Where the statistical evidence fails to report those factors that are critical to its interpretation, such as reliability and validity in that field of research, it is also arguable that such evidence should be inadmissible, or if admitted, its weight severely discounted. Experts are required to specify the assumptions that they make or the facts on which they have relied. Once those assumptions or facts have been identified, there is then a conflict under Australian law whether it is necessary for those assumptions or facts to be proven or provable by other evidence in the proceeding. In *Dasreef v Hawchar*, Heydon J advocated for the existence of 'basis rules'[65] that would mean facts or assumptions relied on by experts must be proven, and a failure to do so would render the opinion inadmissible.[66] The majority in *Dasreef*

[59] *Freckelton, Expert Evidence* (n 4) 120.
[60] Section II.A below.
[61] Section II.B below.
[62] Section II.C.2 below.
[63] Section II.C.1 below.
[64] Section II.B below.
[65] There are commonly said to be three interacting basis rules, being the assumption identification rule, proof of assumption rule and the statement of reasoning rule: see *Dasreef* (n 10) [64] ff. For present purposes the key focus of the inquiry is on the proof of assumption rule.
[66] *Dasreef* (n 10) [102]–[127].

were equivocal on that issue. The existence of such a rule (or set of rules) was previously rejected by the Australian Law Reform Commission.[67] Since *Dasreef* was decided, however, it would appear that the approach taken by Heydon J has been accepted in civil proceedings.[68] By contrast, in criminal proceedings, the existence of a basis rule remains opposed due to the risk that such a rule offends the right to silence.[69] It is unclear whether the different approaches to the interpretation of s 79 of the UEL between criminal and civil proceedings is the product of a valid distinction. Certainly, the existence of a basis rule would appear to be more consistent with how the law is developing, seeing as it provides the most likely basis on which a reliability review of expert evidence can occur as part of its admissibility.[70]

What is clear is that a basis rule for statistical evidence (for civil and criminal proceedings) would be a positive step in the scrutiny of expert evidence. An essential assumption of any statistical measure is that it is valid. Statistical evidence that is entirely invalid is potentially spurious and irrelevant. If it has some validity, but that validity is inappropriate or severely undermines the evidence, it is likely relevant and therefore prima facie admissible under the principles espoused by *Commissioner for Government Transport v Adamcik*[71] and adopted in *Dasreef*, but could be inadmissible if the evidence is likely to be 'misweighted' by the fact-finder (and therefore prejudicial), or be of such minimal probative value that it should be inadmissible either as being too confusing or provocative of undue delay. Importantly, however, by going through that exercise, a gatekeeper, when sitting as fact-finder, would have the evidence of robustness before them so that a proper scrutiny of it can be undertaken as a matter of probative value, or appropriate directions can be given to a jury about that evidence without infringing the general understanding that a gatekeeper cannot tell a fact-finder how evidence should be weighted. There is no such restriction on informing a jury about the potential unreliability of evidence; indeed, where statistical evidence is not robust, such information should be given.[72]

One could, consistently with Edmond's views, claim that this does not go far enough. It does not compel witnesses to explicitly rely on statistical evidence; it simply says that the evidence should be reviewed if it is explicitly relied on. That is a justifiable criticism but offset by current expert evidence jurisprudence. The approach to expert evidence presently suggests that such evidence will be inadmissible if an identifiable basis for the expert's opinion, other than their *ipse dixit*, is

[67] ALRC, *Uniform Evidence Law* (Report 102, 2005), 9.52–9.84.

[68] See, eg, *Dura (Australia) Constructions Pty Ltd v Hue Boutique Living Pty Ltd (No 3)* [2012] VSC 99, [97]–[98] (John Dixon J); *Herron v HarperCollins Publishers Australia Pty Ltd* (2022) 292 FCR 336 at 458 [500]–[501] (Lee J).

[69] eg, *R v Fleming (Costs)* [2023] NSWSC 1258, [22]–[23]; *Taub v R* [2017] NSWCCA 198, [21] ff.

[70] As to the trend in the law, see Edmond, 'Reply' (n 16) 173.

[71] *Adamcik* (n 35).

[72] *Aytugrul v The Queen* (2012) 247 CLR 170, [69]; *R v GK* (2001) 53 NSWLR 317 (NSWCA) [31].

not put into evidence. If that approach survives, then litigants are on notice that the expert must specify the evidentiary basis for every factual contention relied on by that expert. An expert could, in theory, revert to anecdotal evidence. But that will expose the poor basis of the opinion. Anecdote is more readily understood by lay audiences and thereby requires no special protections as long as it is clearly identified. Such an approach is arguably consistent with how the common law and statutory approach to expert evidence is developing. Experts can and do rely on the statistical analysis conducted outside of court. Where empirical evidence is relied on (implicitly or explicitly), that evidence should be explicitly referred to in the opinion 'so that the cogency and probative value of [an expert's] conclusion can be tested and evaluated by reference to it'.[73]

A similar requirement is set out in schedule 7 to the Uniform Civil Procedure Rules 2005 (UCPR), whereby an expert is required to specify 'the reasons for and any literature or other materials utilised in support of each such opinion'. When it is incumbent on the expert to identify the basis for their opinion, and the degree of such references is made clear, it is more likely that parties to litigation will instruct their experts to refer to and analyse that evidence to better protect the opinion. Further, gatekeepers should consider not just the fact of a basis of the opinion, but the reliability of that basis. Expert evidence is at its most useful and reliable, at least in respect of being supported by a body of knowledge supporting that opinion, when it is closely anchored to the underlying research, and not reliant on an impressionistic assessment of the expert's credit.[74]

Courts are becoming more interventionist in regulating the kinds of evidence put forward by parties to litigation. Case management powers are often used to influence and guide how evidence is to be presented at trial. The use of such powers is illustrative of a desire to regulate complex evidence coming before courts. It would not be much of a further step to seek to regulate the reliability of statistical evidence in the way envisioned by this book by updating current practice notes regulating expert evidence.

II. Testing Reliability

If the robustness of statistical evidence is to be assessed as a factor of admissibility and weight, a framework is needed to assist both levels of that review. The most well cited and studied approach comes from the so-called *Daubert* trilogy regarding the admissibility of expert evidence in the US.[75] *Daubert* introduced a requirement that the 'reliability' of expert evidence be considered as a precondition

[73] *Abadom* (n 10) 131.

[74] In the US context of assessing reliability as part of admissibility, see *Merck v Garza* 347 SW3d 256, 262 (TexSC, 2011).

[75] Comprising *Daubert* (n 34), *General Electric Company v Joiner* 522 US 136 (1997) and *Kumho Tire Co v Carmichael* 526 US 137 (1999).

to admissibility of the evidence under r 702 of the Federal Rules of Evidence.[76] *Daubert* has led to an additional obligation on the gatekeeper of conducting a discretionary[77] 'preliminary assessment' of the scientific evidence to ensure that 'the reasoning or methodology underlying the testimony is scientifically valid'.[78]

Daubert, and the worth of an assessment of 'scientific validity', is controversial. What is meant by 'scientific validity' is not always clear, nor is it a uniform concept.[79] This book does not intend to intrude into this debate. *Daubert* concerns the admissibility of scientific evidence generally. The framework proposed by this book concerns the admissibility of statistical evidence, typically in support of expert (and usually scientific) evidence. How each criterion will be assessed will depend on the discipline promulgating the statistics, as different disciplines will have their own conventions and standards of statistical reporting. A gatekeeper and fact-finder will ultimately need to be sensitive to these issues and will rely on the testifying experts to explain why they fit the discipline's conventions. Requiring an explanation of the statistics as a feature of the admissibility of the evidence will ensure that courts have the material available to perform this exercise, as lawyers instructing experts in the preparation of the evidence would be charged with the responsibility of ensuring it is in admissible form.[80] If the information necessary to evaluate the statistical evidence is absent, the evidence will be inadmissible.

In addition to a change in evidentiary approach, *Daubert* evolved into a procedure whereby a preliminary assessment of the scientific evidence was conducted prior to trial.[81] The purpose of this procedural approach (of a kind similar to what Heydon suggests is the consequence of a reliability review for admissibility) is manifest in the US where almost all cases are heard by a jury, and where there was a significant history of problematic 'junk' and 'novel' science being used to found claims.[82] This chapter has already indicated that for the most part, such a procedure is unnecessary in the Australian context, or, if it is necessary, a judge will be able to determine whether the benefits of such a procedure outweigh any detriment at the time the application is proposed. *Daubert* is used here only to identify the factors that gatekeepers and fact-finders should consider when scrutinising statistical evidence for proof of general factual causation.

Daubert postulated five factors in reviewing reliability. These include whether the theory or method can be or has been tested, subject to peer review or publication, has a high 'known or potential error rate', the existence of 'standards

[76] See discussion in DE Bernstein, 'Junk Science in the United States and the Commonwealth' (1996) 21 *Yale Law Journal* 123, 143.

[77] *Joiner* (n 75) 142.

[78] *Daubert* (n 34) 592–93.

[79] See E Beecher-Monas, *Evaluating Scientific Evidence* (Cambridge, Cambridge University Press, 2007) ch 3; Edmond and Mercer (n 17).

[80] *Thiess v Dobbins Contracting* [2016] NSWSC 265, [21]–[22].

[81] See discussion in Federal Judicial Center (FJC), *Reference Manual on Scientific Evidence*, 3rd edn (Washington DC, National Academies Press, 2011) 14.

[82] Bernstein (n 76) 28.

controlling the technique's operation', and whether the theory or technique enjoys general acceptance in the relevant scientific community.[83] The focus of the *Daubert* approach is ascertaining whether the scientific method underpinning the expert evidence is an accurate measure of the relationship the study purports to measure.

The second facet of *Daubert* is 'relevance'.[84] Relevance under *Daubert* appears to mean ascertaining the extent by which the evidence can support a finding of causation in an individual case.[85] To require expert opinion evidence to be relevant is not a novel approach; evidence is admissible only if it is relevant. The *Daubert* approach to relevance appears to extend beyond how relevance is typically understood. There is some suggestion in US scholarship that a *Daubert* analysis permits a judge to assess whether the evidence 'sufficiently' supports the causal proposition.[86] *Daubert* invites the gatekeeper to consider the capacity of the expert evidence to prove a fact-in-issue, for example by looking at the degree to which animal studies are transferrable to general factual causation of human traits.[87] Relevance usually only asks whether the evidence has any capacity at all to rationally affect the existence of a fact-in-issue. This book has already canvassed the fiction about relevance being an 'all or nothing' decision. Relevance is itself a question of degree leading to the decision about whether the evidence has that capacity. But it would be problematic to allow reliability to be assessed on a scale at the admissibility stage. A balance must be struck between assessing statistical evidence 'at its highest' and meaningfully assessing the ability of the evidence to support the existence of general factual causation.

For robustness, the question is only whether, after a proper scrutiny of the evidence, the gatekeeper decides that the statistical evidence can be robust and possess some probative value. This is consistent with the High Court's approach in *IMM* and *Bauer*. Opinions relying on statistical analysis should at least set out (or refer to) an estimate of the effect size, the confidence in that effect size, and methodological factors influencing robustness, the latter including some indication of where this evidence sits within the body of knowledge that comes before it. A court is entitled, as a matter of admissibility, to consider and hear evidence on those features of the evidence that justify its reliability as evidence of general factual causation.

Each of the features of the test of the admissibility of statistical evidence (which then guides how the evidence should be weighted) are to be weighed against one another. A study that has good validity may need to be balanced against a de minimis effect size or a low degree of confidence. Whether the evidence is admissible depends on showing that each of these factors are sufficiently engaged that the evidence is of some weight in the assessment of general factual causation. Although

[83] *Daubert* (n 34) 593–94.
[84] ibid 591.
[85] That is, involving an analysis of sufficiency of the evidence to prove the causal pathway: see Green and Sanders (n 32) 664.
[86] ibid.
[87] *Joiner* (n 75) 146.

this again adopts a test akin to relevance, at least for the admissibility aspect of the test, it is a far more involved process than the present approach to relevance and ultimately requires weighing these different factors so that the gatekeeper believes that the evidence has some probative value and provides a proper basis for expert opinion. The balancing act continues for the assessment of weight where the fact-finder will need to exercise judgement about the usefulness of the evidence in the proof of general factual causation given each of these factors.

A. Effect Size

Statistics are based on a process of hypothesis testing. A researcher might want to test the hypothesis that X causes Y. To do so, the researcher sets a null hypothesis that there is no association between X and Y. Rejecting that null hypothesis means that the study has found that there is an association between X and Y. The degree of that association is the effect size. Often, the greater the degree of association between X and Y, the more believable the inference that X caused Y.[88] If an object (A) causes an event (C) 99 times out of every 100 exposures to A, and a second object (B) causes the same C 30 times out of every 100 exposures to B, evidence showing those causal propensities could allow a person to reasonably believe that A is more likely to be the cause of C than B is, or, at least, that A is more often associated with C than B is. In an epidemiological study testing whether smoking is associated with lung cancer, the effect size is the quantitative difference between the number of those who contract lung cancer and smoke against the number of those who contract lung cancer and who do not smoke. That is, a direct measure of the size of the impact of smoking on lung cancer rates known as the relative risk (RR). The higher the RR, the more comfort a decision-maker can draw that the agent in question caused the disease.[89] A RR of 1 between the variables means that the probability of contracting lung cancer from smoking is no greater than chance because lung cancer rates are not different between smoking and non-smoking conditions. A RR of 2 means that smokers are twice as likely to contract lung cancer than non-smokers.

The similarity in the language of RR>2 and the civil standard of proof has led to a range of legal responses. The approach in *Daubert* and *Merrell Dow Pharmaceuticals v Havner*[90] suggests that unless RR>2, epidemiological evidence will be inadmissible. If RR<2, it is suggested that the evidence cannot establish that Y was more than 50% likely to have been caused by X. Conversely, some courts have gone too far the other way and stated that RR>2 is ipso facto sufficient for specific causation and crossing the inferential gap.[91]

[88] *Amaca v Booth* (2011) 246 CLR 36, [43].
[89] *Seltsam* (n 1) [147], applied at [175].
[90] *Merrell Dow Pharmaceuticals v Havner* 907 SW2d 535 (TexCrtApp, 1994).
[91] See comments in A Broadbent, 'Epidemiological Evidence in Proof of Specific Causation' (2011) 17 *Law Times Reports* 237, 269, 274.

Both of these approaches are flawed. RR is not an absolute measure of the probability of causation even in the general population.[92] Effect sizes are measured in the sample only. Further statistical measures are needed to determine whether it is appropriate to infer the effect in *n* to *N*. Studies showing RR<2 also should not be used to prove the inverse proposition, that there is no relationship between the variables. Such evidence may appropriately be used as a cautionary point in assessing the weight of the evidence. An RR approaching 1 should be approached with some caution in inferring causation because, logically, the degree of magnitude is an important factor in the existence of a connection between variables. But it is not the only factor, and statistical evidence should not be inadmissible, nor without probative value, simply because RR<2. *Seltsam*, correctly, sets out the appropriate approach to effect size:

> [T]he test of actual persuasion does not require epidemiological studies to reach the level of a relative risk of 2.0, even where that is the only evidence available to a court. Nevertheless, the closer the ratio approaches 2.0, the greater the significance that can be attached to the studies for the purposes of drawing an inference of causation in an individual case.[93]

It should also be borne in mind that not all connections are necessarily strong connections. The court may be concerned with very weak associations between events, such as in *Rogers v Whittaker*, where the association between bilateral blindness and the procedure was 1 in 14,000.[94] That effect size was still salient because the evidence was only being used to establish the degree of risk and not any causal attribution between the impugned act (the surgery) and the outcome (bilateral blindness).[95] Causation had been determined by other means. Crafting a catch-all rule about effect size would therefore be arbitrary and counter-productive. It is a factor to be taken into account both for admissibility and weight, and how controlling that factor is will depend on the context of the fact the evidence is adduced to prove, and other factors inherent to the statistical evidence. When adduced to prove causation, even a *de minimis* association may be potentially explained by a causal relationship and so is rightly admissible. A study that shows no association between the variables is prima facie inadmissible as proof of an association.

Effect size is perhaps the closest proxy to the fact weight of statistical evidence. Evidence which displays insufficient strength (but has some association) in the association between the variables may be incapable of establishing general factual causation.[96] This is especially so where there are competing statistical studies pointing in opposite directions.[97] This is why it is especially important that

[92] See C McIvor, 'Debunking Some Judicial Myths about Epidemiology and its Relevance to UK Tort Law' (2013) 21 *Medical Law Review* 553, 573.
[93] *Seltsam* (n 1) [137]. See also Broadbent (n 91) 274–75.
[94] *Rogers v Whitaker* (1992) 175 CLR 479, 482.
[95] ibid.
[96] eg *Cubillo v Commonwealth* [1995] FCA 1749.
[97] *Seltsam* (n 1) [171]–[176].

experts are required to contextualise their reliance on statistical evidence in their opinions.

In balancing these issues, the fact-finder needs to be aware that there may be some overlap between general factual causation and individualising inferences (or specific causation). In *Seltsam*, Spigelman CJ concluded that the epidemiological evidence showing a link between kidney cancer and asbestos may have been sufficient to establish general factual causation, but that the magnitude of the effect was too weak for specific causation:

> When the negative results of the seven studies entitled to be given weight is combined with the small to moderate increased risk of all but two of the positive epidemiological studies, the effect of the evidence when combined as strands in a cable, does not, in my opinion, support an inference of causation in the specific case of the respondent.[98]

The Chief Justice left open the possibility that even in circumstances where only a weak inference to general factual causation could be identified, there may be other evidence that could draw the connection between the individual plaintiff and the proposed effect. There was insufficient evidence in that case. Some care has to be exercised in respect of using extraneous information to bolster causation from general factual causation to the individual. Where the statistical evidence is neutral, or otherwise capable of demonstrating an effect in the population, it is logically valid for a fact-finder to couple that information with evidence about the plaintiff (*p*) to find that X caused Y in *p*. That is, in spite of the weak effect, there are sufficient individuating circumstances that allow the fact-finder to believe causation in this case. But that should not be permitted to overbear evidence demonstrating the absence of an effect in *N*. Even though the question of legal interest is specific causation, courts cannot ignore general factual causation.

As will be explained further, how effect size is ultimately used for admissibility and weight also depends on how other features of the test answer the questions 'does the evidence have the capacity to prove that X causes Y' (for admissibility) or 'by how much is my belief that X causes Y altered by this evidence' (for weight).

B. Confidence

Effect sizes are measured from data sourced from *n*. The ability to then infer from that *n* to *N* depends on the representativeness of *n* and the method and design of the study. For that reason, statistical evidence cannot make statements of certainty about *N*-wide events. An inference that X causes Y in *N* from the same relationship in *n* is necessarily inductive. In circumstances where every possible influence on X and Y is known, and every member of *N* was available for testing, statistical inference would be largely unnecessary. The effect of the variable could be measured

[98] ibid 290–91.

directly and with certainty, as all extraneous influences could be excluded. That would still not provide a certain basis for the prediction of future associations between X and Y, but the probabilities could be extrapolated using classical probability rather than complex statistical techniques.

Such a world does not exist for most research. Human behavioural research, for example, can never rationally assert that all possible influences on behaviour are known or knowable. It is impossible as a practical and resourcing matter to survey every possible member of a population for a study. Statistics bridge the gap by providing a formal means to measure the degree of uncertainty in drawing conclusions about associations between variables. Testing whether those associations are reliable can be done by considering confidence intervals around the effect size and measuring two types of error: type I error, or the risk of a false positive, and type II error, or the risk of a false negative. Reducing both type I and type II errors, and narrowing the confidence interval, can be achieved by exponentially increasing the size of the sample. Usually, that is not feasible and so inference and testing are essential.

Confidence intervals plot the range of the magnitude of the effect given a certain parameter. The typical formulation is a '95%' confidence interval, meaning that 95% of the time, the effect size will be between a certain range. If the RR is 2.3, a 95% confidence interval may be between 2.1 and 2.5. Ideally, that range will be as narrow as possible, as that gives greater confidence in the reported effect. Controversy over confidence intervals in legal proceedings concerns the inclusion of RR of 1 or its equivalent in other forms of testing. Some legal interpretations suggest this means that at least some of the time there is no effect and as such the entire study is unreliable as demonstrating any effect at all.[99] Such reasoning derives from a mistaken view of confidence intervals. If the effect size was 1.01, and the confidence interval was between 0.3 and 1.02, then one might view the presence of an effect with some scepticism, because the vast bulk of the range is well below 1, and the effect size itself is tiny, suggesting a minimal positive association between the variables. That may, in conjunction with other factors, suggest the evidence should not be admitted. Conversely, just because the confidence interval includes 1 (or indeed, if the effect size itself is less than 2) does not mean that the evidence has no capacity to demonstrate general factual causation. Including 1 in the confidence interval means that there is a possibility of no association, but that is a risk that exists ipso facto the decision to choose a 95% confidence interval, meaning that there is already a 5% chance that the range is inaccurate. Of course, this is a further layer of information that may go to the weight of the evidence but is not conclusive of the absence of an effect, where the study otherwise reports an effect size greater than 1.[100]

[99] cf ibid [210] (Stein JA).

[100] E Beecher-Monas, 'Lost in Translation: Statistical Inference in Court' (2014) 46 *Arizona State Law Journal* 1057, 1070.

Type I error is measured by way of statistical significance. A study is statistically significant if there is a chance (typically, and arbitrarily, set at 0.05) that the association between X and Y is false, that is, there is a 0.05 or less probability that the null hypothesis ought to have been accepted (a false positive). The continuing use of statistical significance as an important measure of the quality or robustness of statistical evidence, especially in the social sciences, has been under sustained attack.[101] There is a movement in the social sciences to disavow or minimise the reporting of statistical significance in favour of a more holistic approach.[102] That is partly due to an excessive reliance placed on statistical significance by researchers. All statistical significance stands for is a rate of accepted type 1 error. To say that statistics are 'significant' because the null hypothesis was correctly rejected 95% of the time, but that they are not significant and therefore cannot be relied on if the null hypothesis was correctly rejected 94.9% of the time, seems patently absurd, especially when the accepted rate of error under the standard of proof is only on balance of probabilities. That is not to say that statistical significance has no place in statistical reporting and determining robustness. But its importance should not be overstated, and for the purpose of admitting and weighing statistical evidence, merely finding that evidence is not statistically significant should not ipso facto make it inadmissible,[103] nor excessively dilute its weight.[104]

Type II error concerns the risk that an association between X and Y will be rejected even though it in fact exists (a false negative). Sample size is a key factor in type II error. Type II error is militated by understanding the minimum possible sample size required in light of the significance level. An insufficiently large sample will mean the study lacks 'power' and is of questionable representativeness. Although often overlooked, power is an essential component to statistical evidence. When it comes to litigation-generated statistical evidence (discussed further below), power is one of the most critical factors necessary to balance the rigour of the study against the cost in conducting it.

C. Design and Methodology

Reporting statistics tends to follow different conventions depending on the discipline in which the study is conducted. The American Psychological Association

[101] ibid 1064–66.
[102] eg BB McShane and others, 'Abandon Statistical Significance' (2019) 73 *The American Statistician* 235.
[103] See S Haack, 'Warrant, Causation, and the Atomisim of Evidence Law' (2008) 5 *Episteme* 253, 260. In *Australian Federation of Consumer Organisations v Tobacco Institute of Australia* (1991) 27 FCR 149, 289, Morling J held that statistical significance was a 'guide to thought' and that non-significant results should not be 'rejected from consideration'.
[104] cf RA Posner, 'An Economic Approach to the Law of Evidence' (1999) 51 *Stanford Law Review* 1477, 1511.

(APA) publishes a style guide that includes guidance on how statistics ought to be reported. Although many journals follow APA style, different journals (assuming the evidence is drawn from published research) may have different requirements for reporting statistics. Due to the variability in how statistics can be reported, it is impossible to set general criteria for the evaluation of statistical evidence. The evidence will have to be evaluated against the relevant conventions of the discipline in which it is created and by reference to the reliance placed upon it by the expert.

There is an existing substantial body of scholarly work regarding the interaction between the law and statistical evidence, including how lawyers should understand statistical measures and methodologies.[105] For example, Andretta and others propose a 19 factor 'Structured Statistical Judgment' exercise that interrogates various statistical measures for the review of statistical evidence in legal proceedings including significance, power, reliability and validity.[106] Given its breadth, this chapter does not seek to evaluate this literature. It may be that by a process of consultation between courts and professional disciplines a structured approach to the evaluation of statistical evidence can be achieved. Further, the increasing use of procedural mechanisms such as court-appointed experts and science panels, where courts can more readily set forth their expectations of the evidence, may provide more acceptable accounts of statistical evidence. These procedural mechanisms, along with increased training for judicial officers are likely to have a more positive effect on the use of statistics than any approach centred on what the law can do by its own processes.

In the absence of such mechanisms, this section seeks to establish a basic list of factors that ought to be reported on and taken into account in the assessment of statistical evidence. The design and methodology of any study are essential components in believing that the statistical evidence reliably shows an effect in n, and whether it is justifiable to extend that finding to N. There are certain key methodological factors that underpin most empirical research. By constructing a test of admissibility that specifies these factors, experts will be required to give evidence of each in order for the evidence to be admissible, thereby ensuring that the court is furnished with the material necessary to evaluate the statistical evidence. This review must centre on the reliability, validity and method used by the investigator.

1. *Reliability*

Statistical evidence is measured against its 'reliability'. Statistical reliability refers to the 'reproducibility' of the results, that is, that the measuring device used in

[105] eg Beecher-Monas 'Lost' (n 100); MO Finkelstein, *Basic Concepts of Probability and Statistics in the Law* (New York, Springer, 2009).

[106] JR Andretta and others, 'Applying Statistics to the Gatekeeping of Expert Evidence: Introducing the Structured Statistical Judgment' (2019) 37 *Behavioral Sciences & the Law* 133.

the analysis returns consistent measures under the same or similar conditions.[107] This can be measured across different studies (test-retest reliability), or, if a study uses multiple researchers to collect data, within the same study between different observers (inter-rater reliability) or from the same observer. Reliability can be measured statistically by way of a number of coefficients. When assessing reliability, a degree of judgement is necessary. Reliability as a coefficient will be subject to certain thresholds that may differ depending on the nature of the research. Moreover, a study may trade off reliability against other measurements in the study. For that reason, it is not possible to say categorically that evidence is reliable or not reliable. The gatekeeper, or fact-finder, will need to make a determination in that regard, based on the evidence. Statistical evidence that is unreliable, however, should not be used in the proof of general factual causation.

2. *Validity*

Reliability measures the consistency of the measurement, but it does not test whether the statistical evidence is actually measuring the intended effect. A reliable study could still be wrong or spurious. Validity measures the extent the statistical evidence is measuring the phenomena it was designed to measure.[108] The metric of reliability proposed in *Daubert* is in fact concerned with statistical validity.[109] Although validity may be said to include statistical reliability,[110] statistical reliability can be measured on its own with specific coefficients. For that reason, excluding any consideration of reliability is short-sighted.

There are a number of different types of validity that can be broadly grouped under internal and external validity. Internal validity, or whether the study accurately measures what it purports to measure, is concerned principally with methodology. If a study purported to show a correlation between X and Y in *n*, but *n* was comprised exclusively of male participants, the results would be invalid because one could not exclude the possibility that gender played a role in the effect.

External validity measures accuracy between *n* and *N*. That is, do the results found in the study of *n* really demonstrate an effect existing in the real world? External validity refers to the generalisability of the study from the sample to the population, given the difference in object, space and time between *n* and *N*.[111] There are no statistical measures of external validity within any individual study. Replication is the best test of validity. If the variables are correlated across multiple testing formats (preferably measured by meta-analysis), a researcher is more likely to conclude that the measures are externally valid.

[107] *Reference Manual on Scientific Evidence* (n 81) 71.
[108] ibid.
[109] *Daubert* (n 34) n 9.
[110] *Reference Manual on Scientific Evidence* (n 81) 71.
[111] See J Monahan and L Walker, *Social Science in Law*, 9th edn (New York, Foundation Press, 2017) 73–74.

Ensuring that the domains of object, space and time are controlled for as tightly as possible can also facilitate external validity. Using a randomised sample of sufficient size assists in generalising from *n* to *N*. Randomisation and control are critical elements of inferring causation in empirical research. Testing for other potentially significant variables (Z) means that if Z does play a role in the association between X and Y it will become obvious during the analysis. Failing to control for or explain Z will mean that the results lack external validity.

For that reason, there is a trade-off between internal and external validity. Narrowing the scope of *n* and controlling for more variables increases the internal validity. But that then narrows the reference population, meaning that the scope of any inference is more limited and may not identify a real effect in nature.

3. *Method*

Method is vitally important to the evaluation of any statistical evidence. Measures such as significance, power, reliability and validity are meaningless if the experiment or survey was poorly designed and implemented. This is both a factor of weight and admissibility. A study can be so poorly designed, or so pervaded by bias, that its conclusions are worthless and should be inadmissible. Even if there is some value to the study despite its design defects, more rigorous studies should be given greater weight during the fact-finding exercise. Experts should give some evidence on the method adopted in any study relied on and how this study relates to the existing literature. This ensures that the court has a broad view of the discipline's views on the existence of the causal relationship that is being relied upon. Multiple confirmatory studies should give the court greater comfort that the results are not explained by a methodological error or aberration in results.[112]

The choice of method can have a significant effect on the strength of the conclusion that can be drawn from the study. In 'true' experiments (as opposed to observational and 'quasi-experiments')[113] on immutable constructs, it is possible to isolate variables and establish causal relationships. In human research, where true causal studies are virtually impossible, laboratory settings can help control the number of extraneous variables by keeping various other situation-based factors as constant as possible. But excessive control can also undermine the study's applicability to the real world. Laboratory studies are often criticised in legal proceedings for their artificiality, especially in fields like behavioural research.[114]

True experiments can also be done in the field, although their ability to control for a wider range of variables that could include the causal relationship

[112] cf *Re Zoloft*, 26 FSupp3d 449, II (EDPenn, 2014).

[113] KJ Rothman, S Greenland and TL Lash, *Modern Epidemiology*, 3rd edn (Philadelphia, Wolters Kluwer Health, 2013) 146, ch 6.

[114] eg *Brown v Entertainment Merchants Association* 564 US 786, 800–01 (2011).

becomes more problematic. The most common form of true experiment in the field is the RCT.[115]

By contrast, field research and quasi-experiments, including epidemiological evidence, are better able to reflect what occurs in the real world, but at a cost of being relatively unable to control variation in the sample. That makes causal attribution between variables more difficult. Epidemiological evidence is not experimental but survey-based. Such studies track the development of disease in participants; they do not induce the disease and measure its progression, whereas an RCT will introduce the drug and a placebo to test the efficacy of pharmaceutical products.

Statistical methodology is a vast interdisciplinary topic inapposite for precise formulation. Courts will need assistance on how to best evaluate statistical methods. That assistance should be given by the expert relying on the evidence. If that evidence falls outside their expertise, further expert evidence may be required.

Conclusion

The consequences of non-compliance with the proposed statistical evidence framework are either inadmissibility or a clear basis for why the evidence is lacking in weight in proof of general factual causation. Short of providing a genuine scientific education for all decision-makers, it is unrealistic to assume that this framework can be appropriately navigated by gatekeepers and fact-finders without the assistance of the experts relying on the statistical evidence. Experts should state in clear terms the different causal propositions they rely on and the empirical or anecdotal evidence in support of those causal propositions. Failing to do so may mean that the opinion falls foul of the basis rule.

Having provided those factors, the framework requires the expert to demonstrate how the statistical evidence has an appropriate effect size, confidence in that effect size and method. It should not be enough to just refer to the existence of a study. Statistical evidence should be explained and contextualised within the relevant discipline it emanates from. Experts should articulate why the evidence establishes that X caused Y in *N*. Positive statements by an expert of this kind may increase the length of expert reports and may increase the costs associated with the report's production. It should, however, also increase the quality and reliability of expert evidence in litigation and allow decision-makers to better understand how the expert opinion tracks against the underlying evidence in assessing the worth of that evidence.

[115] For further discussion about the RCT and its role in the law, see DJ Greiner and A Matthews, 'Randomized Control Trials in the US Legal Profession' (2016) 12 *Annual Review Law and Social Sciences* 295.

3

Statistical Proof of General Factual Causation

Introduction

A second set of objections to statistical evidence adduced to prove general factual causation is that some statistics are an insufficient basis to make findings about causal propositions in a state of nature.[1] As Australian law elides general causation as an element in a cause of action, Australian authorities tend to blur lines between evidentiary objections to general factual causation and specific causation. The question 'is the evidence relevant to specific causation because it demonstrates general factual causation' is an aspect of individualising inferences and referred to in this book as 'linkage' in chapter five. Instead, this section deals with the precursor question of how gatekeepers should identify the capacity of statistical evidence to reliably be probative to general factual causation. If statistical evidence does not have the capacity to prove general factual causation, it is irrelevant. Otherwise, unless the evidence falls foul of the admissibility test for statistical evidence suggested above, it should be admissible.

The focus of this section is entirely on factual causation. Causation is both a factual proposition and a key element in many causes of action. It has proven especially invidious for negligence in personal injuries and medical malpractice. This book is not attempting to relitigate the nature of causation. It accepts that 'causation' in law describes two separate outcomes.[2] The first, and of most significance here, is the process of fact-finding leading to a conclusion that, say, action X causes result Y, known as 'factual causation'. Factual causation in this sense is independent of any cause of action or legal complaint. It is a reconstructive or predictive exercise seeking to explain what happened or what will happen. A fact-finder does not need to know that a plaintiff attributes the cause of their mesothelioma to the defendant's actions to know whether those actions were a factor that 'might be

[1] Other reasoning suggests that statistics are insufficient to prove causation at all; that is typically framed as an objection to the capacity of statistical evidence to prove something about an individual and is dealt with in subsequent chapters.

[2] The division between factual and legal causation was proposed for the law of negligence during the process of 'tort reform' in Australia, culminating in D Ipp and others, *Review of the Law of Negligence: Final Report* (Commonwealth of Australia, 2002) recommendation 29. This division was subsequently adopted by, for example, New South Wales in s 5D(1) of the Civil Liability Act 2002 (NSW) and Victoria in s 51(1) of the Wrongs Act 1958 (Vic).

involved' in the plaintiff's mesothelioma.[3] The second aspect of causation is the 'scope of liability' that the law will permit a defendant to be responsible for, also called 'legal causation'. Questions about the scope of liability are important, insofar as they define the limit of where courts are prepared to attribute responsibility for a particular action. They are not exclusively factual inquiries about the variables of interest, but rather can extend to normative judgements based on a variety of factors. This work adopts Professor Stapleton's view, that the law should choose a standard of causation that is 'untainted by normative interrogations and controversies', and instead leave those other factors to be determined by the remainder of the cause of action.[4] Although legal causation is an important feature in establishing liability, it is distinct from the inquiry as to whether X caused (or materially contributed to) Y as a matter of fact.[5] From the perspective of evidence law, the only question that might justify intervention is whether the statistics have the capacity to reliably prove factual causation.

I. Correlation ≠ Causation

An integral aspect of any admissibility or weight criteria for statistical evidence of causation is deciding what is meant by the term 'causation' itself, and how causation is proved by evidence. Statistical evidence is not by itself conclusive of a causal relationship. Statistics report 'correlations', or measures of association, between variables of interest. Correlation is not necessarily causation:

> The existence of an association or a positive statistical correlation between the occurrence of one event and the subsequent occurrence of another may be expressed as a possibility, which may be no greater than a 'real chance' that, if the first event occurs, the second event will also occur. *The mere existence of such an association or correlation does not justify a statement, relevant to factual causation in law, that the first event 'creates' or 'gives rise to' or 'increases' the probability that the second event will occur.* Such a statement contains an assumption that if the second event occurs it will have some causal connection to the first. However, if the association between two events is shown to have a causal explanation, then the conclusion may be open, if the second event should occur, that the first event has been at least a contributing cause of that occurrence.[6]

French CJ is identifying the problem of enumerative induction[7] versus induction by variation.[8] Induction by variation involves looking at not just the magnitude of

[3] J Stapleton, 'Choosing what we Mean by Causation in the Law' (2008) 73 *Missouri Law Review* 433, 441.
[4] ibid 446.
[5] See J Edelman, 'Unnecessary Causation' (2015) 89 *Australian Law Journal* 20, 22.
[6] *Amaca v Booth* (2011) 246 CLR 36, [43] (French CJ) (emphasis added).
[7] Enumerative induction relies on 'calculating the relative frequency of a certain attribute in an initial section of a sequence which is being considered, and *assuming* that the observed frequency will hold approximately, or within certain limits of exactness, for any prolongation of the sequence': MC Galavotti, 'The Origins of Probabilistic Epistemology' in A Hajek and C Hitchcock (eds), *The Oxford Handbook of Probability and Philosophy* (Oxford, Oxford University Press, 2016) 135.
[8] LJ Cohen, *The Implications of Induction* (Yorkshire, Methuen, 1970) 107.

the occurrences, but the conditions surrounding those occurrences.[9] Enumerative induction by itself cannot achieve this because it only looks at the magnitude of the occurrence of X and Y.[10] In order for a causal relationship to exist between X and Y, Y has to follow and be explained by the occurrence of X or a combination of variables including X.

The greater degree of control exercised over a study, the more likely it is that the relationship identified is a true association in nature. Trying to prove causation from statistical evidence is, however, like trying to solve a puzzle with an insufficient number of pieces. There is no means of ever being 'certain' about a causal event. The best a fact-finder can hope for is as complete an image as possible, based on as many pieces of the puzzle as possible, and to fill in the gaps using inference, other evidence and commonsense. For general factual causation, statistics are an essential component of that puzzle. Statistics, and other evidence that general factual causation can be inferred from, are a partial explanation of the whole that can reveal shape and contours of the image. That is why it is imperative that experts explain why the evidence establishes general factual causation. Conclusions about causal propositions should always be supported by an evidence-based approach. Without the evidence, decision-makers are unable to appropriately piece the puzzle together.

The human judgement applied to fill in those gaps is usually set by the conventions around causal associations emanating from the discipline in which the study was conducted. For epidemiology, the 'Bradford Hill' factors of causation are typically applied.[11] These include: the strength of association of the variables (strength); the degree of repetition of the association (consistency); the proximity of the association between variables (specificity); that the effect follows the cause (temporality); the existence of a dose–response curve (biological gradient); the inherent biological plausibility of the association between the variables (plausibility); consistency with previous research about the relationship (coherence); the existence of any experimental research; and the existence of 'similar but slighter' evidence that may give rise to an analogy to the present effect.[12] These factors are indicia of the existence of a causal relationship between variables beyond the correlative conclusions of the statistics, and offer a means of assessing the reliability of the statistical evidence as evidence of causation.

Just because human judgement is required to accept general factual causation does not mean, however, that statistics and correlational findings cannot be used as the basis for causation, including by reason of those studies (and commonsense) alone. Identifying a correlative association between variables is an essential step to inferring causation. In *Brown v EMA*, the US Supreme Court rejected studies

[9] ibid 107.

[10] ibid 106ff.

[11] S Haack, *Evidence Matters* (Cambridge, Cambridge University Press, 2014) ch 10. For an application of the Bradford Hill factors to epidemiological evidence, see *Re Zoloft Products*, 257 FSupp3d 737, II.B (3dCir, 2017); *Seltsam v McGuiness* (2000) 49 NSWLR 262 (NSWCA) [139].

[12] A Bradford Hill, 'The Environment and Disease: Association or Causation?' (1965) 58 *Proceedings of Royal Society of Medicine* 295.

of media violence showing an association with childhood aggression, remarking that '[n]early all of the research is based on correlation, not evidence of causation, and most of the studies suffer from significant, admitted flaws in methodology'.[13]

Putting methodological flaws to one side, rejecting correlational evidence as not 'evidence' of causation is, respectfully, wrong. Correlation is a necessary antecedent to causation, even if it is, by itself, insufficient for causation. Evidence drawn from individuals, even a collective of individuals, cannot reliably exclude the possibility of the post hoc fallacy and may be the product of self-serving statements. The scale and rigour of statistical analysis is a superior tool for that purpose. If courts accept that statistical evidence is sufficiently robust to be admissible, it can serve as evidence of general factual causation even though it may reach no higher than correlation.

II. Proximate Causal Inferences

As a reasoning process, in order for the evidence to have any probative value of general factual causation, a fact-finder has to be able to believe that the evidence is capable of rationally affecting the probability that general factual causation in the population (N) is true. Generalisations from a sample (n) to N are different from individualisations from N (and n) to an individual (p). Whereas individualising to p involves an inductive movement from the general proposition (proven by statistical evidence) to the instant case with other evidence about p, and drawing a connection between them, inferences from n to N depend on accepting that whatever group comprising n is representative of N. This process is governed by the external validity of the evidence. The clarity of this causal pathway is likely to be bolstered by increasing repetition of similar findings in the statistical evidence and by ensuring that each of those studies is founded on an appropriate method and statistical measures.

Accepting the existence of causation is an epistemic process set to the belief of the fact-finder or the gatekeeper's view of what the fact-finder could find from the evidence. Causation in civil proceedings is proven if the fact-finder believes that X causes Y on balance of probabilities. The law does not prescribe how this standard is to be reached, only that the fact-finder must be actually persuaded of the truth of the facts.[14] There are many ways to construct how human beings form a belief in an event. Haack, for example, opines that belief is justified when it is 'warranted', namely, that the accumulated evidence 'warrants' a conclusion depending on the fact-finder's view of the supportiveness (or how well the two propositions 'interlock'), independent security (how solid the evidence is independent of its conclusion), and comprehensiveness (similar to Nance's account of Keynesian weight or the flimsiness of the evidence).[15] Haack's account explains

[13] *Brown v Entertainment Merchants Association* 564 US 786, 800 (2011) (citations omitted).
[14] *Re Day* (2017) 263 CLR 201, [18].
[15] Haack (n 11) 258.

the tipping point between accepting a causal relationship on the evidence, or not, and thereby the reasonableness of decisions made by fact-finders. These theories are not immediately implicated by evidence law, as evidence law does not concern itself with how fact-finders form their beliefs, as long as those beliefs are rational. But Haack's theory of warrant demonstrates how the so-called 'commonsense' approach to causation may in fact be constructed, and how certain features of that evidence may be more or less believable. This better informs the gatekeeper's exercise in predicting what a fact-finder will, or will not, ultimately believe, by reference to some clear criteria beyond simply 'what I would believe'.

The comprehensiveness of evidence depends on an aggregated view of general factual causation. General factual causation is (rationally) more likely to be found where past studies (including lesser evidence such as case studies and anecdotal evidence) are adduced to show how the discipline in question has previously tried to analyse the particular general proposition, or how it might infer from existing evidence to the general proposition if no other research has yet been done. As belief in general factual causation must rest on a fact-finder's impression of how comprehensive the evidence is, courts should not adopt an 'atomised' approach to establishing effect, whereby each study is considered individually without reference to the literature as a whole.[16] The process of proving *p* is not to be conducted by reference to discrete inferences from individual pieces of evidence.[17] Further, the greater the aggregation of previous similar instantiations of the event, the greater the security of the belief, because different independent sources are pointing to the same outcome.[18]

Forming a belief in general factual causation from evidence that does not precisely answer the question in issue depends on showing that the two separate propositions 'interlock', or that the evidence in support of the proposition is sufficiently proximate to the present event in light of the variables of interest. In *General Electric Company v Joiner*, Joiner claimed that he had been exposed to toxic chemicals (PCBs) during his work and that this had caused his lung cancer. The US Supreme Court concluded that the evidence was appropriately rejected by the trial judge because it was based on animal studies that were 'so dissimilar to the facts presented in this litigation', and epidemiological evidence that failed to find the causal proposition asserted by the plaintiff.[19] On one view, the dissimilarity between the animal studies and the facts of the litigation suggested that a individualisation objection was at work. However, the US Supreme Court's conclusion was ultimately that the evidence failed to establish the necessary reliability to support an inference that exposure to PCBs could cause cancer of the plaintiff's type. That is in fact a failure of general factual causation by reason of the dissimilarity in the reference classes between the studies and the hypothetical effect that should be observed in the population.

[16] E Beecher-Monas, 'Lost in Translation: Statistical Inference in Court' (2014) 46 *Arizona State Law Journal* 1057, 1070–74.

[17] *Belhaven and Stenton Peerage* (1875) 1 App Cas 278, 279.

[18] Haack (n 11) 259–60.

[19] *General Electric Company v Joiner* 522 US 136, 144–45 (1997); see further Haack (n 11) 279.

Statistical evidence may be inadmissible in the proof of general factual causation if the evidence is simply incapable of instantiating the effect contended for by the plaintiff. But if there is some rational association between the study and the purported effect, assessed by reference to what the gatekeeper perceives the fact-finder can believe, the evidence will be relevant and admissible on that basis. How that evidence is weighed then becomes a function of the fact-finder's assessment of the causal relationship between the variables in light of other indicators of reliability of the statistical evidence.

III. (A) Commonsense (Standard of) General Factual Causation

Fact-finding is predicated on belief in facts from evidence, and gatekeeping on excluding evidence that does not have the capacity (epistemically or normatively) to allow such a belief to be formed. In the previous section, the focus was on how decision-makers form a belief. Whilst such assessments are a necessary part of determining whether evidence has the capacity to prove facts, when assessing the proof of causation from statistical evidence, it is necessary to have an agreed standard or definition of causation. Variables share a causal relationship when the variable of interest is 'necessary' for the outcome to have occurred, whether by itself, or as a part of a set of conditions.[20] In law, this idea of causation is referred to as a 'but-for' cause. Whether a variable was 'necessary' for the outcome to have resulted is tested by the construct of a hypothetical world that does not contain that variable. If X is alleged to have caused Y, a test of whether X was in a fact a cause depends on whether Y would have occurred in a counterfactual world not containing X. If Y would have resulted regardless of X, then X did not cause Y.

In some respects, the law does not always follow a but-for standard of causation.[21] In *March v E&M H Stramare*, the High Court disavowed a but-for standard of causation to be replaced by a 'commonsense' standard.[22] Causation scholars argue that the problem with the commonsense approach, as opposed to a 'but-for' approach, is that it has led to the blending of the factual and legal causation questions.[23] Edelman argued that the law is increasingly turning away from a commonsense approach towards a but-for standard.[24] Certainly there are

[20] Edelman (n 5) 20; *Strong v Woolworths* (2012) 246 CLR 182, [20]; *Kuwait Airways v Iraqi Airways (Nos 4 and 5)* [2002] 2 AC 883 (HL) [127].

[21] Complex causal phenomena, such as the Hunter problem, where A and B independently fire a gun at C simultaneously causing death, fail the but-for standard: S Steel, *Proof of Causation in Tort Law* (Cambridge, Cambridge University Press, 2015) 20–21. These problems undermine the but-for approach because A's actions are not 'necessary' for C's death, due to the simultaneous conduct of B. These problems are extremely rare in practice and this book does not attempt to enter into the debates around these complex causal problems.

[22] *March v E&M H Stramare* (1991) 171 CLR 506, 509, 514.

[23] Stapleton (n 3) 449; cf *Kuwait Airways* (n 20) [128].

[24] Edelman (n 5) 24.

a number of examples demonstrating an increasing separation of factual and legal causation. Section 5D of the Civil Liability Act 2002 (NSW), in setting out the requirements for causation in negligence, clearly delineates between factual causation as being a 'necessary condition of the occurrence of the harm' which is akin to the but-for test and legal causation as whether 'it is appropriate for the scope of the negligent person's liability to extend to the harm so caused'.[25]

Whilst the law might properly turn away from the commonsense standard of causation, it should be careful to recall that fact-finding itself is also built on notions of commonsense. 'Commonsense', as such, has two usages: first, the impugned use as a legal test of causation described above, and second, as a guide to the process of fact-finding. When deciding whether X caused Y, fact-finders will use all of their available tools including their own prior knowledge, schemas, heuristics and biases. Commonsense does not mean nor require that all facts will be found identically by all fact-finders; the outcome will depend on their individual assessment of the evidence, but by reference to this common approach.[26] A commonsense approach to fact-finding subsumes the definition of causation as an inquiry into but-for consequences. When the High Court in *March* or the House of Lords in *Yorkshire Dale Steamship v Minister of War Transport*[27] decided causation by reference commonsense or 'intuition', those references were fraught by issues of legal causation. For factual causation, however, the reference to commonsense operates as affirmation that the fact-finder is approaching the task of causation under a constrained environment. The information possessed by the fact-finder is limited, the consequences of the decision are enormously important, and the fact-finder must make some kind of choice that is justifiable and, for judicial officers, reasoned. The commonsense approach to factual causation (as opposed to commonsense notions of causation described in *March*) is a standard of fact-finding that the law accepts, knowing that it may produce error, and acts to ameliorate that risk through burdens and standards of proof.

Framing causation in terms of commonsense has led to another curious aspect of factual causation: whether that causal inquiry is somehow different between the law and sciences, where the latter produces the statistical evidence that the former relies on. The genesis of this argument are English authorities, adopted by the High Court, seeking to explain why the law does not need to articulate the totality of the causal relationship, but rather only find the causal connection justifying liability. In *National Insurance Co (NZ) v Espagne*, Windeyer J accepted:

> [Q]uestions of cause and consequence are not the same for law as for philosophy and science. That, it seems to me, is better than saying that law stops short of philosophy in considering causation. Philosophy and science seek the explanation of phenomena and look to relationships and concurrences. Law is not concerned rerum cognoscere causas, but with attributing responsibility to persons.[28]

[25] *Strong v Woolworths* (2012) 246 CLR 182, [18].
[26] L Cohen, *The Probable and the Provable* (Oxford, Clarendon Press, 1977) 275.
[27] *Yorkshire Dale Steamship v Minister of War Transport* [1942] AC 691 (HL).
[28] *National Insurance Co (NZ) v Espagne* (1961) 105 CLR 569, 591, quoting *Simpson v Sinclair* [1917] AC 127 (HL) 135.

In other words, it is not necessary to establish that the impugned conduct comprised the sum total of all factors relevant to the cause of the outcome, as long as it was one factor that was necessary for the outcome to occur.[29] What should be plain from this analysis, however, is that the definition of causation need not change between the law and sciences. Both are still applying a necessity test of whether a thing is a cause of an outcome; what is changing is the scope of that inquiry. There is no reason why a scientist, given the limited question of 'did this conduct cause this outcome', could not fit that question within the broader concept of causation in science, being an explanation of all the relevant events that lead to the outcome. The factual inquiry into whether X caused Y is therefore the same.

Yet, from these authorities has come a line of judicial reasoning that causation in law and science have different standards of causation. Causation can mean a certain outcome. Anything short of causation is a probability.[30] If X causes Y '100%' of the time, it is not true to say that X and Y are probably associated; the conclusion is that X causes Y invariably, without uncertainty. This describes, in the terms used in *Espagne* and *March*, the legal perception of 'philosophical' causation. Scientific causation, by contrast is not metaphysical but probabilistic,[31] in the same way that the law accepts that causation is probabilistic. Like the concept of cause in law described in *Espagne* and *March*, causes in science are also 'sufficient causes' comprised of different 'components' that are necessary to produce the causal effect.[32] Even if the law is only focused on one of those causes, and accepts the other component causes may be necessary to produce the outcome, the concept of causation expressly requires that the cause be necessary for the outcome to have occurred. If it is not necessary, that is, Y could have occurred irrespective of X, it is not 'causal' in the sense recognised either by the law or by science.[33]

It is an oversimplification to say that scientific causation has a 'higher' or 'lower' standard than legal causation. Many cases reveal judicial anxiety over causal statements given by expert witnesses that, in their eyes, lacked the necessary underlying certainty of proof to justify a finding of causation at law.[34] The

[29] *March* (n 22) 509; see also *Gill v Ethicon Sarl (No 5)* [2019] FCA 1905, [4358]–[4361]; *Yorkshire Dale* (n 27) 706; HLA Hart and T Honore, *Causation in the Law*, 2nd edn (Oxford, Oxford University Press, 1985) 1.

[30] See D Gillies, *Philosophical Theories of Probability* (Oxford, Routledge, 2000) 117, 129, 131.

[31] Whilst most scientists would accept that scientific causation is probabilistic, it is equally true that how scientists approach causation may differ depending on the approaches adopted by the scientific discipline: see G Edmond and D Mercer, 'Rebels Without a Cause? Judges, Medical and Scientific Evidence and the Uses of Causation' in I Freckelton and D Mendelson (eds), *Causation in Law and Medicine* (Oxford, Routledge, 2002) 84–87. Those differences will be pertinent to any inquiry into causation from statistical evidence but are not otherwise captured by the purported difference between science and law referred to herein.

[32] KJ Rothman, S Greenland and TL Lash, *Modern Epidemiology*, 3rd edn (Philadelphia, Wolters Kluwer Health, 2013) 6; C Plante and CA Anderson, 'Media Violence, Aggression, and Antisocial Behaviour: Is the Link Causal?' in P Sturmey (ed), *The Wiley Handbook of Aggression and Violence* (Hoboken, Wiley, 2017) 4–5.

[33] With the exception, perhaps, of the Hunter problem: see n 21 above.

[34] eg *King v Western Sydney LHN* [2013] NSWCA 162, [111]–[113], [122]–[124], [130]–[131]. See also J Oosthuizen and M Cross, 'Establishing Cause, What Does That Mean from an Epidemiological

real differences lie in the evidentiary threshold where the scientist and the lawyer accept causation. Science may (but not necessarily) reserve judgement on deciding causation, pending further evidence. Law does not have that luxury; a decision must be made even though a scientist would consider the evidence incomplete. Put another way, a judge may be entitled to infer causation between a contagion and disease even in the absence of (but not against)[35] statistical evidence demonstrating a link between them, as long as the surrounding circumstances make that conclusion more likely than not in the mind of the fact-finder on the facts before the court.[36] That does not suggest there is any difference in approach to the definition of causation, or the reasoning process by which causation is inferred. In *Gill v Ethicon Sarl (No 5)*, Katzmann J stated that 'the determination of [causation in law] does not involve a process of scientific reasoning or mathematical calculation'.[37] Such a statement is apt to mislead. Reasoning about causation is inductive and probabilistic, whether in science or in law. Whereas mere mathematical proofs may not be enough to meet the standard of proof, that does not mean that causation cannot be inferred from evidence expressed in mathematical form. When it comes to weighing evidence of causation, the law adopts a commonsense approach, as it does for all evidentiary matters. But the starting point of what causation is and how it is demonstrated remains the same.

Viewing the jurisprudence about commonsense causation through the lens of evidentiary sufficiency makes clear that the legal approach does not hold a greater or lesser standard of causation. Scientists are no more wedded to an ideation of 'certain' connection when finding that an outcome is 'probably' caused by some variable, than lawyers are.[38] A fact-finder must still accept that the variable is 'causal' in the sense that but for its occurrence the event of interest would not have occurred. What is potentially different is the completeness of the evidence needed to make that judgment. It makes sense that a court would say that '[a]n inference of causation for purposes of the tort of negligence may well be drawn when a scientist, including an epidemiologist, would not draw such an inference'.[39] A court may accept that there is sufficient evidence in the particular case to draw a causation connection between X and Y even though it may be aware of, but not have before it, the potential existence of other evidence, or the lack of other evidence, outside

and Legal Perspective?' (2018) 35 *Environmental and Planning Law Journal* 426. One also has to account for the difference between 'evidence' of a causal proposition and evidence giving rise to sufficient 'proof' of that proposition: *Tobacco Institute of Australia v Australian Federation of Consumer Organisations* (1992) 111 ALR 61 (FCAFC) 66. Usually, statistical evidence will only be evidence of a proposition; proof follows from the fact-finder's impression of the evidence. An expert may have formed a view as to causation based on evidence and experience, whereas the tribunal is limited only to its own impressions built on the instant case. The threshold of proof of a causal relationship may be the same between the expert and the court, but the information on which the decision is to be made may be different.

[35] *EMI (Australia) v Bes* [1970] 2 NSWLR 238 (NSWCA) 242 (Herron CJ).

[36] *Fernandez v Tubemakers of Australia* [1975] 2 NSWLR 190 (NSWCA) 197C.

[37] *Gill* (n 29) [4359].

[38] cf *Gill* (n 29) [4359], [4361] citing *Henville v Walker* (2001) 206 CLR 459, [97].

[39] *Seltsam* (n 11) [143].

the proceeding. A judge is bound by the evidence admitted within the proceeding, inferences appropriately drawn from that evidence and, to an extent, their own knowledge. It is not part of the judicial function to speculate about what might be the case in the absence of evidence before the tribunal. Scientists, however, would not be entitled to blind themselves to the possibility of other evidence in coming to a view based in their own discipline whether there is an association between X and Y. It is the function of the scientist to seek out that evidence, and scientists will not be limited by the same parameters imposed on fact-finders by a system of justice. As such, a fact-finder, per *March*, would be entitled to infer the existence of causation from that limited dataset even though a scientist might withhold judgment pending further information.

Where this information imbalance does not exist, there is no basis to conclude that the approach of scientists or lawyers to standards of causation is different at all. When experts give evidence, they will or ought to give such evidence from the perspective of their own discipline. Experts should identify and engage with the underlying statistical evidence upon which they rely in their opinions. If an expert has formed a view that there is sufficient evidence of causation and gives that opinion in court based on statistical evidence, courts should be wary of approaching the task of finding factual causation from the position that the scientific view of causation is somehow more stringent than the legal approach. Doing so may lead courts to mistakenly apply a stricter standard of causation for expert evidence and undermine the expert evidence by finding that the evidence in that discipline did not provide sufficient support for the expert's opinion.

In *Resi Corporation v Munzer*,[40] the appellant complained that the trial judge had erred in accepting that the respondent's pleural chest plaques were caused by his exposure to asbestos when he worked for the appellant. The appellant claimed that the expert testimony was a 'mere hypothesis' and could not reach a level of causation. The SASCFC correctly rejected the submission that a hypothesis could not reach the level of causation at law because

> it must be borne in mind that proof of a fact in a civil case to the satisfaction of the fact-finding tribunal on the balance of probabilities and proof of a fact for scientific purposes to the satisfaction of those expert in the particular field are different. The latter kind of proof is much more rigorous and demanding than the former.[41]

The problem is how this conclusion was expressed. A 'mere' scientific hypothesis can be sufficient for legal causation. The hypothesis in *Resi Corporation* was itself about causation. Based on clinical experience and research, the expert determined that a causal association between asbestos and pleural plaques existed. Even though expressed as a hypothesis (and therefore attended by some doubt) that conclusion is no different from how the civil standard of proof is articulated: that the fact-finder forms an actual belief in the truth notwithstanding their remaining

[40] *Resi Corporation v Munzer* [2016] SASCFC 15.
[41] ibid [52].

doubt. It would be extraordinary if, when asked the question, 'is it the case that you do not actually believe there is a causal association', the expert would have answered 'yes'. If the expert did so, the probative value of that evidence as proof of causation would be effectively nil.

Conclusion

It is vital that fact-finders do not hold statistics to a higher standard of causation than is warranted, either as a function of admissibility or fact-finding. Rejecting the usefulness of statistics in the proof of general factual causation, where statistics offer the best possible evidence of general factual causation, should only be done where the evidence is demonstrably unreliable. Otherwise, the temptation for fact-finders will be to fall back on evidence of anecdote, heuristics and schematic reasoning based on 'commonsense' that may not have sufficient, or any, empirical basis.

When the law and science refer to causation, they each mean the same thing: is X necessary (by itself, or in conjunction with other factors) for Y? Science can accept that X is causally associated with Y even though other causes may also be operating. The law holds the same view. There is no basis for saying that the standards for causation between the law and the sciences are different. As statistics usually offer the best evidence of causation, they should not be dismissed or disregarded simply because a fact-finder is not satisfied that the statistics are robust enough to meet a non-existent scientific threshold of causation.

4

Individualising Inferences from Statistical Evidence

Introduction

The second stage of the statistical evidence syllogism is to infer from general factual causation to the physical or mental phenomenon in issue. Usually, that involves an inference from a collection of phenomena (a reference class) to establish an individual phenomenon. Or a representative sample drawn from larger populations can be used to infer trends in that population. Such individualising inferences are a feature of statistical inference. The terminology associated with evidence of or derived from such inferences in law is prolix and often inconsistent.[1]

Individualising inferences from statistical evidence are adjuncts to generalisations and follow similar and overlapping inferential pathways. A generalisation involves inferences from specific instances into populations, or inferences about individuals or things based on shared traits with other, similar people or things.[2] It is a form of generalisation to say that 'Australians go to beaches' and also a generalisation to say that 'that person is Australian and therefore goes to the beach'.[3] An individualisation is closely akin to the latter form of generalisation and follows the same syllogistic pathway. For example, inferring the effect of a shared trait across a reference class of people or objects (such as 'most eyewitnesses are reliable')[4] is a

[1] eg, 'group-to-individual' (DL Faigman, J Monahan and C Slobogin, 'Group to Individual (G2i) Inference in Scientific Expert Testimony' (2014) 81 *University of Chicago Law Review* 417); 'population' (R Goldberg, 'Epidemiological Uncertainty, Causation, and Drug Product Liability' (2014) 59 *McGill Law Journal* 777, 795); 'base rate' (JJ Koehler, 'When Do Courts Think Base Rate Statistics are Relevant?' (2002) 42 *Jurimetrics* 373, pt III); 'probability' (C Nesson, 'The Evidence or the Event? On Judicial Proof and the Acceptability of Verdicts' (1985) 98 *Harvard Law Review* 1357, 1386); 'mathematical' (LH Tribe, 'Trial by Mathematics: Precision and Ritual in the Legal Process' (1971) 84 *Harvard Law Review* 1329); 'non-specific' (A Stein, *Foundations of Evidence Law* (Oxford, Oxford University Press, 2005); L Brilmayer and L Kornhauser, 'Quantitative Methods and Legal Decisions' (1978) 46 *University of Chicago Law Review* 116, 145); 'general' (S Steel, *Proof of Causation in Tort Law* (Cambridge, Cambridge University Press, 2015) 66). Each of these labels describe the 'evidence' of general factual causation that is being used to infer from a general proposition to a specific case.

[2] A Pundik, 'Freedom and Generalisation' (2016) 37 *OJLS* 189, 189.

[3] See, eg, C Dahlman and A Pundik, 'The Problem with Naked Statistical Evidence' in C Dahlman, A Stein and G Tuznet (eds), *Philosophical Foundations of Evidence Law* (Oxford, Oxford University Press, 2021) 341.

[4] M Redmayne, 'Exploring Proof Paradoxes' (2008) 14 *Legal Theory* 281, 287.

form of generalisation whereby a general characteristic (reliability) is presupposed to apply broadly to a class (witnesses), which so happens to include an individual (Witness A). Such an inference can also be styled as an 'individualisation', where the general concept (reliability) is inferred specifically from the class (witnesses) to a particular individual (Witness A). Put another way, individualising inferences arise from a generalisation that because a trait is shared by a particular group of people or things, and that trait happens to be present in an individual, the effect seen in the group can be inferred to the individual.

What is significant for the arguments made in this chapter is that individualisations are an inference derived from generalisations. Statistical evidence is capable of supporting both generalising or individualising inferences. For the purpose of this book, the term 'generalisation' is the overarching term used to describe the evidence that produces the objectionable inference, whether that inference is a generalisation or a resulting individualisation. Where it is necessary to distinguish between true generalisations and the process of inferring to an individual, the term 'individualisation' is used.

Individualising inferences require utilising knowledge gained outside the time, space and object of the specific phenomenon. That knowledge can be the product of anecdote or heuristics. Or it could be statistical inference from empirical observations and testing. Logically, both follow the same inferential pathway. To establish the bases of objections to individualisations from statistical evidence, this chapter considers how similar objections are framed against generalisations and individualisations more broadly.

The use of generalisations is a controversial but necessary feature of fact-finding. For statistical evidence, that controversy has been particularly difficult to solve. There are basic disagreements over whether statistical evidence requires individualisation at all, whether generalisations and individualisations should be 'objectionable', and the context of that objection.

This chapter proposes that each of these controversies can be resolved by accepting that the objection to individualising inferences is a product of an epistemological deficiency in generalisations and resulting individualisations called the 'inferential gap', which evidence that is not the product of a generalisation does not appear to possess. Understood in that way, the generalisation objection to statistical evidence can be sensibly resolved. First, this chapter seeks to define what is meant by generalisations and individualising inferences from statistical evidence, where the objection appears to arise and how such inferences implicate evidence law. Second, a category of purported generalisations, called 'no-gap' generalisations, will be distinguished as generalisations that do not possess the same basic inferential structure as objectionable generalisations. Third, a category of generalisations often used as non-objectionable examples of generalisations and individualisations, described as 'background' or 'commonsense' generalisations, will also be shown to possess different and non-objectionable inferential foundations. Fourth, 'factual' objectionable generalisations are distinguished from a subset of purportedly non-objectionable generalisations. Fifth, some extraneous factors will be identified that appear to influence how different theorists subjectively approach the presence or absence of the individualisation objection.

I. The Generalisation Objection

Objections to generalisations and individualisations focus on the 'intuitive' (anti-liability) feeling that something isn't right or proper about relying on generalisations or individualisations to prove the existence of facts in the legal process.[5] The use of the term 'anti-liability' is potentially misleading, as it focuses attention on the end stage of the inferential process. As will be shown below, the discomfit felt by decision-making from generalisations or individualisations arises at stage three of the statistical evidence syllogism. This book refers to this intuitive feeling as 'dissonance'. The existence or non-existence of dissonance begs two further questions, which are the subject of the following sections: what is the nature or source of dissonance, and what effect should dissonance have on the approach of evidence law to generalisations and individualisations?

Sourcing dissonance is problematic. Three basic propositions, each with their own variants, are used to explain dissonance.[6] The most widely debated is an epistemic objection: that individualisations derived from generalisations are less useful for or less accurate in proving facts than specific evidence that are not the product of generalisations. This is often presented as a facet of causal explanations of dissonance, that is, because the events in the reference class were not caused by this phenomenon, it is less useful,[7] or not at all useful,[8] in proving the phenomenon. If an individual testifies that a red car hit a pedestrian, that is 'specific' and prima facie epistemically unobjectionable evidence of a phenomenon. The evidence only exists because an individual witnessed (or claimed to witness) a red car hit the pedestrian. But if a reference class of red cars was used to show that red cars were more accident prone than other colours, an epistemic objection could be argued against such evidence because decision-makers cannot 'know'[9] if it was actually a

[5] Redmayne (n 4) 282–84.

[6] D Enoch and T Fisher, 'Sense and "Sensitivity": Epistemic and Instrumental Approaches to Statistical Evidence' (2015) 67 *Stanford Law Review* 557, 563–64.

[7] M Dant, 'Gambling on the Truth: The Use of Purely Statistical Evidence as a Basis for Civil Liability' (1988) 22 *Columbia Journal of Law & Social Problems* 31. See further I Puppe and RW Wright, 'Causation in the Law: Philosophy, Doctrine and Practice' in M Infantino and E Zervogianni (eds), *Causation in European Tort Law* (Cambridge, Cambridge University Press, 2017) [30].

[8] RW Wright, 'Causation in Tort Law' (1985) 73 *California Law Review* 1735, 1822–23. Green suggests that Wright's argument does not mean that generalisations (exemplified in her discussion by generalisations from epidemiological evidence) are ipso facto redundant: see S Green, *Causation in Negligence* (Oxford, Hart, 2015) 119. The passages that Green cites in fact identify the contention that epidemiological evidence might be admissible where sufficient particularistic evidence is admitted in support of that contention. In substance, this results in the particularistic evidence overtaking any need for reliance on the generalisation. See also M Dore, 'A Commentary on the Use of Epidemiological Evidence in Demonstrating Cause-in-Fact' (1983) 7 *Harvard Environmental Law Review* 429, 434.

[9] HL Ho, *A Philosophy of Evidence Law* (Oxford, Oxford University Press, 2008) 140–41.

red car – the fact-finder has to 'guess' based on the non-specific information available, which is not necessarily associated with the outcome; there is no immediate link between the colour red and accidents. This evidence exists independently of whether the red car did (or is alleged to have) hit the pedestrian, and was therefore not caused by that event.[10]

Others contend that morality is the source of dissonance, or at least the source of dissonance that the law should focus upon. As the driver of the red car cannot respond to or affect the generic probability that red cars cause more accidents, it undermines the driver's individual autonomy[11] or 'free will' to make her liable for that injury.[12] The law is predicated on free will – individuals who are incapable of acting freely are exculpated from liability,[13] or have their culpability reduced if their actions are induced by external phenomena. Morality alone, however, does not appear to explain dissonance. Dissonance remains even where, for example, human drivers are replaced with autonomous driving systems. There is still an epistemic deficit. Uncertainty over the answer to the question of why one should accept that a specific red car caused this accident just because more red cars are involved in accidents still remains.

Finally, contextual and normative factors are used to explain the presence and relevance of dissonance. Among others, it has been said that reliance on generalisations undermines belief in the legal system,[14] fails to contribute to the incentive structure for lawful behaviour,[15] or could lead to 'lazy' litigation practice by allowing litigants to avoid seeking 'specific' evidence.[16] Although these theories perhaps add some pointed questions for the legal system, they do not illuminate the presence or resolution of dissonance. Dissonance is not confined to law. The debates over the causal connection between smoking and lung cancer or human emissions and climate change are apposite examples of strident disagreements about how to apply generalisations (statistical or otherwise) to specific phenomena. Nor do the contextual and normative accounts explain why, in the context of truth-seeking, individualisations and generalisations are perceived as less useful than specific evidence. Nesson argues that belief in a phenomenon is different from a 'statement about the evidence' (meaning inferences from reference classes) because although

[10] JJ Thomson, 'Liability and Individualised Evidence' (1986) 49 *Law and Contemporary Problems* 199, 203.

[11] DT Wasserman, 'The Morality of Statistical Proof and the Risk of Mistaken Liability' (1991) 13 *Cardozo Law Review* 935, 943.

[12] Pundik (n 2) 191.

[13] eg, the complete defence of automaton provides that a person cannot be guilty if their behaviour is 'without conscious volition' and ipso facto beyond the control of the defendant: *R v Quick* [1973] QB 910 (CA) 920. See further discussion in F Picinali, 'Generalisations, Causal Relationships and Moral Responsibility' (2016) 20 *International Journal of Evidence & Proof* 121, 127.

[14] C Nesson, 'The Evidence or the Event? On Judicial Proof and the Acceptability of Verdicts' (1985) 98 *Harvard Law Review* 1357, 1362–63.

[15] C Dahlman, 'Naked Statistical Evidence and Incentives for Lawful Conduct' (2020) 24 *International Journal of Evidence & Proof* 162.

[16] RA Posner, 'An Economic Approach to the Law of Evidence' (1999) 51 *Stanford Law Review* 1477, 1509.

it might be accurate, it doesn't record what an individual believes to be true.[17] But that assumes that an individual would refuse to form a belief from a individualisation or generalisation (for which no justification is given), and that belief is more important than accuracy. It also assumes, again without any apparent justification, that generalisations and individualisations cannot reveal 'what happened'. If that were true, inferences from reference classes would be irrelevant. Nesson does not make that argument, and so as such, Nesson's argument is contradictory. For a belief formed from flimsy specific evidence to be superior to a belief formed from 'strong' statistical evidence or generalisation requires the legal process to devalue the stated accuracy and truth-seeking goals of fact-finding;[18] unless one assumes that statistical evidence is inherently less likely to be accurate than non-statistical evidence, such that the probability of truth of statistical evidence is always lower than non-statistical evidence.

The many obvious inconsistencies with the theories about the objectionable nature of generalisations or individualisations have led to a field of literature that disputes the existence of a recognisable strand of objectionable generalisations or individualisations at all,[19] or that acting upon the objection is counterintuitive,[20] and contrary to the fact-finding goal of 'truth' seeking.[21] In light of these diverging views, the goal of this chapter is to articulate a basis for the individualisation objection, and why evidence law should take account of it. The claim here is that the objection is epistemic in nature, but not because generalisations and individualisations (and especially generalisations and individualisations from statistical evidence) are weaker or less valuable than specific evidence. It is logically (and mathematically) wrong to suggest that probabilistically equivalent statistical evidence has a greater 'risk of error' than specific evidence.[22] Schauer contends that preferring evidence derived from human perception over that of generalisations on the basis that perception evidence is more reliable is (unquestionably) false.[23] Yet this assumption is a frustratingly intractable feature of litigious practice. Where specific evidence is available (in fact or in theory), there is a clear preference in the profession and the judiciary for such evidence to be adduced rather than generalising or individualising from empirical studies.[24] What should be appreciated is that generalisations and specific evidence are not equivalent;

[17] Nesson (n 14) 1362.

[18] *R v War Pensions Entitlement Appeal Tribunal* (1933) 50 CLR 228, 256 (Evatt J).

[19] See P Tillers, 'Introduction: Three Contributions to Three Important Problems in Evidence Scholarship' (1997) 18 *Cardozo Law Review* 1875, 1886–87.

[20] See JJ Koehler and DN Shaviro, 'Veridical Verdicts: Increasing Verdict Accuracy Through the Use of Overtly Probabilistic Evidence and Methods' (1990) 75 *Cornell Law Review* 247, 256.

[21] D Enoch, L Spectre and T Fisher, 'Statistical Evidence, Sensitivity, and the Legal Value of Knowledge' (2012) 40 *Philosophy & Public Affairs* 197, 212.

[22] A Pundik, 'Statistical Evidence and Individual Litigants: A Reconsideration of Wasserman's Arguments from Autonomy' (2008) 12 *International Journal of Evidence & Proof* 303, 311.

[23] FF Schauer, *Profiles, Probabilities and Stereotypes* (Cambridge Mass, Harvard University Press, 2003) 94, 100–01.

[24] See discussion in ch 1.

generalisations and individualisations have an additional inferential hurdle that requires a resolution of the 'inferential gap'. This first section engages with the difficulty in identifying, on a consistent basis, when the inferential gap arises and what impact it has on evidence law.

A. General and Specific Evidence

The first limb in that debate is whether there is any intelligible difference between generalised and specific evidence, also referred to as 'typical', 'particularistic' or 'individualised' evidence.[25] If there is in fact no meaningful difference between a generalisation (which forms the basis of the individualising inference) and specific evidence, or if generalisations are inextricable from specific evidence, then objecting to generalisations because of their generalised character is pointless. Many scholars have cast doubt on the notion that evidence independent of generalisations can ever really exist.[26] Defining what makes evidence 'specific' has proven challenging. Specific evidence is not 'direct evidence' in the sense that direct evidence represents Bentham's *factum probandum*; evidence that by itself proves an element in a cause of action.[27] There is no reason why *probandum* evidence could not be itself comprised of a generalisation. Many scholars make no attempt to define specific evidence,[28] instead relying on a 'know it when we see it' paradigm.[29] Definitions that do exist, for example, 'peculiar to the incident',[30] or 'causally connected to the [putative] fact',[31] add little more detail than the label 'specific evidence'. In *US v Shonubi*, the Court sought to define its requirement of specific evidence by examples such as 'drug records' and 'admissions'.[32] As Tillers identifies, this is tantamount to saying that the only evidence of 'what happened is what happened'.[33] If that is right, specific evidence is evidence of direct observation, such as eyewitness accounts.

Even then, Tillers and others notably derided the possibility of any evidence, including eyewitness evidence, being 'specific'. No evidence, in their view, is free from generalisations.[34] Eyewitness evidence involves an individual identifying an

[25] Thomson (n 10) ('individualised evidence'); Stein (n 1) ('specific evidence').

[26] P Tillers, 'If Wishes were Horses: Discursive Comments on Attempts to Prevent Individuals from Being Unfairly Burdened by their Reference Classes' (2005) 4 *Law, Probability and Risk* 33; C Dahlman, 'Unacceptable Generalisations in Arguments on Legal Evidence' (2017) 31 *Argumentation* 83, 84.

[27] DN Walton, *Legal Argumentation and Evidence* (Pennsylvania, Penn State University Press, 2002) 81–82.

[28] Stein (n 1) 70–72 (conceding that specific and general are inextricably intertwined).

[29] A Pundik, 'Epistemology and the law of evidence: Four doubts about Alex Stein's Foundations of Evidence Law' (2006) 25 *Civil Justice Quarterly* 504, 513–14.

[30] Wasserman (n 11) 955; RJ Allen and MS Pardo, 'The Problematic Value of Mathematical Models of Evidence' (2007) 36 *Journal of Legal Studies* 107, 114 ('what happened specifically at a certain moment of time').

[31] Thomson (n 10) 203.

[32] *US v Shonubi* (*Shonubi IV*) 103 F3d 1085, 1089–90 (2dCir, 1997).

[33] Tillers, 'Reference Classes' (n 26) 44.

[34] ibid; Schauer (n 23) 101ff; Redmayne, 'Proof Paradoxes' (n 4) 293.

object at a particular time and place. But to arrive at that conclusion, a fact-finder has already accepted multiple generalisations. Witness evidence is communicated by words, and those words are given meaning by society outside the time, space and object of the initial phenomenon; in turn allowing room for disagreement about the meaning of the words (per general factual causation) or what those words mean in this particular context (per specific causation). Equally, if one takes the example of a witness giving evidence of seeing a goose, how did the witness 'know' there was a goose? She must have previously seen a goose at a different time or place, or had its features described to her by another person. Again, this information originates outside the time, space and object of the specific phenomenon. Somehow, her evidence that 'that bird is a goose' is viewed differently to evidence that 'I saw six birds in formation, I know that geese fly in formation at this time year, therefore the birds were geese'. The conclusion that the birds were geese is somehow (if only very slightly in this example) more uncertain than if she gave evidence of directly observing that each bird was a goose, notwithstanding the high probability, based on a generalisation from robust empirical sources, that geese in this area fly in formation at this time of year. Dissonance reflects the degree of possibility that some other type of bird was flying in formation.

Maintaining a bright line distinction between evidence of generalisations and specific evidence appears impossible. Even scholars who consider generalisations to be objectionable evidence concede that in many cases there is no clear difference.[35] Generalisations are a ubiquitous feature of legal reasoning. But making that concession does not change the fact that in some circumstances, generalisations are treated as inherently objectionable and are fairly or unfairly disregarded in the fact-finding process. To better explain the role of generalisations in fact-finding, instead of trying to find a distinction between general and specific evidence (which is likely impossible), this chapter focuses on the distinction, if any, between objectionable and unobjectionable generalisations.

B. The Inferential Gap

The cornerstone of the rejection of the epistemic account of the generalisation objection is the 'risk of error' fallacy. The risk of error in establishing truth is a potent worry for any actor within the legal system. It is also unavoidable and a risk present within every fact-finding exercise.[36] It is contrary to logic to claim that that specific evidence of 'X is 80% likely' is somehow less accurate than a statistically derived probability that X is 80% likely. Both present equal possibilities of error.

[35] Stein appears to concede that it is unnecessary to maintain the distinction: (n 1) 70 ('Seemingly, "case-specific" or "individualized" evidence is a misnomer. By its very definition, evidence entails inferential progress. Evidence refers to information from which fact-finders can derive some additional information. A piece of information qualifies as evidence only when it evidences something').

[36] Ho (n 9) 142.

Characterising dissonance as a consequence of risk of error is a mistake. Dissonance does not arise from some inherent epistemological failing in generalisations relative to specific evidence, but from the nature of the inductive inference from generalisations to the specific case. The issue is not risk of error per se, but a perceived inability to assess what the risk of error actually is; whether the probability of X propounded by the generalisations is an accurate reflection of the probability of X. Dissonance reflects the perceived inability of the fact-finder to believe in the truth of probabilities drawn from statistical evidence relative to perceptions (rightly or wrongly) of probabilities derived from individualised evidence. Dissonance is not a product of known-unknowns (the .2 error rate), but unknown-unknowns ('is the probability actually .8?'). Why should the fact-finder accept that the reference class accurately encapsulates the phenomenon in issue or that the probability seen in the reference class is reflected perfectly by the individual?

For that reason, objections to generalisations, and individualising inferences from those generalisations, fluctuate depending upon the degree of applicability or similarity of the reference class to the individual phenomenon.[37] This can be exemplified by a bridge metaphor. Fact A is general factual causation; the probabilities of suffering from lung cancer where it is believed that smoking caused that lung cancer, derived from a sample (*n*) taken from a population (*N*). Fact B is a putative fact; the lung cancer of the plaintiff (*p*) was caused by smoking. The probability of *p*'s lung cancer being caused by smoking is grounded by specific facts about *p* necessary to connect Fact A and Fact B (sometimes referred to as 'primary facts' in expert evidence literature),[38] which serve to justify the basis for the decision that Fact A and Fact B are sufficiently similar for a bridge to be constructed. The process of proving Fact B by inferring from Fact A requires crossing an inferential gap between the reference class and *p* created by differences in time, space and object. If Fact A is ephemeral or non-existent, no bridge can be constructed, and any expert opinion purporting to link Fact A and Fact B is irrelevant.[39] If Fact A is not proven, or not adequately proven, by admissible evidence or assumptions, the opinion that Fact A proves Fact B may be either inadmissible or lacking in weight.[40] Where Fact A is accepted, only by constructing a bridge across the inferential gap can Fact A assist in the proof of Fact B. If Fact A is too dissimilar to Fact B, as a matter of logic, the gap cannot be crossed no matter the strength of the evidence of general factual causation. Mere construction of the bridge does not mean that Fact A proves Fact B, albeit that does not mean that Fact A cannot by itself prove Fact B. Rather, a pathway has been forged that allows the fact-finder to take Fact A into account in Fact B's existence.

[37] Stein (n 1) 94.
[38] I Freckelton, *Expert Evidence*, 6th edn (Sydney, Thomson Reuters, 2019) 124.
[39] See ch 2, n 11.
[40] Freckelton (n 38) [2.20].

Gold divides the probabilities associated with Fact A and Fact B into 'fact' probabilities and 'belief' probabilities, respectively.[41] This concept enjoys support in scholarship and in judicial reasons.[42] Gold's dichotomy of fact and belief probabilities, fixated on Fact A and Fact B, oversimplifies the probabilistic calculus. General factual causation must itself be the subject of fact-finding to justify its place as the basis for the statistical evidence syllogism. There is both a fact and belief probability associated with Fact A. Likewise, one can compute fact probabilities about specific phenomena as long as one forms a belief in the fact probability.[43] It is better to avoid the use of terms like 'fact' and 'belief' probability writ large over fact-finding from statistical evidence.

The inferential gap widens as the differences between Fact A and Fact B multiply. Dissonance associated with the probative value of Fact A to Fact B accordingly increases. Bridges are hard to construct and support over a larger span. The wider the inferential gap, the (potentially) flimsier and less probative support offered by the bridge. As will become clear, understanding the generalisation objection in this way is critical to resolving the many debates that have arisen about its presence or absence.

Objections arising from the inferential gap are not unique to law. They are a common feature of philosophical debates about causation, probability and epistemology. Mill's statement that causal attributions from reference classes to individuals requires an 'assumption of the uniformity of nature'[44] neatly encapsulates the problem. Unless one can establish, or is prepared to believe, that a reference class is uniform in every respect,[45] extrapolating causation from Fact A to Fact B exposes a risk that the fact-finder's reliance on Fact A was misplaced. Fact A may not actually be relevantly 'the same' as Fact B. Uncertainty is the product of the degree of dissimilarity between Facts A and B that now have to be connected by inductive reasoning.

An extension of the problem of the inferential gap gives rise to the even more invidious 'reference class problem'. If the inferential gap causes the fact-finder to question the basis of their belief in Fact B from Fact A, the reference class problem challenges the appropriateness of Fact A's use (or, more precisely, which Fact A to use) in the first place.[46] If the reference class of Fact A is 'smokers', and the reference class for Fact A1 is '40 year old male smokers', which fact should be used to prove Fact B, when p is a 40 year old male? The logical answer is Fact A1. But sometimes the differences between the facts are harder to detect, making the choice between Fact A and Fact A1 unclear. To make matters more confusing,

[41] S Gold, 'Causation in Toxic Torts: Burdens of Proof, Standards of Persuasion, and Statistical Evidence' (1986) 96 *Yale Law Journal* 376, 383–84.

[42] Green (n 8) 12–13, 114; *Sienkiewicz v Greif* [2011] 2 AC 229 (UKSC) [217]–[218] (Lord Dyson).

[43] See ch 7, section IV.A.

[44] See S Zabell, 'Symmetry Arguments in Probability' in A Hajek and C Hitchcock (eds), *The Oxford Handbook of Probability and Philosophy* (Oxford, Oxford University Press 2016) 325.

[45] eg if the causal relationship existed for every participant.

[46] Redmayne, 'Proof Paradoxes' (n 4) 286.

the probabilities for Fact A and Fact A1 may not be the same; indeed, they may be entirely contradictory,[47] and these contradictions may replicate ad infinitum.[48]

This gives rise to two problems. First, if presented with two sets of data from two or more different reference classes, which should be used? Second, if we only have one set of data, why should we use that reference class if there could be a vast array of other hypothetical reference classes in existence, some of which potentially contradict the probability of the current reference class? This book engages with this second problem in chapter seven. But the first presents a more difficult challenge and requires a holistic view of the evidence. For statistical evidence, that means looking at the robustness of the statistics, the generalisability of those statistics to the individual case, and their ability (in tandem with other evidence) to prove the facts-in-issue, in order to assess why that reference class from that evidence is superior to another. Choosing between reference classes is a subjective judgement grounded in rationality well known to evidence law. Reasonable minds can and will disagree. Acknowledging that subjectivity does not, however, resolve the array of objections that can be levelled against generalisations. That is partly because what is meant by 'objection' is often argued in the abstract and without reference to how evidence and objections to evidence are dealt with by evidence law.

C. Generalisations in Evidence Law

Dissonance and uncertainty are not, by themselves, a basis for objection in evidence law. Describing the objection as an anti-liability feeling suggests that objection is to the ability of generalisations to prove facts. That is, even if we accept the generalisation is 'true', why should the fact-finder accept that this evidence, by itself, is sufficient to meet the burden of proof? This raises questions about how the standards of proof ought to be interpreted, and the weight of the evidence. Dissonance is much broader. Proof is only one component in the evidentiary process. Relevance, weight and admissibility are also implicated by objections to generalisations. Dissonance is a bundle of objections that arise at different levels of the evidentiary process.[49]

1. *Relevance*

Dissonance implicates the relevance of generalisations by two interrelated processes. First, evidence can be dissonant where general factual causation fails to

[47] MS Pardo and RJ Allen, 'Juridical Proof and the Best Explanation' (2008) 27 *Law & Philosophy* 223, 259–60.

[48] MS Pardo and RJ Allen, 'Generalizations and Reference Classes' in C Dahlman, A Stein and G Tuznet, *Philosophical Foundations of Evidence Law* (Oxford, Oxford University Press, 2021) 304.

[49] cf Pundik, 'Generalisation' (n 2) 192, who claims that the anti-liability intuition is distinct from admissibility concerns.

be appropriately convincing, either because the evidence is insufficiently reliable or fails to instantiate the general causal proposition it is adduced to prove. Where the evidence is incapable of proving general factual causation, such as where the association between X and Y is spurious, or where the statistics so lack robustness that they cannot be relied on, the evidence will be irrelevant.

The second aspect of relevance arises at the poles (*n* and *p*) of the inferential gap. This book argues in chapter five that the relevance of statistical generalisations is analogous to the relevance of similar fact evidence. Ultimately, the inferential gap is a scale; the closer the poles of the scale are together, the less dissonance is occasioned. In the unlikely event that the poles overlap, there can be no dissonance because the phenomena must be identical.[50] Following that logic, at the other extreme, completely disparate phenomena from which no bridge could span are entirely non-generalisable and irrelevant. The reference phenomenon is so removed in space, time and object from the phenomenon in issue that no support can be derived for the existence of the specific phenomenon whatsoever. A great deal of scholarship has focused on this stage in the inferential process. For example, Wright claims that ex ante probabilities (a form of 'factual generalisation')[51] cannot be 'evidence of what actually happened on the particular occasion because it provides *no information* on whether the … causal generalisation … actually [was] instantiated on the particular occasion'.[52] If evidence provides *no* information for the proposition it is adduced in support of, that evidence is irrelevant.

The more nuanced view – that factual generalisations of this type can be helpful but only when supported by specific evidence[53] – takes the same approach by converting the problem from relevance to conditional relevance. Under either theory, the generalisation in question is irrelevant but for the tender of specific evidence. To make matters even more convoluted, Wright (and others) have opined that tendering statistical evidence almost always involves identifying some specific evidence that can be used to connect the generalisation to the specific proposition.[54] It is unclear how that approach is consistent with Wright's claim about ex ante probabilities since, almost by definition, a relevant ex ante probability will have some link to the specific case as a necessary consequence of the determination of relevance.

The difficulty seems to arise from trying to categorise the objection as a single phenomenon. All ex ante probabilities (employing Wright's parlance) are equally objectionable by virtue of their nature as ex ante probabilities. That cannot be the correct approach. From time-to-time courts do reject ex ante probabilities,

[50] See Allen and Pardo (n 30) 114.

[51] See further section IV below.

[52] R Wright, 'Causation, Responsibility, Risk, Probability, Naked Statistics, and Proof: Pruning the Bramble Bush by Clarifying the Concepts' (1988) 73 *Iowa Law Review* 1001, 1071 (emphasis added).

[53] Tribe (n 1) 1349–50; Dant (n 7) 63–64. It is noteworthy that in subsequent writings, Wright would appear to adopt this view: see RW Wright, 'Proving Causation: Probability versus Belief' in R Goldberg (ed), *Perspectives on Causation* (Oxford, Hart, 2011) n 67.

[54] Wright, 'Proving' (n 53) n 67.

sometimes for reasons that are less than clear. But not all ex ante probabilities are treated equally. Where ex ante probabilities are so removed from the present phenomena (and would therefore not implicate any particular characteristics of the specific phenomenon), that evidence would be irrelevant. But where there is some connection to the facts-in-issue, the key criterion for relevance – that the evidence could rationally affect the probability of the existence of a fact-in-issue – is fulfilled.

Relevance objections to generalisations should be distinguished from 'error' objections. It is not claimed that ex ante probabilities are more likely to be erroneous than specific evidence where the 'probabilities' of the phenomena occurring are the same. Rather, what is claimed is that it is harder to assess what support ex ante probabilities can provide. If the fact-finder cannot perceive what support is provided, the generalisation is irrelevant. Generalisations that are perceived as wrong as they apply to the specific case are not, however, irrelevant.[55] The law accepts that fact-finding is inherently uncertain and can remain so even after the legal label of certainty is bestowed. Error does not ordinarily result in irrelevance unless that error is so profound and obvious to cast the generalisation as effectively spurious. There are, however, some suggestions to the contrary. In *Commonwealth v Amann Aviation*, Deane J suggested that the approach to fact-finding about past events was such that 'a 50 per cent probability represents a dividing line between certainty *and non-existence or irrelevance*'.[56] With respect, that statement is inconsistent with prevailing authority and logic.[57] The burden of proof does not straddle certainty and irrelevance, but rather, belief in the probable truth and the failure to so believe. To prefer one version of events to another, where those events conflict, implicitly rejects the truth of the disbelieved account.[58] But that does not render those disbelieved events 'irrelevant'. This is especially because the burden is set up as a threshold to be overcome by weight of evidence. It would be wrong to suggest that 'there is insufficient evidence for a judicial officer to make a positive decision' is the same as saying 'I believe one version of events to be manifestly and entirely wrong'. Events that are not and cannot ever be correct are irrelevant. Otherwise, events that fail to meet the standard of proof are relevant, they are just not persuasive or sufficient at that time.

2. *Weight and Sufficiency*

Once generalisations are accepted as relevant, the inquiry shifts to the degree of support the evidence offers. The terminus of that scale is the appropriate standard of proof and the capacity of the evidence to be sufficient. This book examines the proof objection levelled at statistical evidence in chapter seven, that is, the capacity of statistical evidence to be sufficient by itself.

[55] eg *Commissioner for Government Transport v Adamcik* (1961) 106 CLR 292, 303.
[56] *Commonwealth v Amann Aviation* (1991) 174 CLR 64, 123.
[57] eg I Dennis, *The Law of Evidence*, 6th edn (London, Sweet & Maxwell, 2017) 114.
[58] See *Coote v Kelly* [2013] NSWCA 357, [46].

Generalisations (especially generalisations from statistical evidence) pose a challenge to the assessment of weight. Assessing probative value for any evidence, or the degree of support from the evidence for the phenomenon in issue, gives rise to at least two separate weight inquiries. First, to what extent does the fact-finder believe the putative fact to be true (an analogue for credit weight of the fact-in-issue)? Second, to what extent does the putative fact support the existence of the specific phenomenon in issue (fact weight to the fact-in-issue)? Generalisations pose a third question; to what extent is the generalisation a good representation of the specific phenomenon (Keynesian weight to the fact-in-issue)? The book introduces these questions, and how the law approaches the mathematical interaction between statistical evidence and other evidence in chapter eight.

3. *Prejudice and Admissibility*

If statistical evidence is relevant to general factual causation and specific causation, and is not otherwise inadmissible, it is prima facie admissible evidence of both. Dissonance caused by the inferential gap is epistemic. It arises from the decision-maker's belief that the generalisation entirely fails to encompass the phenomenon in question and is therefore irrelevant. Or, it arises from the fact-finder's doubt about the degree to which the generalisation explains the specific phenomenon. But, as established in chapter one, there is no rule of evidence that explicitly excludes generalisations at large from the fact-finding process.

Common law and statutory rules of evidence also permit or require gatekeepers to exclude prejudicial evidence. Evidence is prejudicial if fact-finders could use it 'improperly'.[59] Chapter six provides a detailed analysis of the role of prejudice from statistical evidence.

When placed alongside the full gamut of evidence law, it becomes clear that dissonance produced by generalisations and statistical evidence is not just one holistic objection. Dissonance is a collection of objections concerning the relevance, weight, admissibility and sufficiency of the evidence. These objections are not unidimensional – often, they will occur together. Accounts that limit themselves to sufficiency (such as those derived from the proof paradox) or admissibility[60] miss this crucial element in the nature of the objection and cannot offer a complete account of objections to generalisations.

This chapter is dedicated to establishing the existence of an identifiable epistemic objection arising from generalisations that acts as a precursor to all generalisation objections, and the circumstances in which that objection arises. It

[59] *HML v The Queen* (2008) 235 CLR 334, [12].

[60] Pundik, 'Generalisation' (n 2) 192. A further difficulty with Pundik's claim that generalisations supporting culpability ought to be inadmissible fails to take into account the test for inadmissibility in that context; that the prejudice flowing from that evidence should outweigh its probative value. The question of admissibility is not just 'is the evidence prejudicial' but 'is the evidence so prejudicial that this outweighs the knowledge gained from it'.

demonstrates that a rational epistemic basis to the generalisation objection can be coherently distinguished from other generalisations in fact-finding.

II. 'No Gap' Generalisations

Pundik correctly points out that not all generalisations are epistemologically objectionable. That does not mean that an epistemological objection does not exist, or that the law should be unconcerned by it. Dissonance arises from the group to individual inference. Even if a particular trait or effect is observed in *n*, why should the decision-maker accept that this trait or effect equally exists in *p*?

It stands to reason that in the absence of this gap, no dissonance can arise. What determines the presence of the gap is not just the existence of a generalisation but the use that generalisation is put to in the fact-finding process. Some generalisations do not provoke dissonance because their use does not require the fact-finder to turn their mind to crossing the inferential gap. Pundik, however, asserts that a theory of objectionable generalisations cannot account for the fact that some decisions are made based on generalised evidence that should be objectionable, but are not.[61] In his hypothetical 'Richard', the protagonist is exposed to radiation, causing a unique skin rash and a propensity towards violence. Pundik suggests that it would be unobjectionable to restrain Richard in hospital for his risk of violence. But it would be objectionable to convict him of a violent offence for displaying the same rash.[62] This, it is said, belies the coherency of the epistemic objection to generalisations.

What differentiates these two scenarios is the purpose of the generalisation. For restraint, no inferential gap is occasioned because Richard's individual propensity for violence is irrelevant. Richard 'the individual' is not being regulated but rather a general class of patients possessing a skin rash that uniformly poses a risk of violence. The inquiry remains at the level of generalisation despite its specific effect on Richard because a risk is inherent to a class of people and all people in the class can be regulated equally. This would only be objectionable if Richard was being restrained ostensibly for his skin rash, but other similar skin rash patients were not, leading the fact-finder to query why Richard warranted different treatment. By contrast, convicting Richard of a crime requires the fact-finder to accept a likelihood of criminal offending in skin rash patients and that this likelihood predicts Richard's chances of having committed an offence. In that scenario there is an inferential gap between other skin rash patients and Richard. Dissonance results from the use of the generalisation to prove a specific phenomenon (where other phenomena may operate to interfere with the causal pathway between Richard's rash and the crime), rather than a uniform trait.

[61] See ibid 210.
[62] ibid 204.

There are three principal forms of non-objectionable generalisations in law. The first, concerning regulatory decision-making or liability by way of risk allocation, operates on identical footing to Richard's case by focusing exclusively on proof of an effect in the group. The court is only concerned with general rather than specific causation. A court may accept that Executive power was validly exercised in banning a particular dangerous additive. It would not be epistemologically objectionable[63] to rely on evidence of the additive's dangerousness in making that decision because the subject of the evidence (the additive) is entirely encapsulated in the response (banning the additive). Regulation is not concerned with 'what happened' but rather 'what could happen' to a particular population. By contrast, using that same evidence to say that a particular instance of that additive caused harm would be dissonant.

Similar reasoning supports certain exceptions to the common law of causation in order to overcome evidentiary hurdles. Section 15 of the Tobacco-Related Damages and Health Care Costs Recovery Act 2009 (Quebec) (TRDA-Q) was enacted to facilitate the recovery of damages from tobacco companies and provides:

> In an action brought on a collective basis, proof of causation between alleged facts, in particular between the defendant's wrong or failure and the health care costs whose recovery is being sought, or between exposure to a tobacco product and the disease suffered by, or the general deterioration of health of, the recipients of that health care, may be established on the sole basis of statistical information or information derived from epidemiological, sociological or any other relevant studies, including information derived from a sampling.

Section 15 is intentionally and explicitly designed to overcome the historical arguments made by tobacco manufactures and accepted Canadian jurisprudence that epidemiologic evidence cannot amount to specific causation.[64] For class actions for damages against tobacco companies, the TRDA-Q purports to change the nature of the inference. Usually, epidemiologic evidence forms part of a chain of proof that relevantly includes personal information about the disease in the individual. If the epidemiology establishes the basis for the risk (and thus the overall causal framework), the individualised evidence fills out the causal structure. By removing the requirement for specific proof, the Quebec legislature have displaced the ordinary inferential process from n to N to p. With somewhat similar effect to the *Fairchild* exception,[65] the TRDA-Q permits causal findings when there is only

[63] Even Wright concedes that statistical evidence is useful for causes of action predicated on the allocation of risk: Wright, 'Causation' (n 8) 1826.

[64] *Letourneau v JTI-MacDonald* 2015 QCCS 2382, [691]–[692], and authorities at fn 314.

[65] Derived from the principles in *Fairchild v Glenhaven Funeral Services* [2003] AC 32 (HL), the *Fairchild* exception permits findings of liability in English law against defendants where medical science is insufficient to establish a 'but-for' causal connection. Instead, it is enough that the defendant 'materially increased the risk of harm to the employee': at [44] (Lord Nicholls). The status of the *Fairchild* exception is more uncertain in Australia law, although the concept of causation also includes 'material contribution': *Amaca v Booth* (2011) 246 CLR 36, [52], [70].

evidence of an increase in risk for an individual.[66] That means the inferential gap between the general (*n* and *N*) and the specific (*p*) is greatly diminished. One only needs to establish that *p* smoked, and fits somewhat into the framework of *n* and *N*. At trial (and upheld on appeal) the Superior Court of Quebec (QCCS) went on to reject much of the countervailing expert evidence adduced in *Letourneau v JTI-MacDonald* (concerning an action for damages under TRDA-Q) because those experts 'preferred to blinder their opinions within the confines of individual cases, even though [they] should have known of the critical role that [s 15 TRDA-Q] plays with respect to the use of epidemiological evidence'.[67]

Of course, as a matter of logic, the generalisation objection still exists for proof of individual causation for members of the class. TRDA-Q merely creates a legal platform for ignoring or minimising that objection. The same can be said for *Fairchild*, whereby liability can be found against a 'defendant who has materially increased the risk that the claimant will suffer damage and may have caused that damage, but cannot be proved to have done so because it is impossible to show, on a balance of probability, that some other exposure to the same risk may not have caused it'.[68] That regime means that proof of the causal nexus between exposure and disease is unnecessary; it is enough that exposure, occasioned by a breach of duty, increased the risk of disease in the individual plaintiff. A legal construct is created that largely avoids the need for a generalisation inference by artificially minimising the generalisation objection. Causation can be assumed across the inferential gap as long as the plaintiff fits broadly within the reference class.

The second form of non-objectionable generalisations are 'deterministic phenomena'. Phenomena that are deterministically associated – that is, one must follow the other – cannot produce dissonance because *n* and *p* are identical. These situations are extremely rare, because there are few circumstances where every possible manifestation of a phenomenon is known or knowable.[69] One potential example could be 'human beings will die without oxygen'. This is not the same as 'person X died from a lack of oxygen when deprived of it', because some other circumstance may have caused death even where the individual was in an environment with no oxygen. The generalisation here can only be used to establish that where an individual is deprived of oxygen in whatever form, they will eventually die of asphyxiation or some other cause; but they will be dead. No dissonance arises from that evidence despite the use of inference from general to the specific because the possibility of error to the underlying probabilities that attracts dissonance no longer exists.

[66] The Australian Consumer Law also permits recovery of damages where there is an increased risk of harm leading to damage. In *Medtel v Courtney* (2003) 130 FCR 182 (FCAFC), the Full Court of the Federal Court of Australia (FCAFC) held, concerning similar provisions of the former Trade Practices Act 1975 (Cth), that it was sufficient that the plaintiff's pacemaker bore a risk of being defective; he did not need to prove that it was in fact defective to recover damages on the basis that the product was 'unfit for its intended purpose'.

[67] *Letourneau* (n 64) [737].

[68] *Barker v Corus UK* [2006] 2 AC 572 (HL) [17] (Lord Hoffmann).

[69] Picinali (n 13) 127–28.

The third form of unobjectionable generalisations are referred to here as 'direct generalisations', where statistical evidence is adduced to prove statistical facts, or facts unconcerned by causation. Such generalisations are used to 'prove' the probable conduct of hypothetical persons, sometimes referred to as the 'reasonable person'.[70] The statistical evidence in *Rogers* showed that the risk of bilateral blindness arising from a procedure performed by her ophthalmic surgeon on one eye was 1 in 14,000.[71] This evidence was used to establish the degree of appreciable risk and whether it would be 'significant' to the patient.[72] That is, would a reasonable person view those rates as significant and, if warned of that risk, chose not to undertake the surgery. Used in this way, the generalisation is not epistemologically objectionable. There is no point of comparison between the general and specific, only a general view that a hypothetical individual would consider that probability sufficiently concerning. By contrast, using blindness rates to establish that the plaintiff's blindness was caused by the surgery would be objectionable as there is a comparison between the general probability of something going wrong, and something going wrong in this particular instance.

III. Commonsense and Background Generalisations

One area of strident disagreement in the literature concerning epistemological objections to generalisations is the role played by 'background generalisations'. Despite, it is argued, following an identical inferential structure to objectionable generalisations, background generalisations are sometimes regarded as not objectionable.[73] There have been many attempts to classify what differentiates a background generalisation from an objectionable generalisation. None of these attempts has succeeded, principally because the scope and variety of possible background generalisations used in fact-finding are infinite and inherently resistant to like treatment.

What is agreed is that background generalisations are an indispensable element in fact-finding.[74] Background generalisations facilitate fact-finding by infilling gaps in evidence. For example, a witness gives evidence that a red car entered a street, and another gives evidence that a red car left the street shortly after. The fact-finder could be asked to infer that the car in fact drove down the street that

[70] Caveats can be attached to the reasonable person concept to narrow the field of inquiry; eg the loss of control defence in English law requires the decision-maker to find that a person of the same age and sex as the accused would have 'lost control': Coroners and Justice Act 2009 (UK) s 54(1)(c). That requires a generalisation about individuals in the position of the accused. But, by itself, it is not a generalisation about the accused and therefore does not result in an inferential gap unless one seeks to infer a difference between the reasonable person (in the same position as the accused) and the accused.

[71] *Rogers v Whitaker* (1992) 175 CLR 479, 482.

[72] ibid.

[73] Pundik, 'Generalisation' (n 2) 194–96.

[74] Stein (n 1) 94.

it entered, and then exited the street, even though there is no 'direct' evidence it drove down the street. Equally, background generalisations allow fact-finders to interpret evidence. Identifying the cars seen by the two witnesses as the same vehicle may rest on evidence of what the number-plate of that car was. To understand why that evidence is significant in identifying a motor vehicle, the fact-finder needs to appreciate what a number-plate is and its role in identifying vehicles; such knowledge being the product of a generalisation 'cars have unique identifiers recorded on a number-plate'. Without this ability to fill evidentiary gaps and interpret evidence, fact-finding would become functionally impossible.

To explain the difference between background and objectionable generalisations, Pundik suggests that although the content of eyewitness testimony does not (usually) involve objectionable generalisations, assessing the credibility of that evidence appears to.[75] Yet, for some reason, generalisations about credit do not seem to provoke the same kind of epistemic objection despite following the same inferential pathway as objectionable generalisations.[76] Pundik gives the example described in the film *Twelve Angry Men*:[77] a woman who gave evidence about seeing an event in the distance was later discredited because it was revealed that she was short-sighted and was not wearing her glasses at the relevant time. Pundik claims that the generalisation 'short-sighted people cannot see well' and the specific inference discrediting her evidence because she could not see well is unobjectionable.[78]

Pundik's example actually contains two stages. The first is an inference that because short-sighted people are vision impaired, and the old lady is accepted to be short-sighted, her vision is generally impaired.[79] Pundik is right to claim that this inference doesn't seem to provoke dissonance. By contrast, taking that inference one step further to infer that because she is short-sighted she could not see the event, is objectionable. There is an inferential gap between the sample group (n) (short-sighted people) and the individual (p) (the short-sighted woman) because this second step involves a specific inference about what she actually saw based on what other people could or could not see. There are a great many competing factors that could differentiate the reference class from the individual, such as distance or lighting and individual differences in the degree of myopia. Pundik might be right that the objection to the second stage would not result in the discrediting evidence being inadmissible on epistemological or moral grounds. But it would give rise to a question concerning the weight of that inference by reason of epistemological uncertainty.

[75] Pundik, 'Generalisation' (n 2) 193.
[76] ibid 194.
[77] Directed by Sidney Lumet, Orion-Nova Productions, 1957.
[78] ibid 194, 211.
[79] Had there been no acceptance that the witness was short-sighted, a further generalisation would be needed to establish that her short-sightedness meant she was vision impaired. That inference would be dissonant.

The more intriguing question from *Twelve Angry Men* is why the first stage of the inference is apparently unobjectionable. Pundik provides a clue when he concludes that background generalisations hold the same inferential structure as naked statistical evidence (albeit that Pundik is seeking to demonstrate why background generalisations ought to be objectionable and are not).[80] Naked statistical evidence, contrary to Pundik's view, does not contain an objectionable generalisation because the proof paradoxes that exemplify naked statistical evidence are designed so that the probabilities of *p* and *n* are necessarily identical, precluding the existence of an inferential gap. Unlike naked statistical evidence however, background generalisations would rarely involve the actors in the reference class and the individual being identical. Some other means of connecting the two is necessary. This work argues that this connection is the product of a 'uniform rebuttable presumption', a distinct method of understanding inferences from generalisations that are typically couched in the language of 'commonsense'.

A. Commonsense Inferences

Stein distinguishes between non-objectionable background generalisations (called 'inferential evidence')[81] and objectionable generalisations (called 'fact-generating evidence').[82] Stein offers four bases for making this distinction: inferential evidence 'encompasses general regularities that fact-finders extract from common knowledge and experience' and '[reveal] nothing about the specifics of any individual case',[83] whereas fact-generating evidence requires inferring from the general case to a specific case, and concern 'new domains, unaccounted for by past experience' causing 'deep epistemological problems'.[84] These in turn represent two domains: first, whether the evidence is 'commonsense' or 'novel', and second, the use of the evidence to explain individual occurrences. However, neither of these categories is capable of distinguishing between background and objectionable generalisations.

Commonsense is the glue that holds fact-finding together. Evidence is interpretable because of 'commonsense' inferences about the existence of phenomena.[85] Estimating what might have occurred from evidence is only possible by reason of extrapolating commonsense conclusions from an existing state of affairs.[86] Even complex factual inquiries like causation are determined by reason of a 'commonsense' understanding of how the world operates.[87] Commonsense

[80] Pundik, 'Generalisation' (n 2) 211.
[81] Stein (n 1) 93.
[82] ibid 95–96.
[83] ibid 94.
[84] ibid 96–97.
[85] *Jones v Great Western Railway Company* [1930] All ER Ext 830 (HL) 842.
[86] *Amann* (n 56) 120.
[87] See ch 3.

allows fact-finder(s) to resolve factual uncertainties by reference to what 'everyone' knows.[88] Stein's account suggests that the difference between background and objectionable generalisations is explained by the difference between commonsense and ex ante uncertain factual inferences. There is some logic to this approach. The inferential gap produces dissonance because of the uncertainty between the general and the specific. But if the connection were a product of commonsense, that is, 'everyone' believed that the evidence was generalisable, then dissonance could not arise.

The obvious difficulty for Stein's approach is that it relies on every hypothetical fact-finder believing the same thing equally. He suggests that commonsense is 'ruled by consensus' and that 'individuals with common experience always have ways of moulding [commonsense inferences] into generalisations'.[89] That seems intrinsically implausible given the plurality of beliefs between individuals. Roberts and Zuckerman suggest '[c]ommon sense … is highly acculturated and differentially distributed. Only a limited number of factual generalisations are truly common to the bulk of humanity, and even within smaller communities, "common sense" may be contested terrain'.[90] Differentiating objectionable from background generalisations by way of commonsense becomes futile if there is limited agreement over what commonsense means. What is meant by 'common' is not a genuinely uniform concept. Fact-finding is a subjective task. Facts are not found because they exist but because the fact-finder believes they exist. Commonsense is better understood as what an individual fact-finder rationally believes everyone else thinks. Anchoring the analysis to rationality means, in legal parlance, that a reviewer of the commonsense conclusion could also accept that people think in that way, permitting an element of consensus into the analysis of commonsense. That does not detract from its subjective nature and the likelihood that one fact-finder's commonsense is different to another's.

Stein counters that differences of opinion are issues of 'definition' that can ultimately be the subject of agreement by rendering the generalisation more or less strong, such as 'all witnesses uninterested in the outcome do not lie' may be changed to 'some witnesses disinterested in the outcome do not lie'.[91] The difficulty with that approach is that background generalisations ultimately rely on categorical inferences irrespective of their phrasing. Evidence of an accused's flight from a crime scene can be used to support that the accused committed the act and intended to do so. The strength of the inference 'guilty people run away' can be adjusted to 'some people', but either the fact-finder accepts the inference that guilty people have a special propensity to run, and therefore a particular individual who ran is likely to be guilty, or they do not accept it. Graded strength is unhelpful when

[88] eg *Briginshaw v Briginshaw* (1938) 60 CLR 336, 362.

[89] Stein (n 1) 95.

[90] P Roberts, *Roberts & Zuckerman's Criminal Evidence*, 3rd edn (Oxford, Oxford University Press, 2022) 146–47.

[91] Stein (n 1) 95.

there is no evidence to test the application of that generalisation in the particular case. Moreover, no matter how the inference is phrased, 'everyone' must accept the general proposition as being a true representation in that particular case. Some people may be unwilling to draw such general inferences or may not agree that the inference applies in this case. For example, if a bomb had gone off at the scene, it would be illogical to conclude that all running people were guilty. The argument over what constitutes commonsense in the first place defeats any possibility that commonsense can account for why background generalisations are unobjectionable. In this regard, commonsense is likely an empty doctrine in all but the rarest of instances.[92]

Equally, there is no reason why 'fact-generating' evidence cannot be the subject of commonsense. First, evidence could be adduced to prove a fact that otherwise fits into the rubric of commonsense and that evidence produces an inferential gap based on 'the similarity between the factual patterns that the generalisation and the [specific evidence] exhibit respectively'.[93] Second, in light of the subjective account of commonsense described above, Stein's claim that fact-generating evidence only concerns new domains is equally doubtful. What might be common for one person may be new to another.

Stein also argues that inferential evidence is non-dissonant because it is never used to make claims about individual cases. Stein's basis for this claim is unclear. If the claim is that inferential evidence only operates over group inferences (such as general factual causation), then the account is broadly correct. But that cannot be what Stein intended. Background generalisations are used to 'move cases forward' and fill in empty details. Those details will often relate back to individual phenomena. It would be an entirely artificial exercise to distinguish between an inference that is used to support another inference that is purportedly more specific, when both ultimately form part of the corpus of the evidence. In any event, inferential evidence is regularly used to make claims about individuals.

In *Jones v Great Western Railway Company*, a railway worker was crushed between two train cars.[94] In the absence of any evidence of the movements of the deceased, the case on breach of duty turned on whether the court could infer that the defendant employer had issued a warning that the train trucks were about to move, and thus the deceased was caught between the train trucks by his own negligence.[95] To infer that no warning had been given, the House of Lords used the generalisation that 'had he received a warning he would not have entered the gap'.[96] It was only by reason of commonsense that one could infer that people who hear warnings do not disobey them. That generalisation was specifically attributed to the deceased. Whilst one might query the justification for accepting the

[92] RJ Allen, 'Common Sense, Rationality and the Legal Process' (2001) 22 *Cardozo Law Review* 1417, 1424–25.
[93] Stein (n 1) 97.
[94] *Jones* (n 85).
[95] ibid 831–32.
[96] ibid 840.

reliability of the generalisation that all people listen and obey warnings (unless contrary evidence establishes otherwise), it does not seem to raise an epistemological problem of distinguishing between the individual deceased and a reference class of individuals who do follow such instructions. Such rules of convenience are commonplace in the law under the rubric of evidence of 'past practice' or 'habit',[97] and are used to support the existence of phenomena that accord with popular psychological notions of human behaviour, which, in the sense raised by Stein, permit the litigation to move forward.[98]

B. Uniform Rebuttable Presumptions

Stein's commonsense account of background generalisations fails because it is too restrictive in scope. Background generalisations occur in a far wider variety of contexts than those covered by Stein's categories. Many of the categories Stein identifies could also fall into fact-generating situations. The problems with defining commonsense make it difficult to determine if uncertainty about the objectionable nature of the generalisation is from an epistemological objection or a challenge to its commonsense status. Whether a generalisation is a matter of commonsense is more appropriately evaluated by the ability of the evidence to establish general factual causation than the applicability of that evidence to the individual case.

Assumptions of uniformity offer a more consistent means of distinguishing background generalisations from objectionable generalisations. Stein does refer to this feature, but it is distinct from his inferential and fact-generating theories. Stein states that non-objectionable inferential evidence covers 'uniformities'.[99] Although it should not be limited to inferential evidence as Stein construes it, categorising a phenomenon as uniform has the effect of removing the inferential gap and dissonance. Stein's example that 'all disinterested witnesses tell the truth', Pundik's claim that 'all short-sighted people are not credible' because they cannot see, and the example that 'all guilty people run away from crime scenes' possess a common theme; these background generalisations purport to offer a uniform explanation of the phenomenon. For the generalisation about 'short-sighted witnesses' to apply to the individual case, the claim is made about all short-sighted witnesses as an entire class, including the individual in question. There is no need to generalise the evidence to a specific case because the trait itself includes witnesses within the class (short-sighted people) about whom the generalisation is assumed (correctly or not) to be true. This is distinct from relying on commonsense; it is unnecessary to show that 'everyone knows' the fact to be uniform. Instead, all that is necessary is that the decision-maker is prepared to assume, rightly or wrongly, that the trait is uniform across all possible circumstances.

[97] JD Heydon, *Cross on Evidence*, 14th edn (Chatswood, LexisNexis, 2023) [1135].
[98] *Potts v Miller* (1940) 64 CLR 282, 304.
[99] Stein (n 1) 94.

Where generalisations can be uniform (for example, the dead cannot perform mathematical calculations), controversy is unlikely to arise. But where the generalisations are equivocal or fuzzy, arguments about the potential uniformity of a phenomenon could be infinite. Background generalisations offering conclusions mirroring the 'natural and probable consequence'[100] of actions are more likely to be accepted as valid uniform generalisations than controversial generalisations. The less obvious the generalisation, the less likely it is that it will capture a universal snapshot of the class of phenomena about whom it is made. Moreover, real proof of uniformity would require evidence of every available transaction. Such evidence is rarely, if ever, available. To avoid metaphysical impossibility, courts adopt a 'rebuttable presumption' approach. An inductive inference from a particular phenomenon or reference class is assumed to cover the entire gamut of possibilities. Any contrary evidence undermines the uniformity of the generalisation, and the generalisation returns to an objectionable state.

Using uniformity as a means of bypassing evidentiary objections is common practice. In *R v Sadique*, a defendant was charged with inchoate offences concerning the supply of precursor, but not inherently illegal, drugs to alleged drug dealers.[101] In rejecting the defendant's claim that he supplied these drugs legitimately and without any intention to supply for the purposes of drug offences, the prosecution adduced evidence that 'no business records, client lists or delivery records were ever discovered or produced'.[102] For this evidence to be relevant to proving his illegitimate supply at least two generalisations are required: legitimate businesses (typically) produce business records and an absence of business records suggests the business is acting illegitimately. No evidence was raised to support this inference; no population study of legitimate businesses was conducted to show the proportion that produce legitimate records. The generalisation seems to follow a doctrine of commonsense that modern business practices require businesses to produce records. If evidence had been tendered to support the inference that the business was acting illegitimately, by reference to others' business and reporting practices,[103] an (objectionable) generalisation inference would need to be drawn by reason of this evidence's separation from the present facts by time, space and object or personality. How do we know that because those other businesses produced records, that the accused's business is illegitimate because it did not? In the absence of evidence, the inference has universal application – all legitimate businesses produce business records, and their absence places the defendant's operation outside the scope of 'legitimate business'. The defendant's

[100] eg *Parfitt v Lawless* (1872) 2 P&D 462, 472 (Lord Penzance).

[101] *Sadique v R* [2013] 4 All ER 924.

[102] ibid [2].

[103] Such evidence is often referred to as evidence of 'custom': *Fleet v Murton* (1871) LR 7 QB 126, 134–35. The line between assuming or proving a custom is blurred. It depends in large part on how generic the custom is. The more general and applicable the custom, the more likely it will fall under the rubric of 'common experience' within a judicial officer's personal knowledge: *Adelaide Stevedoring v Forst* (1940) 64 CLR 538, 570.

exclusion from the class of 'legitimate business' means that there is no need to generalise the evidence to the defendant and thus dissonance is avoided.

Whereas uniform rebuttable presumptions may not be epistemologically objectionable, they are certainly empirically objectionable. The claim that 'all short-sighted people have impaired vision' is arguably correct. But that generalisation may be so broad as to be unhelpful. If the question is not 'was the person's vision impaired' but 'could that person see a certain event', merely being short-sighted proffers very little information. Not all short-sighted people require corrected vision for all things. The circumstances of witnessing the event may render their short-sightedness moot. The more generic the reference class, the less weight it has, even though it might be epistemologically unobjectionable.

Notwithstanding substantial empirical doubt, the law has been prepared to assume the existence of uniform phenomena from time to time. For example, courts import local customs into contractual relationships to fill gaps in that relationship. The existence of these customs

> is a question of fact which must be strictly proved. It must be so notorious that everybody in the trade enters into a contract with that usage as an implied term. It must be uniform as well as reasonable ...[104]

The proffered evidence in support of the uniform presumption is usually flimsy in scope and could not rationally serve as empirical proof of a uniform trait. It would not be feasible or even possible to require all parties to every transaction in a particular field to give evidence of their customs. Nor is any inquiry undertaken into why the evidence supporting the custom is entirely representative of 'everybody in the trade'. Instead, a selection of witnesses (or even a single witness) can give evidence of the purportedly uniform custom. An inductive generalisation is then used to infer the uniform characteristic over the custom. Any inference from this evidence must assume uniformity. Such evidence is flimsy because any contrary evidence should show that the custom is not uniform, and the inference must fail.[105]

In Pundik's *Twelve Angry Men* example, his principal claim is that background generalisations ought to be objectionable as generalisations but they are not. Coincidentally, he compares the inferential structure of the reliability of the eyewitness to naked statistical evidence to demonstrate why reliability ought to be objectionable.[106] There are two problems with this approach. The first is that naked statistical evidence does not give rise to a generalisability objection. As such, it would make sense that, compared in that way, the evidence is not epistemologically objectionable because all members of the sample (using Pundik's example, all attendees at a rodeo) are assumed to be uniform. Second, he misconstrues the nature of the inference. Pundik asserts that the property short-sighted people

[104] *Nelson v Dahl* [1879] 12 ChD 568, 575 (Lord Jessel MR).
[105] *Thornley v Tilley* (1925) 36 CLR 1, 8.
[106] Pundik, 'Generalisation' (n 2) 211.

exhibit is 'misidentifying the murderer'. Evidence that a certain class of people have myopia does not give rise to a rational inference that they also possess a trait of misidentifying accused killers. Instead, the highest the evidence goes in establishing a particular property is that the eyewitness has impaired vision, the extent of which is unknown. In fact, had the inferential pathway been identical to naked statistical evidence, the property the witness would have exhibited was short-sightedness. To get to misidentifying the murder, a further inference is needed that does require crossing the inferential gap and is highly objectionable, especially in the absence of any information about her short-sightedness.

There is an element of counter-intuitiveness to this logic. It would seem that inferences made without the support of evidence are assumed to be true whereas evidence supporting those inferences are required to go through two levels, despite their likely greater accuracy,[107] reliability and objectivity,[108] and lesser susceptibility to bias. Unlike facts supported by uniform rebuttable presumptions, generalising inferences involve an element of comparison between the reference class and the specific phenomenon. This contrast allows the fact-finder to latch onto, rightly or wrongly, points of departure between the two sets of facts. That said, if the evidence is generalisable, objectionable generalisations are much harder to refute than background generalisations. The merest contrary evidence ought to be capable of undermining the uniformity assumption. By contrast, risk of error is factored into inferences from objectionable generalisations. Contrary evidence does not automatically negate such evidence.

IV. Factual Generalisations

Background generalisations rely almost exclusively on assumptions (rather than inferences from evidence) made about world events. Factual generalisations instead rely on specific items of evidence to prove general factual causation and specific causation. The inductive leap from the general to the specific is highly unlikely to be, and need not be, uniform, because there is an identifiable class from where the evidence is drawn. From this evidence, a comparison is made between n and N, and p, and it is that process that results in the epistemic objection. The potential gap between the sample and population, and the individual, is plain to see.

Pundik (and others) object to this account of dissonance, at least as a complete account, because there appear to be factual generalisations that do not, but ought to, produce dissonance. He gives two examples: DNA evidence (as an example of the broader category of 'forensic evidence of identification'); and evidence of future matters. However, for the reasons that follow, both forensic and future evidence fit comfortably within the proposed paradigm of an epistemological objection.

[107] Enoch and Fisher (n 6) 579.
[108] eg D Davis and WC Follette, 'Toward an Empirical Approach to Evidentiary Ruling' (2003) 27 *Law and Human Behaviour* 661, 668.

A. Forensic Evidence of Identification

What is meant by the term 'forensic evidence' (sometimes referred to as 'scientific evidence')[109] is not entirely clear. It typically describes the evidence of an expert witness about the probable identification of an individual based on certain features or characteristics of that individual. DNA evidence typifies this category. This book uses the term 'forensic evidence', as 'scientific evidence' has the capacity to incorporate all evidence derived from an empirical or quasi-empirical process. As will become clear, the inferential structure of forensic evidence is distinct from other forms of statistical evidence, such as epidemiology.

Pundik claims otherwise; in his view, DNA evidence is the ideal example of statistical evidence, built upon generalisations, that is otherwise 'unobjectionable'.[110] Putting to one side the problematic claim that DNA evidence is in fact 'unobjectionable',[111] it is arguably true that 'good' DNA evidence[112] (and other similar forensic evidence) does not raise an epistemological generalisation objection. Forensic evidence is often 'highly probabilifying',[113] and DNA evidence in particular is often cast as very reliable.[114] The fact of this high probability and perception of reliability (spurious or otherwise) could be confounding factors in identifying the epistemic objection. Forensic evidence, and DNA evidence in particular, however, does not raise a generalisation objection in the same way as other statistical evidence because of its inferential structure about *p*.

There is not one process of obtaining DNA evidence.[115] The means of collection, source and analysis of the DNA evidence should not impact on the inferential structure for any evidence of the identification of an individual. To simplify the discussion here, identification from a DNA database will be the primary means of source identification and a random match probability the method of analysis.

The purpose of DNA evidence is to be able to uniquely (or very close to uniquely) identify a particular person to the exclusion of all others in the general population. To do this, a sample of an individual (J) is taken and entered into a database (JKL) comprised of data relating to numerous other individuals. Consider a scenario where a DNA sample is found at a relevant crime scene, and that sample is compared to JKL. It is found that the sample matches J's DNA stored in JKL to

[109] Freckelton (n 38) [12.0.02].

[110] Pundik, 'Generalisation' (n 2) 212; see also Enoch and Fisher (n 6) 591 (unlike forms of statistical evidence, DNA evidence satisfies sensitivity); cf MS Pardo, 'Safety vs Sensitivity: Possible Worlds and the Law' (2018) 24 *Legal Theory* 50, 63–64 (DNA and other forms of statistical evidence are sensitive and admissible).

[111] Whereas this may be increasingly true, it was by no means true when such evidence was first used in legal proceedings: see *R v Galli* (2001) 127 A Crim R 493 (NSWCCA) [98].

[112] If the DNA evidence is incomplete and contaminated, the reliability of the evidence is severely undermined: see *R v Juric* (2002) 4 VR 411 (VCA) [20].

[113] Enoch and Fisher (n 6) 589.

[114] Which, as Edmond identifies, and as discussed in ch 2, is not always the case for forensic evidence.

[115] For a comprehensive account of DNA evidence, see C Adam, *Forensic Evidence in Court* (Hoboken, Wiley-Blackwell, 2016) ch 10.

the exclusion of any other person recorded in the database. But simply proving a match is not enough as it says very little about the probabilities of finding a unique match in the population at large. If a brown hair was found at the scene, and the accused also had brown hair, one could hardly rely on that to establish that J was at the scene, because billions of human beings could also have brown hair. DNA draws its strength from being effectively unique to each individual person shown by means of probabilistic evaluation against a particular population to which the individual belongs.[116] As such, DNA evidence contains two parts. First, matching the DNA sample from the crime scene to J's DNA stored in the database (content). Whereas the match could in theory be probabilistic, convention dictates that the probability is 1, that is, there is no possible error in matching the two samples, or that two people within the database could have identical DNA. Second, the probability of another human being possessing identical DNA in the population (reliability). Given DNA's relative uniqueness, that probability is usually spectacularly low; for example, in *Pfennig (No 2)*, purportedly 1 in 7,537 billion.[117]

DNA evidence becomes statistically complex when assessing the probabilities of the reliability component. Multiple approaches can be adopted in how to assess the evidence. The two most common are the random match probability (RMP) (or the 'probability that a person other than the suspect, randomly selected from the population, will have the same profile as that found at the crime scene')[118] and the likelihood ratio (LR) ('the probability of finding a match on the database, given that the suspect is not the source of the crime scene').[119] LR is typically calculated by the probability of a match in DNA profiles (usually assumed to be 1) over the RMP.[120] RMP and LR look at the same information from different angles. In simple terms, RMP provides the probability of no-match, and LR the probability of a match in the general population. Both can be used in conjunction, although they are subject to different assumptions. LR is commonly seen in Australian litigation and is widely accepted in scientific literature.[121]

Pundik correctly states that the content element of DNA evidence is not objectionable. It is 'specific evidence' comprising the comparison of the alleles of the

[116] ibid 132–33.

[117] *R v Pfennig (No 2)* [2016] SASC 171, [242].

[118] Australian Law Reform Commission (ALRC), *The Protection of Human Genetic Information in Australia* (Report 96, 2003) [44.22].

[119] Adam (n 115) 134; ALRC Report 96 (n 118) [44.23]; National Research Council, *The Evaluation of Forensic DNA Evidence* (Washington DC, National Academy Press, 1996) 127–31. It should be noted that Australian and English jurisprudence is clouded by the use of non-standard terminology. In *Aytugrul v The Queen* (2012) 247 CLR 170, the High Court of Australia (HCA) was confronted with a 'frequency ratio' and an 'exclusion percentage'. The frequency ratio, sometimes referred to as a 'random occurrence ratio' (*Doheny & Adams* [1997] Cr App R 369 (CA)), is another way of saying the 'frequency of occurrence' (M Goode, 'Some Observations on Evidence of DNA Frequency' (2002) 23 *Adelaide Law Review* 45, 63) which in turn identifies the RMP (Adam (n 115) 143). The exclusion percentage is an inverse expression of the frequency ratio as a percentage.

[120] Adam (n 115) 133; *R v Karger* (2002) 83 SASR 135 (SASCCCA) [67].

[121] eg *Perryman v The Queen* [2019] VSCA 252; *Pfennig (No 2)* (n 117); *Aytugrul* (n 119); *R v Keir* [2002] NSWCCA 30; *R v GK* (2001) 53 NSWLR 317 (NSWCCA).

sample to the database. He argues, however, that the reliability component takes the form of an objectionable generalisation (but is not otherwise objectionable). With respect, that is not quite correct. In *Pfennig (No 2)*, the accused was granted permission to appeal against his conviction on the basis that it was rendered unsafe by DNA evidence. The circumstances of the leave application are not significant for the present analysis. What is significant is the presentation of the RMP and LR. The DNA was extracted from the victim's clothing and compared directly to the accused. From the 'tape lift' component of the evidence, the evidence was summarised as follows:

> (a) using the random match probability analysis and a Dutch Caucasian database, the chance of finding someone in the Dutch Caucasian population with the profile obtained from the tape lift was 1 in 5,766 billion;
> (b) by use of the same random match probability analysis, recalculating (a) but using the Australian Caucasian database, that figure was 1 in 7,537 billion;
> (c) using the LRmix Studio probabilistic method, a likelihood ratio for material from the tape lift in support of the proposition that the accused and one other person contributed to the DNA on the tape lift, as opposed to the proposition that the tape lift contained the DNA of *two unknown individuals* is between 9.6 billion and 36.9 billion.[122]

Neither RMP nor LR requires a generalisation inference about the accused. DNA evidence assumes its significance from an empirically justified inference about the probability of DNA's uniqueness in the population.[123] This inference can be facilitated by databases of other persons (and the accused's) DNA. Databases serve two functions. The first is confirmatory, in that alongside the generalisation that there is no repetition of the individual in the population, a specific test against the database can be used.[124] The second is, if reliably constructed, supportive of the proposition that within the population, the individual's DNA is unique. That is, because the database is representative of the population, an inference can be made that the same level of uniqueness would be seen in the population as in the database.[125] In *Pfennig (No 2)*, because the accused was identified as Caucasian, and of Germanic origin, the databases, and populations, could be confined to specific ethnic and geographical origins.

This analysis shows that although there are generalisations at work, there is no generalisation of the kind producing dissonance. Indeed, those generalisations are more akin to generalisations within general factual causation rather than specific causation. The evidence about p is direct evidence; the identification of the match between samples derived from observation and perception. There is no inference about n or N that is inferred back to p. It may be epistemologically objectionable to

[122] *Pfennig (No 2)* (n 117) [362] (emphasis added).
[123] See E Beecher-Monas, 'Lost in Translation: Statistical Inference in Court' (2014) 46 *Arizona State Law Journal* 1057, 1059.
[124] B Robertson, GA Vignaux and CEH Berger, *Interpreting Evidence* (Hoboken, Wiley, 2016) 109–10.
[125] This structure is made clear from the recount of the evidence in *Aytugrul* (n 119) [11].

assume that match rates in a sample (or scientifically examined in empirical literature) reflect the population; but such objections are complaints directed against the assumptions of uniqueness of DNA evidence, and not whether the individual's DNA has been identified. As such, it is not the case that DNA evidence is an example of a generalisation that is not objectionable per se. If there is a generalisation in DNA evidence, it is a generalisation between *n* and *N*. That *N* captures *p* is assumed. To use DNA evidence as the standard bearer for why no epistemic generalisation objection exists is invalid.

Forensic evidence of identification becomes more problematic (in the sense raised by Edmond and discussed in chapter three) as the degree of confidence in the underlying data lessens. In the series of cases concerning Sally Clark,[126] the accused was convicted of killing her two children having claimed they died from sudden infant death syndrome (SIDS). At first instance and on first appeal, evidence was received and accepted that the probability that two children in any one family died of SIDS was 1 in 73 million.[127] The statistical evidence, and the purported data that justified its calculation, were deeply flawed.[128] But one objection that could not and was not taken was a generalisation objection. There was no generalisation from a particular reference class of 'families with two SIDS deaths', because such events were extraordinarily rare. Instead, to arrive at that (erroneous) figure and to apply it to that case relied on an assumption that the probability of two SIDS deaths were equally spread amongst *N*. Whereas rigorous testing has been done to substantiate the assumption in DNA evidence, no such testing had been done for dual SIDS occurrences. To put it another way, there was no *n* to compare to *p*.

In chapter two, it was noted that one of the controversies around forensic evidence is the lack of scientific rigour and analysis of such evidence.[129] Even when such evidence is correctly given, judges fail to understand it.[130] Footprint analysis, handwriting and other forms of individual identification are all examples of highly controversial fields that are sometimes used to identify individuals in the context of legal trials by purportedly scientific means. While there are a great many objections to establishing general factual causation and the reliability of these techniques, inferences about identification from the use of those techniques are not dissonant because of a generalisation to an individual.

[126] Similar examples where evidence is treated in this way are *People v Collins*, 68 Cal2d 319 (CalSC, 1968) (probability of physical traits being seen in a couple) and the 'Dutch Nurse Case', where Lucia de Berk was convicted of killing her patients from evidence the extremely low probability that one nurse would have been present at all impugned deaths and resuscitations: see B Verheij, 'To Catch a Thief With and Without Numbers: Arguments, Scenarios and Probabilities in Evidential Reasoning' (2014) 13 *Law, Probability and Risk* 307.

[127] *R v Clark (No 1)* [2000] EWCA Crim 54, [149]–[168].

[128] *R v Clark (No 2)* [2003] EWCA Crim 1020, [172]–[180]; see further C Aitken, P Roberts and G Jackson, *Fundamentals of Probability and Statistical Evidence in Criminal Proceedings* (London, Royal Statistical Society, 2010) [3.41]–[3.43].

[129] Beecher-Monas (n 123) 1059; G Edmond, 'What Lawyers Should Know about the Forensic "Sciences"' (2015) 36 *Adelaide Law Review* 33, 79.

[130] B Robertson, GA Vignaux and CEH Berger, 'Extending the Confusion About Bayes' (2011) 74 *MLR* 444, 449–50.

B. Future Evidence

Pundik suggests that 'future' evidence is not an objectionable form of generalisation.[131] That future evidence is based on generalisations is without doubt: future damages are drawn from estimates that are based almost entirely on the progression and needs of populations of injured persons who are similar to the individual in question. Pundik uses the example of life expectancy tables that rely on population data.[132] An inferential gap is present between the observed consequences in other individuals and the individual about whom the prediction is made. Despite the recognition that the reasoning processes are quite different between past and future fact-finding,[133] and avoid other evidentiary features such as probabilistic proof of past certain events,[134] a process of generalisation is still apparent.

The basis for the claim that future estimates are epistemologically unobjectionable is not clear, nor does it seem consistent with how judges approach such evidence. Pundik suggests that life expectancy estimates are not objectionable because they do not undermine the free will of the individual; dying is not what someone does, it is what 'happens' to a person.[135] This chapter does not comment on that distinction, because it is plain that the common law has long recognised the existence of an epistemic deficit in future estimation, including the use of actuarial tables for working life expectancy.[136]

Where the difference lies between factual generalisations concerning past (or contemporaneous) phenomena, and future phenomena, is in the type of available evidence to prove the phenomenon. For past phenomena, 'better', more specific evidence, may exist that supports or rejects the existence of the phenomenon. By contrast, there can be no specific evidence of what will happen because it has not yet happened.[137] Predicting what might happen in the future is wholly speculative. Unlike past and contemporaneous phenomena, fact-finding as to future (and past hypothetical)[138] phenomena involve gambling on probabilities. Reasoning about future phenomena is permissible (and the evidence in support of such reasoning, such as actuarial tables, is not usually objected to) due to the unavailability of any other evidence from which to infer future outcomes.[139] Where the evidence relied on for the purpose of the future inference departs from the present case, an epistemological objection arises. Actuarial tables are typically immune from

[131] Pundik, 'Generalisation' (n 2) 196, 198.
[132] ibid 196.
[133] See D Gillies, *Philosophical Theories of Probability* (Oxford, Routledge, 2000) 99.
[134] *Gregg v Scott* [2005] 2 AC 176 (HL) [10].
[135] Pundik, 'Generalisation' (n 2) 207.
[136] *Todorovic v Waller* (1981) 150 CLR 402, 412 (Gibbs CJ and Wilson J).
[137] Tribe (n 1) 1345–46.
[138] *Sellars v Adelaide Petroleum* (1994) 179 CLR 332, 360.
[139] *Todorovic* (n 135) 412. Certain preventative orders also depend on proof of future matters, such as 'control orders' sought to prevent terrorist attacks (Criminal Code Act 1995 (Cth) s 104.2) and orders seeking to involuntarily detain mentally ill persons (Mental Health Act 2007 (NSW) s 14).

this objection because they are so generic and offer no explanation of the various features of individuals who comprise the data. *N* subsumes *n* and *p* for the reason that there is no means of distinguishing between *n* and *p*. For that reason, courts require practitioners to discount damages for the 'vicissitudes of life',[140] to allow for the possibility, based on the specific facts of each case, that the individual will not follow the average course of life expectancy.

V. Confounding Variables on the Generalisation Objection

The second element of Pundik's attack on an epistemic account of objectionable generalisations is the supposed inability of this theory to account for the presence or absence of the objection by reason of context.[141] Context certainly has a role in the strength of dissonance. But that may not have anything to do with the inferential gap per se. Some facts are, despite all other things being equal, harder to establish than others. In *Briginshaw*, Dixon J set down the widely adopted principle that fraudulent behaviours require more cogent evidence to prove.[142] The standard of proof remains the same, but the degree of evidence needed to satisfy that standard and form the belief that an individual acted fraudulently is higher. Individuals may also have different thresholds of belief. Some people might be willing to accept the existence of a certain state of affairs, and more readily cross the inferential gap than those who are more sceptical. Subjectivity therefore plays a large role in the presence or absence of dissonance.

A. Layers of Objection

Many of the examples Pundik provides that purport to show the inexplicable presence or absence of dissonance are explained by the occlusion of dissonance by some factor or the presence of an additional layer of controversy that, whilst itself objectionable, is not related to the epistemological objection to generalisations. This chapter has already referred to a number of examples of extraneous factors that influence the way the epistemological objection is perceived, such as reliability objections to DNA evidence and future evidence.

The reliability of general factual causation as the basis for the generalisation is an important influencing factor on the presence of the epistemological objection. The more readily the fact-finder believes the reference phenomenon, the easier that phenomenon will be to extrapolate to the individual case. No reasonable fact-finder

[140] *Wynn v NSW Insurance Ministerial Co* (1995) 184 CLR 485, [18].
[141] Pundik, 'Generalisation' (n 2) 196.
[142] *Briginshaw* (n 88) 361.

would generalise an obviously spurious association because the inference as a whole would be nonsensical.[143] Logic and commonsense, rather than statistical artefacts, play a key role in screening out spurious associations. Attributing causation from evidence of general factual causation is a reasoning process, criteria for which are set by the professional discipline generating the evidence.

Whilst reliability influences the ability to generalise, reliability is independent of generalisability. Spurious associations are generalisable notwithstanding their complete non-association. For example, 'expert opinion' linking breast implants and autoimmune disease, vaccinations and autism, or the non-association between HIV and AIDS,[144] could be generalisable if one takes a selective approach to the 'evidence'. All generalisability requires is that there is a connection between the reference class and the individual. If the individual (and the occurrence to that individual) seems to follow the same pattern as the occurrence in the reference class, notwithstanding the complete non-association in the reference class itself, that evidence could be generalisable. The critical stage for screening out spurious or tenuous associations is not generalisability, but when considering how general factual causation is established and the reliability of the evidence purporting to do so (including, inter alia, perceptions of the expert giving the opinion).

B. Strength of Association

As has been noted above, dissonance is not a once-and-for-all concept. Dissonance is a scale that is highly dependent on the content of the generalisation and influenced by an array of factors both internal and external to the fact-finder. The more probable the generalisation, or the more similar the circumstances of the reference class to the individual, the less dissonance a fact-finder will feel.[145] Conversely, the more improbable the generalisation, or the more distinct the reference class from the individual event, the more pronounced the objection.[146] Something that is so likely to occur that it would be absurd not to accept it as true (for example, consuming arsenic could have health consequences) might suggest that no generalisation objection exists. As long as the outcome is not deterministic, the generalisation objection does exist in some infinitesimal form. The philosopher might point out the existence of the objection. But for the more rudimentary construct of evidence law and fact-finding, it would barely be noticeable.

External factors also influence the presence or absence of dissonance. Knowledge and attitude towards certain subjects can greatly affect the fact-finder's willingness to accept the underlying facts, and that in turn affects how the evidence is perceived. A climate scientist, for example, may be more likely

[143] Picinali (n 13) 123.
[144] *R v Parenzee* [2007] SASC 143, [12], [36]–[50].
[145] See Stein (n 1) 81.
[146] ibid 97.

to accept that human-produced emissions can cause or contribute to a particular climate event than a climate change denier. Equally, the surrounding circumstances can be used to buttress the bridge across the inferential gap. Epidemiology can be supported by specific evidence of causation, such as tissue samples and medical histories. Such evidence stands on its own in support of the causal proposition as well as bolstering the likelihood that the generalisation applies to *p*.[147] That does not mean, however, that the generalisation is unobjectionable; simply that the avenue for resolving the objection is easier and perhaps the degree of objection is less noticeable.

The distinction between unobjectionable and 'less objectionable' is made plain by Pundik's hypothetical, 'Anne's Case'. Anne is charged with blowing up a building by a bomb that Anne planted.[148] The question is whether the bomb or a machinery malfunction caused the explosion. The evidence is the presence of a 'specific type of gas' that is more likely to be produced by a bomb than by a malfunction. Pundik suggests that using the generalisation from other circumstances of gas present on explosion to the present is 'intuitively unobjectionable'.[149]

The supposedly unobjectionable nature of this evidence suggests that subjective perceptions of dissonance are playing more of a role than perhaps intended. Even though, as an individual, Pundik may not view that this scenario as objectionable, another person might. There doesn't appear to be any reason why this example is necessarily any less objectionable than a generalisation from epidemiological evidence. In Anne's Case, the gas is associated with bombs (where past explosions form the reference class), the explosion occurred contemporaneously with the gas (the specific event), and we infer that the bomb caused the explosion. Similarly, lung cancer is associated with cigarette smoke, exposure to cigarette smoke occurred 'contemporaneously' with the development of lung cancer, therefore we infer that smoking caused the individual's lung cancer. The difference between the two examples is better explained by the relative level of contemporaneity between gas and explosion and lung cancer and smoking. Pundik refers to a 'specific type of gas' where there are only two options for explosion, bomb or malfunction. The inferential gap between the reference class and the specific phenomenon is much narrower than for epidemiology because there may be multiple causes of lung cancer that have not been excluded, such as the environment or genetics. Nevertheless, both are dissonant generalisations.

The extent to which subjective intuitions play a role in the presence or absence of dissonance is a challenge that exists in numerous accounts. For example, Moss argues that moral encroachment – that moral features can affect the epistemic status of an opinion – may explain distinctions between various propositions. She compares reactions, derived from statistical evidence based on racial profiling, with those to certain breeds of dog, and suggests that whereas reacting to a

[147] Dant (n 7) 64–65.
[148] Pundik, 'Generalisation' (n 2) 206.
[149] ibid.

statistically dangerous dog breed is capable of being 'knowledge' (albeit perhaps not for legal fact-finding if based solely on statistical evidence),[150] reactions based on racial profiling would not be capable of being knowledge.[151] The problem with the moral encroachment account is that it can explain why some evidence may be more objectionable than other evidence by reason of, first, the wider harm it can have on individuals and societies[152] and, second, its less robust nature. But it fails to explain away the epistemic objection that remains against the evidence of dog breeds which are labelled dangerous. A fact-finder is still required to cross an inferential gap between the individual dog and the reference class on which the evidence is based.

Conclusion

The goal of this chapter was to refute the argument that the epistemic account of objectionable generalisations could not explain why some generalisations do not appear to be objectionable, and why the objection was sensitive to context. It has sought to address these two criticisms by demonstrating that the objection is a product of the inferential gap between the general and the specific, and that the objection is itself a multifaceted concept that arises in various ways in evidence law. It is clear that many of the criticisms of the epistemic account fail to appreciate that not all 'generalisations' are used for the same purpose. When generalisations do not give rise to an inferential gap, there can be no dissonance and no epistemological objection. Moreover, the content of the generalisation and the knowledge and attitude of the fact-finder towards the evidence play an important role in how dissonance is perceived but does not cause it to exist or disappear. The presence or absence of dissonance, as opposed to the degree of dissonance, is a consequence of inferential structure.

[150] cf S Moss, 'IX – Moral Encroachment' (2018) 123 Proceedings of the Aristotelian Society 177, 189.
[151] ibid 179–80.
[152] ibid 197.

5

Statistics and Similar Facts

Introduction

Understanding and resolving generalisation objections to statistical evidence requires establishing a theory of and criteria for crossing the inferential gap between the statistical evidence and the present facts. In evidence law, dissonance induces a tri-layered objection. First, if the inferential gap cannot be crossed, the statistical evidence is irrelevant. This is the principal subject of this chapter. Second, if the gap can be crossed but the support provided by the statistical evidence for the proposition is weak, the evidence may lack sufficient probative value compared to the cost or delay associated with its receipt into evidence to justify its admissibility. If the evidence is admissible, however, any further objection to the statistical evidence is a question of weight for the fact-finder. Third, if the gap can be crossed and there is sufficient probative value for admissibility and reliance, there may nevertheless be epistemic and moral prejudice arising from admitting the evidence.

Successful individualisation is the key to the relevance of statistical evidence used to prove causation. In *Amaca v Ellis*, the High Court of Australia (HCA) identified that

> [t]o draw an inference about causation from what was established by the epidemiological studies, it would be necessary to decide whether the particular case under consideration should be treated as conforming to the pattern described by the epidemiological studies. Absent evidence which suggests that the individual may stand apart from the ordinary, there may be sufficient reason to assume conformity, but whether or not that is so, *it is important to recognize that the first step that must be taken, if an inference is to be drawn from epidemiological studies, is to relate the results of studies of populations to the particular case at hand.* That step is not inevitable.[1]

The HCA did not expand on what role evidence law plays in taking that step. It is also not clear if this process is different to fact-finding from non-statistical evidence. Identifying a 'first step' appears to be a differentiating factor between statistical and non-statistical evidence. Yet in *Seltsam v McGuiness*, the New South Wales Court of Appeal (NSWCA) referred to statistical evidence that relies on

[1] *Amaca v Ellis* (2010) 240 CLR 111, 135 [62] (emphasis added).

inductive principles as a 'strand in a cable of proof' alongside other circumstantial evidence.[2]

Few attempts have been made in scholarship or judicial reasons to provide a practicable theoretical framework for understanding how the law ought to approach individualisations from statistical evidence.[3] This work contends that if statistical evidence is a form of 'circumstantial evidence',[4] it should be treated as a special sub-category of circumstantial evidence to which particular inferential considerations attach. The process of generalising statistical evidence to facts-in-issue requires the acceptance of a 'propensity' inference.[5] That is, the variable or trait X has a tendency to cause outcome Y. By drawing this inference, the statistical evidence is no longer separate from the present facts by time, space or object. The statistical evidence is identifying a trait that operates as a contemporaneous feature directly impacting the fact-in-issue; establishing a propensity inference as such individualises the evidence.[6] Without that inference, statistical evidence is irrelevant to prove facts about particular events.

Common law jurisdictions all regulate in various ways inferences from evidence that suggests a person is more likely to have committed a particular act or possessed a state of mind because of the existence of a 'separate' act or state of mind ('similar fact evidence').[7] While the rules between jurisdictions are different, the underlying approach is broadly similar. Under the Australian Uniform Evidence Law (UEL), even if the evidence is relevant it is inadmissible unless it possesses 'significant probative value' ('similar fact rule') and, in criminal proceedings, its probative value outweighs any prejudicial effect ('criminal similar fact rule').[8] In the UK, similar fact evidence as to the character of the accused is only admissible under the Criminal Justice Act 2003 which sets out certain conditions that are not dissimilar to those regulating 'character evidence' under the UEL.[9] Whereas in civil

[2] *Seltsam v McGuiness* (2000) 49 NSWLR 262 (NSWCA) 276 [91] (Spigelman CJ), cited favourably in *RTA (NSW) v Royal* (2008) 82 ALJR 870 (HCA) 898 and other Australian intermediate courts of appeal: *Merck Sharp & Dohme v Peterson* (2011) 196 FCR 145 (FCAFC) 172–73; *King v Western Sydney LHN* [2013] NSWCA 162, [150].

[3] DL Faigman, J Monahan and C Slobogin, 'Group to Individual (G2i) Inference in Scientific Expert Testimony' (2014) 81 *University of Chicago Law Review* 417, 420.

[4] I Freckelton, *Expert Evidence*, 6th edn (Sydney, Thomson Reuters, 2019) 1071.

[5] Derived from a propensity theory of probability: see D Gillies, 'The Propensity Interpretation' in A Hajek and C Hitchcock (eds), *The Oxford Handbook of Probability and Philosophy* (Oxford, Oxford University Press, 2016) 407.

[6] LJ Cohen, 'Subjective Probability and the Paradox of the Gatecrasher' [1981] *Arizona State Law Journal* 627, 633–34.

[7] See J Stone, 'The Rule of Exclusion of Similar Fact Evidence: England' (1932) 46 *Harvard Law Review* 954, 957; discussion in HL Ho, 'An Introduction to Similar Fact Evidence' (1998) 19 *Singapore Law Review* 166, 196. Similar fact inferences are defined by a collection of overlapping terminologies, eg 'propensity', 'tendency', 'improbability', 'similar fact', etc: *R v Ellis* (2003) 58 NSWLR 700, [75]. These inferences are better understood to be minute variations under the common rubric of inferences from similar facts: see Z Cowen and PB Carter, *Essays on the Law of Evidence* (Oxford, Oxford University Press, 1956) 110–11.

[8] Uniform Evidence Law (UEL) ss 97, 98, 101. Not all Australian states have adopted the UEL, eg Queensland: *BBH v The Queen* (2012) 245 CLR 499.

[9] Criminal Justice Act 2003 (UK) ss 98–113. For a short summary of how the exclusionary rules have been interpreted, see P Mirfield, 'Bad Character Evidence – Again' (2023) 82 *CLJ* 395.

cases, the test for the admissibility of similar fact evidence remains at common law and has proven to be controversial.[10] In the US, evidence of bad character is prima facie inadmissible under the Federal Rules of Evidence (FRE) in both civil and criminal proceedings, subject to certain exceptions.[11]

Similar fact rules regulate the admissibility of relevant similar fact evidence. The focus of this chapter is on the process by which similar fact evidence is construed as relevant. But relevance and probative value are intertwined concepts; relevance simply means the evidence possesses some probative value, however low or high.[12] There will inevitably be some crossover of discussion for how relevance and probative value are assessed. The next chapter focuses on how statistical evidence might fit under the rubric of the similar fact rules.

Applying analogies to statistical and similar fact evidence is not novel. Philosophical, probability and statistical literature have long recognised that statistical inferences rely on establishing 'dispositions', 'propensities' and 'tendencies'.[13] Nor has legal scholarship neglected the similarities between statistics and similar facts. Redmayne acknowledges that similar fact reasoning is 'rather like a process of hypothesis testing' in that both doctrines seek to reject a null hypothesis that the occurrence of the present and similar fact is mere 'coincidence' or 'luck'.[14] Levanon characterises this similarity on the grounds that both similar fact evidence and statistical evidence present a risk of 'eliminable errors'.[15] Statistical evidence per se is not tendency or coincidence evidence as the UEL defines those concepts.[16] But the inferential structure of statistical evidence and tendency and coincidence evidence is the same.[17] By explicitly recognising statistical evidence's relevance for a purpose akin to similar fact evidence, the disputation within legal scholarship and decisions about the generalisation objection can be contextualised and dealt with in a principled fashion.

What this chapter articulates is that, as with many aspects of evidence law, underlying formal legal rules are the logical processes of decision-making. For proof, that process is the point where the fact-finder believes that factor X probably caused outcome Y in the individual (*p*).[18] For relevance, it is the point where the evidence is believed to have a rational effect on the probability of the existence of the effect in *p*. It is the approach to rationality that governs when evidence

[10] HL Ho, 'Similar Facts in Civil Cases' (2006) 26 *OJLS* 131, commenting on the House of Lords decision in *O'Brien v Chief Constable of South Wales Police* [2005] 2 AC 534.

[11] Federal Rules of Evidence (FRE) rr 404–05.

[12] *Hughes v The Queen* (2017) 263 CLR 338, [41]; *IMM v The Queen* (2016) 257 CLR 300, 313 [43], citing *Festa* v *The Queen* (2001) 208 CLR 593, 599 [14]; *Smith v Rapid Transit*, 58 NE2d 754, [6] (MassSJC, 1945).

[13] D Gillies, *Philosophical Theories of Probability* (Oxford, Routledge, 2000) ch 6.

[14] M Redmayne, *Character in the Criminal Trial* (Oxford, Oxford University Press, 2015) 116.

[15] L Levanon, *Evidence, Respect and Truth: Knowledge and Justice in Legal Trials* (Oxford, Hart, 2022) 122.

[16] *R v Villalon* [2014] NSWSC 725, [8], [22].

[17] D Enoch, L Spectre and T Fisher, 'Statistical Evidence, Sensitivity, and the Legal Value of Knowledge' (2012) 40 *Philosophy & Public Affairs* 197, 212, 217.

[18] As noted earlier, the term '*p*' is used in this book to denote both the individual and an event associated with that individual.

will be considered relevant to the existence of a fact. Whilst rationality has an element of objectivity insofar as the decision to describe something as rational must be reasoned and defensible, there is nonetheless the potential for subjective differences of opinion between decision-makers that cannot be entirely avoided. Although the law relies on logical processes underlying the decision-making process, it does not regulate the application of logic to decisions nor (usually) how inferences are made.

First, this chapter establishes the common inferential structure of statistical and similar fact evidence. Second, it identifies the process of gauging the relevance of similar fact evidence and the criteria it must fulfil. Third, the parallels between similar fact and statistical evidence are demonstrated and the inconsistencies arising from judicial decisions about statistical evidence are shown to be a consequence of departing from, or mistaking, the tendency purpose for which statistical evidence is relevant. Ultimately, however, inconsistencies cannot be entirely excluded as they arise from the nature of relevance as a 'logical' exercise of individual decision-making that the law cannot entirely control.

I. A Common Inferential Structure

Similar fact evidence ('bad character evidence' in the US and UK and 'tendency' and 'coincidence' evidence in Australia) is where the previous conduct of an individual is used to prove some further conduct of that individual. If A is accused of murdering B, it may be relevant to adduce evidence of A's previous murder of C and D. The deaths of C and D are evidence of other transactions that may impact the existence or non-existence of A's involvement in B's death, if evidence of C and D's murder is suggestive of A's propensity to murder.

Statistical evidence shares a similar inferential basis to similar fact evidence. Both rest on a proposition that events extraneous to the individual in issue can explain something about that individual – that is, the extraneous events are relevant because they can be individualised. When evidence that X causes Y in a sample (n) is used to prove that X also caused Y in p, where n is separated from p by time, space and object, an identical inferential form to similar fact evidence is created. Similar fact evidence is only differentiated from statistical evidence by the specificity of substance. Whereas similar fact evidence concerns the past actions or intentions of a single individual, statistical evidence typically relies on the conduct of other people or objects.[19]

[19] Although, statistical evidence about an individual's past conduct could be introduced as the basis for a tendency inference. In *BDS17 v Minister for Immigration and Border Protection* [2018] FCA 1683, [11], [24] ff, the applicant alleged that the judicial officer's decision was pervaded by actual bias on the basis of, inter alia, statistical evidence drawn from the judicial officer's past decisions and adduced as coincidence evidence.

Outside the similar fact rules, there is no specific exclusionary rule that applies to statistical evidence or evidence requiring individualising inferences from other conduct. Assuming that such evidence survives the hearsay rule (if it applies at all), gatekeeper exclusion of statistical evidence, as opposed to being declared insufficient for proof by the fact-finder, is typically on grounds of irrelevance, procedure, policy and prejudice. If evidence of an effect in *n* does not rationally affect the assessment of the probability of the existence of an effect in *p*, the evidence is irrelevant. But a great deal of evidence that may not necessarily arise from the individuals or events in issue is prima facie relevant, even though it might not typically form part of the record of legal proceedings:

> It cannot be said [that evidence that 95% of all motorists cut a particular corner] has no bearing on the probabilities with regard to the question whether the [motorist] defendant cut the corner, for if the jury were allowed to hear the evidence it might well conclude that it was more probable that the defendant did as most of his fellow citizens do ...[20]

Instead of irrelevance, Eggleston contends that such evidence is inadmissible on policy grounds because admitting it would 'turn every case into a piece of sociological research'.[21] But policy grounds of this type are wearing thin. The trend towards free proof[22] and the increasing emphasis on cost-effective accuracy has meant that statistical evidence is becoming a more common feature in contemporary litigation. Parties are more willing to invest in complex expert evidence to prosecute their cases. Statistical analyses provide the bases for a great deal of that professional knowledge. Indeed, class actions that depend on 'indirect causation' can only be proved by econometric evidence such as event studies.

A further difficulty is the ongoing failure to recognise the commonality between statistical and similar fact evidence. When similar fact evidence is adduced, its 'individualised' character is accepted; for such evidence to be relevant it must shed light on the probabilities of the individual's alleged actions. Yet, courts continue to refer to statistical evidence as lesser than 'direct evidence' because statistical evidence lacks individualisation.[23] This doesn't take into account the logical reality that for evidence to be relevant to an individual case, it must be individualised to some degree. If the question concerns *p*, and the evidence is about *n*, it is necessary to either accept that something about *n* helps explain *p*, or that *n* and *p* are entirely distinct. Concluding the latter means that *n* is irrelevant to *p*.

[20] R Eggleston, *Evidence, Proof and Probability*, 2nd edn (London, Weidenfeld and Nicolson, 1983) 59.

[21] ibid 60.

[22] See discussion in A Choo, 'Evidence, (In)efficiency, and Freedom of Proof: A Perspective from England and Wales' (2015) 66 *University Alabama Law Review* 493, 502.

[23] eg *King* (n 2) [85]. See C Williams, 'Burdens and Standards in Civil Litigation' (2003) 25 *Sydney Law Review* 165, 180–85, arguing in support of the proposition (purportedly accepted by the HCA) that statistical evidence cannot be used to make individualised findings.

This failure occurs even when statistical evidence is substantively identical to similar fact evidence. In *Vietnam Veterans' Association of Australia v Gallagher*,[24] 'statistical' evidence was tendered showing that when the tribunal was constituted with a particular member, that tribunal was more likely to make unfavourable decisions against applicants than similar tribunals constituted without that person. This evidence was used to press a disqualification application against the tribunal member for reasonable apprehension of bias. When the member refused, the matter was appealed to the Federal Court of Australia (FCA), where the appeal was dismissed, and the statistical evidence found irrelevant. At no time did the FCA recognise this evidence as similar fact evidence. In one illuminating passage, Heerey J commented that

> it is no use tendering statistical evidence, or any other evidence, to show merely that a judge is likely, from what could be colloquially called a track record, to decide a case in a particular way.[25]

'Track records' are exactly what similar fact evidence is adduced to prove; that an individual acted in a particular way in the past and has continued to so act. That is not to say at this juncture that Heerey J was necessarily incorrect on the evidence in that case. Irrelevance in *Vietnam Veterans' Assoc* rested, rightly or wrongly, on the inability of the evidence to meet the substantive elements of reasonable apprehension of bias. But it is necessary to explain why these two strands of evidence would appear to be treated differently.

II. Inferential Structure of Similar Fact Evidence

Evidence is epistemologically justified and therefore relevant when the evidence can rationally make the existence of a fact-in-issue more or less probable to any degree.[26] Most evidence derives relevance from its direct proximity in time, space and object to the facts-in-issue. For example, A is accused of slaying B. B was stabbed to death with a knife. A is known to possess a knife fitting the description of the murder weapon. A's possession of a similar looking knife is circumstantial evidence relevant to A's guilt. A is, rationally, more likely to have been involved in B's death than someone who did not possess the knife; possession puts A in a likely more proximate position to the death than a non-possessor, increasing the probability A was involved.[27] The probative value of this evidence fluctuates depending on the degree of proximity of possession. Evidence that A held an identical knife just before B is stabbed is likely very probative compared to evidence showing A's possession of an identical knife two weeks after the murder in a separate country.

[24] *Vietnam Veterans' Association of Australia v Gallagher* (1994) 34 ALD 205 (FCA).
[25] ibid 213.
[26] See UEL s 55; *IMM* (n 12) 312 [40]–[41], 313[43], citing *Festa* (n 12) 599 [14]; *Smith* (n 12) [6].
[27] Cowen and Carter (n 7) 133.

Both circumstances are still relevant 'directly' to possession, an integral element of the *res gestae* of the offence. A's possession even when overseas is not a separate transaction because possession is a continuum that includes, but is not limited to, the exact time of the offence. There is a rational explanation consistent with A's possession and guilt; A could have killed B and fled without disposing of the weapon. If, however, A owned a knife that could not be the murder weapon, there is no rational explanation for A's 'possession' of that knife to be relevant to B's death.

Similar fact evidence about the conduct of individuals operates under the same evidentiary mandates as circumstantial evidence: the ultimate goal is still to explain A's role in the facts-in-issue. But the inferential process needed to realise that goal is different.[28] To explain why A killed C is relevant to A killed B, the fact-finder not only must accept that A in fact killed C, but infer that because of some feature of that event he is also more likely to have killed B. Such inferences are not inevitable but require a rational basis for why C is relevant to B.

A. Frequentist Accounts of Similar Fact Evidence

One method of linking the existence of a current event with a collection of past events is by a frequentist account of probability. Frequentism rests on principles of enumerative induction. Naked statistical evidence, for example, is premised on enumerative induction. The Blue Bus proof paradox[29] relies on the number of buses owned by Blue independent of any evidence of accident involvement. Unlike similar fact or statistical evidence, naked statistical evidence does not need an assumption that the observed frequency will continue from the sample into the population – that is guaranteed by entirely defining the population itself.

Enumerative logic fails for similar fact evidence because the sequences of conduct are insufficiently long to make any reasonable conclusion. It is impossible to establish the existence of a single event from an infinite class of similar events simply because those events seem to occur at an identifiable rate. Counting the number of times an event occurs in a given sample does not mean that it continues at that rate indefinitely into the population unless that sample is in fact, or very nearly, the size of the population (which almost never occurs in reality).[30] Nor is it usually possible to infer the cause of the event simply by its mere occurrence in conjunction with another event.[31] A causal theory is needed that is based on an

[28] *Sutton v The Queen* (1984) 152 CLR 528 558–59; *Pfennig v The Queen* (1994) 182 CLR 461, 482; *HML v The Queen* (2008) 235 CLR 334, 355–56. Contra M Bagaric and K Amarasekara, 'The Prejudice Against Similar Fact Evidence' (2001) 5 *International Journal of Evidence & Proof* 71, 85–87.

[29] See ch 7, section II.

[30] M Galavotti, '*The Origins of Probabilistic Epistemology*' in A Hajek and C Hitchcock (eds), *The Oxford Handbook of Probability and Philosophy* (Oxford, Oxford University Press, 2016) 138; A La Caze, 'Frequentism' in A Hajek and C Hitchcock (eds), *The Oxford Handbook of Probability and Philosophy* (Oxford, Oxford University Press, 2016) 353.

[31] The fallacy *post hoc ergo propter hoc*: K Rothman, S Greenland and T Lash, *Modern Epidemiology*, 3rd edn (Philadelphia, Wolters Kluwer Health, 2013) 19.

assumption that whatever occurred in the past is continuing at or about the same rate into the future, known as an 'assumption of continuance'.[32] Frequentism cannot account for the assumption of continuance because it doesn't provide any logical connection between the variables, only the frequency of their occurrence. Merely counting the number of times smoking is associated with lung cancer does not provide a justifiable explanation for 'smoking causes lung cancer' – it may be a coincidence, and other genetic or environmental factors may be responsible, especially given that not all smokers develop lung cancer. Without a reason for accepting the assumption of continuance,[33] there is no possibility of accepting frequency explanations about *p* from *n*, or that A is more likely to kill B because A killed C.[34]

These doubts about the assumption of continuance clearly explain the historical reluctance to accept similar fact evidence.[35] In *Hollingham v Head*, terms of prior contracts between the defendant and third parties were irrelevant to prove the existence of terms between the plaintiff and the defendant.[36] Evidence proving 'a person having once or many times in his life done a particular act in a particular way [adduced to] make it more probable that he has done the same thing in the same way upon another and different occasion' was inadmissible as unwarranted speculation.[37] Without an explanation for why the past practices made current actions more probable,[38] courts were unwilling accept that such evidence was relevant.[39]

[32] See AE Acorn, 'Similar Fact Evidence and the Principle of Inductive Reasoning: Makin Sense' (1991) 11 *OJLS* 63, 65; *Martin v Osborne* (1936) 55 CLR 367, 383–85 (Evatt J). In philosophy this is referred to as an assumption about the uniformity of nature, often ascribed to Hume, Bacon and Mill (see S Zabell, 'Symmetry Arguments in Probability' in A Hajek and C Hitchcock (eds), *The Oxford Handbook of Probability and Philosophy* (Oxford, Oxford University Press, 2016) 325; L Cohen, *The Implications of Induction* (Yorkshire, Methuen, 1970) 204. This assumption has borne the brunt of philosophical and especially empirical derision for centuries: Rothman, Greenland and Lash (n 31) 19–24.

[33] Rothman, Greenland and Lash (n 31) 20–22.

[34] One may, however, be able to predict the probability of that effect in any future *n*: Gillies (n 13) 118, citing Von Mises' frequentist view of probability.

[35] eg Stone (n 7). For discussion of the development of the Australian approach, including treatment by various attempts at law reform, see *Ellis* (n 7).

[36] *Hollingham v Head* [1858] 140 ER 1135, 1136 (Willies J). In *Holocombe v Hewson* [1810] 170 ER 1194, the Court was asked to find that the beer supplied by a brewer to a particular publican was 'good beer' because beer of quality had been supplied to other publicans. Lord Ellenborough rejected that evidence on the basis that '[t]his is *res inter alios acta*. We cannot here enquire into the quality of different beer furnished to different persons. The plaintiff might deal well with one, and not with the others … I cannot admit witnesses to his general character and habits as a brewer.' Although inconsistently used, the inferential structure giving rise to *res inter alios acta* is similar to the individualisation of statistical evidence.

[37] *Hollingham* (n 36) 1137.

[38] This book does not suggest that no explanation was in fact available in these cases. There is a rational basis for saying that the past defective supply of goods makes the present defective supply more probable. What is important about these cases is that the courts did not recognise that a theory connecting the events existed and it was the absence of recognition of that theory that caused the evidence to be irrelevant.

[39] How to describe this principle at common law is the subject of some uncertainty. In *Makin v A-G (NSW)* [1894] AC 57 (PC) 65, the Privy Council stipulated that character-based assumptions were forbidden unless adduced within a certain category. The House of Lords retreated from the categories approach to similar fact evidence in *DPP v Boardman* [1975] AC 421 (HL): see P Mirfield, 'Similar Facts – Makin Out?' (1987) 46 *CLJ* 83.

Missing in *Hollingham* and cases like it was a logical explanation for why contracting at time one predicts contracting at time two. James uses an example involving a breach of warrant for defective paint:

> Proof of the condition of the paint in the first drum was of negligible value in judging the probable character of the paint in the second, unopened drum. It merely showed that plaintiff company sometimes sold bad paint. If the issue was whether the paint in the second drum was bad, an issue on which the defendant had the burden, the trial judge's ruling [that the evidence was irrelevant] seems sound.[40]

James' conclusion on relevance is correct if each tin of paint is independent from every other batch. If that were true, then a very long sequence of bad batches would be needed to satisfy a fact-finder that an individual can of paint from the supplier was bad. But if the fact-finder could have reasoned from the evidence a common cause for defective paint, such as evidence of a manufacturing defect at the plant, or even that the supplier was in the habit of selling defective paint, then James' conclusion on relevance would be logically incorrect.

A's prior killing behaviour (exemplified by the death of C) is relevant if it can be assumed to continue into and thus help explain the death of B. Such an assumption is predicated on a belief that something about B's death is inherent to A, such that when under similar conditions A is likely to repeat the behaviour. This is a partial extrapolation from a causal law.[41] If a causal law about A's conduct could be identified (and assuming that human free will can be bound by causal laws)[42] then one could identify A's behaviour in those conditions with certainty.[43] Knowledge of causal laws is, however, almost always imperfect. Inferences made in such conditions are inductive and probabilistic because their accuracy is ex ante uncertain. Simply repeating the behaviour is not enough to identify the conditions of the causal law. Some other interpretation is needed.

B. Propensity Accounts of Similar Fact Evidence

Looking beyond frequencies to the conditions producing those frequencies allows one to draw a rational link between the similar fact and the present fact. 'Induction by variation in circumstance' takes the basic premise of enumeration but adds to it the identification of the conditions surrounding the frequency.[44] Propensity theories of probability best represent this process.[45] They assert that 'the generating

[40] GF James, 'Relevancy, Probability and the Law' (1941) 29 *California Law Review* 689, 692–93.

[41] 'Causal generalisation' in Wright's parlance: see R Wright, 'Causation, Responsibility, Risk, Probability, Naked Statistics, and Proof: Pruning the Bramble Bush by Clarifying the Concepts' (1988) 73 *Iowa Law Review* 1001, 1045.

[42] cf H Ho, *A Philosophy of Evidence Law* (Oxford, Oxford University Press, 2008) 301–03.

[43] See discussion of Fretzer's propensity account in Gillies (n 13) 128–29, where it is hypothesised that objective probabilities could be fashioned if one could identify a complete set of relevant variables.

[44] Cohen, *Implications* (n 32) 107.

[45] There is no unifying propensity theory of probability: see Gillies (n 13) 127. But for present purposes it is enough to note that each of these theories relies on an underlying premise that an individual's actions can be related to other actions by reason of the conditions under which both actions occur.

conditions [of an event] are … endowed with a propensity to produce observed frequencies'.[46] The probability of an event occurring depends on the identified conditions of its occurrence. The advantage of such a theory is that causal conclusions can be generated from far smaller samples; as long as there is one other instance of the event, or some behaviour connected to the event, a tendency can be inferred.[47]

Similar fact evidence tendered for a tendency purpose relies on a propensity theory of probability through the assumption of continuance. Nomothetic generalisations about human behaviour lead to the conclusion that individuals who act in a certain way or have a certain belief are likely to act that way again.[48] An individual possessing this trait can be believed to be more likely to commit the action than someone in the same position without that trait.[49] This overcomes, or at least ameliorates, the causation deficit in enumerative induction by ex ante proposing the cause of the subsequent event; the accused has a certain character or character trait that causes a tendency to act in a certain way under certain conditions.[50] Identifying those conditions at both time points gives the fact-finder a rational basis for the assumption of continuance. Linking the past behaviour to the present means the evidence is no longer separated by time, space and object but has a contemporaneous impact on current behaviour; both sets of behaviour are explained by a tendency operating at both time points.

One flaw in using propensity theories of probability is the potential inability to calculate single-case probabilities 'objectively'.[51] Both philosophy and law identify that fact-finding probabilistically about single cases is problematic because, at least for past events, the probability of the event being true is 1 (it did occur) or 0 (it did not occur). It makes little sense to speak of a past event probably occurring because either it did or did not occur. This questions whether it is ever appropriate to extrapolate from probabilities identified in a population to individual events that have occurred but are presently unknown. The fatal flaw in this argument is

[46] ibid 115. That view of propensity theory is contested. Miller suggests that one cannot use similar events to fashion a propensity. Only the exact circumstances at the time are relevant indicia of propensity. For a criticism of this approach, see ibid 127.

[47] ibid 118.

[48] AAS Zuckerman, 'Similar Fact Evidence – The Unobservable Rule' (1987) 103 *LQR* 187, 190. For a discussion of the development of these principles in psychological literature and their relevance to similar fact evidence, see M Redmayne, 'The Relevance of Bad Character' (2002) 61 *CLJ* 684, 687–89, 695. For philosophical support, see L Cohen, *The Probable and the Provable* (Oxford, Clarendon Press, 1977) 284–85. cf Bagaric and Amarasekara (n 27) 91 (human conduct is not sufficiently consistent to justify a 'propensity' inference); A Cossins, 'The Legacy of the Makin Case 120 Years on: Legal Fictions, Circular Reasoning and Some Solutions' (2013) 35 *Sydney Law Review* 731, 739–41 (using propensity inferences relies on heuristic assumptions of behaviour that are often wrong).

[49] M Redmayne, 'Recognising Propensity' (2011) 3 *Criminal Law Review* 177, 178.

[50] Ho (n 10) 137, 146–47. The notion that prevailing conditions control or influence the probability of the event is a key theme of the propensity theory: see K Popper, 'The Propensity Interpretation of Probability' (1959) 10 *British Journal for the Philosophy of Science* 25, 34.

[51] See Gillies (n 13) 114–15, who notes that frequentist accounts reject 'objective' single-case probabilities, whereas propensity accounts may permit such probabilities.

the notion that the discovery of legal facts can ever be proved true or false absolutely. Unlike gambling or predictions, where ultimately the odds of an event occurring will be resolved once the event occurs (assuming that there is consensus about the occurrence), there is no ultimate source of information independent of the fact-finder that can confirm or deny the truth or falsity of a past uncertain fact. Fact-finding does not and cannot require the absolute truth to be ascertained. Absolute truth is an impossible standard because

> [f]actual uncertainty is a chronic condition of human existence. Since omniscience is denied to human beings, all fact-finders can ever do is extrapolate from current knowledge and past experience to produce probabilist conclusions.[52]

That philosophical quandary is not resolved even with the further expenditure of resources after the trial process as the same epistemic challenges to establishing the truth in the absence of evidence demonstrating 'what happened' remain.[53] Unless the individual decision-maker can observe or experience the event, the 'truth', insofar as the law is prepared to apply that label to the existence of a fact, is the result of the belief of the fact-finder in the existence of the event based on the (potentially incomplete) evidence the parties put before the decision-maker.[54]

Nor does fact-finding require objective probabilities of truth. A subjective and rational belief in the propensity is enough. Different fact-finders can reach different answers on the same facts without undermining legal fact-finding and is an accepted part of the administration of justice.[55] The assessment of single-case probabilities in law under a propensity theory of probability appears to be something of a hybrid between the calculation of objective and subjective probabilities,[56] and that reflects the nature of the relevance assessment at law.

Once a rational basis for the continuity of character is asserted, relevance objections ought to dissipate.[57] *Blake v The Albion Life Assurance Society* concerned a scheme of fraud committed by an individual in conjunction with a life insurance company on unsuspecting loan-seekers.[58] A fictitious person would agree to loan the unsuspecting victim a sum of money in return for, amongst

[52] P Roberts, *Roberts & Zuckerman's Criminal Evidence*, 3rd edn (Oxford, Oxford University Press, 2022) 157.

[53] cf D Kaye, 'The Laws of Probability and the Law of the Land' (1979) 47 *University of Chicago Law Review* 34, 45.

[54] eg *Air Canada v Secretary of State for Trade* [1983] 2 AC 394 (HL) 438 (Lord Wilberforce); S Gageler, 'Evidence and Truth' (2017) 13 *The Judicial Review* 249, 253.

[55] See *HML* (n 28) 373 [73]; *Vietnam Veterans' Assoc* (n 24) 213.

[56] Gillies (n 13) 124–25. For a discussion on the place of subjective probabilities in legal proceedings, see Kaye (n 53) 41–52.

[57] Albeit that depends on courts accepting that the nomothetic generalisation about the probable continuity of character: see Ho (n 10) 137–38. Because the belief in continuity need only be rational and non-absolute, the relevance and probative value implications of similar fact evidence are sometimes described as being of little difficulty: see Zuckerman (n 47) 194. As this chapter demonstrates, however, relevance and probative value still occupy a great deal of attention in cases and literature concerning similar fact evidence: eg *Hughes* (n 12).

[58] *Blake v The Albion Life Assurance Society* [1878] 4 CPD 94.

other things, depositing a life insurance policy with Albion. No money was ever lent. The scheme was allegedly an agreement between the person and Albion to share in the life insurance proceeds. To prove that this was in fact a scheme of fraud involving the defendants and not a mere aberration, the plaintiff adduced a number of similar instances where loan-seekers had been defrauded by the same means. Albion objected to this evidence because the 'course of business of the defendants in transactions with different persons was not relevant to the cause of action, nor even evidence to support it'.[59] That is, the defendants' act at time one was irrelevant to their subsequent act at time two, much like the conclusion in *Hollingham*.

The Court rejected this submission:

> [I]n order to prove that A has committed a fraud on B, it is neither sufficient nor even relevant to prove that A committed fraud upon C, D, and E … But let it be shewn that the fraud on B is *one of a class* of other transactions, *having common features*, then I disagree altogether with that proposition.[60]

Blake identifies two mechanisms to explain the relevance of similar fact evidence. The first is where the evidence is necessary to establish an intention behind a scheme. Fraud is an intentional act. In addition to acts depriving victims of property, the moving party must show that the fraudster acted deliberately. That is very hard to do if only one bad transaction is put forward – it can be explained away as a mistake or an aberration. But if multiple instances of similar conduct are put forward, these can amount to direct evidence of a scheme to unlawfully deprive victims of their property and circumstantial evidence of intention. This is one instance of a 'non-tendency' use of tendency evidence.[61] As noted previously, the purpose for which the evidence is used is a vital consideration. Used directly in this way, similar fact evidence does not give rise to a generalisation objection. But it should be borne in mind that similar fact evidence used directly might still permit a fact-finder to use the evidence for its propensity purpose.[62]

The second method that *Blake* identifies rests firmly on inductive principles and prompts the generalisation objection. Given the totality of the conduct involving multiple parties, a fact-finder may determine that an innocent explanation is improbable. The weight of the defendant's past conduct suggests they have a

[59] ibid 98.

[60] ibid 106 (Lindley J) (emphasis added).

[61] *HML* (n 28) 396 [160] warns against bifurcating purposes too readily. But it appears now to be accepted practice that evidence displaying a tendency purpose can be admissible for its non-tendency purpose if accompanied by appropriate warnings: *Roach v The Queen* (2011) 242 CLR 610, [47]. Evidence of state of mind can be used for a tendency purpose (that an individual has a tendency to support a particular cause) or for a circumstantial purpose (the individual 'in fact' supports the cause): *Elomar v The Queen* (2014) 316 ALR 206 (NSWCCA) [367]. There is ongoing controversy over whether a practical distinction really exists between tendency and non-tendency purposes, especially in light of the relative inadequacy of warnings: see D Hamer, 'The Legal Structure of Propensity Evidence' (2016) 20 *International Journal of Evidence & Proof* 136; Redmayne, 'Recognising' (n 49) 188ff.

[62] Zuckerman (n 48) 199–200.

tendency to act in a fraudulent manner; something about their past practices suggests they have developed a modus operandi and the existence of further, similar events are explained by this tendency. The evidence is relevant because the tendency suggests that the impugned conduct is more probably fraudulent than if the present behaviour was viewed in isolation.

Such tendencies can be generated prospectively or retrospectively. In *Blake*, the tendency was prospective; the accumulating evidence gave rise to a logical conclusion that the defendants were in the business of fraud. By contrast, scientific research is not always premised on ex ante hypotheses. The discovery of the efficacious effect of drugs has been the product of unexpected relationships between the compound and observed effects.[63] This still entails the creation of a tendency – the compound has a tendency to have a particular effect – but this theory of connection is constructed retrospectively by way of the improbable association between the compound and the observed effect. This is both enumeration (Y keeps happening after X) and variation (X logically explains Y because no other variable could have this effect). Legal reasoning permits this form of reasoning despite its similarity to the logical fallacy *post hoc ergo propter hoc*.[64] But the conditions upon which such reasoning is permitted are, to varying degrees, controlled.

1. *Prior and Present Acts*

Propensity inferences rely on ascertaining causal laws. The conditions for a potential causal law (that a person has a tendency to act) are assumed from an existing body of evidence (the 'prior acts'). The fact-in-issue (the 'present act') is compared to this causal law to ascertain its fit. That is, by reason of the propensity that is inferred from the collection of prior acts, the present act was caused by that propensity. The syllogism, strikingly similar to the statistical evidence syllogism outlined in the Introduction to this book, operates in the following way:

> C and D have been killed.
>
> C and D share some common features that can be connected to A, or the circumstances of their death can be connected to A, such that 'A killed C and D'.
>
> It is rational to infer that A has a 'tendency' to kill people like 'C and D'.
>
> B has been killed and B, or the conditions surrounding the death of B, are similar to C and D.
>
> It is rational to infer that A is more likely than another individual to have killed B because A has a propensity to kill people like C and D (tendency), or the death of B and C and D share common features such that it is improbable that the deaths of B, C and D were not commonly caused (coincidence).

[63] Famously, aspirin and heart disease: PC Elwood and others, 'A Randomized Controlled Trial of Acetyl Salicylic Acid in the Secondary Prevention of Mortality from Myocardial Infarction' (1974) 1 *British Medical Journal* 436.

[64] *Sienkiewicz v Greif* [2011] 2 AC 229 (UKSC) [6]–[10] (Lord Phillips P).

Where the prior acts 'A killed C and D' are proven, the UEL describes such evidence as 'tendency evidence'.[65] Tendency evidence uses past similar behaviour to establish that A has a character trait predisposing A to commit certain acts and that tendency helps explain A's involvement in the putative act.[66] 'Coincidence evidence' is where the prior facts are not proven but putative and form the basis of further charges.[67] A is accused of the murder of B and C. Even though neither B's or C's murders are proved prior to the trial, the circumstances of each are so similar that it is improbable that the two events occurred coincidentally.[68] Coincidence evidence seeks to establish that C (separate in time, space and object from B) makes the existence of B (and vice versa) more probable because it is unlikely that A's involvement with B and C was a product of coincidence or luck.[69]

When to label evidence as tendency or coincidence is not always clear, and there is some potential for overlap. Both tendency and coincidence rely ultimately on the construction of a 'propensity' by way of an assumption of continuance. The difference between them is when that propensity is believed to exist. Tendency evidence alleges that A is more likely to have killed B because A's past behaviour reveals a peculiar character trait – a propensity to kill. It is necessary to show that A possesses this trait to connect C and B. Coincidence evidence cannot rely on an established tendency because the facts giving rise to it have not yet been proven. To construct a tendency at that point would commit a logical fallacy of circular reasoning.[70] Instead, coincidence evidence suggests that an innocent explanation of A's involvement in the deaths of B and C is so improbable that C's death means A is likely to have murdered B. Unlike tendency evidence, the propensity in coincidence evidence is a consequence of connecting B and C. In *Blake*, the occurrence of multiple, similar impugned acts gave rise to an inference that the defendant was 'in the habit of carrying on business in that way' even though the 'habit' was constructed from a collection of putative events and as such serves as an explanation for the coincidence rather than a means of proof of it.[71]

There are two potential logical flaws to constructing propensities from the syllogistic pathway described above. First, constructing a propensity from proven prior acts alone logically requires at least one repetition of the prior acts. As referred to above, there is a movement in probability philosophy to construct 'objective' 'single case' probabilities. To say that an event is likely to occur again because it has a tendency to so occur, in the absence of any evidence of reoccurrence of that event, is a fraught exercise.

[65] UEL s 97.

[66] See *Gipp v The Queen* (1998) 194 CLR 106, 111–12.

[67] UEL s 98. Also known at common law as 'improbability' reasoning.

[68] eg *DSJ v R* (2012) 215 A Crim R 349; Cowen and Carter (n 7) 112. For a discussion of the interrelationship between coincidence reasoning (also referred to as the 'doctrine of chances') and tendency reasoning, see Redmayne, *Character* (n 14) 116–20.

[69] See Redmayne, 'Recognising' (n 49) 192.

[70] *Perry v The Queen* (1982) 150 CLR 580, 612.

[71] *Blake* (n 58) 106.

That said, a great deal depends on what the fact-finder is prepared to accept as evidence of a propensity. A single, unique event could hardly be said to have a propensity to repeat itself without any evidence of that repetition – a factual finding devoid of any evidence whatsoever is prima facie irrational. However, a singular, unique event that shared some characteristics with another type of event could, subject to what those factors were, be inferred to have a propensity of some kind by reason of that extraneous evidence. The appropriateness of inferring a propensity from a unique event is the subject of some controversy in philosophy and law. But it is also commonplace. Similar fact evidence by definition collects singular events that can be explained, in part, by a common cause. The deaths of C and D are unique events that will probably have some differences. It is the degree of their similarity that connects them together, and ultimately allows for A's tendency to be inferred. The problem for single-case probabilities is that the narrative of tendency is lacking. Where an event is so disconnected from the events said to give rise to a tendency, it simply cannot form a part of that chain – it is too dissimilar.[72]

What is more difficult is whether it is permissible to use the present act as part of the evidence to establish the tendency including where, for example, there is only one instance of the prior act. Usually, a propensity is relied on to prove the existence of the present act. In *Perry*, Brennan J stated that '[t]o seek to prove a fact-in-issue by a chain of reasoning which assumes the truth of that fact is, of course, a fallacy, repugnant alike to logic and to the practice processes of criminal courts'.[73] If a present act is to be included in the evidence establishing the tendency, the existence (to the standard of proof) of the present act is being assumed in order to prove that act. Reasoning of this kind is akin to 'bootstrapping', and there are vociferous arguments against its use.[74]

Reasoning of this type is unavoidable for coincidence evidence. The propensity to commit the unproven acts is established by way of a propensity account formed post hoc,[75] rather than from an ex ante tendency. This problem is encountered by statistical evidence when the sample used in the analysis is drawn from the litigation directly. More typically, statistical evidence is published outside the litigation context and as such the tendency established by evidence other than the present acts. That is, the tendency is established by prior acts from a sample that does not overlap with p.

Litigation-generated statistical evidence, especially prevalent in class actions, takes present and unproven acts as a collective and seeks to explain causal laws through statistical analyses. In *Wal-Mart Stores v Dukes*,[76] this consisted of evidence

[72] *Perry* (n 70) 611–12.

[73] ibid 612.

[74] See Cossins (n 48) 744 ('circular reasoning'); cf D Hamer, 'Structure and Strength of the Propensity Inference – Singularity, Linkage and the Other Evidence' (2003) 29 *Monash Law Review* 137, 159, who suggests that coincidence evidence is in fact less problematic, or that the difference between tendency and coincidence evidence is illusory.

[75] See discussion in Hamer, 'Structure' (n 74) 159–60.

[76] *Wal-Mart Stores v Dukes* 564 US 338 (2011).

of gender-based discriminatory promotion practices. Samples of individuals from various Wal-Mart stores were used to found a claim that a discriminatory promotion practice existed. The bootstrapping problem is clear. An attempt was being made to say that employees were not promoted because of their gender by adducing the existence (on a huge scale) of similar instances of non-promotion, the inference being that the fact of non-promotion of these similarly situated employees could be explained by a discriminatory practice. This relies on assuming non-promotion in each case was a decision taken because of (whether consciously or unconsciously) their gender, which had not been proved.[77]

Although this is a logical flaw in how this evidence was presented, it does not by itself invalidate an argument that such evidence is relevant to the existence of the impunged propensity. It does nonetheless pose its own special risks, which will be discussed in chapter six, concerning how the generalisation problem should be regulated by evidence law.

2. *Linkage*

If, for present purposes, the discussion is confined to circumstances where the tendency is constructed exclusively from prior acts, the fact-finder is still confronted by an incomplete causal law. Inferring from specific past actions in a sample (n) to a generic causal law in the population (N) and back to the fact-in-issue (p) is made under conditions of uncertainty. Such inferences are therefore inductive in nature.[78]

Hughes v The Queen usefully sets out the basic inferential structure of similar fact evidence.[79] When similar fact evidence is tendered to prove that an act is more probable because of the existence of a prior act, there are two epistemic questions to resolve before that evidence is relevant. First, does the evidence give rise to a rational inference that the events in question are the product of a tendency of action? Second, if such a tendency could exist, does that tendency make the fact-in-issue more probable – in other words, is the present fact explained, in whole or in part, by the prior facts?[80] This work adopts the terminology proposed by Hamer in identifying the indicia of this inferential pathway for similar fact evidence. The first question is 'linkage', that is, the evidence establishing that the defendant committed the prior acts from which a tendency can be inferred. The second question is 'singularity'. Singularity describes the consistency between the prior acts and the present acts that can be explained by the tendency.[81] In the above

[77] ibid 356–57.
[78] *Hughes* (n 12) [71].
[79] *Hughes* (n 12).
[80] These criteria are effectively identical to those in the assessment of significant probative value, save for under that assessment, the gatekeeper is looking to the degree of support under each limb: ibid [41]. For relevance, the only questions are whether there is any rational basis for the existence of a tendency, and does it have some effect on a fact-in-issue.
[81] Hamer, 'Structure' (n 74) 151.

syllogism, singularity is the identification of the conditions common to C and D on the one hand, and B on the other. Hamer's further criterion, 'other evidence' is the additional available direct and circumstantial factors linking the defendant to the present and prior acts.

The existence of the assumption of continuance about a character trait is the product of linkage. Once the trait is assumed to continue across time and place, it can be inferred that the present act was caused by that trait. Linkage, as such, is akin to general factual causation in statistical evidence, in that it refers to the fact-finder's belief in the causal law that exists prior to and sometimes because of the instant act. For coincidence evidence, singularity and linkage become effectively one inference, because the individual's tendency is said to explain the existence of the present acts, rather than being a necessary ingredient in their proof.[82] Put another way, coincidence reasoning may be considered a form of frequentist logic that is ultimately justified by a propensity.

Establishing the assumption of continuance by linkage is composed of at least two heuristic processes: magnitude and similarity. As heuristics, these factors are the product of rough generalisations about human behaviour; evidence is not typically adduced in support of them. The only limit on such reasoning is that it must be 'rational'. Rationality is a highly contextualised inquiry that is decided on a case-by-case, fact-by-fact basis.[83] Rationality is not a legal construct.[84] The rational existence of a tendency, necessary for the evidence to be relevant,[85] is a matter for 'logic and human experience'[86] and 'commonsense'.[87] Establishing the rational basis for a tendency is an individualised judgement[88] that rests on psychological and subjective factors rather than objective indicators.[89] The law does not attempt to prescribe indicia of rationality. Ultimately, this is a question of judgement for the individual or collective fact-finders that the law does not intrude upon.[90] This explains in part why similar fact evidence continues to be a controversial evidentiary doctrine and troubles appellate courts on a regular basis. But relying on the worldly knowledge of fact-finders is an essential and unavoidable part of legal fact-finding.[91]

The controversy about the use of heuristics in similar fact reasoning is long-standing. Commonsense is premised on a basic repository of knowledge reasonably

[82] ibid; Cossins (n 48) 755.

[83] *R v Guney* [1998] 2 Cr App R 242, 265–67; *HML* (n 28) 427 [279].

[84] J Heydon, *Cross on Evidence*, 11th edn (Chatswood, LexisNexis, 2017) [3205], citing JB Thayer, *A Preliminary Treatise on Evidence at the Common Law* (1898) 134, 265.

[85] *Martin* (n 32) 375; see Roberts (n 52) 110–11.

[86] *Hughes* (n 12) [40]; James (n 40) 701–02. How one ascertains 'human experience' is in itself a difficult question not entered into here, but see Eggleston (n 20) 89, ch 11.

[87] *HML* (n 28) [6] (Gleeson CJ); *R v Randall* [2004] All ER 467, 474 [20].

[88] R Pattenden, 'Similar Fact Evidence and Proof of Identity' (1996) 112 *LQR* 446, 456.

[89] Acorn (n 32) 74–75.

[90] Roberts (n 52) 111.

[91] *Lyons Sons v Gulliver* [1914] Ch 631 (CA) 641 (Lord Cozens-Hardy MR).

common to all individuals.[92] But human behaviour is remarkably resistant to simple characterisations. Individuals can differ markedly in their assessment of how people ought to react in different situations. To add another layer of controversy, these assumptions change over time.[93] Despite relying on heuristics, the law has identified some basic ingredients that inform the existence of behavioural tendencies by way of an assumption of continuance about character; the degree of repetition of the behaviour (magnitude) and the logical connection between those behaviours (similarity). These are not 'legal' rules as such, but factors of the evidence that guide the logical process of determining whether the assumption of continuance ought to be made.

i. Magnitude

The magnitude heuristic suggests that an event is more probable if an identical or sufficiently similar event has occurred previously than if it had not previously occurred. A is more likely to be guilty of killing B if A killed C and D because

> [t]he repetition of acts or occurrences is often the very thing which makes it probable that they are accompanied by some further fact. The frequency with which a set of circumstances recurs or the regularity with which a course of conduct is pursued may exclude, as unreasonable, any other explanation or hypothesis than the truth of the fact to be proved.[94]

Fewer repetitions make it harder to dispel the claim that the events occurred coincidentally.[95] Prolonging the sequence of events (or the behaviour repeated) increases the inductive warrant that the frequency in the sample holds true in the population.[96] Frequentist logic of this type cannot by itself generate a causal conclusion. Something more is needed to bind the events together.

ii. Similarity

In *Hughes*, the majority of the HCA established that the first step in establishing the relevance and admissibility of tendency evidence is the 'extent to which the

[92] A Stein, *Foundations of Evidence Law* (Oxford, Oxford University Press, 2005) 94; T Anderson, D Schum and W Twining, *Analysis of Evidence*, 2nd edn (Cambridge, Cambridge University Press, 2005) 269–75, 277; Cohen, *Probable* (n 48) 275.

[93] See O Holmes, 'The Path of the Law' (1897) 10 *Harvard Law Review* 457, 466. In *Thompson v R* [1918] AC 221 (HL), Lord Sumner commented that because the offender was homosexual, he was more likely to have committed a child sex offence. Those conclusions about the nature of homosexuality were rejected in *Boardman* (n 39) 458 as '[sounding] nowadays like a voice from another world' (Lord Cross). Homosexuality and paedophilia are not (at least without cogent evidence) the same type of behaviour: Pattenden (n 88) 469. But prejudice against homosexual activity is an ongoing feature of some individual judicial reasons: see *Ex parte HH*, 830 So2d 21, 27–28 (AlaSC, 2002) (Moore CJ). Imagining a standard relying on truly universal social mores that 'everyone believes' is a fools' errand.

[94] *Martin* (n 32) 376 (Dixon J). See further *Perry* (n 70) 610; Cohen, *Implications* (n 32) 106.

[95] Mirfield (n 39) 84; *Dingley v Chief Constable Strathclyde Police* 1998 SC 548, 604–05. This reasoning was not cavilled with on appeal to the House: *Dingley v The Chief Constable, Strathclyde Police* 2000 SC 77, 86–89 (Lord Hope).

[96] *Martin* (n 32) 353; Cohen, *Implications* (n 32) 106.

evidence supports the tendency'.[97] The underlying principles governing whether there is sufficient similarity to justify the existence of a tendency in the prior acts are governed by the same basic ideas concerning similarity for the purpose of 'singularity' – that is, whether the decision-maker is prepared to accept that the evidence demonstrates a sufficiently logical connection between each of the prior acts to justify the existence of a common cause. It is for the gatekeeper to determine if there is some connection, and therefore whether the evidence is relevant. Fact-finders are then charged with determining the strength of the tendency. Yet, the gatekeeper can also play a role in determining whether the evidence has sufficient probative value to be admitted and, in criminal cases, whether that probative value outweighs its prejudicial effect.[98]

Of course, the trait doesn't have to be entirely unique. But generic tendencies have less discriminatory power and are of less probative value.[99] 'Too' generic tendencies will be irrelevant because they cannot explain the specific behaviour in question. For example, males commit the vast majority of crimes in society. But the probative value of 'the defendant's gender' would be negligible for its tendency purpose because there doesn't appear to be a rational connection between 'male' and 'propensity for crime' in the context of all males, the majority of whom don't commit crimes. This evidence may have epistemic value, however, if 'male' were a salient feature and if there were only two potential perpetrators – one male and one female. In such circumstances, the discriminatory potential of the generic class is high.

More generic tendencies also leave greater scope for the application of individualised 'commonsense' reasoning. This opens the fact-finding process to a greater risk of infection from bias and incorrect character imputations. The heightened risk of biased reasoning is one reason why some scholars have called for the outright rejection of similar fact reasoning, or greater curtailment of its use.[100]

[97] *Hughes* (n 12) [41].

[98] How far the gatekeeper can go in assessing the degree of connection, and the basis upon which it ought to be done, is the subject of some controversy: see N Lennings, 'Assessing Significant Probative Value for the Purposes of Admitting Coincidence Evidence: *DSJ v R; NS v R*' (2013) 17 *International Journal of Evidence & Proof* 202, 211–12. The debate focuses on the extent the gatekeeper can take into account the 'reliability' of the evidence in assessing significant probative value. There existed a split in approach between the New South Wales Court of Criminal Appeal and Victorian Court of Appeal: J Heydon, 'Is the Weight of Evidence Material to its Admissibility?' (2014) 26 *Current Issues in Criminal Justice* 219. The HCA attempted to resolve this controversy in *IMM* (n 12), but that decision was bedevilled by a split in the Court 4-1-2: G Edmond, 'Icarus and the Evidence Act: Section 137, Probative Value and taking Forensic Science Evidence "at its highest"' (2017) 41 *Melbourne University Law Review* 106, 118–19. Subsequently, in *R v Bauer* (2018) 266 CLR 56 at [69], the HCA recognised that its prior jurisprudence had left the state of the law unclear and the Court unanimously opined that 'unless the risk of contamination, concoction or collusion is so great that it would not be open to the jury rationally to accept the evidence, the determination of probative value excludes consideration of credibility and reliability'.

[99] *Sokolowskyj v The Queen* (2014) 239 A Crim R 528 (NSWCCA) 537–38.

[100] See Cossins (n 48) 751ff; R Nair, 'Weighing Similar Fact and Avoiding Prejudice' (1996) 112 *LQR* 262, 283–84.

The general position at law is to refuse, or warn against, tendency evidence that amounts to a general 'criminal' disposition. If A is accused of murdering B, it seems prima facie implausible to adduce evidence that A defrauded C. At best, the tendency one could infer is that A has a criminal disposition. Ironically perhaps, empirical evidence suggests that criminals are 'generalists' and that prior criminality of any sort is a good predictor of future criminality generally.[101] How robust that conclusion is in relation to very disparate offences (speeding and murder, for example) is unclear. In any event, generic 'bad character' evidence is usually inadmissible in criminal proceedings as a matter of statute and common law.

Taken together, similarity and magnitude are synergistic. Two similar events are more likely to be connected if there is a prior history of those same events occurring, in turn increasing the inductive warrant for the inference that B and C share a common cause.[102] Magnitude and similarity do also operate with a degree of independence. If there is only limited repetition, increasing similarity will reduce the impact that has, especially where the conduct is considered unique or a signature. Equally, events that appear reasonably disparate can be connected because the concurrence of multiple events in conjunction with a single causative agent makes it improbable that they are not connected.

3. *Singularity*

The second stage of the *Hughes* test requires connecting the tendency to the present act. Just like linkage, singularity involves two stages. First, there must be sufficient similarity between the identified tendency and the impugned conduct for the tendency to rationally affect the existence of the conduct at all.[103] Second, the degree of similarity will determine the level of probative value the tendency evidence possesses. Again, the gatekeeper plays a role at this stage, with the power to refuse the admission of that evidence if the connection is insufficient, or incapable of overcoming the prejudice the evidence might cause.

How to assess 'similarity' in singularity is controversial. Similar fact evidence does not need to be identical, 'strikingly similar' or possess an 'unusual feature' to the present fact to have some explanatory power.[104] It does, however, need to traverse the same substantive territory in order for a logical connection to exist between the prior fact and the event.[105] Some degree of similarity or logical connection is necessary for a tendency to exist.[106] If there is no similarity or logical connection, similar fact evidence possesses no probative value and is irrelevant.[107]

[101] Redmayne, 'Relevance' (n 48) 698.
[102] S Haack, 'Warrant, Causation, and the Atomisim of Evidence Law' (2008) 5 *Episteme* 253, 259.
[103] *Sutton* (n 28) 548–49.
[104] *Bauer* (n 98) [48]; *B v The Queen* (1992) 175 CLR 599, 618; *DPP v P* [1991] 2 AC 447, 462D–H.
[105] *Hughes* (n 12) [92], citing *Saoud v R* (2014) 87 NSWLR 481 (NSWCCA) 491 [44].
[106] Gillies (n 13) 119.
[107] *Boardman* (n 39) 451.

As the degree of similarity between the similar fact and present fact increases, the less likely it is those events are coincidental. If A killed C and D in a particular fashion, and that same method was used to kill B, it is easier to accept that A killed B, C and D, than if B and C and D had been killed by different methods.[108]

In this example, either one infers that A has a propensity to kill in a particular manner from C and D, such that the probability that A killed B is increased (tendency evidence), or that the conditions B, C and D, and A's association with each, are so similar that A is rationally the common cause (tendency or coincidence evidence).[109] In *Laughton v Shalaby*, evidence of negligence in knee, wrist and foot operations was 'too far removed' to be relevant similar fact evidence to negligence of hip operations.[110] In Longmore LJ's mind there was insufficient similarity between negligence in knee, wrist and foot operations to infer anything about negligence in hip operations. No reasons were given for why these procedures were considered dissimilar, but one can speculate on the existence of anatomical and surgical technique differences. Having decided that the appropriate reference class for the causal law was 'hip surgeries' (even though the broader category of 'human surgery' may have been available) the CA determined that surgeries to another part of the body were insufficiently similar.

Once the conditions for the causal law have been identified, the applicability of this causal law need not be certain nor unequivocally inculpate A in the criminal behaviour.[111] A's association with B, C and D could ultimately be found to be a coincidence (that is, there is no real association), and yet similar fact evidence

[108] See Pattenden (n 88) 451, 464; *The Queen v Dickens* [2016] NTSC 7, [66].

[109] Similar fact evidence is likely to hold more probative value for crimes that are uncommon than crimes that are common: see Redmayne, 'Relevance' (n 48) 693. Bagaric and Amarasekara (n 28) suggest that similar fact evidence does not, in fact, rely on establishing propensities of action at all. Logical inferences from similar fact evidence are said to be no different to any other form of evidence (at 85) and that 'information stemming from our previous conduct impacts upon our belief forming calculus in the same way as other "observable" facts' (at 86). Similar fact evidence is relevant not because (at 87):

> we engage in reasoning along the lines that A has previously committed a similar offence, therefore he must be the culprit. Rather, we reason that A has by his previous conduct shown that he is one of a very small proportion of the community that is willing to go to such lengths as robbing a bank in order to satisfy his desire to increase his financial wealth.

This approach seems to ignore the fact that in order to be compartmentalised into a particular category of people, some factual basis for doing so is necessary, and that factual basis relies on possessing either a propensity to rob or that it would be improbable that the facts were such and the individual in question were not the robber. This approach effectively ignores the first stage of similar fact inferences. The second stage is identical to any other form of evidence, and could perceptibly be used to categorise the individual; a person who possesses a tendency to act (and thereby belong to a class of people with that tendency) possesses that tendency at the time of the offending and can be relied on in the same way as other evidence. But the first stage to that process is accepting the existence of a tendency at all. See further Redmayne, *Character* (n 14) 128ff.

[110] *Laughton v Shalaby* [2014] EWCA Civ 1450, [22]–[26] (Longmore LJ).

[111] There is a great deal of possible variation in and reasons for behaviour that may be taken into account in assessing the likelihood of action across points in time: see Redmayne, 'Relevance' (n 48) 689–90.

of B, C and D can still be relevant.[112] Part of the early resistance to similar fact evidence was based on a presupposition that because it could not be guaranteed that A acted in the same way towards B as A acted towards C, the similar fact evidence was not probative of the second event.[113] The mistake in this reasoning, and the subsequent basis for its rejection, was that propensity is not a measure of absolute conduct.[114] Requiring 'certainty' of action mistakes relevance for proof and sets a higher than necessary standard of proof.[115] A person does not always need to act in a certain way in a certain situation for a fact-finder to be satisfied that they nevertheless possess a propensity to act in that way.[116] This is consistent with the inductive principles that comprise legal reasoning. Inductive inferences cannot be, and need not be, immutable and therefore conclusive to be relevant.[117] It is the responsibility of the standards of proof, and in extreme cases like tendency evidence, admissibility rules, to control epistemic uncertainty, not relevance. It is enough for similar fact inferences that a rational person could conclude that A probably had a tendency to act in a particular way such that B's death is made more probable, to any degree, by C's death.

C. Similar Fact Rules

The historic similar fact rule prohibited the admission of evidence concerning the past or contemporaneous acts or states of mind of the accused that occurred separately to the instant dispute. Under the UEL, coincidence is prima facie admissible if the events are 'similar'. Tendency evidence has no such requirement, although *Hughes* demonstrates that there is an implicit requirement of similarity or connection between the events. Disputes arise over how far this scale can be pushed. As events become increasingly dissimilar, their predictive power for each other should, in theory, lessen. But, as discussed above, generalisations about character leave significant scope for highly dissimilar events to be used to impugn the general character of the individual. Because perceptions of magnitude and similarity are ultimately subjective, there is no easy resolution to the approach to similar fact evidence. That, in part, explains why statistical evidence has been so problematic.

[112] *Commissioner for Government Transport v Adamcik* (1961) 106 CLR 292, 303 (expert evidence need not be correct to be admissible); Heydon, 'Weight' (n 98) 225.

[113] Stone (n 7) 977.

[114] See *R v Handy* (2003) 213 DLR(4th) 385 (CanSC) [94]–[97]. This comports with a propensity probability perspective that the conditions that cause the events have 'a propensity to produce frequencies which are approximately equal to the [objective] probabilities': Gillies (n 13) 116.

[115] Redmayne, 'Relevance' (n 48) 690.

[116] Zuckerman (n 48) 190. Zuckerman says character is the aggregate of peculiar qualities which constitute personal individuality. As long as we believe human behaviour is not entirely arbitrary and unpredictable but dictated to some degree by the individual's mentality, character has both predictive force and probabilistic significance concerning a person's past acts or omissions. See also Acorn (n 32) 70–71.

[117] Ho (n 10) 137–38.

III. Inferential Structure of Statistical Evidence

Whereas similar fact evidence requires an assumption of continuance between A's conduct towards C and then B, the inferential gap in statistical evidence is between the observed occurrence in *n*, inferred to exist generally in *N*, and the purportedly similar occurrence in *p*. Linking *n* to *p* requires the acceptance of propensities and dispositions of traits and effects across populations.[118] Inductively connecting *n* and *p* relies on a 'leap of faith … that, because things have happened in a certain way, or have been observed to be a certain way in the past, they will continue to happen or be observed in the same way in the present and the future'.[119] If the fact-finder accepts the assumption of continuance, the statistical evidence is 'individualised' because the tendency itself is not separate by time, space and object but contemporaneous to the facts-in-issue.

This, it is argued, demonstrates the fallacy in the ongoing claim that statistical evidence can only ever be corroborative because it is not individualised.[120] Cohen claimed that on a mathematical account of fact-finding, a risk of injustice would lie against an individual because even though that person's circumstances placed them within a particular reference class, they may not in fact belong to that reference class.[121] That is, the statistical evidence might be insensitive and in fact contrary to the truth. He referred to this as the problem of negation. His solution to negation was to claim that under an inductive approach to fact-finding, adducing statistical evidence alone meant

> that there just is no inductive evidence against that particular man. So, if inductive probabilities are at issue, we can say quite simply that there is no evidence against him.[122]

Cohen's solution oversimplifies the nature of the inference from statistical evidence. Statistical evidence itself can be individualised by a propensity inference. Even though prima facie it concerns a population, it can be individualised by a process of reasoning. Once a propensity is constructed, it is no longer true that '[t]he different way other patients responded in a similar position [evidenced statistically] *says nothing* about how the claimant would have responded'.[123] Similar objections are made both in law and science, and appear to arise from the idea that

> statistical inference from the general to the specific is simply not something science can do. Statistical inference is a useful tool for describing average effects on populations …

[118] Gillies (n 5) 408.

[119] Acorn (n 32) 68–69, citing LJ Cohen, *An Introduction to the Philosophy of Induction and Probability* (Oxford, Oxford University Press, 1989).

[120] *Sienkiewicz* (n 64) [163]; *King* (n 2) [85]; G Turton, *Evidential Uncertainty in Causation in Negligence* (Oxford, Hart, 2016) 86.

[121] Cohen, *Probable* (n 48) 270.

[122] ibid 271; *McTear v Imperial Tobacco* [2005] CSOH 69 [6.180]–[6.184]; *Amaca v Booth* (2011) 246 CLR 36, 80 [118].

[123] *Gregg v Scott* [2005] 2 AC 176, 186 (Lord Nicholls) (emphasis added).

> But it cannot tell us whether a particular individual within that population suffered the effect in question from exposure or for some other reason.[124]

With respect, the statement is correct only if one assumes that legal proceedings are conducted in a vacuum and that statistical evidence is truly 'naked'. When the decision-maker comes to decide causation about *p*, they must form a belief that X caused Y. If there is statistical evidence that X causes Y, but no other evidence whatsoever, a fact-finder would be justifiably reluctant to find that the association between X and Y in *p* was causal. That does not mean that even in that scenario, statistical evidence cannot tilt the decision-maker towards causation. If there is evidence that *p* was exposed to X, and now has Y, it seems absurd to say that the population information does not inform what might have happened to *p* where *n* and *p* share salient commonalities. In some circumstances, the degree of connectivity between X and Y and *n* and *p*, may be so strong that a rational decision-maker could believe, based only on the population data, that X caused Y in *p*. The question turns on the strength and cogency of the propensity the evidence can establish. It is simply wrong, as a matter of logic and practice, to say that statistical evidence cannot, or should not, be used to justify inferences about causation in individuals. Indeed, there is an inherent logical tension in the claim that evidence can be admitted to establish associations between variables in populations but then cannot or should not also be used to establish those same associations in individuals.[125] If the law really is only concerned with specific causation, the only function general factual causation has is to support, or to be evidence of, specific causation. If a doctor testified that the evidence shows that X caused Y in *n*, but that there was no way in which X could be shown to cause Y in *p* from that evidence, both the statistics and the doctor's evidence should be irrelevant.

On that basis, epidemiology can 'by itself' support the existence of a condition in an individual.[126] If the question is 'did asbestos cause renal cancer', establishing that asbestos has a propensity to cause renal cancer is individualised evidence because it explains a particular trait of asbestos that is open to have eventuated in this individual. Likewise, the infamous conclusion in *US v Shonubi* that evidence of the quantity of drugs other Nigerian drug smugglers had swallowed was not 'specific' evidence of what the defendant swallowed is logically tenuous.[127] The probative value of the evidence to quantity may have been limited, but it is evidence logically capable of individualisation under certain conditions. A better characterisation would be that the evidence was 'insufficiently specific' as the basis

[124] E Beecher-Monas, 'Lost in Translation: Statistical Inference in Court' (2014) 46 *Arizona State Law Journal* 1057, 1077.

[125] Contra ibid 1062.

[126] *Seltsam* (n 2) [89] (Spigelman CJ) ('evidence of possibility, including epidemiological studies, should be regarded as circumstantial evidence which may, alone or in combination with other evidence, establish causation in a specific case'). Contra Beecher-Monas (n 124) 1076–77 and M Dant, 'Gambling on the Truth: The Use of Purely Statistical Evidence as a Basis for Civil Liability' (1988) 22 *Columbia Journal of Law and Social Problems* 31, 64.

[127] *US v Shonubi* (*Shonubi IV*) 103 F3d 1085, 1091 (2dCir, 1997).

for why it was specific was not revealed. Testimony from Nigerian drug smugglers saying that *x* amount was routinely swallowed may have pushed the evidence from the reference class towards being sufficiently specific, as that evidence may have revealed the indicia of a propensity connecting members of and those similar to the reference class.

If statistical evidence lacks any individuating capacity, no propensity inference will be possible, and the evidence must be irrelevant. Evidence of the cancerous properties of asbestos would be irrelevant if there was no evidence linking the victim to asbestos. If the evidence is relevant but not dispositive, it is no different from any other form of relevant but individually insufficient evidence. Statistical evidence can be evidence of possibility or probability;[128] it can be sufficient if the fact-finder believes it to be so. No principle of logic supports the claim that statistical evidence is necessarily insufficient once a propensity is established. Such arguments are a relic of the naked statistical evidence debates and should be rejected.

The division of similar fact evidence in *Hughes* into two levels of linkage and singularity works equally well to explain the process of generalising from statistical evidence.

A. Linkage (General Factual Causation)

Linkage identifies the factual basis for a propensity inference. In similar fact evidence, linkage is the connection between the similar facts that are said to give rise to a tendency. That connection might arise directly (for example, when adducing past proven offences), or indirectly under coincidence reasoning (A is more likely to have killed B because it is unlikely that B died coincidentally in similar circumstances to C). There must be some basis for believing the defendant committed or is associated with the similar acts to establish a tendency.[129]

In statistical evidence, linkage refers to the hypothesis X caused Y in *n*: general factual causation. Accepting that hypothesis invites an inductive inference either that X causes Y in absolute terms, or that X causes Y under those conditions and perhaps similar conditions. The established conditions where X causes Y are represented by *n*, which provides the platform for a tendency inference. Before any inference to *p* it must be shown that 'it was an accepted medical fact' X could cause Y 'in some cases'.[130] If such evidence does not exist, or the preponderance of evidence suggests that X does not cause Y, general factual causation fails.[131]

Linkage in statistical evidence is also based on degrees of magnitude and similarity in the statistical evidence, and are part of the general concept of robustness.

[128] cf *Seltsam* (n 2) [89]–[98].
[129] *Sutton* (n 28) 550–52.
[130] *Kay's Tutor v Ayrshire and Arran Health Board* (1987) SC (HL) 168 (Lord Griffiths).
[131] *Cubillo v Commonwealth* [1995] FCA 1749, [221]–[223], [319]–[320].

More instances of a statistical effect being found in the literature (Bradford Hill's 'consistency') will lend more credibility to the claim that there is a general causal principle in a state of nature. That is why meta-analyses are seen as the apex of proof of general causal laws in medicine and other disciplines. Likewise, the degree of similarity of the findings between those studies lends support to the existence of a causal phenomenon. Smaller reference classes mean the inference is more specific and controlled and therefore more likely to be accepted.

As a causal proposition, linkage cannot just be an associative or correlative relationship between X and Y. The fact-finder must actually believe, on the balance of probabilities, that X caused or materially contributed to Y.[132] A logical theory causally connecting X to Y is necessary. Similar fact evidence achieves this connection by holding the individual constant across various situations. A's association with the prior acts and the present act is explained by A's tendency to kill.

Statistical evidence is far broader. The ability to believe in general factual causation has been canvassed in chapter three. The mere existence of a statistically significant association between X and Y does not, ipso facto, establish a causal theory. But that does not mean that an association is not evidence of causation. Ultimately, the question returns to what the decision-maker is prepared to believe about causation based on the knowledge they bring to the process and the admissible evidence. Differences in the belief of the causal association between smoking and lung cancer or human carbon emissions and climate change are a product of different actors construing the evidence with different knowledge sets. Given the commonsense nature of causation, it is no surprise that the controversies these judgments provoke in popular discourse are replicated in legal decision-making. Failures of linkage or general factual causation explain why statistical evidence has failed to prove, or even be admissible for, facts-in-issue in legal proceedings.

1. Non-Existent Linkage

Linkage completely fails where there is no basis in the evidence to find that the causal proposition exists. Infamous examples of these failures, such as litigation asserting a causal association between certain vaccines and autism,[133] abound. In *Re Zoloft*, the plaintiffs alleged that the antidepressant Zoloft caused birth defects. The Court found, inter alia, that the epidemiological evidence adduced in support of general factual causation was insufficient because the availability of epidemiology showed very few statistically significant associations, and that there was inadequate repetition of those associations between studies.[134]

[132] eg *Strong v Woolworths* (2012) 246 CLR 182, [25]–[30]. The definition of causation does not change for criminal law (see *R v Pagett* (1983) 76 Cr App R 279 (CA) 288) but a higher standard of proof is imposed.

[133] eg *Blackmon v American Home Products Corporation* 346 FSupp2d 907 (SDTex, 2004).

[134] *Re Zoloft* 26 F Supp 3d 449, III.B (EDPenn, 2014).

But there are more complicated examples too that raise questions of principle of how judges approach linkage inferences in statistical evidence. In *Wal-Mart*, the Supreme Court of the United States declined to certify a class action under Rule 23(a) of the Federal Rules of Civil Procedure on the basis that the putative class lacked common issues of law or fact. Scalia J, for the majority, explained that commonality required

> a common contention – for example, the assertion of discriminatory bias on the part of the same supervisor. That common contention, moreover, must be of such a nature that it is capable of classwide resolution – which means that determination of its truth or falsity will resolve an issue that is central to the validity of each one of the claims in one stroke.[135]

The statistical evidence tendered in this case could not achieve this level of commonality. No 'pattern or practice of discrimination'[136] was established and '[w]ithout some glue holding the alleged reasons for all those decisions together, it will be impossible to say that examination of all the class members' claims for relief will produce a common answer to the crucial question "why was I disfavored"'.[137] As the statistical evidence could not identify a 'common mode' of discrimination, there was insufficient similarity to justify a claim between claimants that Wal-Mart policy had a tendency to discriminate in a particular way that gave rise to common questions.

Employment cases like *Wal-Mart* are further examples of the crossover between statistical evidence and kinds of similar fact evidence. The sample used in that case was group members in the litigation. Assuming that the statistics had been acceptable, the inference to be drawn was that because there was a pattern of discrimination in one sample of group members, all group members were prima facie discriminated against. For those group members not a part of the sample, the inference follows the traditional form of n to p where n and p are separated by time, space and object. But for those who were sampled, a putative circumstance is being used in support of the proposition directly and utilises a form of bootstrapping logic.

One controversial area where statistical evidence is introduced is in support of disqualification applications against judicial officers for 'reasonable apprehension of bias' (RAB). For RAB 'there must be an identification of what … might lead a judge to decide a case other than on its legal and factual merits and … an articulation of the *logical connection* between the matter and the feared deviation from a course of deciding a case on its merits'.[138] Even if evidence was capable of showing that a judge had a tendency to decide certain decisions in a particular way, that could not establish that this pattern was a product of unlawful decision-making. Such evidence is only relevant to RAB if the tendency demonstrates some unlawful conduct.

[135] *Wal-Mart* (n 76) 350.
[136] ibid 352.
[137] ibid.
[138] *ALA15 v Minister for Immigration and Border Protection* [2016] FCAFC 30, [36] (emphasis added).

This was precisely the problem with the statistical evidence tendered in *Vietnam Veterans' Assoc*, and more recently in *ALA15 v Minister for Immigration and Border Protection*. In *ALA15*, statistical evidence that the trial judge decided 99.21 per cent of cases against refugee applicants in favour of the Minister was regarded by the trial judge and on appeal as irrelevant to RAB. At first blush, this seems troubling. The evidence is clearly in the nature of similar fact evidence; prior acts of the individual are being used to prove that the individual is likely to make similar decisions in the future.[139] Usually the past acts of individuals are relevant to the probability of the same or a similar future act being performed. The applicant appeared to invite the court to draw such an inference – that it was improbable that a judge would show such marked one-sidedness against a particular class of applicants.

Nevertheless, the Full Court of the Federal Court of Australia (FCAFC) gave five reasons for the statistical evidence's irrelevance. Only one is important for present purposes: that even though the trial judge could be said to have a tendency to act, that tendency was not itself evidence of bias that would be reasonably apprehended.[140] Similar fact evidence typically (but not universally) ensures connectivity because the acts used to form the tendency are themselves illegal, for example, evidence of a tendency to commit sexual assault.[141] Or, if the prior acts are not illegal, the act that the tendency purportedly proves is illegal. It may not be illegal to research on the internet 'how to administer poison', but such evidence may be relevant to prove that an individual had a tendency to kill illegally by poisoning.

Even though a tendency to decide against applicants in *ALA15* was arguably a rational inference to draw,[142] merely deciding against applicants was not evidence of RAB. There could be any number of explanations for why the judicial officer's decisions fell in that pattern and the statistical evidence did not, by itself, give rise to any causal theory for the pattern that the trial judge was more likely to reject the

[139] Indeed, *BDS17* (n 18) concerned a similar application brought from a decision of the same trial judge on the basis of actual bias supported by coincidence evidence.

[140] Encapsulated by reasons 2 and 4: ibid [39], [41]. See also *Vietnam Veterans' Assoc* (n 24) 213.

[141] cf *Bauer* (n 98) [49].

[142] It should be noted that the FCAFC in fact held that the data the applicant relied on, the previous decisions, were themselves irrelevant to establishing RAB: *ALA15* (n 138) [44]. This appears to be because, first, the stage of dismissal of this appeal was different to that data (which was derived from dismissals at the first return date), and second, because a differently constituted FCAFC had ruled that the trial judge's method of dismissal at the first return date was invalid. Whilst these factors may discount the presence of a tendency, it is hard to see how they make past decision-making irrelevant. The cause of action concerned RAB in the proceeding as a whole, not the particular risk the decision would be dismissed at the first return date. The pattern as such holds irrespective of when the judge found against the prior applicants and, per *Hughes* (n 12), there is no need for the tendency to be identical in nature. Further, the presence of the 'corrective' decisions of the FCAFC do not undermine the thesis of a latent bias; it would be bizarre to say that evidence of past murders cannot be used to infer the probability of future murders merely because the defendant was punished for murder in the intervening period. This is a factor that may be taken into account in deciding whether the tendency in fact manifested in this case, but it does not undermine the relevance of the evidence.

applicant's case unlawfully on another occasion. The FCAFC rejected the factual inference that it was improbable that a trial judge would decide the overwhelming proportion of cases in one way without being biased.

ALA15 demonstrates some of the invidious problems of statistical evidence. The FCAFC here is rejecting a frequentist explanation of the evidence; simply because a judge has decided a number of cases one way does not justify the conclusion that the judge will decide the same way in the future and, importantly, that such decision would be unlawfully decided. Even so, it seems unnecessarily strident for such evidence to be irrelevant. The FCAFC appears to have committed the same error of principle warned against in *Hughes*: that 'it is not necessary that the disputed evidence [make the *factum probandum* more likely] *by itself*.'[143] The FCAFC's statement that 'raw statistics concerning the outcome of immigration matters which have been determined by the primary judge compared with other FCCA judges or the outcome of MRT-RRT decisions generally *does not necessarily* indicate prejudgment'[144] clearly falls afoul of that statement. Statistical evidence does not need to 'necessarily indicate prejudgment' to be relevant.

This was particularly problematic in *ALA15* because there were other factual matters that could rationally have provided the necessary contextualisation. The FCAFC also held that prior decisions of the FCAFC criticising the process adopted by the trial judge were irrelevant to the present proceeding.[145] Such evidence, if admitted, could have provided the context the FCAFC required, although it is highly unlikely that such evidence would have been 'sufficient' to meet the RAB threshold. It seems likely that the irrelevance decision in *ALA15* stems from the policy rationale articulated in *Vietnam Veterans' Assoc* that to allow this sort of evidence in would invite litigants to engage in 'judge shopping'.[146] By declaring it to be irrelevant, the FCAFC constructed a barrier against these applications. It is not necessary for present purposes to explore the basis for this rationale and the consequences of it. But the FCAFC's approach to, admittedly poor, statistical evidence demonstrates a theoretical inconsistency in the way courts approach linkage in statistical evidence.

2. *Weak Linkage*

Even if linkage can be established to some degree, the proposition that X caused Y may be very weak. In *Kay's Tutor v Ayrshire and Arran Health Board*, the House rejected on appeal a finding at first instance that the plaintiff's neurological deafness was caused by a penicillin overdose. Both courts rejected linkage on the bases that, first, there was no evidence in that case establishing that penicillin can cause

[143] *Hughes* (n 12) [40] (emphasis in original).
[144] *ALA15* (n 138) [39] (emphasis added).
[145] ibid [44].
[146] *Vietnam Veterans' Assoc* (n 24) 213.

neurological deafness,[147] and second, that a revision of the reference class to 'penicillin can cause neurological damage' from some scant evidence was simply too broad to be justified in the circumstances:

> [I]t is [in]correct to say that because [statistical] evidence shows that an overdose of penicillin increases the risk of particular types of neurological damage found in these cases that an overdose of penicillin materially increases the risk of a different type of neurological damage, namely that which causes deafness when no such deafness has been shown to have resulted from such overdose.[148]

Whereas in *Kay* the House rejected linkage due to the insufficient basis for concluding that neurological damage of the kind suffered by the plaintiff could have been caused by penicillin, that does not mean that all weak linkages will be insufficient. This raises two sets of considerations. The first, dealt with in the proceeding section, is how to infer singularity inferences from weak linkage. The second concerns whether it is appropriate to even ask that question given the potential minimal value the statistical evidence possesses.

Evidence of weak linkage and potential unreliability is still prima facie relevant. Relevance is assessed 'at its highest'. While the reliability of statistical evidence should be taken into account in its admissibility, presently it is not. Assessing the merits of that evidence is a question of weight for fact-finders. But there are procedural and cost consequences for allowing such evidence to be led. A great deal of controversy has arisen in the wake of this laissez-faire approach to, in particular, expert evidence relying on statistical evidence.[149] How these issues are to be balanced is argued in chapter two.

B. Singularity

Linkage establishes a causal proposition in *n*. If X can cause Y under *n* conditions, a framework for what possibly occurred in *p* is created. What type of causal relationship is needed depends on the substantive law in issue. For causation in tort, that framework may be sufficient by itself, or in conjunction with other evidence. But for certain specific exceptions to normal causation principles,[150] it is not enough just to demonstrate the capacity for X to cause Y generally, such that there was a risk that X caused Y in *p*. It must be shown that X actually caused Y in *p* to the standard of proof; the risk must have eventuated.[151] This too necessitates an absolute inference for relevance (*n* reveals something, however small, about *p*), and a graded inference for probative value (the degree of probative value

[147] *Kay's Tutor* (n 130) 167.
[148] ibid 172.
[149] See G Edmond, 'Against Oracular Pronouncement: A Reply to Heydon' (2015) 36 *Adelaide Law Review* 173.
[150] See ch 4, section II.
[151] *Seltsam* (n 2) [108]; *TC v NSW* [2001] NSWCA 380, [59].

n possesses in explaining the existence of *p*). Other substantive legal tests may adopt different standards of causation. Certain regulatory proceedings typically only require the identification of an increased risk of harm, rather than the eventuation of that harm.[152] Equally, there are special categories of causation in tort law where the cause of the injury cannot be established under ordinary principles, but would otherwise result in an injustice to the parties. In such cases, it is enough that the negligence 'materially increased the risk' of injury.[153] This section focuses on causation in civil wrongs because of the increased complexity in identifying causal propositions about past events. But the conclusions reached may be adjusted depending on the substantive causal questions in issue.

To explain the singularity (or 'G2i') inference in expert evidence, Faigman, Monahan and Slobogin distinguish between 'framework evidence' (evidence of general factual causation derived from group studies, or *n* to *N*) and 'diagnostic evidence' (the application of that group evidence to the individual, or *n* to *N* to *p*).[154] Singularity is the process of going from framework to diagnostic. One difficulty in proposing a distinction between framework and diagnostic evidence is how to meaningfully compartmentalise the different forms. It is accepted in US jurisprudence that experts can be confined to giving framework evidence only, and that any subsequent connecting inference is to be made exclusively by the decision-maker. But that claim turns a blind eye to the reality that in order for the framework evidence to be relevant at all, it has to comment in some way on what occurred in the individual.

Faigman, Monahan and Slobogin suggest that '[e]ven if framework evidence is admissible, extrapolation from it to the individual case may not be scientifically or legally justifiable'.[155] This suggests that framework evidence can be admitted even if an inference to the individual case cannot be made by the expert. With respect, that cannot be right. Experts may be prevented from drawing connecting inferences for fear of trespassing on the fact-finder's exclusive province; if an expert is in no better position to make that leap than the fact-finder, then expert opinion crossing the gap may be inadmissible.[156] But if an expert is entitled to give framework evidence, an essential component of that evidence is that it will have some bearing on the individual. At the very least it must be legally justifiable to extrapolate the framework to the individual case to some degree, even if the expert cannot explicitly draw that link. Otherwise, the framework evidence is irrelevant. Dividing expert evidence into framework and diagnostic categories is a prima facie helpful way of decoding what experts do in a courtroom. The reality of the inferential process, however, suggests that in order for framework evidence to be admissible it must have some diagnostic effect.

[152] eg *Cain v Australian Red Cross Society* [2009] TASADT 3, [386].
[153] *Sienkiewicz* (n 64) [243].
[154] Faigman, Monahan and Slobogin (n 3) 424. See also Beecher-Monas (n 124) 1080.
[155] Faigman, Monahan and Slobogin (n 3) 425.
[156] Albeit the relevant question is whether the evidence would be 'useful' even if otherwise traversing matters of commonsense: *Murphy v The Queen* (1989) 167 CLR 94, 112; UEL s 80(b).

Singularity between n and p (assuming that n is representative of N) is a necessary condition for a relevant tendency. Although n may be capable of demonstrating other tendencies, it is only those tendencies with sufficient connection to the present acts that are relevant. Singularity is also the product of assessing magnitude and similarity between the sample and the individual that is first performed by the gatekeeper (on the questions of relevance and admissibility) and then the fact-finder (for weight and proof). There are some differences in this process between similar fact and statistical evidence. Similar fact inferences are not empirical. No reliance is placed on evidence of recidivism and the empirical rationale for inferring from past criminal behaviour. Statistical evidence, by contrast, concerns the tender of evidence about the continuity of the variable of interest that is alleged to have been established empirically. The process of connecting n to p still involves an 'inductive' commonsense comparison and is thus exposed to heuristic processes.

1. *Magnitude*

For the singularity of statistical evidence, magnitude may not necessarily be inherent to the case at hand. Similar fact evidence draws its strength from the repetition of certain similar behaviours in an individual. Statistical evidence may be adduced to prove an event that only occurs in the individual once; for example, proof of the cause of cancer from epidemiological studies. Some cases may turn on the repetition of certain individual events that can be explained statistically, such as allegations of anti-competitive conduct, where proof derives not just from showing how a reference class of similar behaviour is anti-competitive, but also by the interrogation of individual transactions that fit the rubric created by inferences from the reference class.[157]

Class actions also serve as examples where specific causation can be bolstered by evidence of an outcome in multiple plaintiffs. Class actions are typically brought by individual plaintiffs on behalf of group members who have similar claims. Whereas the claim of the lead plaintiff is meant to be representative of group members (and so evidence from group members is prima facie unnecessary unless individual questions arise), the fact that more than one person has the same claim may provide the basis for inferences about causation, and influence the probability that the defendant engaged in wrongdoing. In much the same way that fraud in *Blake* was proven by the existence of multiple, similar claims,[158] causation in toxic torts cases can be influenced not just by epidemiological evidence, but by the higher incidence of cancers in a defined population that all share some feature that inculpates the defendant, such as employment or proximity to a contamination site. Larger than expected effects in a discrete population connected to a

[157] C Beaton-Wells, *Proof of Antitrust Markets in Australia* (Sydney, Federation Press, 2003) 270–72, describing the evidence relied on in *TPC v Australia Meat Holdings* (1988) ATPR 40-876 (FCA).
[158] *Blake* (n 58) 98.

particular location and event can give rise to an inference that the common situation is not coincidental.

2. *Similarity*

Evidence that logically demonstrates some similarity will be relevant, but, in the view of the fact-finder, may not be sufficient. In *King v Western Sydney LHN*, the plaintiff child developed foetal varicella syndrome contracted from her mother, who had become infected with varicella (chickenpox) while pregnant.[159] The plaintiff claimed that failing to offer her mother a vaccine was negligent and caused her syndrome. The principal evidence of causation was an observational study performed in Germany that reported the vaccine was successful in preventing the onset of chickenpox in 54 per cent of cases. On the question of specific causation, the trial judge and a majority of the NSWCA rejected the statistical evidence because, purportedly relying on *Seltsam*,

> [t]he essential question to be answered was 'what would have happened to Mrs King as an identified individual and not just what would have happened across a population?' That question was not to be answered simply by translating the scientific results to the legal test of causation, e.g., if on the [statistical evidence], 54 per cent were found not to have any varicella infection. General causation which was the only conclusion open on the [statistical evidence], whether adjusted or not, was only evidence of possibility and not probability …[160]

The trial judge and NSWCA accepted the statistical evidence was relevant; it was 'possibility' evidence that could be used as a framework for what might have happened. The trial judge and the NSWCA rejected that the evidence was sufficient for factual causation in the present case because 'it was by no means clear that the appellant constituted a "typical" member of the cohort on which the [statistical evidence] was based'.[161] The reasoning of the majority of the NSWCA was pervaded by a logical error that

> the statistical fact that a particular proposition is true of the majority of persons *cannot of itself* amount to legal proof on the balance of probabilities that the proposition is true of any given individual.[162]

That statement, despite the widely held belief in its truth,[163] is incorrect as a matter of logic[164] and on the current state of the law.[165] Or, at least, it overstates the objection. Statistical evidence derived from a sample may not, by itself, establish

[159] *King* (n 2) [2]–[4].
[160] ibid [85], summarising the opinion of the trial judge.
[161] ibid [138].
[162] *State Government Insurance Commission (SA) v Laube* (1984) 37 SASR 31 (SASCFC) 33 (emphasis added), cited favourably in *Merck v Peterson* (n 2) [106] and *King* (n 2) [136].
[163] Beecher-Monas (n 124) 1076; *McTear* (n 122) 6.180.
[164] A Broadbent, 'Epidemiological Evidence in Proof of Specific Causation' (2011) 17 *Legal Theory* 237, 245–47.
[165] *Seltsam* (n 2) [89].

a proposition in any individual, where the singularity inference fails, and the evidence is not generalisable at all. It is contrary to logic and the propensity basis on which such evidence is relevant to say that it cannot.

In *Medtel v Courtney*, the appellant contended that the respondent had failed to demonstrate that his pacemaker was 'unmerchantable' under s 74D of the Trade Practices Act 1974 (Cth) because even though it may have belonged to a category of pacemakers that were prone to a particular defect, that did not mean that his particular pacemaker was defective.[166] This was a 'failure of singularity' submission. The appellant at trial had demonstrated that the respondent's pacemaker had not failed and would not fail in the manner complained of.[167] The FCAFC rejected the failure of singularity submissions on the basis that unmerchantability had to be assessed at the time of the acquisition of the product and not necessarily in light of all the evidence presented at trial (albeit that such evidence is relevant to the question of whether the goods were merchantable).[168] As it was not known to the respondent at the time of the extraction that his pacemaker was not actually defective, the FCAFC considered that his loss was caused by the 'superadded risk of premature failure' that was believed to be present at the time.

The problem in this case, on the question of singularity, is how the FCAFC approached the evidence of defect in the respondent's pacemaker. The appellant had submitted evidence that the type of pacemaker first implanted into the respondent only had a 2 per cent risk of failure. In suggesting that such evidence was unhelpful in the circumstances, Branson J noted that

> the parties accept that s 74D(1) is concerned with the quality of the particular goods, or product, supplied to the consumer who seeks to recover compensation … It follows, in my view, that for the purposes of the subsection, it is not appropriate to attribute to Mr Courtney's pacemaker any qualities derived by statistical analysis of the total population … of pacemakers from which Mr Courtney's pacemaker came … while statistical analysis of the total population of pacemakers from which Mr Courtney's pacemaker came might show that pacemakers of that type have a 2% chance of premature failure, that analysis would *reveal nothing* about the quality of Mr Courtney's particular pacemaker.[169]

This dictum goes much further than what was necessary in the circumstances. The FCAFC had determined that the actual state of the pacemaker was, if not irrelevant, certainly not controlling of the outcome. By virtue of that finding, it was unnecessary for Branson J to consider whether or not the statistical evidence was capable of revealing anything about the respondent's pacemaker. Addressing the actual state of the respondent's pacemaker in this way reveals a fallacy about singularity and the means by which statistical evidence derives relevance towards proof of facts-in-issue.

[166] *Medtel v Courtney* (2003) 130 FCR 182, [28].
[167] ibid [40].
[168] ibid [38]–[40].
[169] ibid [58] (emphasis added).

Branson J's conclusion appears to rest on an assumption that all products that are otherwise identifiable parts of unified (and potentially uniform) class are nevertheless entirely separate and that no 'propensity' can connect them. This conclusion is reminiscent of Professor James' paint tin analogy that rests on a rejection of frequentism and fails to consider propensity. Branson J's reasoning appears to conflict with established authority that justifies the use of statistical evidence. *Seltsam* (decided before *Medtel*) explicitly recognises that statistical evidence can 'alone' amount to sufficient evidence of causation about an individual event from evidence derived from a class.[170] If a propensity can be established, statistical evidence is relevant to the individual and potentially dispositive. Branson J purported to deny singularity (in circumstances where singularity was otherwise unnecessary) and in so doing failed to consider a propensity approach to the use of the statistical evidence.

Her Honour's reasoning also appears to be contradictory. Branson J concludes that the trial judge's decision that the product was not merchantable was appropriate because '[the pacemaker] had the physical characteristic of having been manufactured with yellow spool solder'.[171] But that very conclusion was reached because the trial judge accepted that 'the background or random rate of failure … was substantially greater for' for pacemakers manufactured with yellow spool solder.[172] That is, the pacemaker was not merchantable because it had a greater risk of failure by reason of the rate of failure demonstrated by other, similarly manufactured pacemakers. Not only does that conclusion rest on a propensity account of the effect of yellow spool solder across the class of pacemakers, it relies directly on statistical evidence. No reasons are given for why the negative singularity inference about the total population failed, but the positive singularity inference about yellow spool solder succeeded. This apparently irreconcilable position has not been scrutinised – indeed the proposition that statistical evidence does not provide any evidence of the quality of goods is still construed as good law in eminent commentaries despite the contradiction in that finding.[173]

C. Synergism between Linkage and Singularity

The strength of the tendency propounded by linkage is an important factor in singularity. As this book has previously demonstrated, the strength of association between the variables of interest in n plays an important role in generalising from that relationship to p. The stronger the pre-existing tendency, the more likely the generalising inference can be made. In *Seltsam*, the plaintiff alleged, and the

[170] ibid [89].
[171] ibid [77].
[172] ibid [61], [75].
[173] R Miller, *Miller's Australian Competition and Consumer Law*, 45th edn (Sydney, Lawbook, 2023) 1672.

Dust Diseases Tribunal accepted at first instance, that his renal cell carcinoma was caused by his negligent exposure to asbestos at the defendant's workplace. The NSWCA reversed this finding of liability in the defendant's favour. It held that the trial judge had not sufficiently considered the state of the epidemiological evidence tendered at trial. This case is not a gatekeeper decision, but rather a de novo assessment of the evidence of causation by the appellate court. Nevertheless, it provides some insights into the mechanics of singularity inferences from statistical evidence.

Substantial expert evidence was tendered for and against the proposition that the plaintiff's renal cell carcinoma was caused by his exposure to asbestos. Those experts relied on epidemiological evidence that was inconclusive. Some studies showed an increased risk of renal cell carcinoma consequent on exposure to asbestos, but the majority showed no significant increase in risk.[174] Despite this weak effect, Stein JA found sufficient evidence for linkage so that the trial judge was right to conclude that asbestos could, in general, 'cause or materially contribute to renal cell carcinoma'.[175]

Spigelman CJ's language is more difficult to interpret. On the one hand, it could be argued that the Chief Justice denied linkage because 'the extent of increased risk indicated by all but one, or perhaps two, of the epidemiological studies is too small to justify an inference of causation'.[176] But Spigelman CJ qualified this statement. What could not be justified was an inference from the epidemiological evidence to causation in the 'individual case'. As the strength of association in the pre-existing tendency was weak or subject to doubt, a higher threshold of justification in the present case was required.[177] The degree of magnitude (Bradford Hill's 'consistency') in the empirical evidence was insufficient to justify an inference to the individual case without some further corroborative material, such as the presence of asbestos in the plaintiff's kidney.[178] Evidence that more closely tied the plaintiff to the hypothesis that *his* renal cell cancer was caused by asbestos was needed. *Seltsam* clearly shows the synergy between singularity and linkage. Had the evidence demonstrated a closer logical link between asbestos exposure and renal cell carcinoma shown by some studies, perhaps a tendency could have been formulated that would have encompassed the plaintiff.

D. Subjectivity of Singularity

Decisions about tendency inferences are neither inevitable nor objective. They are matters of judgement to be exercised by individuals. Individuality in

[174] *Seltsam* (n 2) [172].
[175] ibid [250] (Stein JA).
[176] ibid [174].
[177] Similarly, *Cubillo* (n 131) [247]–[321].
[178] *Seltsam* (n 2) [171].

decision-making is a key area of dispute for similar fact evidence. It is equally problematic for statistical evidence. The assessment of magnitude and similarity are subjective questions of 'logic and human experience' that necessarily differ from person to person.[179] Just like similar fact evidence, the problem for generalisation inferences is as much one of application as of principle.[180]

In an ideal world, probability could be calculated objectively if all possible variables impacting a particular decision were known ex ante. Controlling for all possible variables allows an individual to identify the fullest extent of the causal laws operating over a variable's tendencies of action and to objectively predict with exactitude the outcomes in individual cases. But it is highly improbable that all possible effects on a particular variable can be accurately identified and controlled for.[181] As a consequence, probabilistic interpretations about individual cases are based on partial understandings of causal laws and any predictions following from them are influenced by subjective factors.

The law accepts that reasonable minds can disagree over the existence or non-existence of facts and such disagreement does not negate the availability of justice.[182] This acceptance conflicts with the metaphysical certainty expressed by the definition of logical relevance in *Smith* that 'evidence is either relevant or it is not'.[183] Taken literally, that definition assumes that right and wrong answers to relevance questions exist as a matter of principle. Logical relevance appears to suggest that a bright threshold of similarity must exist. Identifying that threshold is effectively impossible due to the subjectivity in the assessment. The standard of relevance is 'rationality'; evidence is relevant if, as a matter of 'logic' and 'commonsense', the fact-finder believes it to be relevant. In light of the following point about standards of relevance, the most appropriate response would be for courts to adopt lenient assessments of relevance to avoid this conflict.

E. Standards of Relevance

Amaca v Ellis does not identify the consequences of the initial generalisation inference.[184] At the extremes of the singularity scale, the outcomes should be fairly obvious. If evidence is so dissimilar that no logical connection exists between the tendency in n and p's conduct, the evidence will be irrelevant. Equally, if

[179] Although there are facts and norms that a wide body of society may purport to know, generalisations made from commonsense reasoning relies ultimately on the 'stock of knowledge and beliefs' and experiences an individual holds and that may vary between individuals: Anderson, Schum and Twining (n 92) 277. See further Roberts (n 52) 158–59; J Edelman, 'Unnecessary Causation' (2015) 89 *Australian Law Journal* 20, 24 (there is no real commonsense basis to causation in fact).

[180] LH Hoffmann, 'Similar Facts after Boardman' (1975) 91 *LQR* 193, 196.

[181] Rothman, Greenland and Lash (n 31) 10.

[182] See *Vietnam Veterans' Assoc* (n 24) [26]; *HML* (n 28) 373 [73]. See also *Smith* (n 12) 653 [6], where the process of ascertaining relevance is described as involving 'nice questions of judgment'.

[183] *Smith* (n 12) 653 [6] (Gleeson CJ, Gaudron, Gummow and Hayne JJ); Roberts (n 52) 111.

[184] *Amaca v Ellis* (n 1) 134–36.

the evidence is so similar that it would be illogical to distinguish between it, the evidence will be both relevant and dispositive. Legal proceedings rarely concern such obvious questions of fact. The kind of inferences courts need to draw usually will involve degrees of dissimilarity between *n* and *p*. To what extent should gatekeepers be involved in regulating such evidence from the perspective of relevance?

Crucial to understanding how relevance should be assessed is identifying the scope of the inductive inference. One potential pitfall of the language used in *Amaca v Ellis* is an overreliance on the reference to relating the 'results of studies of populations to the particular case at hand'.[185] The exact conditions of *n* (as a representative sample of *N*) are important. But it would be a mistake to construe inductive inferences as only being permissible between two sets of identical facts. Induction takes an effect found in a segment of the population and attempts to extrapolate a generic causal law that applies broadly. Even though *n* represents the strongest case for the effect identified in the study, fact-finders are entitled to infer that the effect X caused Y can apply to situations other than *n* as long as the inference is rational.

Cases involving statistical evidence reflect the difficulties identified in similar fact evidence concerning the assessment of singularity. In *Merck v Peterson*, epidemiological evidence was tendered to support the allegation that Vioxx increased the risk of heart attack.[186] At trial and on appeal, the generalisability of that evidence to the individual was rejected:

> [T]here was a clear basis for concluding that Mr Peterson does indeed stand apart from the ordinary case. His personal circumstances [afforded] a ready explanation for … his injury independent of … Vioxx. The *strength* of the epidemiological evidence as a strand in the cable of circumstantial proof is *seriously diminished* by this consideration. The *epidemiological studies do not provide assistance* …[187]

The FCAFC was concerned by the number of pre-existing conditions the plaintiff suffered that also could have been concomitantly responsible for his heart attack.[188] One expert opined that heart attack could have occurred with or without the presence of Vioxx.[189] But the FCAFCs language does not make it clear on what basis it rejected the evidence. If the evidence had some weight, but ultimately was inconclusive in its own right in light of multiple other potential causes, that suggests it was evidence of possibility only and without more insufficient.[190] Evidence that is by itself insufficient is not, however, incapable of providing assistance. Evidence that cannot provide assistance is irrelevant. Only evidence that lacks any rational capacity to assist is irrelevant. The FCAFC appears to have accepted linkage, but the conditions in the present case were so far removed from

[185] ibid [62].
[186] *Merck* (n 2) 149.
[187] ibid 174 (emphasis added).
[188] ibid 163–64.
[189] Precluding Vioxx as a causative factor: see Edelman (n 179) 22, 24–25.
[190] *Luxton v Vines* (1952) 85 CLR 352, 360.

the statistical evidence that this tendency could not carry over to the plaintiff and denied singularity entirely.

It seems likely that the evidence in *Merck v Peterson* was treated analogously to *Laughton*. In *Laughton*, the CA determined that there was insufficient similarity between 'hip surgery' and 'knee, foot and wrist surgery' to justify a similar fact inference.[191] The CA treated the evidence as irrelevant. From a procedural standpoint it could not be declared irrelevant after receiving it into evidence as it '[added] nothing of any persuasive weight'.[192]

Laughton rested on identifying dissimilarity between surgical types. This is a matter of degree supported ideally by evidence, or in its absence, commonsense. If, on closer examination, the negligence was attributed to a particular technique or failing, it would be strange to conclude that the presence of that failing was irrelevant to its presence in another surgical context. As evidence was not adduced to explain the difference, another judicial officer may have been inclined to permit a tendency inference between the surgical types. To call the evidence irrelevant, that is, without rational connection, probably overstates the degree of dissimilarity. Both *Merck v Peterson* and *Laughton* may be the consequence of an excessive focus on the precise conditions of the similar fact or *n*, as opposed to other rationally available inferences from that evidence.

For the evidence in *Merck v Peterson* and *Laughton* to be irrelevant suggests a stricter standard than logical relevance was applied. In 1941, James promulgated the distinction between legal and logical relevance.[193] Logical relevance refers to the basic intellectual proposition that evidence can affect the assessment of probative value. Legal relevance incorporates various normative and legal standards into that process, for example, the degree of probative value or the cost of accepting the evidence. James eloquently and decisively argued against a legal relevance standard. The US, UK and Australia all purport to adopt logical relevance.

In 1971, Hoffmann, prior to his judicial career, promulgated a different view:

> [W]hen a lawyer says that evidence is irrelevant, he does not necessarily mean that it is incapable of having any probative value whatever. He always means that it is insufficiently relevant. [I]t shows that the degree of relevance needed to qualify for admissibility is not a fixed standard, like a point of some mathematical scale of persuasiveness. It is a variable standard, the probative value of the evidence being balanced against the disadvantages of receiving it such as taking up a lot of time or causing confusion.[194]

Hoffmann's definition (noteworthy because of its appearance in conjunction with a discussion of similar fact evidence) conflicts sharply with logical relevance. Despite the widespread acceptance of logical relevance, legal relevance subverts how courts construct the epistemic justification of similar fact and statistical

[191] *Laughton* (n 110) [26].
[192] ibid [28].
[193] James (n 40) 700.
[194] Hoffmann (n 180) 205.

evidence. Judicial officers appear to be applying a standard of sufficient rather than logical relevance. Practical consequences follow this approach;[195] courts declare similar fact and statistical evidence irrelevant despite the apparent conflict with the logical relevance standard.[196]

This temptation should be avoided. The moral and procedural concerns identified by Hoffmann that could justify the exclusion of evidence are more appropriately couched in rules of admissibility and should not be permitted to intrude and confuse how relevance is assessed.[197] The continuum of permissible intrusion for non-epistemic concerns would be difficult to identify and to replicate across fact-finders, making the fact-finding process even more subjective.[198] This problem is amplified by the general acceptance that questions of fact and relevance are the exclusive province of the trial judge, save where 'clearly erroneous'.[199]

Overturning relevance decisions is difficult and can have a substantial impact on the quality of the evidence ultimately tendered at trial. James noted that

> [v]irtually never would an appellate court be justified in reversing a trial judge for the admission of remote [that is, relevant but low probative value] but non-prejudicial evidence.[200]

There are a number of competing factors that make appellate assessment of relevance decisions difficult. Appellate courts can overturn erroneous fact-finding decisions made at trial.[201] But that step is seen as the exception rather than the rule because appellate courts cannot institute their own view of the facts in place of the original fact-finder, and it is generally accepted that trial courts are in a better position to assess the evidence.[202] As relevance is a question of logic rather than law, it is even more difficult to justify appellate intervention in a gatekeeper's view on relevance without reverting to opinion. By contrast, admissibility rules, such as the similar fact rule, are questions of law and a misapplication of such rules are a more appropriate question for appellate review.[203] Courts should exercise a great deal of caution in labelling evidence as irrelevant given the very low threshold of relevance and the availability of admissibility rules to achieve the same effect.

[195] Contra Heydon (n 83) fn 814.

[196] See *Phillips* (2006) 225 CLR 303, 318–19 and criticism in D Hamer, 'Similar Fact Reasoning in Phillips: Artificial, Disjointed and Pernicious' (2007) 30 *University of New South Wales Law Journal* 609.

[197] Coincidentally, a similar complaint is directed against Lord Hoffmann by Edelman J in relation to causation, where his Lordship is accused of 'extensive bundling of different rules within the nomenclature of causation': Edelman (n 179) 25.

[198] Roberts (n 52) 113–14.

[199] See *RTA (NSW) v Dederer* (2007) 234 CLR 330, [42]; *NSW v Ryan* (2002) 211 CLR 540, [53]–[55]; *Adamcik* (n 112) 308.

[200] James (n 40) 704.

[201] eg *M v The Queen* (1994) 181 CLR 487, 494; *Fox v Percy* (2003) 214 CLR 118, 126–28; *HML* (n 28) 381; discussion in *ACCC v TPG* (2013) 250 CLR 640, [32]–[33].

[202] *Chamberlain v The Queen* (1984) 153 CLR 521, 607.

[203] *Pfennig* (n 28) 515.

Conclusion

Generalisation objections to statistical evidence mirror the inferential process of similar fact evidence. Statistical evidence is 'individualised' if the gatekeeper accepts linkage and singularity. Statistical evidence that does not logically meet these factors is irrelevant. Objections in this field are difficult to resolve because the logic-based test of relevance is inapposite for regulation. Identifying the basis for relevance of statistical evidence as a tendency can introduce some common principles and consistency in reasoning that is currently lacking. There will always be individual differences and unsatisfactory decisions. But if the proper standards of relevance are adhered to, that is, evidence is relevant if it has any impact at all on the assessment of the probability of a fact-in-issue, where the errors have occurred should be more obvious. What follows from accepting the forgoing epistemic justifications of statistical evidence is how to assess the quantum of probative value and the consequent epistemic and moral prejudice that arises from doing so.

6

Prejudicial Statistical Evidence

Introduction

Statistical evidence used to prove facts about individual circumstances conjures dissonance in the minds of decision-makers. Scholarship about statistical evidence has historically focused on the role of dissonance in objections to the proof of facts from statistical evidence.[1] Scholarship has more recently tended to consider both the relevance and admissibility of such evidence, but usually in the absence of how the law in fact applies relevance and admissibility rules.[2] This book contends that dissonance underlies a bundle of objections arising at each level of the evidentiary process. It arises from an inability of the fact-finder to trust that the probabilities in the reference class (*n*) apply at all to the individual (*p*) and how those probabilities inform the probability of the event concerning *p*. This has its greatest effect during the assessment of the weight of the evidence and ultimately whether the evidence proves (in whole or in part) the fact-in-issue.

Evidence law does not usually regulate how fact-finders weigh evidence. It does not explain to the fact-finder the approach to take to evidence where probative value is uncertain. Evidence law, nonetheless, imposes a failsafe mechanism; where the gatekeeper forms the view that the evidence is likely to mislead or in fact misled the fact-finder in coming to a view that was not supportable by that evidence, the evidence may be declared 'prejudicial' and rendered inadmissible. This chapter seeks to articulate how statistical evidence might be prejudicial.

Perhaps due to the decreasing use of juries in the UK and Australia, and the lesser role played by an independent gatekeeper in regulating evidence, there has been limited consideration of how statistical evidence could be prejudicial under

[1] The literature frames this objection variously, with principles suggesting that statistical evidence is (a) effectively irrelevant despite the evidence being apparently logically relevant (R Wright, 'Causation, Responsibility, Risk, Probability, Naked Statistics, and Proof: Pruning the Bramble Bush by Clarifying the Concepts' (1988) 73 *Iowa Law Review* 1001); (b) necessarily inadmissible (L Levanon, 'Statistical Evidence, Assertions and Responsibility' (2019) 82 *MLR* 269, 271–72; A Pundik, 'Freedom and Generalisation' (2016) 37 *OJLS* 189); (c) conditionally admissible pending the admissibility of case-specific evidence (M Dant, 'Gambling on the Truth: The Use of Purely Statistical Evidence as a Basis for Civil Liability' (1988) 22 *Columbia Journal of Law and Social Problems* 31); or (d) some nebulous standard of reducing the weight of the evidence in the face of 'case-specific' evidence (L Tribe, 'Trial by Mathematics: Precision and Ritual in the Legal Process' (1971) 84 *Harvard Law Review* 1329), thereby extending the purview of evidence law into the weighting of evidence.

[2] eg, ZA Johnson King, 'Sensitivity, Safety and Admissibility' (2022) 200 *Synthese* 1.

the law of evidence. The usual practice in judicial reasons is simply to undermine its significance to the facts-in-issue. But that approach is problematic where statistical evidence is likely to be useful, or indeed essential, to the fact-finding process. If the pillars of evidence law are accurate and reliable decision-making and the appropriate allocation of error, statistics can provide a valuable contribution to that endeavour. That statistical evidence requires crossing an inferential gap does not necessarily mean it is inaccurate or will result in the erroneous allocation of the risk of error. Only if it can be shown that statistical evidence poses an *unacceptable* risk of undermining the fact-finding process should it be excluded.

Prejudice is the basis of the ex ante inadmissibility of similar fact evidence. Statistical evidence shares an identical inferential structure to similar fact evidence. It too may be (but often is not) excluded as prejudicial but there is no ex ante rule or presumption against statistical evidence, at least arising from its inferential structure. If statistical evidence is to be excluded from the corpus of evidence, it should be because of some identifiable prejudice that causes an unacceptable risk that the fact-finding process will miscarry.

To assess the theoretical and practical implications of prejudice arising from statistical evidence, first, this chapter will consider the basis for the inadmissibility of similar fact evidence for prejudice and the operation of the similar fact rule. This shows that prejudice is divided into two apparently distinct forms: epistemic (or 'reasoning') prejudice and moral prejudice.[3] Second, it will consider the basis of epistemic prejudice arising from statistical evidence. Epistemic prejudice is in fact a collection of different attacks on statistical evidence that may, or may not, demonstrate an 'unacceptable' risk of prejudice from the evidence. Third, it will consider the basis of moral prejudice from statistical evidence. Moral prejudice can be divided into two forms: moral influences on epistemic prejudice, and objections to evidence emanating from moral philosophy. This book argues that whilst moral considerations on epistemic prejudice warrant some consideration in determining prejudice, arguments from moral philosophy do not. Fourth, if statistical evidence can be potentially prejudicial, what kind of response is warranted? Should an ex ante rule operate to exclude statistical evidence subject to its probative value, or should the status quo remain and require an identifiable form of prejudice to warrant its exclusion?

I. Regulating Similar Fact Evidence

At first blush, evidence of a tendency constructed from data outside the space, time and object of the present can be (very) probative to present facts. That high degree of probative value is also the source of concern. Whereas past conduct seems instructive as to future behaviour, the inferential gap seems to undermine confidence that the probative value ascribed to that evidence is correct. Such inferences

[3] M Redmayne, *Character in the Criminal Trial* (Oxford, Oxford University Press, 2015) 33ff.

rely on a continuity of behaviours across time and space. Doubt about the accuracy of such an inference is manifested in evidence law as prejudice.

A. Prejudice and Probative Value

Prejudice arises from similar fact evidence by the risk that fact-finders may unjustifiably believe that the evidence was of more probative value than it in fact possessed.[4] In *DPP v Kilbourne*, Lord Simon stated the common law justification for the exclusion of similar fact evidence as 'not because it is irrelevant, but because its logically probative significance is considered to be grossly outweighed by its prejudice to the accused, so that a fair trial is endangered if it is admitted'.[5] The probability that the evidence can accurately represent the truth is outweighed by the risk that it does not. Lord Simon's concern for the endangerment of a fair trial was explained in *DPP v Boardman* as the belief that 'if it were generally admitted jurors would in many cases think that it was more relevant than it was, so that, as it is put, its prejudicial effect would outweigh its probative value'.[6] Of course, it is not the evidence as such that produces prejudice, but its use.[7] Similar fact evidence can be used for non-propensity purposes. If so, no inferential gap, and as such no prejudice from the inferential gap, arises.

There are two distinct forms of prejudice. Epistemic prejudice refers to the risk that the jury will overestimate the weight that can be attached to the tendency supposedly proven by way of similar facts.[8] This is characterised as a 'logical' error[9] from

> cognitive bias, amounting to an inclination observable on the part of most persons to overvalue dispositional or personality-based explanations for another person's conduct and to undervalue situational explanations for that conduct. The bias is towards over-estimating the probability of another person acting consistently with a tendency that the person is thought to have – of treating the person as more consistent than he or she actually is.[10]

Such prejudice (whether arising from similar fact evidence, statistical evidence or otherwise) is epistemic because it concerns the perceived inaccuracy of a

[4] *Hughes v The Queen* (2017) 263 CLR 338, [71]; *Festa v The Queen* (2001) 208 CLR 593, 603; *R v BD* (1997) 94 A Crim R 131 (NSWCCA) 139. See further discussion in D Hamer, 'Similar Fact Reasoning in *Phillips*: Artificial, Disjointed and Pernicious' (2007) 30 *University of New South Wales Law Journal* 609, 611–12; FL Stow, 'Evidence of Similar Facts' (1922) 38 *LQR* 63, 63; P Roberts, *Roberts & Zuckerman's Criminal Evidence*, 3rd edn (Oxford, Oxford University Press, 2022) 587 (for similar fact evidence, prejudice means 'contrary to the interests of the accused … [or prejudice] can also imply a detriment to accurate fact-finding').

[5] *DPP v Kilbourne* [1973] AC 729, 757C–D.

[6] *DPP v Boardman* [1975] AC 421, 456G–H (Lord Cross).

[7] A Palmer, 'The Scope of the Similar Fact Rule' (1994) 16 *Adelaide Law Review* 161, 169.

[8] ibid 169–70.

[9] ibid 170.

[10] *Hughes* (n 4) [72] (Gageler J).

fact-finder's belief in the 'truth'. There are at least two accounts in epistemology that could be used to identify a source of epistemic prejudice identified in the authorities: the notion that statistical evidence (or similar fact evidence) is 'insensitive' or that it is 'unsafe'. A belief is sensitive if the person holding that belief would not hold it if the belief was in fact false.[11] A belief is safe if person holding the belief could not 'easily' do so if the belief was erroneous.[12] There is presently a grand debate in the literature as to whether sensitivity, safety or neither can explain the nature of the epistemic objection to statistical evidence, and whether that debate concerns the sufficiency of the evidence or its admissibility.[13] Whilst that debate is interesting, it isn't necessary to resolve for the purpose of assessing prejudice arising from statistical evidence at law. It would oversimplify the approach to gatekeeping simply to say that evidence which is insensitive, unsafe, or both should be inadmissible, or insufficient for that matter. Sensitivity and safety are not of themselves criteria of inadmissibility,[14] but rather potential explanators of the existence of prejudice, which may in turn lead to the inadmissibility of the evidence. That is, what these debates can show is that evidence that is insensitive or unsafe can be epistemically prejudicial because both accounts may identify circumstances where a fact-finder's belief in the truth is potentially inaccurate.[15]

A belief from evidence infected by the cognitive bias identified in *Hughes v The Queen*[16] can be 'insensitive'[17] or 'unsafe'.[18] The evidence could be insensitive because in a close possible world where in fact the further alleged event did not occur, it still may be believed by reason of the alleged predisposition to act in that way.[19] The evidence could equally be unsafe because the person could easily believe that the predisposition was operating when in fact it was not.[20] For the determination of prejudice by a gatekeeper in assessing the admissibility of the evidence, what is key to that assessment is the probability of the fact-in-issue being potentially independent of the probability of the reference class. Insensitive or unsafe beliefs may be prejudicial, and therefore inadmissible, where the probability of the reference class assumes more importance in the proof of the fact-in-issue than it ought to have.

[11] D Enoch and L Spectre, 'Sensitivity, Safety, and the Law: A Reply to Pardo' (2019) 25 *Legal Theory* 178, 178.

[12] MS Pardo, 'Safety vs Sensitivity: Possible Worlds and the Law of Evidence' (2018) 24 *Legal Theory* 50, 52.

[13] See Johnson King (n 2) 4–5.

[14] ibid 18.

[15] For a discussion of the complementary nature of sensitivity and safety as forms of epistemic error from statistical evidence and inference, see G Gardiner and B Zaharatos, 'The Safe, the Sensitive, and the Severely Tested: A Unified Account' (2022) 200 *Synthese* 1, 19–20.

[16] *Hughes* (n 4).

[17] Enoch and Spectre (n 11) 207.

[18] Pardo (n 12).

[19] Gardiner and Zaharatos (n 15) 14.

[20] cf Johnson King (n 2) 5.

The authorities reveal a fundamental distrust of relying on past actions to support the existence of present behaviour.[21] Interestingly, empirical and scholarly research suggests that, at least with respect to recidivism of criminal conduct (where the most controversy around similar fact evidence arises) the risk of epistemic prejudice is overinflated, or at least contrary to the empirical realities that people do tend to behave consistently.[22] Despite that research, epistemic prejudice from similar fact evidence remains a key concern, especially in criminal proceedings.

Epistemic prejudice is not simply the product of a fact-finder deciding to give a certain weight to the evidence. The assignment of weight is a quasi-discretionary function of the fact-finder. Weight, irrespective of how much, cannot be an error in and of itself because the weight that is assigned by the trial judge cannot be varied subsequently only because another decision-maker has a different opinion on weight.[23] What can be erroneous is the process of weighing. When the process of weighing miscarries, then the weight assigned to the evidence can be erroneous and reviewable.[24] Epistemic prejudice arises from the ability of the evidence to produce a defect in reasoning about the evidence; for example, by the evidence assuming greater importance relative to other evidence in the proceeding. This line between an error of reasoning and mere disagreement in the weight assigned to a fact is far from clear and is perhaps more a question of degree than a true difference in kind.

Moral prejudice supposedly refers to a different kind of risk. In *Perry v The Queen*, Murphy J noted that similar fact evidence 'immediately conjures up a highly suspicious prejudicial atmosphere in which the presumption of innocence tends to be replaced with a presumption of guilt'.[25] Instead of being a flawed belief in the importance of the propensity brought about by a disconnect between belief and empirical reality, moral prejudice arises from the fact-finder's negative impression of the accused's character.

Whereas epistemic prejudice is the risk that evidence will be weighed erroneously, evidence can be morally prejudicial even though the evidence itself is weighed correctly. Moral prejudice flows from a potential rejection of the presumption of the innocence irrespective of any other evidence in the case.[26] As the focus is on the risk that something about the tendency will infect the minds of the fact-finders against the accused, Palmer suggests that this risk can only arise from 'morally repugnant conduct' of an individual.[27]

[21] eg *Makin v A-G (NSW)* [1894] AC 57 and authorities referred to at 61.

[22] M Redmayne, 'The Relevance of Bad Character' (2002) 61 *CLJ* 684; cf A Cossins, 'The Legacy of the Makin Case 120 Years on: Legal Fictions, Circular Reasoning and Some Solutions' (2013) 35 *Sydney Law Review* 731, 739–40, who complains that similar fact evidence (notwithstanding the empirical support) leads to heuristic reasoning.

[23] *Carr v The Queen* (1988) 165 CLR 314, 331.

[24] *Fox v Percy* (2003) 214 CLR 118, 127–28.

[25] *Perry v The Queen* (1982) 150 CLR 580, 593.

[26] *Sutton v The Queen* (1984) 152 CLR 528, 545.

[27] Palmer (n 7) 171.

B. Similar Fact Rules

How to balance the potentially highly probative force of similar fact evidence against any potential prejudice is a controversial topic in Australian evidence law.[28] It is not, however, necessary to canvass the debate around similar fact evidence here. In evaluating the appropriate forms of regulation of (the inferentially similar) statistical evidence, this work uses the currently settled approach to similar fact evidence. There are also now sufficient jurisdictional differences between Australia and the UK to evaluate the operation of different approaches.

The Uniform Evidence Law (UEL) reforms in Australia converted the common law similar facts approach to the contentious[29] division between tendency[30] and coincidence evidence,[31] described in chapter five. Tendency and coincidence evidence are inadmissible unless notice is provided and the evidence has 'significant probative value'.[32] Significant probative value is not defined, but it is usually taken to mean something more than mere relevance.[33] How relevant the evidence must be is also the subject of some debate.

Criminal trials introduce an additional hurdle. If the prosecution wishes to rely on tendency or coincidence evidence against an accused, the probative value of the evidence must 'substantially outweigh any prejudicial effect' on the accused.[34] Codifying the approach to similar fact evidence in this way broadly reflects the development of the common law approach to similar fact evidence.

Despite the UEL definition, prejudice is not a static 'all-or-nothing' concept. It is a matter of degree. All evidence, whether similar fact or not, presents a risk of error through misconstruing the 'true' weight of the evidence. Any risk of such error is a form of prejudice. The question is at what point does mere risk of error give rise to prejudice justifying intervention? Judges have a great deal of (necessary) latitude in setting the threshold for when and how prejudice ought to be considered unacceptable.

[28] eg *R v Bauer* (2018) 266 CLR 56; *IMM v The Queen* (2016) 257 CLR 300; *TL v The King* (2022) 275 CLR 83.

[29] See D Hamer, '"Tendency Evidence" and "Coincidence Evidence" in the criminal trial: What's the Difference?' in A Roberts and J Gans (eds), *Critical Perspectives on the Uniform Evidence Law* (Sydney, Federation Press, 2017).

[30] s 97(1) ('Evidence of the character, reputation or conduct of a person, or a tendency that a person has or had … to act in a particular way, or to have a particular state of mind').

[31] ibid s 98(1) ('Evidence that 2 or more events occurred … to prove that a person did a particular act or had a particular state of mind on the basis that, having regard to any similarities in the events or the circumstances in which they occurred, or any similarities in both the events and the circumstances in which they occurred, it is improbable that the events occurred coincidentally').

[32] ibid ss 97(1)(a)–(b), 98(1)(a)–(b).

[33] *IMM* (n 28) [103]; *Hughes* (n 4) [215]; *R v Zhang* (2005) 158 A Crim R 504, [33], all citing *R v Lockyer* (1996) 89 A Crim R 457 (NSWSC).

[34] UEL s 101.

The UK approach to evidence is more laissez-faire. For civil trials, the standard for the admissibility of similar fact evidence now appears to be relevance.[35] For criminal trials, s 101(1) of the Criminal Justice Act 2003 provides for a series of alternative 'gateways'[36] for the admissibility of evidence of a defendant's 'bad character'; for example, at (c), that the evidence is 'important explanatory evidence', or, at (d), 'relevant to an important matter in issue between the defendant and the prosecution'. Admission under s 101(1)(d) is qualified by a requirement under (3) that the 'admission of the evidence would have such an adverse effect on the fairness of the proceedings that the court ought not to admit it'. Although this formulation sounds like a radical departure from the common law weighing exercise, and judicial officers have been at pains to explain that difference,[37] there remains a marked similarity in the reasoning process for evaluating the admissibility of the evidence. First, the evidence must be more than merely relevant. Second, if the evidence could render the trial unfair, it should be rejected. The 'adverse effect' in s 101(3) traverses substantially identical territory to the common law's 'prejudicial effect'. The difference lies in the breadth of the inquiry. Prejudice is limited to risk of error that causes unfairness and the potential miscarriage of justice. The Criminal Justice Act 2003 is arguably broader. Focusing on unfairness allows for factors beyond prejudice that could cause the trial to miscarry.

Although the similar fact rules are designed to assess prejudice arising from the inferential gap, their scope is limited. Such rules only exist in respect of a person's 'character', inferred from their actions or mental state. Evidence about non-human character tendencies are not covered by the similar fact rule. Evidence of the manufacturing process of pacemakers can be adduced to prove that a type of pacemaker was manufactured with defective materials (being evidence of a general circumstance), and that one such defective pacemaker was probably inserted into a particular individual (being a specific circumstance). The generic evidence is not prima facie inadmissible even though inferring the defective nature of the individual pacemaker requires an inductive step across the inferential gap and an assumption of continuance about the defective nature of the manufacturing process across all pacemakers of the impugned type.[38] Even so, this inferential structure is identical to similar fact evidence. Epistemic prejudice can arise from that structure. The perception of the risk of error, being a potential error in the degree of probative value to be assigned to the evidence, equally arises from the evidence regardless of the subject being human or non-human.[39]

[35] *O'Brien v Chief Constable of South Wales Police* [2005] 2 AC 534 (HL) [53], and discussion in H Ho, 'Similar Facts in Civil Cases' (2006) 26 *OJLS* 131, 139.

[36] Redmayne, *Character* (n 3) 145.

[37] *R v Chopra* [2007] Cr App R 16 (CA) [12]; see also Redmayne, *Character* (n 3) 148–52.

[38] cf *Medtel v Courtney* (2003) 130 FCR 182 (FCAFC); *Seeley International v Jeffrey* [2013] VSCA 288, [109].

[39] Although the focus of this work is statistical evidence, for the purpose of this chapter at least, the principles espoused apply equally to statistical evidence and individual (or case studies) of non-human similar facts.

In the absence of a rule of admissibility for statistical evidence, courts concerned by a risk of error from statistical evidence tend to discount or disregard statistical evidence, often in favour of non-empirical and anecdotal conclusions drawn from (limited) personal experiences.[40] Only rarely is the admissibility of statistical evidence directly considered. In part, this is because statistical evidence is usually adduced only in support of expert opinion and not admitted in its own right.[41] Little attention is paid to the ability of the statistical evidence to prove facts-in-issue directly, even though the expert opinion may be exclusively derived from the statistical evidence. The exception was, for some time, DNA evidence. Now, however, objections to the admissibility of DNA evidence rarely focus on the nature of the inference and the probabilities associated therewith, as opposed to the soundness of the match conclusions.[42]

There is utility in considering the admissibility of statistical evidence by examining the risk of error in fact-finding from such evidence. Even if the evidence is admissible despite its prejudice, risk of error is a factor that must be taken into account in establishing fact and credit weight. Understanding how statistical evidence might be prejudicial can inform what considerations need to be taken into account when it is weighed and will highlight points of weakness and strength. That, in turn, may help guide judicial officers in making decisions, and lawyers in preparing evidence for trial, in understanding the key areas of dispute about statistical evidence.

II. Epistemic Prejudice

Similar fact evidence uses assumptions of constancy about character as the vehicle for crossing the inferential gap. Statistical evidence tries to bridge the gap by using empirical analyses of the relationships between variables to demonstrate 'constancy' of certain variables across conditions. The probative value of the evidence is derived by comparing those conditions to ascertain their similarity to the case at hand. A risk remains, as the effect in the population may not carry over to the individual case meaning that the degree of belief in constancy is wrong. Epistemic prejudice from statistical evidence is the risk that *n* assumes a disproportionate role in the minds of the fact-finder in proving *p* by reason of the evidence's insensitive or unsafe nature. How to understand this risk of error from the perspective of evidence law is a question of degree. Where there is no connection, the evidence is irrelevant in inferring to the individual. Assessing the degree of connection thereafter is a fact-finding function that evidence law does not usually interfere with. But, if the evidence poses a risk that this assessment

[40] See ch 1.
[41] See I Freckelton, *The Trial of the Expert* (Oxford, Oxford University Press, 1987) 120.
[42] cf arguments in *R v GK* (2001) 53 NSWLR 317 (NSWCA) [35]–[61] and *Pfennig v The Queen* [2017] SASCFC 26, [51]ff.

of probative value could be overvalued because of some fault in the inference, evidence law may exclude that evidence as prejudicial.

Misplaced or undue reliance on statistics appears to arise from at least four interrelated and potentially contemporaneous reasoning processes. First, that *n* is an inappropriate basis for making findings about *p* (appropriate basis prejudice). Second, that the probability of *n* will be construed erroneously as the probability of *p* (compression prejudice). Third, the probability of *n* is given greater prominence than other evidence about the existence of *p* (inflated value prejudice). Fourth, the probability of *n*, especially when that probability is extremely high, may disguise defects in how the probability of *n* was calculated with respect to its generalisability to *p* (incredible coincidence prejudice). Each of these processes arises from the inferential gap between the fact to be proved and the evidence adduced to prove it. That in turn increases the risk that the evidence is insensitive or unsafe. Just because evidence is insensitive or unsafe does not in and of itself mean that the evidence is so prejudicial that it warrants exclusion. What still has to be determined, at least in respect of the law of evidence and the identification of prejudice, is what impact on the fact-finding process may manifest from the insensitive or unsafe nature of the evidence.

A. Appropriate Basis Prejudice

Appropriate basis prejudice arises from the widely expressed idea that fact-finding from statistical evidence is dangerous or causes an affront to the legal system.[43] It is argued that fact-finding about individuals should be based on evidence that is directly about those individuals, and not derived from sources outside the time, space and object of the issues under consideration.

Underlying this fear of fact-finding from statistical evidence is the idea that statistical evidence is 'flimsy' and lacking in Keynesian weight, that is, the 'relative completeness of the evidence, [and] the extent to which the evidence address important inferential questions that are raised by competing hypotheses'.[44] Even though statistical evidence may have substantial probative value in the proof of *p*, when put into the context of making a decision about *p*, it can leave a lot of specific questions about *p* unanswered.

Flimsiness is a particular issue for naked statistical evidence. Meyerson gives the example of the 'Prisoner One' hypothetical.[45] There are 25 prisoners in a yard. The evidence shows, and a fact-finder would rationally believe beyond a

[43] Of the many proponents of this thesis, see C Nesson, 'The Evidence or the Event? On Judicial Proof and the Acceptability of Verdicts' (1985) 98 *Harvard Law Review* 1357.

[44] D Nance, 'The Weights of Evidence' (2008) 5 *Episteme* 267, 268. Wasserman describes Keynesian weight as 'resilient odds': D Wasserman, 'The Morality of Statistical Proof and the Risk of Mistaken Liability' (1991) 13 *Cardozo Law Review* 935, 938.

[45] D Meyerson, 'Risks, Rights, Statistics and Compulsory Measures' (2009) 31 *Sydney Law Review* 507, 515ff.

reasonable doubt, that 24 prisoners were involved in an altercation with a guard who was murdered. One prisoner had no involvement. There is no way to separate the uninvolved prisoner from the guilty prisoners, assuming all protest their innocence. Probabilistically, there is a 4% chance that any one prisoner was not involved, and a 96% chance that any one prisoner was involved. Is that probability high enough to justify a conviction for murder or liability for some civil wrong when at least one such finding would be wrong? The problem of flimsiness is manifested by the absence of knowledge about other factors that might be relevant; such as one of the prisoners being imprisoned for non-violent offences. As those facts are not in evidence, only the probabilities based on membership of a particular class are available.

Class membership evidence raises legitimate concerns about appropriate basis prejudice because the salience of the evidence of class may be de minimus. In Prisoner One, there must be sufficient evidence supporting the conclusion that one prisoner did not participate. If no further evidence is proffered, that is a rational basis upon which to say that any individual prisoner taken in isolation did not commit the offence. To secure a conviction, the prosecution must find additional evidence. The obligation to put forward contradictory evidence would be reversed for civil liability; as the probability that any one person committed the act is substantially above the balance of probabilities threshold, any one individual may produce additional evidence seeking to offset or discount the probabilities that they were in fact involved.

Appropriate basis prejudice arises for criminal liability from Prisoner One because a fact-finder may decide to convict regardless of the rational possibility of innocence. That is, the probability of guilt reflected by the evidence is insufficient for the purpose to which it is adduced. By contrast, compression prejudice does not arise. It is true that the fact-finder is assuming that the probabilities in the population (the 25 prisoners) hold true for the individual (a 96% chance of guilt). What distinguishes Prisoner One, and other paradigms of naked statistical evidence, is that the individual is ipso facto a member of the sample; that person is one of the 25. The probability based on that evidence is, therefore, 'correct'.

Appropriate basis prejudice does not arise for civil liability. The burden of proof in civil cases has been met by the party adducing the evidence, assuming the naked statistical evidence paradigm. The chance of inflated value prejudice, insofar as the probabilities may overbear any other evidence adduced in favour of innocence, however, remains very real.

This book later provides a rationale for the problems raised by the flimsiness of naked statistical evidence.[46] For this chapter, it is acknowledged that naked statistical evidence is a poor basis for making judgements about the generalisation objection to statistical evidence, but just because evidence is flimsy does not necessarily mean it is erroneous or unhelpful. An increase or decrease in Keynesian

[46] See ch 7, section III.

weight may be entirely independent of the probative value of the evidence.[47] Flimsy evidence will only be considered prejudicial if it also presents a risk of the probative value being assigned to the statistical evidence being wrong. Keynesian weight may be a marker for that analysis, but in and of itself it does not give rise to prejudice of the kind the law is ordinarily concerned with.

Flimsiness may purportedly be offset by 'case-specific evidence'. Adducing additional evidence in support of a proposition will, as a matter of logic, discount the risk that some evidence of that proposition is wrong, because the overall probability the proposition is true is improved. Care should be taken to avoid assuming that this logical paradigm is interpreted as a rule that statistical evidence is only admissible with case-specific evidence. Such a rule rests on an assumption that no case-specific evidence is already in evidence. Statistical evidence cannot be relevant unless there is case-specific evidence to give it context. Any so-called rule about case-specific evidence would therefore be a rule about the sufficiency of the case-specific evidence that has been adduced. Such a rule is unnecessary as the degree of appropriate basis prejudice will depend greatly on the evidence that is adduced, the facts to be proved, and the connection between them. A hard and fast rule requiring 'sufficient' case-specific evidence is immaterial to resolving flimsiness. A better formulation is to require gatekeepers to consider the potential for appropriate basis prejudice, and to make a determination based on the evidence and facts at hand.

As demonstrated in chapter five, the distinction between case-specific and statistical evidence has no real meaning for propensity. Requirements for case-specific evidence are otiose. Flimsiness may contribute to dissonance, but it does not by itself warrant a finding that evidence lacking in Keynesian weight is prejudicial. The real issue is whether flimsiness contributes to a risk of error in the assessment of the probative value of the evidence.

B. Compression Prejudice

In the process of inferring the probabilities about p, it is necessary to revise the probability of n in light of the specific circumstances of p. Failing to so could result in an over (or under) estimation of the probative value of the statistical evidence to p. Gold draws a distinction between 'belief probability' and 'fact probability' in proof of causation.[48] Belief probability is the degree of probability the fact-finder assigns to the evidence against the standard of proof; the probability of p. Fact probability is the objective probability expressed by the evidence that is independent of any belief by the fact-finder; the probability of n. Gold's

[47] Nance (n 44) 268.

[48] S Gold, 'Causation in Toxic Torts: Burdens of Proof, Standards of Persuasion, and Statistical Evidence' (1986) 96 *Yale Law Journal* 376, 383.

hypothesis was that, especially in toxic tort cases where non-statistical evidence of causation was scant or even non-existent, fact-finders had collapsed the belief and fact probabilities such that it was sufficient to prove causation based on the objective probabilities alone.[49]

Collapsing of the type referred to by Gold is a well-known risk of using statistical evidence.[50] Gold suggested that the result of collapsing the belief and fact standard would be that fact-finders may focus on the statistical evidence to the exclusion of other evidence,[51] and that courts would adopt a rigid focus on the underlying probabilities.[52] Both of these concerns are direct consequences of failing to appropriately account for the statistical evidence in light of the other evidence in the proceeding, and potentially gives rise to a form of epistemic prejudice.

Some caution needs to be exercised when considering Gold's hypothesis as a basis for epistemic prejudice. Failing to take into account the differences between *n* and *p* before assessing the probability of *p* is an error, and evidence that poses a risk of such is potentially prejudicial. But that should not lead to a conclusion that the probability of *n* cannot inform the probability of *p*, or that such excessive caution should be used before relying on statistical evidence that it is effectively disregarded. Lord Dyson in *Sienkiewicz v Greif* stipulated that there is no reason why fact-finders could not 'infer belief probability from fact probability'.[53] This mirrors the conclusion this book draws concerning the use of objective probabilities in chapter seven. As long as there is no basis for contradiction, or the evidence is generalisable by way of a propensity of causation, there is no reason why statistical evidence cannot be used to prove specific events.[54] Fact probability, in whole or in part, can be the basis for belief probability. Before belief probability can be settled, the fact-finder must perform their duty of considering the fact probability against the other fact probabilities in the proceeding, whether statistical or not. There are two well-known examples of the manifestation of this compression prejudice: the idea that epidemiology demonstrating a 'doubling of risk' amounts to proof of specific causation in *p*, and, by a true error in the reasoning process, the 'prosecutor's fallacy'.

1. *Epidemiology and Doubling of Risk*

Relative risk (RR) measures the likelihood that a contagion caused a disorder against the probability that the disorder was due to something else.[55] It is neither

[49] ibid 385–86.
[50] eg *R v Karger* (2002) 83 SASR 135, [11].
[51] Gold (n 48) 392.
[52] ibid 390.
[53] *Sienkiewicz v Greif* [2011] 2 AC 229 (UKSC) [222].
[54] A similar sentiment was expressed by Spigelman CJ in *Seltsam v McGuiness* (2000) 49 NSWLR 262 (NSWCA) 276.
[55] See ch 2, section II.A.

an absolute measure of incidence in the general population, as the inference from the sample to the population is inductive, and nor does it represent the precise probability of specific causation in *p*.[56] RR is, however, evidence of both of those things. It would be wrong, and an example of compression prejudice bearing fruit, for a fact-finder to assume that any RR derived from statistical evidence represents the probabilities of causation in an individual; unless, of course, the fact-finder turned their mind to the probability of *p*, decided that the statistical evidence was directly and absolutely representative of *p*, and had a rational basis for doing so. The approach adopted by Australian courts is outlined in *Seltsam v McGuiness*, where RR and effect size generally is correctly identified as a significant piece of statistical evidence, but not an overbearing one, especially on the subject of admissibility.[57]

Seltsam nonetheless leaves one important question begging: what if the fact-finder is unsure how to construe the probability of *n* by reference to the factual milieu to come to a conclusion about the probability of *p*? What evidence should be adduced to explain that probability, and what sources can the fact-finder consult? Without that information and given the clear risk of misconceiving what RR means, there remains a risk that the evidence will not be appropriately used.[58] The function of the gatekeeper ends once it is determined that the prejudice does not outweigh the probative value of the evidence. But there remains a risk of compression prejudice even after the gatekeeper has determined that such prejudice does not outweigh its probative value (if that is the test to be employed). If the evidence is nevertheless permitted, that risk of error is in no way ameliorated.

2. *Prosecutor's Fallacy*

Forensic evidence of identification does not follow the same inferential pathway as generalisations from statistical evidence.[59] Generalisations from forensic evidence are between the sample and the population, rather than the individual. The fallacy of 'transposing the conditional', or 'false positive inversion',[60] commonly referred to as the prosecutor's fallacy,[61] appears to collapse the probabilities about *n* (being the product of statistical generalisations) into the probability of *p* without paying regard to the fact that the probabilities attaching to an individual are distinct from

[56] A Broadbent, 'Epidemiological Evidence in Proof of Specific Causation' (2011) 17 *Legal Theory* 237, 246 (statistical evidence is relevant to, but not the same as, the probability of specific causation).

[57] *Seltsam* (n 54) [137].

[58] A Dawid, D Faigman and S Feinberg, 'Fitting Science Into Legal Contexts: Assessing Effects of Causes or Causes of Effects?' (2014) 43 *Sociological Methods Research* 359, 369.

[59] See ch 4, section IV.A.

[60] C Dahlman, 'A Systematic Account of Probabilistic Fallacies in Legal Fact-finding' (2024) 28 *International Journal of Evidence & Proof* 45, 52.

[61] See N Fenton and M Neil, 'Avoiding Probabilistic Reasoning Fallacies in Legal Practice using Bayesian Networks' (2011) 36 *Australian Journal Legal Philosophy* 114, 120.

probabilities about samples or populations.[62] *Doheny & Adams* describes the reasoning process amounting to the prosecutor's fallacy as:

1. Only one person in a million will have a DNA profile which matches that of the crime stain.
2. The defendant has a DNA profile which matches the crime stain.
3. Ergo there is a million to one probability that the defendant left the crime stain and is guilty of the crime.[63]

Put another way, the prosecutor's fallacy is the risk that the fact-finder will transpose the probability that a random person is the source of the DNA sample with the probability that the person of interest committed the crime because they were the source of the DNA sample.[64] In so doing, the fact-finder has disregarded the proper use of forensic evidence of identification. *Doheny & Adams* demonstrates the real risk of the prosecutor's fallacy is that a conclusion by the fact-finder of the probability of a match in DNA evidence becomes the probability of guilt of the accused, and, by extension, to the exclusion of or overwhelming other evidence.[65] In cases like *Pfennig v The Queen*,[66] where the probabilities expressed by the DNA are in the trillions, transposing the conditional would result in a fundamentally flawed reasoning process.

The prosecutor's fallacy is not so much a failure of statistical inference but of reasoning heuristically. Fact-finding that is pervaded by the prosecutor's fallacy will necessarily overinflate the importance of the forensic evidence. DNA evidence can be highly probative because there is cogent empirical support for the view that it is very unlikely that a match would be found unless the matching individual was responsible for leaving the evidence collected from the crime scene. By itself, however, the probability of a match is not the same as a probability of guilt.

The problem becomes far more acute where there are doubts about the reliability of the forensic evidence. At its worst, the prosecutor's fallacy could lead a fact-finder fundamentally astray in assessing the probabilities of a fact-in-issue. This is a particular risk for Australian proceedings as Australian courts are far more permissive of the use of likelihood ratios and random match probabilities in DNA evidence than, for example, the UK.[67] Indeed, subject to any particular issues arising in the case at hand, Australian courts have generally held that it is unnecessary to provide specific directions about the use of DNA or statistical

[62] R Eggleston, 'Similar Facts and Bayes Theorem' (1991) 31 *Jurimetrics* 275, 284.

[63] *Doheny & Adams* [1997] Cr App R 369, 373; adopted by the HCA in *Aytugrul v The Queen* (2012) 247 CLR 170.

[64] A Ligertwood, 'Avoiding Bayes in DNA Cases' (2003) 77 *Australian Law Journal* 317, 318; P Donnelly and DJ Balding, 'The Prosecutor's Fallacy and DNA Evidence' (1994) *Criminal Law Review* 711, 716.

[65] C Adam, *Forensic Evidence in Court* (Hoboken, Wiley-Blackwell, 2016) 100; D Hodgson, 'A Lawyer looks at Bayes' Theorem' (2002) 76 *Australian Law Journal* 109, 114.

[66] *Pfennig* (n 42) [242].

[67] cf *R v T* [2011] Cr App R 9 (CA) (expert not permitted to use likelihood ratios in expert opinion); *R v Volpe* [2018] VSC 796, [63]ff.

evidence to avoid transposing the conditional.[68] Equally, Australian courts have considered and rejected the proposition that DNA evidence is ipso facto prejudicial by reason of this risk,[69] but can be otherwise prejudicial depending on the circumstances.[70]

Consideration of the prosecutor's fallacy is mainly confined to appeals from the adequacy of warnings and not from the commission of the prosecutor's fallacy itself. That is hardly surprising when DNA evidence is commonly adduced before juries who do not give reasons for their verdicts. That leaves open the real risk that if fact-finders do not understand the evidence the prosecutor's fallacy will occur without any real prospect of review. To some degree, that risk is unavoidable where reasons for decisions are not being given. Even where reasons are being given, there could be an implicit and unstated effect of misunderstanding the probabilities of the other evidence in the proceeding.[71] Clearly, there remains a potential for prejudice arising from the prosecutor's fallacy. Failing to provide specific warnings can only mean that the court must have formed a view that this risk is not of a sufficiently high degree to warrant intervention.

C. Inflated Value Prejudice

Inflated value prejudice is the overvaluing of the probative value of statistical evidence. First, overvaluing can occur if the fact-finder ignores the potential deficit in the evidence occasioned by the need to generalise the evidence across the inferential gap.[72] Second, a fact-finder could place too much reliance on the quantitative expression of the statistical evidence over and above other qualitative evidence in support of *p*.[73]

Either way, the probative value of the statistical evidence is said to be greater than what it should reasonably possess. Consequentially, other qualitative evidence is pushed into the periphery which can result in inaccurate decisions being made. The question for evidence law is whether, and under what conditions, does statistical evidence pose a 'real',[74] 'serious'[75] or 'unacceptable'[76] risk that fact-finders will overinflate the probative value of the statistical evidence?

[68] *Karger* (n 50) [182]; Ligertwood (n 64) 326.

[69] *Aytugrul* (n 63) 183.

[70] *R v Carpenter* [2019] ACTSC 169.

[71] Hodgson, 'Lawyer' (n 65) 113–14.

[72] This risk is equally true in the opposite direction. A fact-finder could unduly discount the value of the evidence because of its non-specific nature. This latter risk does not give rise to prejudice as typically defined because it does not inflate the probative value of the evidence. Nonetheless, it is a source of reasoning error.

[73] Tribe (n 1) 1361.

[74] *Jackson v R* [2020] NSWCCA 5, [111]; *Hughes* (n 4) [71].

[75] *HML v The Queen* (2008) 235 CLR 334, [13].

[76] A Ligertwood, 'What Lawyers Should and Can do Now that They Know about the Forensic Sciences' (2015) 36 *Adelaide Law Review* 153, 163.

There is some evidence to suggest that the risk of inflated value prejudice identified in the literature is overstated. The available empirical evidence suggests that fact-finders are more likely to prefer non-statistical or personalised evidence to evidence drawn from circumstances outside the time, place or object of the present facts; even if that non-statistical evidence is 'less accurate' than the statistical evidence.[77] Although that evidence is important, it does not capture the essential problem presented by inflated value prejudice. The problem is not just that fact-finders might prefer one form of evidence to another but, in the attempt to incorporate that quantitative and probabilistic evidence with qualitative evidence, they may err in the assessment of probative value. It would still give rise to epistemic prejudice if the statistical evidence caused non-statistical evidence to be inflated relative to the real probative value of the statistical evidence.

The most common example of how statistical evidence is immiscible with qualitative evidence is Cohen's finding that fact-finding does not, and cannot, follow mathematical rules.[78] Cohen argues instead that legal fact-finding is inductive.[79] Cohen's thesis largely mirrors the views expressed by Dixon J in *Briginshaw v Briginshaw* that facts are found by reference to a fact-finder's belief, not quixotic decisions based on objective probabilities independent of belief.[80] Whether Cohen's thesis overemphasises the problems of mathematical fact-finding has been the subject of much debate.[81] But what Cohen's work identifies is that even when operating within an inductive model, statistical evidence can present a difficulty in rationalising numerical probabilities against beliefs predicated on qualitative evidence. If numerical probabilities are introduced and then combined with qualitative evidence, there is a risk that mathematical concepts will be misunderstood, or the mathematical information given more importance than it deserves to the detriment of the other evidence.[82] This risk is the root cause of inflated value prejudice from statistical evidence.

Inflated value prejudice is easy to identify in theory, but almost impossible to discern in practice. Prejudice arises from the risk that the probative value of the evidence, or an inference drawn from that evidence, is erroneous, and concomitantly increases the probability that a wrong decision will be made. Not all risk of error is, however, prejudicial. The risk of error from evidence can be thought of

[77] GL Wells, 'Naked Statistical Evidence of Liability: Is Subjective Probability Enough?' (1992) 62 *Journal of Personality and Social Psychology* 739, 748; J Koehler and D Shaviro, 'Veridical Verdicts: Increasing Verdict Accuracy Through the Use of Overtly Probabilistic Evidence and Methods' (1990) 75 *Cornell Law Review* 247, 264–65; A Tversky and D Kahneman, '*Causal Schemas in Judgments under Uncertainty*' in D Kahneman, P Slovic and A Tversky (eds), *Judgment under Uncertainty: Heuristics and Biases* (Cambridge, Cambridge University Press, 1982).

[78] L Cohen, *The Probable and the Provable* (Oxford, Clarendon Press 1977) ch 11.

[79] ibid 246.

[80] *Briginshaw v Briginshaw* (1938) 60 CLR 336.

[81] See N Fenton, M Neil and D Berger, 'Bayes and the Law' (2016) 3 *Annual Review of Statistics and its Application* 51 pt 3; AP Dawid, 'The Difficulty about Conjunction' (1987) 36 *Statistician* 91; Eggleston (n 62) ch 3.

[82] Tribe (n 1) 1361.

as a continuous scale from 0 (no risk of error) to 1 (certain error). It is difficult to imagine evidence that poses no risk of error whatsoever, because error arises both from the nature of the evidence and how it is perceived by the individual fact-finder. Risk of error becomes prejudicial in the eyes of the law when the evidence poses a risk that the evidence will be given a disproportionate weight and misused.[83] Notwithstanding the empirical evidence that suggests fact-finders do not overvalue statistical evidence, there is at least some theoretical risk that the admixture of quantitative and qualitative probabilities could give rise to some misconception about the probative value of the evidence. Even if that is correct, courts should be very reluctant to find statistical evidence inadmissible, and appellate courts equally reluctant to find error in factual findings at first instance for inflated value prejudice.

First, where a judicial officer is sitting as both gatekeeper and fact-finder, it makes very little sense to contend that evidence should be excluded from the corpus of evidence just because it presents a risk of epistemic prejudice. Once the judge has been exposed to that evidence during the process of deciding about prejudice, the chance of that prejudice having some impact has already been felt. Whether legitimate or not, judges are given a degree of latitude in making gatekeeper decisions and treated as being inoculated from infection by that evidence.[84] Given that position, it seems arbitrary and wasteful to say that a judge cannot then consider potentially highly probative evidence simply because there is a chance that its probative value will be misconstrued. If the risk is that the numbers cannot be understood, or the basis for the calculation of those numbers uncertain, a judge is entitled to make their own inquiries of witnesses giving that evidence to resolve those conflicts. If the evidence is still unclear, its weight can be discounted because at that point its probative value is minimal. Evidence that cannot be understood serves no useful purpose in the proof of p, because its relevance and probative value to p cannot be ascertained. Likewise, despite the greater concern regarding the ability of juries to understand complex statistical evidence, the ability to give warnings to juries and directions should, in the absence of something further, be a sufficient safeguard against a mere risk of being uncertain as to how to construe the probative value of the evidence.

A more difficult risk to prevent is if the fact-finder misuses the evidence without realising they have misunderstood it. Warding against this risk would require a gatekeeper to form the view that the fact-finder would not understand the evidence, or that the fact-finder would be incapable of understanding it when fully explained. Courts have generally approached exclusion for miscomprehension with caution. Just because evidence is itself complicated is not usually enough to warrant its exclusion.[85] Regulating the admissibility of evidence for complexity

[83] *Hughes* (n 4) [17].
[84] *O'Brien* (n 35) [11], [55].
[85] *GK* (n 42) [2]–[3]. UEL ss 135–36 give judges a discretion to exclude evidence that is misleading or confusing as against its probative value.

is difficult and presents real risks of idiosyncrasies of gatekeepers operating to exclude evidence simply because the gatekeeper (who is usually not armed with a full view of the evidence) concludes that the fact-finder cannot understand it. That is not to discount the possibility that some evidence will be too complex to warrant admission into legal proceedings. But the more salient reason for its inadmissibility is that the resources it would consume far outweigh its likely probative value.

Second, there is a basic problem of principle in assessing prejudice by reason of the erroneous assignment of probative value to a particular item of evidence. Fact-finders bear the responsibility of deciding the probative value of evidence. That decision is subjective, tempered only by a requirement that the decision has a reasonable or rational basis.[86] The fact-finder rationally decides what probative value the evidence has without any other legal interference.[87] If that statement is correct, it raises the question of how or why any further assessment of the probative value of the evidence is any more likely to be 'correct' than the former assessment. If probative value is in the eye of the beholder, there is theoretically at least no basis for error by the assignment of some probative value, as long as that assignment is rationally based.

An assessment of probative value can be legitimately cavilled with when it has no rational basis. Giving evidence a particular weight that it cannot reasonably or rationally bear is an error of the kind similar to that associated with setting aside a jury's verdict where the decision is said to be unreasonable and unsupported by the evidence,[88] or an error in the exercise of judicial discretion.[89] The bar set for such review should, at least theoretically, be high. The court should be satisfied that the evidence will, or did, present such a risk of being irrationally construed, or, having been admitted, it was relied upon in such a way that is demonstrative of irrational thinking. Evidence that is spurious but somehow survives review for reliability might fit within this category. Likewise, evidence that encourages biases or very strong emotions might equally pose a risk of irrational dealing, especially where the underlying connection to the facts-in-issue is weak.[90] This could include, in the context of similar fact evidence, evidence of prior heinous offending of an entirely different sort to the charged conduct. Assessments of prejudice predicated on irrationality also carry a real risk of mere differences of opinion accounting for the findings of prejudice or error. Reasonable minds can disagree over whether evidence can bear rational relationships to facts. But the fact that a principle cannot always prevent error entirely is not a reason to abandon it. Some

[86] *Martin v Osborne* (1936) 55 CLR 367, 375.

[87] T Anderson, D Schum and W Twining, *Analysis of Evidence*, 2nd edn (Cambridge, Cambridge University Press, 2005) 226ff.

[88] *M v The Queen* (1994) 181 CLR 487, 492–93.

[89] *House v The King* (1936) 55 CLR 499, 505.

[90] *R v H* [1995] 2 AC 596 (HL) 613.

safeguard is necessary to protect against overtly 'wrong' decisions. Otherwise, it would be virtually impossible to ever screen out biases in fact-finding.

Outside of irrational decision-making, however, the regulation of evidence because it could allegedly be assigned a 'wrong' probative value relative to or at the expense of other evidence in the proceeding is very problematic. If the evidence is capable of rationally supporting the probative value that is, or is potentially, assigned to it, the dividing line between substituting the reviewer's opinion for the fact-finder, or pre-judging what the fact-finder might do with the evidence and allowing fact-finders to make their own assessment of the evidence, begins to break down. It is for that reason that appeals based on the inadequate weighting of evidence in the exercise of judicial discretion are 'narrowly confined' because '[q]uestions of weight in the exercise of discretion are matters for the [fact-finder]'.[91] A ground of appeal that is framed only in terms of the 'correctness' of the weight (unless the weight that was given has no rational or reasonable basis) cannot, by itself, establish an error in the process of fact-finding,[92] or the exercise of judicial discretion.[93] Gatekeepers and appellate courts are unlikely to have a superior basis for assigning probative value than a lower court. Courts recognise that it is fact-finders who are usually in a better position to assess the evidence in its full and proper context.[94] Both gatekeepers and appellate reviewers are exposed to a more limited sample of the evidence when these decisions are made.[95] It is only after an error is established that an appellate court may reconsider, in whole, the factual findings of a fact-finder.[96]

Despite this otherwise unequivocal recognition that appellate courts and gatekeepers should not interfere with the weighing of evidence (unless the process of weighing itself miscarries), courts do appear to engage in such revisionary or anticipatory tasks based on their own opinion of the evidence, especially with respect to similar fact and statistical evidence.

This book does not attempt to comment on the admissibility or review of similar fact evidence. However, where statistical evidence is concerned, courts should be very reluctant to find, in the absence of a risk of irrationality, that the evidence should be excluded simply because there is a risk that probative value might be overvalued. In extreme circumstances where statistical evidence does demonstrate an unequivocal and unavoidable risk of being overvalued, it may be justifiably excluded. No rule can be created identifying when the evidence presents such a risk. The decision will depend on the type of evidence and the context of its use. The ability to identify or exclude such evidence is an important function of the judicial role, but one that should be exercised judiciously.

[91] *R v Barker* [2000] NSWCCA 85, [11] (Spigelman CJ).
[92] *M* (n 88) 501.
[93] *Morgan v R* [2017] NSWCCA 269, [69], citing *Bugmy v The Queen* (2013) 249 CLR 571.
[94] *Fox* (n 24) [23]–[27].
[95] *DSJ v R; NS v R* (2012) 215 A Crim R 349, [94]; *GLJ v Trustees of the Roman Catholic Church* [2023] HCA 32, [27].
[96] *Fox* (n 24) [27].

D. Incredible Coincidence Prejudice

Statistical evidence can be presented so that the probabilities of the putative fact having occurred are extraordinarily high. Extremely high probabilities may in turn lead to an inference that the fact is almost certainly true. Just because evidence is strongly probative of a fact, and more likely to lead to a verdict, does not mean it is prejudicial.[97] Sometimes, however, high probabilities can be misleading because they give a false impression of certainty. This appears especially problematic when coincidence evidence is given in terms of numerical probabilities. The three cases commonly cited as examples are *People v Collins*,[98] *R v Clark*[99] and *de Berk*.[100] In each case, an expert gave evidence of the improbability that the accused would be associated with a particular collection of variables. In *Collins*, this concerned the improbability that more than one couple bearing certain features would be in the vicinity of the crime.[101] In *Clark*, the defendant was charged with the murder of her two children. She claimed they had died from sudden infant death syndrome (SIDS). The prosecution led evidence of incidence rates of SIDS, and that the chance of two infant deaths by SIDS was 1 in 73 million.[102] This invited an inference about the improbability of an innocent explanation for the deaths of the accused's children, that is, in the absence of any other causes, the probability of SIDS was extremely low, suggesting that the children did not die of natural causes. In *de Berk*, a nurse was convicted on the evidence that the probability of her being present for seven deaths and three resuscitations on a ward was 1 in 342 million (revised downwards from the first estimate of 1 in 7 billion), suggesting her presence at all of these events could not be mere chance.[103]

The immediate concern of using statistical evidence in this way is that the extremely high probabilities may obscure the fact that the evidence actually has very little probative value to the facts-in-issue.[104] In *Collins*, the prosecution had a compelling circumstantial case built on inconsistent records of interview that the defendants had committed the offence.[105] But the evidence placing the accused at

[97] *Festa* (n 4) 603; A Zuckerman, 'Similar Fact Evidence – The Unobservable Rule' (1987) 103 *LQR* 187, 194.
[98] *People v Collins*, 68 Cal2d 319 (CalSC, 1968); Tribe (n 1) 1334.
[99] *R v Clark (No 2)* [2003] EWCA Crim 1020; *R v Clark (No 1)* [2000] EWCA Crim 54; B Verheij, 'To Catch a Thief With and Without Numbers: Arguments, Scenarios and Probabilities in Evidential Reasoning' (2014) 13 *Law Probability and Risk* 307, 307.
[100] For a detailed discussion of this case and the impugned evidence, see T Derksen and M Meijsing, 'The Fabrication of Facts: The Lure of the Incredible Coincidence' in H Kaptein, H Prakken and B Verheij (eds), *Legal Evidence and Proof: Statistics, Stories, Logic* (Hampshire, Ashgate, 2009).
[101] *Collins* (n 98) 325–26; A Pundik, 'The Epistemology of Statistical Evidence' (2011) 15 *International Journal of Evidence & Proof* 117, 119, fn 11; Tribe (n 1) 1350.
[102] *Clark (No 2)* (n 99) [118].
[103] Derksen and Meijsing (n 100).
[104] *Collins* (n 98) 332.
[105] ibid 324.

the scene of the robbery was relatively weak. Probabilistic evidence was adduced to fill that gap. The prosecution submitted, based on the workings of a mathematician, the probability of a Black man with a beard and moustache, and a blonde woman with a ponytail being together was said to be 1 in 12 million, that there was a 'one chance in 12 million that defendants were innocent and that another equally distinctive couple actually committed the robbery'.[106] The probative value of this evidence depended on the fact-finder accepting that the couple's shared characteristics were capable of identifying them, at least to the standard of proof. DNA evidence supports such an inference because it has been rigorously empirically tested and is widely accepted as being uniquely identifying. As the Supreme Court of California made clear, the evidence could not rise to that level; it could not exclude the possibility, nor even quantify the possibility, of other similar couples being present in the area.[107] Incredible coincidences as such are only probative where, in fact, the coincidence is genuinely and demonstrably incredible, that is, the probabilities of the coincidence relate directly to the relevant offending. That was not the case in either *Collins*,[108] or *de Berk*.[109] In contrast, the probabilities in *Clark*, that there was only a 1 in 73 million chance of the accused's children both dying of SIDS, could have provided that connection to the criminal activity, in that it was used to rebut a defensive explanation predicated on natural causes.

Incredible coincidences are often prejudicial because the mathematics on which they rely are spurious. The probabilities relied on in *Collins*, *Clark* and *de Berk* were fundamentally flawed. In *Collins*, there was apparently no empirical basis whatsoever to the probabilities in the reference classes used to compute the specific probabilities.[110] No empirical evidence of dual SIDS deaths was adduced in *Clark*. The 1 in 73 million was instead a 'theoretical' probability derived by multiplying the 'base rate' of SIDS deaths of 1 in 8,534.[111] Nor was any evidence of the probabilities associated with nurses who injured or killed their patients adduced in *de Berk*.[112] In the absence of empirical evidence and probabilities derived from appropriate reference classes the experts in each case proffered probabilities plagued by a flawed empirical and mathematical approach due to a misunderstanding of the 'product rule'. Where different variables are truly independent, the product rule provides that a valid way of calculating the probability of the association of those variables is to multiply them together.[113] On no rational basis could

[106] ibid 325.
[107] ibid 330.
[108] ibid 330 ('At best, it might yield an estimate as to how infrequently bearded Negroes drive yellow cars in the company of blonde females with ponytails').
[109] See Fenton, Neil and Berger (n 81) 3.4. The statistics only showed the probability of being on the ward for each of the impugned resuscitations or deaths.
[110] *Collins* (n 98) 325, 327–28 ('we find the record devoid of any evidence relating to any of the six individual probability factors used by the prosecutor and ascribed by him to the six characteristics').
[111] *Clark (No 1)* (n 99) [102]–[121]ff.
[112] Derksen and Meijsing (n 100).
[113] M Finkelstein and W Fairley, 'A Bayesian Approach to Identification Evidence' (1970) 83 *Harvard Law Review* 489, 491.

the evidence in *Collins*,[114] *Clark*[115] or *de Berk*[116] be considered truly independent, making the multiplication of the probabilities wholly spurious. And, as occurred in *Collins*, the high probabilities of incredible coincidences make the consequence of transposing the conditional far greater. As such, a great deal of caution should be used before admitting evidence of incredible coincidences expressed probabilistically, and such evidence should only be received where it can be evaluated in the context of a substantial literature and robust empirical testing.

III. Moral Prejudice

Moral prejudice is said to be different in kind to epistemic prejudice.[117] Both statistical evidence and similar fact evidence raise potential moral objections arising from a convergence of two errors: first, the fact-finder will seek to punish the accused for past misdeeds notwithstanding the evidence in the present case, and second, that the standard of proof will be lowered in respect of the present offending by reason of the past misconduct.[118] These errors are said to be different from the logical defects of epistemic prejudice because they arise from a rejection of the presumption of innocence.[119] Palmer argues that because of the rejection of this fundamental tenet of law, moral prejudice, therefore, can only arise against an offender in criminal proceedings, and cannot be cured by warnings.[120]

With respect, it is not clear why the kinds of defects in reasoning associated with moral prejudice are limited to criminal proceedings and are incurable by warnings. The suggestion that criminal proceedings are generally more serious than civil proceedings that is sometimes the basis of that justification is patently untrue. First, negative findings about the character or propensity of a witness or individual involved in the proceedings can be just as reputationally harmful as if they were convicted. This is an especially palpable concern in defamation proceedings. Second, civil proceedings may cause individuals to lose not just their reputations and cost significant sums to prosecute or defend, but a loss can have a crushing impact on their livelihoods. Whereas sentences for serious indictable

[114] *Collins* (n 98) 328–29.

[115] *Clark (No 1)* (n 99) [106]. The figure of 1 in 73 million was not taken from a reference class of cases where families had suffered two SIDS deaths, but rather a mere multiplication of the probability of a family suffering one SIDS death given certain factors. At the second appeal, it was revealed that the authors of the study that underpinned the 1 in 73 million figure did not agree that it was permissible to multiply the figures in this way: *Clark (No 2)* (n 99) [103].

[116] R Gill, P Groeneboom and P de Jong, 'Elementary Statistics on Trial (the case of Lucia de Berk)' (2018) 31 *Chance* 9.

[117] D Hamer, 'The Legal Structure of Propensity Evidence' (2016) 20 *International Journal of Evidence & Proof* 136, 137–38.

[118] Zuckerman (n 97) 195.

[119] Palmer (n 7) 171.

[120] ibid 163, 171, 178ff.

offences can be extremely serious, less serious offences may not necessarily be world-ending. Comparing the seriousness of the outcomes of criminal and civil proceedings is a relative exercise. It remains essential to setting the approach allocating the burden and standards of proof, and how some evidence is admitted. But by itself it should not lead to a suggestion that the risk of prejudicial in civil proceedings is somehow muted or non-existent.

Both facets of moral prejudice have the same result; an overemphasis on the importance of the past conduct which, in turn, may undermine the pursuit of the truth if the assumption of continuance from the past to the present is false. Fact-finders may disregard or minimise present exculpatory evidence in favour of punishing the accused for their past actions; for example, the fact-finder may reason that whether the accused is guilty this time is moot because of the nature of their past offending. This requires the fact-finder to suspend any sufficient consideration of the present facts in favour of that view of the past. Or, a fact-finder may inflate the value of the inculpatory past evidence in order to meet the standard of proof even if, rationally, it could not do so. Whereas these concerns are often associated with past human behaviours, there doesn't appear to be any logical explanation for why similar reasoning processes couldn't apply to a non-human actor outside the criminal context.

For example, a dog could be declared dangerous because it has attacked small children on repeated occasions. When presented with two animals said to have attacked a small child, it seems logical that in the absence of anything else, the dog with the past history of attacking small children would be considered more likely to have attacked the child than a dog with no such history. Moral prejudice may arise where that evidence is used by the fact-finder to find that the dog with the past history committed the present act by reason of a desire to punish the dog (or protect future victims from the dog) but where there is otherwise insufficient or contradictory evidence tending against the rational probability that the dog committed the act on this occasion.

Likewise, a company that previously engaged in misconduct may be subject to a risk that their past conduct will override any countervailing inferences or evidence about the present conduct by reason of that past behaviour. The same could apply to a product which has been found to be faulty in the past. Such reasoning mirrors moral prejudice (to the extent it is actually prejudicial) but is quite clearly epistemic in its effect because evidence of the past is irrationally or unreasonably dictating the probabilities of an event outside the time, space or object of that past event. Moral prejudice, as defined by Palmer, is simply a more granular understanding of what may occur when a fact-finder overemphasises the importance of the past acts relative to the present. Whereas epistemic prejudice alone is focused on the overbearing impact of the past conduct on the facts to be found, moral prejudice is the risk that fact-finders will abdicate the fact-finding task to the putative facts and focus exclusively or excessively on what previously occurred. The problem with doing so is that it irrationally discounts 'the defendant's capacity to diverge from his associates or from his past, thereby demeaning his individuality and autonomy'.[121] So, whilst moral prejudice is rooted in the same defective reasoning processes as epistemic prejudice, the moral element presents a heightened risk that the fact-finding task will miscarry. This could be more accurately described as moral-epistemic prejudice.

Moral prejudice is also said to arise independently of any epistemic defect in the evidence. Such arguments have tended to arise from moral philosophy. For statistical evidence, Wasserman identifies that such evidence, based on a behavioural trait of a person but derived from that person's membership in a class of similar persons, is problematic because the evidence could 'demean the defendant or expose him to a wide ranging risk of false liability'.[122] Concerns about autonomy and individuality are a moral gloss on the process of fact-finding; the truth does not care if the individuality of the person of interest is undermined. Even so, Wasserman clearly links the risks to autonomy to the risk of error, reinforcing the epistemic character of moral prejudice.

Evidence law is not exclusively concerned with truth and risk of error. Rules preventing the admission of evidence of illegality or legal professional privilege are anathema to a truth-seeking exercise but recognise that certain public policy goals may override the search for the truth.[123] There is precedent therefore for creating a rule that excludes evidence otherwise probative of the truth that 'demeans' individuality and autonomy. These concerns about statistical evidence are often bundled as moral and normative objections to statistical evidence. Permitting the use of statistical evidence devoid of individualised evidence, it is argued, undermines the legal system and casts it into disrepute.[124] Litigants may distrust a system that gives insufficient credence to individualised proof,[125] or could be conducive of parties reverting to statistical evidence when further research, time and effort might produce more case-specific evidence.[126] This chapter argues, however, that such objections are not prejudicial to a litigant per se, as the objection in fact involves an encroachment by the substantive law into the law of evidence. Whereas such normative concerns may be justified for other forms of evidence, they should not be used, absent any real epistemic concerns, to label statistical evidence as prejudicial.

Similar fact evidence may be morally prejudicial because the evidence exposes the litigant to their past misdeeds and makes them account for what they have done in the past (which is not per se on trial).[127] Statistical evidence equally presents a risk that the litigant is being held to account for something

[121] Wasserman (n 44) 942–43.
[122] ibid 935.
[123] *McGuinness v A-G (Vic)* (1940) 63 CLR 73, 87.
[124] For a recent discussion of this concept, see generally Levanon (n 1).
[125] Generally, Nesson (n 43).
[126] R Posner, 'An Economic Approach to the Law of Evidence' (1999) 51 *Stanford Law Review* 1477, 1509.
[127] Roberts (n 4) 671, discussing 'bad man' prejudice. cf Redmayne, *Character* (n 3) 67–68.

now beyond their control; their membership in a reference class.[128] Take Pundik's example of Stephen. Stephen is exposed to radiation. This radiation is shown to cause distinctive skin marks and an irresistible urge to go berserk in 80% of cases of exposure.[129]

If adducing evidence of the effects of radiation exposure to prove that Stephen attacked a certain person, Pundik suggests this gives risk to a contradiction that Stephen's behaviour is taken to be both free (for the purpose of attributing culpability to him) and unfree (together with another unknown variable, his violent behaviour was determined by the radiation). That contradiction arises from

> an objection whenever a generalisation is used to attribute culpability to an individual and this use requires presupposing the existence of some causal factor outside the agent's control. This is because, for libertarians, the very presupposition of a causal factor outside the agent's control suffices to render the behaviour unfree, and this remains true even if the causal factor is unspecified or unknown. To avoid the contradiction, either the evidence has to be accepted as probative [and the accused] … not culpable, or it has to be considered not probative, in which case it should be rendered inadmissible.[130]

This formulation appears to elide the substance of the allegation and the evidence used in support of it. It is asserted that because the evidence uses statistical frequencies of behaviours from a common trait, the evidence demonstrates that the individual cannot be responsible for their own conduct and should therefore not be culpable for their behaviour. That seems to overstate the likely importance of the statistical evidence. Just because statistical evidence could, in theory, point to some behaviours as being influenced by certain common traits, that does not mean that the behaviour in question was in fact controlled by that trait. Further, the objection to the evidence inculpating Stephen likely arises from that fact that he has a strong basis for the automaton defence. A conviction is not being jeopardised by some defect in the evidence per se, but by the potential inability to establish the actus reus of the offence.[131]

Further, it seems to overstate the position that the probabilistic generalisation about Stephen is 'irrelevant' if he happens to be one of the few who are not predisposed to violence by the radiation.[132] The fact-finder's task is to establish whether Stephen committed the offence. Evidence that he has a propensity towards violence may be relevant where the fact-finder is ex ante unsure that Stephen in fact has that propensity. It is for the fact-finder to decide on the evidence whether Stephen is one of the 20% of people who are not violent after radiation exposure. The fact-finder could not make that determination unless they have access to that evidence.

[128] L Brilmayer and L Kornhauser, 'Quantitative Methods and Legal Decisions' (1978) 46 *University of Chicago Law Review* 116, 149.

[129] Pundik, 'Generalisation' (n 1) 203.

[130] ibid 203–04.

[131] *A-G's Reference (No 2 of 1992)* [1994] QB 91 (CA) 103–04 (Lord Taylor CJ).

[132] Pundik, 'Generalisation' (n 1) 204.

Perhaps a more revealing example is gang membership. A gang member is accused of committing murder. Evidence is received at trial that the defendant is a member of G1, that G1 operates exclusively in the area of the murder, and that crime statistics show that G1 members are 10 times more likely to commit murder than non-G1 members. Should the latter evidence be prevented from being used due to the moral prejudice associated with forming an inference to guilt by reason of a propensity to murder derived from their membership of G1? It seems to fall foul of Wasserman's admonition that it denies the individual an opportunity to demonstrate their difference from the group to which they belong. The individual may have been a non-violent member of G1. Even so, the evidence seems to be highly probative given the violent tendencies of at least some members of G1. A normative judgement needs to be made between the potentially high probative value of the evidence and the risk it poses to the individual that their autonomy may not be respected. This work argues that moral considerations of this kind have no place in evidence law where the statistical evidence is empirically based and robust. Evidence suggesting that people with personal or inherent traits have a greater propensity to commit certain acts by reason of that trait should be admissible if, and only if, there is good evidence to suggest that the trait is associated with the propensity.

Race is one of the more controversial examples. Without a robust empirical basis, evidence of associations between race and certain behaviours is problematic given the risk of abuse and the historical and contemporary context of disenfranchisement. The existence of these connections would properly be outside what may be fairly construed as commonsense unless one is actually prepared to accept a racist generalisation as a notorious fact. Or, if they are based on commonsense and heuristic reasoning, psychological evidence suggests that such heuristics are overused and contrary to the empirical evidence of such generalisations.[133] Such evidence would not have probative (or significant probative) value; and the risk of error and epistemic prejudice must outweigh whatever slender probative value could be given to such evidence in the absence of strong empirical support. In light of the tendency to overemphasise the importance of racial generalisations (or other generalisations about inherent or personal traits), a rational fact-finder would hold the evidentiary threshold necessary to actually believe in race-based generalisations higher than might be the case for generalisations from other characteristics.[134] The starting point of the fact-finder should be that for any trait to be causal of a certain behaviour, evidence, not heuristics, is required to show that relationship. Per the *Briginshaw* approach to fact-finding about unlikely events,[135] the degree of evidence (as distinct from the standard of proof) required to satisfy the fact-finder that inherent traits are causal of maladaptive behaviours should be significantly more than for non-inherent traits.

[133] See A Pundik, 'Against racial profiling' (2017) 67 *University of Toronto Law Journal* 175, 193–94.

[134] This is consonant with Dixon J's stipulation in *Briginshaw* (n 80) 361 that fraud need be proved by more compelling evidence as it is inherently less likely.

[135] ibid.

Gang membership is somewhat different to a true inherent trait; one would normally expect that membership and participation in the activities of a gang is by choice. The kind of error is the same; that the evidence fails to capture the individual member's potential differences to the base rates of the reference class. The statistical evidence of gang membership referred to above is capable of giving rise to at least two inferences: that the person's behaviour was 'unfree' because of their membership in a gang, or that because of their gang membership, they were more likely to have been involved in the criminal conduct. These inferences can be drawn simultaneously and without contradiction. The latter is the concern of evidence law, as it can affect the probative value of the evidence in support of a fact-in-issue. The admissibility of and weight from such evidence depends on the rigour of the statistical evidence supporting the inference. Fact-finders are charged with determining the accuracy of that evidence as long as the evidence itself is not flawed and incapable of proving general factual causation. The former, however, is not an evidentiary concern. If the evidence demonstrates that the behaviour is unfree, that is a substantive matter that, in the criminal context, may serve as a defence to the actus reus or mens rea elements of the offence. In civil law, such evidence may be relevant to a defence of duress or necessity. There is no basis to exclude the evidence for 'moral prejudice' as such, because the concerns of moral prejudice are already featured in the substantive law.

Statistical evidence does present a risk of moral-epistemic prejudice. Fact-finders could undermine the standard of proof or punish the accused for (perceived) past misconduct, for their membership in a violent gang. Adduced with robust statistics, however, gang membership may be powerful evidence in the proceeding. Moral-epistemic prejudice is a real risk, but not an unanswerable one. Using, and encouraging the use of, statistical evidence requires finding a principled line between acceptable and unacceptable risk of prejudice in light of the probative value of the evidence and a court's appetite for risk.

IV. Balancing Probative Value and Prejudice

As statistical evidence is not usually admitted in its own right, or indirectly even where relied on to support an expert opinion, there is no Australian rule regulating the admissibility of statistical evidence. Statistical evidence can, however, pose some risk of prejudice. How should evidence law ameliorate that risk? There are at least two options. An ex ante presumption of inadmissibility could be created against statistical evidence, akin to that against similar fact evidence. Statistical evidence would be inadmissible unless it possessed significant probative value, and, in criminal proceedings, its probative value outweighed its prejudicial effect. Alternately, the status quo could remain but with an increased understanding of the nature of the generalisation objection as a product of the inferential nature of statistical evidence. The usual presumption that relevant evidence is admissible would apply. But a party would be entitled to object to that evidence on the basis that the potential prejudice of that evidence outweighs its probative value.[136] Such objection would be heard in the context of an increased focus on and understanding of the statistics in issue. At least in respect of when prejudice is weighed, the difference between these rules is only how that process is commenced. Under an ex ante approach, weighing prejudice and probative value is mandatory. Under an ex post approach, it is the parties or the court that must decide whether the evidence should be tested for its prejudice and excluded. Otherwise, the test is the same.

There are at least three reasons why an ex ante rule for statistical evidence should be avoided. First, the variety of circumstances for which statistical evidence is employed is vast. The Supreme Court of the United States rejected the imposition of any categorical rule of inadmissibility for statistical evidence in *Tyson Foods v Bouaphakeo* on the grounds that the variety of circumstances that statistical evidence is used in would make any such rule impracticable, especially where statistical evidence is the only way liability can be proved.[137] Equally, it can be difficult to identify when evidence is inherently 'statistical' such that it would give rise to prejudice justifying exclusion. Prejudice stems from the generalisation objection. That objection exists in evidence that is not statistical; indeed, one could justifiably argue that non-statistical generalisations are far more likely to be inaccurate than rigorous empirical analyses. A principled approach would dictate that such a rule would extend well beyond just statistical evidence, but to any evidence relying on generalisations. That could capture a vast swathe of evidence that would potentially disrupt the process of admitting evidence and unnecessarily increase the costs associated with litigation.

Second, the cornerstone of the similar fact rule in Australian law is the requirement of 'significant probative value'. Chapter five examined judicial statements suggesting that statistical evidence may be subjected to a 'greater than relevance' requirement for admissibility, or to be considered helpful in the context of fact-finding. A greater than relevance approach generally accords with Hoffmann's view of relevance in the context of similar fact evidence.[138] The tension between Hoffmann's approach and the approach generally considered to be appropriate for a relevance analysis can perhaps be articulated as the difference between the assessment of probative value and the assessment of significant probative value. But this suggests that a requirement of significant probative value for statistical evidence would not be without practical precedent.

A tacit or explicit ex ante requirement for significant probative value for statistical evidence to be admissible should be rejected. Although the requirement of significant probative value, in civil cases at least, is purportedly independent of its prejudicial effect, epistemic prejudice is the reason why such a requirement exists.[139] Given the supposed risk that tendency evidence will be over-weighted,

[136] eg, UEL ss 135, 137, or their common law equivalents.
[137] *Tyson Foods v Bouaphakeo* 577 US 442, 454, 460 (2016).
[138] L Hoffmann, 'Similar Facts After Boardman' (1975) 91 *LQR* 193, 200ff.
[139] See discussion of the legislative history of the tendency rule at *Hughes* (n 4) [81]–[84].

one response is to limit the introduction of barely relevant similar fact evidence. That way, the risk of overreliance is confined to evidence that is very useful to the fact-finder. There is, however, a logical flaw in that approach. If similar fact evidence derives its probative value from the closeness of fit between the tendency and the facts-in-issue and the risk is that too much weight will be placed on the tendency in proof of the present facts if the accused has no such propensity, that risk is being maximised as the tendency and present facts become more proximate. A fact-finder is more likely to feel that the tendency explains the present facts over and above any other supportive or contrary evidence in the proceeding. In *Perry*, Murphy J noted that '[t]he allegation that a number of the accused's relatives died or suffered from arsenic poisoning immediately conjures up a highly suspicious prejudicial atmosphere in which the presumption of innocence tends to be replaced with a presumption of guilt'.[140] That atmosphere may not have been so compelling had the evidence been less incredibly coincidental.

Of course, that risk must be set against, first, the logical conclusion that the greater the similarity between the tendency and the underlying facts, the more likely the tendency is to be true and second, that the greater dissimilarity between the facts, the less likely the tendency is to be real, making any reliance upon it more likely to be prejudicial. Even so, it must also be true that greater dissimilarity would reduce the likelihood that the tendency will be accepted.

There is also a challenge in identifying what is added by the word 'significant'. In *Hughes*, a plurality of the High Court of Australia (HCA) held that significant probative value means 'if [the evidence] could rationally affect the assessment of the probability of the existence of a fact-in-issue to a significant extent'.[141] This rather uninformative statement was used in the context of finding that evidence may not have significant probative value when it is insufficiently similar, but that tendency evidence can have significant probative value even if it cannot rise to the level of showing, for example, a modus operandi.[142] The HCA reinforced that the reasoning process for significant probative value is identical to the assessment of relevance.[143] So, if the reasoning process is the same, where is the line between when evidence is said to be significant or not?

With respect, there does not appear to be a sensible way of saying that evidence of similar facts is 'significantly probative' that does not depend on the gatekeeper's intuition. In *R v Lockyer*, Hunt CJ at CL stated that 'the significance of the probative value … must depend upon the nature of the fact-in-issue to which it is relevant and the significance (or importance) which that evidence may have in establishing that fact'.[144] But to say that evidence is significant has to be anchored to some kind of reasoning process with the evidence itself. *Hughes* suggests that the process is an assessment of the similarity between the tendency and the present

[140] *Perry* (n 25) 594.
[141] *Hughes* (n 4) [16] (Kiefel CJ, Bell, Keane and Edelman JJ).
[142] ibid [34].
[143] ibid [42].
[144] *Lockyer* (n 33) 459.

facts. If that is correct, then the process of the assessment of significant probative value has been entirely subsumed by the assessment of probative value. For statistical evidence to be relevant, it must possess a sufficient degree of similarity in order to justify crossing the inferential gap. That is an exercise in judgement about the strength of the evidence. If the gap is crossed, the fact-finder has formed the view that the evidence does contribute to the truth of the fact. If it does so weakly, and could pose a risk of prejudice, or excessive costs and waste, the evidence could be excluded under s 135 of the UEL or its equivalents. If the reason for requiring significant probative value is because of the risk of epistemic prejudice, or elongating the trial with potentially marginally relevant information, then the addition of the word significant doesn't seem to add to the reasoning process at all. The trial judge will have already undertaken the exact same exercise in the process of deciding the relevance of the evidence. Without first understanding the nature of the inference and the applicability of *n* to *p* there is a real risk that inconsequential and prejudicial evidence would be admitted.

Third, identifying an 'unacceptable' risk of error from statistical evidence ex ante the fact-finding process that would justify a presumption against the admissibility of that evidence seems impossible. Statistical evidence can be epistemically prejudicial. In establishing relevance, the gatekeeper has already assessed the degree of applicability of *n* to *p* and therefore the likelihood that any association is spurious. If the responsibility for setting the weight of evidence is left to the fact-finder, and not the gatekeeper, there seems to be no basis for saying that the potential weight rationally perceived from any particular item of evidence is likely to be prejudicial. Only if the evidence had some feature that increased the risk of irrational use would an ex ante approach to prejudice be justified. For similar fact evidence, that seems to be the (questionable) risk of the inflation of the importance of character. For statistical evidence (at least, statistical evidence that is not also similar fact evidence), there is no reason to import an assumption about irrational dealing in the absence of empirical evidence. Epistemic prejudice may occur. But it is likely to be difficult to identify that prejudice prior to the completion of the fact-finding process. Rather than establishing an ex ante rule of inadmissibility, it is preferable to presume that statistical evidence is admissible unless it gives rise to an identifiable risk of prejudice, or, is sufficiently unreliable to warrant inadmissibility.

Identifying and weighing statistical evidence for prejudice (whether ex ante or ex post) does not provide a panacea against the misuse of statistical evidence. The similar fact rules are supposed to manage that prejudice by ensuring that the probative value of that evidence is high enough to offset the risk of its misuse. Gageler J explained the exercise as follows:

> For a court to think that tendency evidence has significant probative value, it must be satisfied that using the evidence for tendency reasoning makes the existence of a fact-in-issue significantly more probable or improbable. If the question is just how much more probable or improbable, the answer is enough to justify the ever-present risk that the objective probability will be subjectively overestimated. Putting the

> same point more colloquially, the court must be comfortable that the evidence is of sufficient weight to justify the risk of the evidence unwittingly being given too much weight.[145]

The challenge for this weighing exercise is that probative value and prejudice are incommensurate.[146] The weighing exercise is not a mathematical equation where probative value and risk of error can be computed, especially where moral-epistemic prejudice presents a risk that the weighing exercise will entirely miscarry. Instead, it is a comparison of the 'probative strength of the evidence with the degree of risk of an unfair trial if the evidence is admitted', and 'only if the judge concludes that the probative force of the evidence compared to the degree of risk of an unfair trial is such that fair minded people would think that the public interest in adducing all relevant evidence of guilt must have priority over the risk of an unfair trial'.[147]

Even though the gatekeeper has weighed the probative value against its potential prejudice, and found the evidence important enough to admit, admitting the evidence still leaves open the possibility of prejudice and misuse of the evidence.[148] The similar fact rule, or ex post exclusion of statistical evidence, are not solutions to prejudice as such, but a process undergone to justify and recognise the risk of prejudice that admitting the evidence will involve.

Conclusion

Objections to statistical evidence are often conveyed in epistemic and moral terms. It is logical to consider such objections in terms of similar objections arising from similar fact evidence. Whilst similar fact evidence is subject to the similar fact rule, that rule is a creature of tradition rather than logic. Epistemic prejudice is a real concern for statistical evidence, albeit that it does not rise to the level of prejudice warranting exclusion ex ante the fact-finding process. Moral prejudice as described by the similar fact rule is in fact a form of epistemic prejudice. The moral objection to statistical evidence on the other hand is not an evidentiary objection per se but is better understood as a problem of substantive law. It poses, or should pose, no challenge to the admissibility of statistical evidence. Given the division of labour between the fact-finder and gatekeeper, even where the identity of the officer in both roles is the same, there is no basis for construing the objections to generalisations from statistical evidence as prejudice for the purpose of evidence law and thereby the admission of statistical evidence on grounds of prejudice. To the extent such objections exist, for the most part, they will be questions for the fact-finder to address.

[145] *Hughes* (n 4) [87].
[146] *Pfennig* (n 42) 528.
[147] ibid 529.
[148] R Nair, 'Weighing Similar Fact and Avoiding Prejudice' (1996) 112 *LQR* 262, 263–64.

7

Objective Probabilities and Naked Statistical Evidence

Introduction

Is it permissible to find facts about *p* based only on the 'objective probability' of those facts being true? There is no consistent answer to this question because the question itself is unclear. Naked statistical evidence (NSE) comprises objective probabilities derived from the reference class. A great deal of philosophical and evidentiary scholarship has tried to explain the appropriateness of fact-finding from NSE. No real consensus has emerged. Unhelpfully, NSE dominates discussion of statistical evidence. This chapter argues that NSE possesses little significance in explaining objections to statistical evidence. First, theories of probability in fact-finding are explained. Second, the NSE debate is introduced. Third, a resolution to that debate, premised on the law of evidence, is proposed. Fourth, the chapter demonstrates how and where NSE has misled analyses of statistical evidence for legal fact-finding.

I. Subjective Probability in Fact-Finding

A fact-finder's own belief in the existence of a phenomenon (*p*) is an integral component to the standard of proof.[1] A fact is not found just because it is true (that-*p*), or even probably true (probably-*p*), in the absence of the fact-finder's belief in *p*. Dixon J's canonical formulation in *Briginshaw v Briginshaw* is that

> when the law requires the proof of any fact, the tribunal must *feel* an actual persuasion of its occurrence or existence before it can be found. It cannot be found as a result of a mere mechanical comparison of probabilities *independent of any belief in its reality*.[2]

[1] Quintessentially, *Briginshaw v Briginshaw* (1938) 60 CLR 336, 361. See further H Ho, *A Philosophy of Evidence Law* (Oxford, Oxford University Press, 2008) 107–09.

[2] *Briginshaw* (n 1) 361 (emphasis added). Some scholarship has suggested that there may be competing views of the standard of proof that could allow for a purely mathematical account of fact-finding from probabilities: see D Hodgson, 'The Scales of Justice: Probability and Proof in Legal Fact-Finding' (1995) 69 *Australian Law Journal* 731, 738–39. However, the authorities justifying those arguments are ad idem with *Briginshaw*'s ratio. In *Davies v Taylor* [1974] AC 207 (HL), Lord Simon stated that proof

The *Briginshaw* standard does not permit belief without some objective basis.[3] Fact-finding is not entirely capricious nor the product of idiosyncratic beliefs. Some individual differences are allowed, but on the condition that there is a rational basis for the fact-finder's belief.[4] Even where 'reasonable minds' are permitted to disagree on the existence or non-existence of an event, that difference in opinion must be rationalised such that the disagreement can be explained. This grounding in rationality is not 'objective' per se. After all, what is rational to one individual may not be for another. Nevertheless, there is some objective basis to fact-finding beyond true subjectivity. Fact-finding has both objective and subjective elements.[5] Belief must have some epistemological backing.

The *Briginshaw* standard can be summarised into a basic matrix. First, the fact-finder must form an actual belief in the existence of an event. That belief can either be categorical (believe that-*p*); a probability – that is, the event is believed to be more likely than not to be true (believe that probably-*p*); or less than a probability (believe less than probably-*p* or possibly-*p*). Second, the fact-finder's belief must be rational. There must be some kind of objective basis to the belief that can be believed by reasonable people, even if all reasonable people may not agree.

Whether the standard of proof is expressed as a belief 'that-*p*' or as 'probably-*p*' has important consequences for fact-finding from statistical evidence and to the nature of fact-finding itself. In Ho's analysis, the law requires fact-finders to believe in events categorically, or that-*p*, as opposed to partially, or probably-*p*.[6] The difference between categorical and partial beliefs, in Ho's analysis, is that a categorical belief is binary such that '[e]ither one believes *p* or one does not', whereas a partial belief is a belief in *p* to 'a greater or lesser extent'.[7] Whilst there appears to be some symmetry in this categorisation of belief, the distinction between categorical and partial beliefs, at least when considered against the express standard of proof, is illusory. Even though Ho defines partial beliefs by express reference to a degree of belief, he also acknowledges that categorical beliefs can have greater or lesser strengths.[8] Ho also explains that categorical beliefs are not absolutist statements of certainty,[9] but equally suggests that '[o]ne believes categorically that *p* when one

may be obtained from 'showing odds of at least 51 to 49' (at 219F). His Lordship caveats that view when he notes the test for 'past' fact-finding depends on 'whether [the trial judge] was satisfied that it was more likely than not', clearly endorsing the requirement of belief: at 220C. Satisfaction is a subjective, perhaps even neurobiological, phenomenon: see H Bennett and GA Broe, 'The Civil Standard of Proof and the "Test" in *Briginshaw*: Is There a Neurobiological Basis to Being "Comfortably Satisfied"?' (2012) 86 *Australian Law Journal* 258.

[3] *Malec v JC Hutton* (1990) 169 CLR 638, 639–40; Hodgson, 'Scales' (n 2) 731–32; R Eggleston, *Evidence, Proof and Probability*, 2nd edn (London, Weidenfeld and Nicolson, 1983) 42.

[4] *Nulty v Milton Keynes BC* [2013] WLR 1183 (CA) [35].

[5] D Nance, *The Burdens of Proof* (Cambridge, Cambridge University Press, 2016) 270.

[6] Ho (n 1) 127.

[7] ibid 124.

[8] ibid 128.

[9] ibid 110.

judges that *p* is, in fact, true'.[10] For *p* to be 'true', the fact-finder cannot also believe that *p* might be (but not necessarily believed to be) false.

How this formulation works in practice in conjunction with the standards of proof is unclear. Is it acting on a categorical belief that a judge decides that X is 'true' because the judge believes, based on the evidence before the court, that-*p* is more probable than not-*p*, despite some lingering uncertainty? It seems likely that the presence of any uncertainty undermines the categorical nature of the belief. If so, it is hard to reconcile Ho's statement that fact-finding need not be the product of certainties.[11] It also conflicts with how judges typically describe their factual findings as probabilities and likelihoods. Even more troubling is how to account for the civil standard. Where does the 'balance of probabilities' test come into a categorical belief? Does it mean that a judge forms an actual, positive belief in *p*, but does so with an appreciation of possible error? If so, that too doesn't seem to be any different from a degree of belief in *p* where that degree of belief outweighs not-*p* (which Ho rejects as being sufficient for fact-finding).[12]

If the belief must be something higher than a probability such that *p* actually occurred without any remaining doubt, how is that any different from the criminal standard that requires a '[generation of] full belief of the fact to the exclusion of all reasonable doubt]'?[13] A belief 'beyond reasonable doubt' is categorical. The fact-finder must believe that-*p* because an unreasonable or irrational doubt would not be enough to undermine the belief in that-*p*. If a doubt lowers the probability of *p* in any way it must ipso facto be reasonable. That standard is inappropriate for civil fact-finding, where the standard of proof expressly asks what is more likely in the circumstances. The statement 'I believe, on balance of probabilities, that-*p*', is identical to the statement 'I believe probably-*p*'. In both scenarios *p* is qualified as a probability – the fact-finder still must believe that-*p* is more likely than not-*p*, and can therefore assert a belief that-*p*, but nevertheless accepts the risk that not-*p* is possibly true.

The critical element in understanding the civil standard is what is meant by a 'reasonable' satisfaction. The term reasonable in this context can be used interchangeably with 'rational', that is, there must be a rational basis to the fact-finder's belief that probably-*p*. How is rationality determined? Cohen hypothesised that legal fact-finding was 'inductive' (or 'Baconian').[14] Fact-finders use commonsense interpretations of the evidence informed by 'roughly qualified generalisations [from everyday life] or rebuttable presumptions'[15] that every fact-finder possesses, albeit not uniformly.[16] Evidence in the proceeding is measured against these

[10] ibid 127.
[11] ibid 110.
[12] ibid 109.
[13] *Briginshaw* (n 1) 360.
[14] L Cohen, *The Probable and the Provable* (Oxford, Clarendon Press, 1977) 245.
[15] ibid 247.
[16] P Roberts, *Roberts & Zuckerman's Criminal Evidence*, 3rd edn (Oxford, Oxford University Press, 2022) 158–59.

generalisations of how the world ought to work and 'proof' is arrived at when every 'relevant feature of the situation' necessary to fulfil the cause of action is explained by the evidence in light of those generalisations.[17] Rationality, as such, depends on the degree of agreement between fact-finders on these generalisations. Even if reasonable minds disagree as to the ultimate outcome of the fact-finding process, a decision will be considered to have a rational basis if the generalisations employed in support of that decision are broadly accepted by the fact-finder. A decision will be irrational where those generalisations fail to be accepted.

Probably-*p* (or partial belief) is the appropriate interpretation of the civil standard of proof. *Briginshaw* made clear that certainty is not required for the civil standard.[18] The civil standard only required that the fact-finder be 'reasonably satisfied' that the event is true.[19] If 'satisfaction' refers to the fact-finder's belief in the truth, the addition of the qualifier 'reasonable' clearly anchors the standard of belief to a probability. A fact-finder need not be absolutely satisfied or satisfied beyond a reasonable doubt. Instead, a fact-finder can be satisfied the event occurred notwithstanding the possibility of other explanations. Expressed as the standard of proof, the fact-finder believes 'on balance of probabilities, that-*p*'.

Ho's rejection of a probabilistic belief in that-*p* seems prima facie inconsistent with his insistence that a categorical belief can be revised and possess different strengths.[20] If that-*p* does not mean 'definitely-*p*', then what else is left for that-*p* to mean other than probably-*p*? Probability as a mathematical construct is simply a representation of the absence of certainty. If p is not certainly true such that $p=1$, or certainly false such that $p=0$ (neither of which are probabilities per se),[21] then the truth or falsity of p is a probability. The error in a that-*p* formulation of belief can be clearly seen from the speech of Lord Diplock in *Mallett*.[22] His Lordship recounted the fact-finding process such that

> [i]n determining what did happen in the past a court decides on the balance of probabilities. Anything that is more probable than not it treats as certain.[23]

Plainly, certainty is a product of the legal process, not of the certain belief of the fact-finder. The fact-finder need only believe that-*p* is more probably than not true. The law still requires a fact-finder to believe that-*p* actually occurred, but only as the greater probability, and not as an unimpeachable fact. There is widespread support for commonsense fact-finding, both in judicial reasons and

[17] Cohen, *Probable* (n 14) 249.
[18] *Briginshaw* (n 1) 360, citing T Starkie, *Law of Evidence* (1876).
[19] *Helton v Allen* (1940) 63 CLR 681, 712.
[20] Ho (n 1) 131.
[21] cf D Enoch and T Fisher, 'Sense and "Sensitivity": Epistemic and Instrumental Approaches to Statistical Evidence' (2015) 67 *Stanford Law Review* 557, 567.
[22] *Mallett v McMonagle* [1970] AC 166, 176.
[23] ibid 176F. See further S Gageler, 'Evidence and Truth' (2017) 13 *The Judicial Review* 249, 254.

in scholarship.[24] Haack's theory of 'warrant' identifies that the degree of support evidence has for a proposition depends on 'how snugly its component elements interlock to form an explanatory account, or how tightly they interweave to form an explanatory picture'.[25] Hodgson (writing extra-judicially) suggests that '[fact-finding] depends very much more on commonsense, experience of the world, and beliefs as to how people *generally behave* (folk psychology), than on mathematical computations'.[26] Proof, whether of a single fact or a case as a whole, depends on the extent to which the contention fits or not into the fact-finder's belief about what is likely to have occurred. The more generalisations satisfied, the more likely the fact is true because '[w]hat ultimately leads to [proof] is the improbability of an innocent person belonging to so many independent classes'.[27]

II. Objective Probabilities

A system of belief based on a probably-*p* standard should rarely encounter problems of principle with the standard of proof. Fact-finders can differ in the extent of their belief in *p*, and whether that belief is rationally based. Such debates are consistent with the principle of a system of proof that relies on ultimately subjective judgements about the truth of events. By accepting that reasonable minds can disagree about the existence of facts, the standard of proof is not undermined by two individual fact-finders coming to opposite conclusions about the same factual milieu.

Of course, fact-finders can disagree about subjective probabilities as well. Direct evidence can be given by a witness that 'A did act B'. A fact-finder's belief in the probability of that fact is the fact weight of the evidence, commonly called a first-order fact. The degree of belief in the probability that the witness is lying or mistaken is the credit weight of the evidence, and usually known as a second-order fact. The probabilities of first and second-order facts are related but deal with different things. Some scholars suggest that the problem of objective probabilities is that such evidence causes special dissonance at the level of second-order facts.[28] But that oversimplifies the problem.[29] Evidence of objective probabilities

[24] *Henderson v Queensland* (2014) 255 CLR 1, [33] (French CJ) ('commonexperience'); *R v Clinton* [2013] QB 1 (CA) [46]; *R v Galli* (2001) 127 A Crim R 493, [55]. Objections to Cohen's Baconian approach are more concerned with his rejection of classical probability in legal fact-finding than the inductive approach per se: Roberts, *Roberts & Zuckerman* (n 16) 152.

[25] S Haack, 'Warrant, Causation, and the Atomisim of Evidence Law' (2008) 5 *Episteme* 253, 258.

[26] Hodgson, 'Scales' (n 2) 736.

[27] Eggleston (n 3) 80.

[28] eg L Brilmayer, 'Second-Order Evidence and Bayesian Logic' in P Tillers and E Green (eds), *Probability and Inference in the Law of Evidence: The Uses and Limits of Bayesianism* (New York, Springer 1988) 150.

[29] A Pundik, 'Freedom and Generalisation' (2016) 37 *OJLS* 189, 195–96; JJ Koehler, 'The Probity/Policy Distinction in the Statistical Evidence Debate' (1991) 66 *Tulsa Law Review* 141, 143–44.

comprises evidence from the reference class (*n*) that '*n* do act B'. The probability is objective because it exists independently from any probability of *p*. *n* has its own components of fact and credit weight and its own first and second order facts.[30] The problem therefore is not the fact-finder's degree of belief in the second-order of *p* per se, but how to establish the fact or credit weight of *p* given the fact and credit weight of *n* which exist independent of *p*. It is especially acute where a belief in the probability of *p* differs from the probability of *n* assuming that no further adjustments to *p* given *n* need to be made.

This problem most commonly occurs in the interpretation of numerically presented objective probabilities. Objective probability objections arise from any scenario where the probability of *p*, given the individual's connection to *n*, being true is greater than .5 but without the subjective belief of the fact-finder that *p* is probably true. This is especially so when the objective probability of *p*, arising from the evidence, can exist independently of *p*'s existence. As such, the evidence of the objective probability is 'insensitive' to the event in question.[31] Just because a study concludes that there is a reasonable likelihood that smoking causes cancer in *n* does not mean that the individual's cancer was caused by smoking. If that cancer was caused by something else (Z), the study would still suggest that the cancer was more probably caused by smoking.

An objective probability only becomes objectionable where the fact-finder has not yet been able to align their subjective belief with the objective probability, such that the fact-finder does not accept that the objective probability is probably true for the individual. Where *n* is not corroborated by other evidence it can be difficult to accept why the objective and insensitive probability of *n* being true is sufficient for a subjective belief in *p* to be formed.

NSE is the tool commonly used to provoke and explain objections to objective probabilities. Theorising about NSE plagues the debates about statistical evidence.[32] What the following sections seek to demonstrate is that the debate around NSE helps inform interesting and important aspects of the standard of proof that are not difficult to resolve. But the way that debate has been carried into the debates about statistical evidence is unhelpful.[33]

NSE refers to evidence of *n* expressed as an objective probability, in the absence of any other evidence used to satisfy the balance of probabilities, of the

[30] J Koehler and D Shaviro, 'Veridical Verdicts: Increasing Verdict Accuracy Through the Use of Overtly Probabilistic Evidence and Methods' (1990) 75 *Cornell Law Review* 247, 251.

[31] D Enoch, L Spectre and T Fisher, 'Statistical Evidence, Sensitivity, and the Legal Value of Knowledge' (2012) 40 *Journal of Philosophy and Public Affairs* 197, 204–05; M Pardo, 'Safety vs Sensitivity: Possible Worlds and the Law' (2018) 24 *Legal Theory* 50, 58; M Di Bello, 'When Statistical Evidence is not Specific Enough' (2021) 199 *Synthese* 12251, 12257 (using the term 'unspecified').

[32] See discussion of the reliance on NSE by D Enoch and L Spectre, 'Sensitivity, Safety, and the Law: A Reply to Pardo' (2019) 25 *Legal Theory* 178 at section IV.B below.

[33] cf Di Bello (n 31) 12254–55, who argues that hypotheticals remain useful tools in explaining the anti-liability intuitions. The problem that Di Bello does not confront is that the anti-liability intuitions that are provoked by the proof paradoxes are not the same as those generated by statistical evidence that could be used by courts.

existence of *p*.[34] NSE is best represented by a series of hypothetical scenarios called the 'proof paradoxes'.[35] Two that have captured the most attention are the 'Blue Bus Company'[36] and 'Gatecrasher'.[37]

The Blue Bus Company scenario proposes the following: within an exclusive zone, the Blue Bus Company (Blue) and the Red Bus Company (Red) are the sole owners and operators of all buses. Blue owns 60% of all buses within the zone, all coloured blue. Red owns 40%, all coloured red. The plaintiff's accepted testimony is that a bus struck her, but she could offer no specific evidence of colour. The proof paradox asks, in the absence of direct colour evidence, should there be a finding of liability against Blue because more than 50% of buses are blue, prima facie satisfying the standard of proof?

The Gatecrasher scenario, proposed by Cohen, asks whether an individual could be liable for the cost of a ticket to a ticketing company if

> 499 people paid for admission to a rodeo, and that 1,000 are counted on the seats, of whom [the individual] is one. Suppose no tickets were issued and there can be no testimony as to whether [the individual] paid for admission or climbed over the fence. So, by any plausible criterion of mathematical probability there is a .501 probability, on the admitted facts, that he did not pay.[38]

Proof paradoxes render the distinction between fact, inference, element and cause of action moot. By assuming all other relevant factual and elemental questions as either 'proven' or non-existent, the paradox ensures that all responsibility for success or failure rests on the objective probability.

Proof paradoxes only produce a functionally identifiable objection intuition if all countervailing legal and evidentiary objections outside of NSE being adduced are dismissed. Some of the objections to the proof paradoxes in fact relate to a failure to control for other objections not related to NSE per se. Take, for example, Di Bello's 'Workers' hypothetical, where 99 of 100 workers kill a guard, and a conviction is sought against one random worker for murder based on the purported 99% probability that the worker was involved.[39] Di Bello argues that the evidence in Worker is insufficient (as opposed to inadmissible) because it is not specific – it says very little about what in fact happened, other than perhaps the accused was in attendance. As Di Bello recognises, the problem he is identifying in Worker is not one that is inherent to the NSE, but rather it is a problem of any evidence that is not capable of supporting the necessary inferences to prove essential facts. The problem in Worker is not the nature of the evidence as such, but rather that the

[34] See G Wells, 'Naked Statistical Evidence of Liability: Is Subjective Probability Enough?' (1992) 62 *Journal of Personality and Social Psychology* 739, 739.

[35] Generally, M Redmayne, 'Exploring the Proof Paradoxes' (2008) 14 *Legal Theory* 281.

[36] F Schauer, *Profiles, Probabilities and Stereotypes* (Cambridge, Harvard University Press, 2003) 81–82.

[37] Cohen, *Probable* (n 14) 78.

[38] ibid 75.

[39] Di Bello (n 32) 12253. This example is closely related to Nesson's Prison Riot hypothetical.

paradox put forward does not identify sufficient evidence to meet the elements of murder – in particular, there is no evidence of *mens rea*. The alternative specific evidence examples given by Di Bello, such the worker punching the guard, provide a better 'accusatory narrative' not because of their specificity as such, but because they are capable of informing inferences that satisfy the elements in the offence. Equally, his solution to the problem of specificity, that statistical evidence can be sufficient where it is 'informative enough to address all relevant questions in a case' simply identifies the point at which the evidence can satisfy the elements of the offence.[40] In this way, such objections to NSE are not identifying an inherent weakness in the evidence itself, but rather than such evidence is inapt for the facts that it is adduced to prove.

If there is to be a debate about these hypotheticals, the question can be construed narrowly as 'is it appropriate to find a defendant liable on balance of probabilities *exclusively* on statistical evidence' and without additional 'case-specific'[41] or 'individualised'[42] evidence?[43] But what does this question actually mean for the law of evidence and how should it affect courts' approach to statistical evidence?

A. Evidentiary Objections to the Proof Paradox

The objection to the proof paradoxes has been variously described but is commonly referred to as an 'anti-liability' intuition.[44] Anti-liability intuition is not an objection known to the law of evidence. If a proof paradox-like situation occurred in a legal proceeding, any objection would have to be managed by the gatekeeper by way of evidence law. There are four areas of interaction between the proof paradoxes and evidence law: relevance; inadmissibility for procedural reasons; inadmissibility for prejudice; and insufficient for proof.

It is easy enough to dismiss relevance and procedure. Relevance sets a low standard. Even if one objects strenuously to fact-finding from objective probabilities, it would be difficult to say that an objective probability is irrelevant to the existence or non-existence of a fact-in-issue,[45] as long as the relationship between the fact and the probabilistic evidence was rational. Second, as the proof paradox

[40] ibid 12261.

[41] A Stein, 'The New Doctrinalism: Implications for Evidence Theory' (2015) 163 *University of Pennsylvania Law Review* 2085, 2091.

[42] J Thomson, 'Liability and Individualised Evidence' (1986) 49 *Law and Contemporary Problems* 199, 204.

[43] D Hodgson, 'Probability: the Logic of the Law – A Response' (1995) 15 *OJLS* 51, 60.

[44] A Pundik, 'The Epistemology of Statistical Evidence' (2011) 15 *International Journal of Evidence & Proof* 117, 119; Redmayne, 'Proof Paradoxes' (n 34) 287; A Stein, *Foundations of Evidence Law* (Oxford, Oxford University Press, 2005) 77; D Shaviro, 'Statistical-Probability Evidence and the Appearance of Justice' (1989) 103 *Harvard Law Review* 530, 545.

[45] Contra L Cohen, 'Subjective Probability and the Paradox of the Gatecrasher' [1981] *Arizona State Law Journal* 627, 633–34.

removes all possible questions of reliability, and evidence itself is easy to identify (by attendance records or company books), it would seem unlikely that the evidence would cause excessive cost or delay to produce.

There is, however, a very good case to make on prejudice.[46] If epistemic prejudice means the potential to misconstrue the weight of evidence,[47] then the objections to objective probability seem apposite. If evidence is usually processed qualitatively, how are fact-finders meant to interpret quantitative evidence? What rough generalisation explains precise probabilities? Tribe hypothesised that objective probabilities would overbear on important qualitative evidence due to the 'overbearing impressiveness of numbers'.[48] But the construction of the proof paradox largely prevents epistemic prejudice. Deliberately excluding any other item of evidence means that other evidence cannot be discounted or ignored. Moreover, it is difficult to argue that NSE could confuse a fact-finder. There is only one source of data expressed as a simple numerical probability. If the law accepts that fact-finders possess a host of pre-existing generalisations to inductively assess the existence of facts, surely basic numerical probabilities are a part of that knowledge? For the reasons explained in section III below, moral-epistemic prejudice is avoided within the tight confines of the proof paradox. Section IV below, however, demonstrates that epistemic and moral-epistemic prejudice plays a significant role in statistical evidence.

The final evidentiary objection to NSE, and the subject of this chapter, is on the insufficiency of proof; notwithstanding the objective probability, no reasonable fact-finder would (or ought to) be actually persuaded of liability.[49]

[46] For a summary of these arguments, see C Dahlman and A Pundik, 'The Problem with Naked Statistical Evidence' in C Dahlman, A Stein and G Tuznet (eds), *Philosophical Foundations of Evidence Law* (Oxford, Oxford University Press, 2021) 332ff.

[47] See ch 6, section I.A.

[48] L Tribe, 'Trial by Mathematics: Precision and Ritual in the Legal Process' (1971) 84 *Harvard Law Review* 1329, 1361. Kahneman and Tversky's studies are often cited as suggesting that objectively probabilities do not overbear specific probabilities; indeed, specific probabilities are usually preferred: see Koehler and Shaviro (n 30) 255–56. These studies do not respond to Tribe's argument. First, the 'specific' probabilities relied on are not specific in the inductive sense. Witness accuracy rates based on past identification attempts also require a generalising inference from the data informing those rates to the present identification. Second, the comparison between the objective and 'specific' probabilities is only a comparison of Keynesian weight. Because the witness has attested to seeing the event, and is supported by an objective probability of accuracy, there is far more weighty evidence in the 'specific' scenario, making the comparison unequal. Third, Tribe's argument is that quantification itself impedes the fact-finding process. Presenting two quantified items, one specific and one general, doesn't say anything about that initial criticism. The participants can rely on the witnesses' direct identification of the event and would probably do so under the inductive approach irrespective of any further probabilities of accuracy.

[49] This objection can manifest in two forms. First, a summary application to terminate the proceedings for a want of evidence, per *Smith v Rapid Transit*, 58 NE2d 754 (MassSJC, 1945). See further Stein, *Foundations* (n 44) 77–78; C Nesson, 'The Evidence or the Event? On Judicial Proof and the Acceptability of Verdicts' (1985) 98 *Harvard Law Review* 1357, 1380. Second, by way of appeal from a decision based on finding facts from such evidence as an error of law: *M v The Queen* (1994) 181 CLR 487, 493–95, qualified by *Libke v The Queen* (2007) 230 CLR 559, [113], in light of *Morris v The Queen* (1987) 163 CLR 454, 472–74 (criminal law); *Fox v Percy* (2003) 214 CLR 118, 125–28 (civil law).

B. Insufficient Weight and Proof

The genesis of the proof paradox is from a series of cases in the US that have various reflections in Commonwealth countries.[50] Proof paradoxes challenge the belief standard of proof by purportedly undermining the ability of fact-finders to form a belief, or the appropriateness of that belief if it can be formed. But not all of the objections attributed to the proof paradox are in fact of this type. Some are simply objections to the sufficiency of evidence independent of its probabilistic expression. There are three forms of proof objections that have been variously attributed to the proof paradox, but it is only the latter that has the potential to produce the proof paradox's 'anti-liability' intuition.

1. Rule Against Possibilities

If the 'actual' circumstances of an event are unknown, the civil standard is not satisfied by a possible explanation that is no more likely than any other possibility.[51] In *Day v Boston*, the deceased's estate argued that the deceased's probable movements in approaching a railway line could counteract the deceased's contributory negligence.[52] The Court noted that 'it may be quantitatively probable'[53] (although no such quantification was attempted) that the deceased noticed a handcar shortly before his death and could have relied on the presence of the handcar in assuming that no trains were in the vicinity. Absent any evidence of the deceased's actions toward or knowledge of the train that killed him, weighing these probabilities was mere speculation that gave no more certainty about what actually occurred as would predicting the result of a die cast: '[w]ithout something more, the actual result of [the throw] would still be utterly unknown'.[54] The die analogy is apposite. This rule prohibits fact-finding where the choice of any one possibility is indiscriminate or a product of random chance. The proof paradox objection is different. The chance of the bus being Blue is not 'random' on this evidence because there is a .6 probability that the bus was Blue in the absence of any other evidence. It is not equally likely that the bus was Blue or Red.

[50] *Day v Boston*, 52 A 771, 774 (MeSJC, 1902) (Emery J); *Sargent v Massachusetts Accident Company*, 307 Mass 246, 250 (MassSJC, 1940) (Lummus J); *Smith* (n 49) 755 (Spalding J); *People v Collins*, 68 Cal2d 319 (CalSC, 1968) 330ff (Sullivan J); see further I Puppe and R Wright, 'Causation in the Law: Philosophy, Doctrine and Practice' in M Infantino and E Zervogianni (eds), *Causation in European Tort Law* (Cambridge, Cambridge University Press, 2017) 30–31.

[51] *ASIC v Healey* (2011) 196 FCR 291 (FCA) [103] (Middleton J) ('it is not enough for the circumstances to give rise to conflicting inferences of equal degrees of probability') citing *Bradshaw v McEwans* (1951) 217 ALR 1 (HCA) 5; *Luxton v Vines* (1952) 85 CLR 352, 359–60; *Miller v Minister of Pensions* [1947] 2 All ER 372, 373–74; *Sargent* (n 50) 251.

[52] *Day* (n 50) 773.

[53] ibid 774.

[54] ibid.

2. *Rule Against Better Possibilities*

A belief that one scenario is more likely than another will still fail the civil standard if X is not more likely than not-X. In *Smith v Rapid Transit*, the 'mathematical probabilities *somewhat favour[ed]* the proposition that a bus of the defendant caused the accident', but failed to convince the appellate court that the accident was caused by the defendant's bus.[55] Unlike the rule against mere possibilities, these explanations are not randomly associated to the event. A fact-finder could point to a more likely explanation set against any other. But the fact-finder still cannot say this scenario is more likely than not to have occurred.[56] Represented probabilistically, the rule prevents the plaintiff's recovery where 40 buses were owned by Blue, 30 owned by Red and 30 owned by a 'Green Bus Company'. Blue is more likely than Red or Green, but Blue is not more likely than 'not-Blue'.

3. *Rule Against Mere Probabilities*

Can evidence that the probability of X is 'objectively' greater than .5 fail to adequately persuade the fact-finder of the civil burden? At what point does an objective probability become subjectively believed? Even though the proof paradox should mathematically satisfy the civil standard, the fact-finder's intuition is against the plaintiff. *Briginshaw* appears to mirror Tribe's account of a spilt between the objective probabilities represented by NSE that a blue bus is more likely responsible for the accident than a red bus, and the fact-finder's subjective belief that the accident was caused by Blue.[57] Tribe asserts that these two probabilities need not and do not align for NSE. Resolving the proof paradox requires either some mechanism of converting the objective probability into a subjective belief or displacing or augmenting the objective probability by case-specific evidence.

One riposte to a purely mathematical or objective account of legal fact-finding comes from the assumption that some facts, such as fraud or judicial bias,[58] are more inherently improbable than others and require clearer and more convincing proof than other facts. Fact-finding is contextually sensitive to the fact under consideration.[59] If so, one could argue the civil standard is not purely mathematical and that objective probabilities cannot of themselves be sufficient to form subjective beliefs. Otherwise how could the standard also be sensitive to the type of fact to be found?

[55] *Smith* (n 49) 755 (emphasis added).

[56] *Jones v Dunkel* (1959) 101 CLR 298, 305.

[57] Tribe (n 48) 1349.

[58] *Re Day* (2017) 263 CLR 201, [15]–[16]. The High Court of Australia (HCA) explained at [18] (referring to *Bradshaw* (n 51) the need to demonstrate more than mere equal possibilities. That is a different rule. Any fact, whether ex ante improbable or not, has to be demonstrated as being more than one of a number of equal possibilities.

[59] *Briginshaw* (n 1) 362. The same point has been made in English law: *Re H* [1996] AC 563 (HL) 586–87. For an analysis of this concept, see M Redmayne, 'Standards of Proof in Civil Litigation' (1999) 62 *MLR* 167.

It is critical that this principle does not regard the standard of proof as any higher.[60] Instead, more or more cogent material is needed to justify an actual belief in the existence of an inherently more improbable event. Fraud is assumed (as no evidence is tendered to prove this) to be improbable.[61] On an inductive approach, a subjective belief that fraud occurred on balance of probabilities would need to displace that ex ante improbability. That does not contradict the ability to find the existence of fraud from objective probabilities alone. The standard is still more probable than not. If the fact to be proved could be demonstrated to possess an objective probability of greater than 50%, and the fact-finder subjectively believed that probability, then the *Briginshaw* standard has been satisfied because the objective probabilities are not then independent of belief. The higher threshold of belief for fraud must have been met if the subjective belief was formed. There may need to be a more compelling reason to accept the objective probability adequately reflects the truth.[62] As long as the fact-finder forms that belief there is no reason why objective probabilities cannot be sufficient for improbable facts like fraud or judicial bias.

III. Resolving the Proof Paradox

Resolving the proof paradox depends on understanding the necessary conditions for forming a subjective belief from an objective probability. Objectors to mere probabilities argue that, by itself, NSE cannot reasonably satisfy the fact-finder of the truth. A collection of theories support this point of view, divided into epistemic (NSE lacks Keynesian weight compared to direct evidence),[63] moral (it is unjust to hold individuals liable merely because they possess a common characteristic)[64] and normative (litigants might engage in 'lazy' litigation and not search for better evidence, or belief in legal systems might be undermined)[65]

[60] *Re Day* (n 58) [15], fn 18.

[61] Described in ibid [16] as a 'conventional perception'. See also *Re H* (n 59) 586 (Lord Nicholls).

[62] A similar formulation was adopted by the House of Lords in *Re H* (n 59) 586–87. The irony in Dixon J's formulation is that although he suggests fact-finding ought to be subjective, his statement that improbable facts should only be proved when 'everybody feels' reasonable satisfaction is more akin to an objective standard: *Briginshaw* (n 1) 362. Subjective standards explicitly recognise the possibility of disagreements; objective standards are designed to avoid such differences: M Galavotti, 'The Origins of Probabilistic Epistemology' in A Hajek and C Hitchcock (eds), *The Oxford Handbook of Probability and Philosophy* (Oxford, Oxford University Press, 2016) 136 (frequentism); D Gillies, 'The Propensity Interpretation' in A Hajek and C Hitchcock (eds), *The Oxford Handbook of Probability and Philosophy* (Oxford, Oxford University Press, 2016) 115–16 (Popper's objective propensity account). It cannot be correct that fact-finding rests on the proposition that 'everyone' must feel that the fact is proved in order for it to be legally so. That standard would be rationally impossible to reach. Not even the criminal law requires unanimous agreement.

[63] Cohen, *Probable* (n 14) ch 7; Stein, *Foundations* (n 44) 92.

[64] D Wasserman, 'The Morality of Statistical Proof and the Risk of Mistaken Liability' (1991) 13 *Cardozo Law Review* 935, 952; Pundik, 'Generalisation' (n 29) 197, 201, 203–05.

[65] Tribe (n 48) 1349; Nesson (n 49) 1366ff; R Posner, 'An Economic Approach to the Law of Evidence' (1999) 51 *Stanford Law Review* 1477, 1509.

domains. Dividing the objections in this way is, however, unhelpful because it perpetuates the confusion between statistical evidence and NSE, discussed in section IV below. Instead, the objections to the proof paradoxes can be more specifically defined as the risk of unavoidable liability, and the roles of 'certainty' and 'individuality'.

For abundant caution, this chapter does not argue that any proof paradox evidence by itself could be sufficient for legal fact-finding. The 'naked' paradigm is effectively impossible to generate in a legal proceeding because it relies on taking every constituent fact in the proof paradox at face value. But, on an assumption of nakedness, the objective probability created by the proof paradox can be converted into a subjective belief to satisfy the *Briginshaw* standard.

A. Unavoidable Liability

There are two parts to unavoidable liability. The first consists of the economic and accuracy concern that all potential cases will be decided in favour of the party with the greatest market share. If Blue owns 60 of 100 buses, under the 'all-or-nothing'[66] rule of civil proof Blue would always be liable even though, statistically, Blue should only be liable 60% of the time. Levanon raises a related objection. If the evidence is that 90% of tall people steal cars, there is a necessary error rate of 10%. When extended across the entire reference class, this means that 10% of all decisions are necessarily wrong.[67] This is said to be an objection to reliance on NSE as individualised evidence is not necessarily guaranteed to be incorrect through a process of narrowing reference classes to an almost individual level meaning that individualised evidence could, logically, be correct in every instance.

In later writing, Levanon draws a distinction between NSE that indicates propensity, and NSE that does not.[68] Under the paradigm of NSE that is adopted in this work, such a distinction cannot exist. Either NSE arises exclusively from a probabilistic extrapolation that is entirely frequentist, or there is an (unquantifiable) additional factor that involves inferring a propensity to act by reason of a statistical association. The former meets the criteria for NSE because the probability is individualised to the question in issue. The latter does not because it necessarily involves crossing an inferential gap.

These objections can be dealt with by way of individualised justice. It is a stated assumption in law that each case is decided on its own merits.[69] The rule of law requires that individual cases be decided on the evidence in that proceeding.[70]

[66] *Tabet v Gett* (2010) 240 CLR 537, 578 [113].

[67] L Levanon, 'Statistical Evidence, Assertions and Responsibility' (2019) 82 *MLR* 269, 285–87.

[68] L Levanon, *Evidence, Respect and Truth: Knowledge and Justice in Legal Trials* (Oxford, Hart, 2022) 135ff.

[69] Ho (n 1) 142–43.

[70] ibid 143.

The law should not take into account the evidence in or outcomes of potential cases especially where there is no evidence that such cases have commenced or could be commenced.[71]

But even if the law did take those matters into account, such objections cannot stand. Collective multiple actions in Blue Bus are less problematic because of the single source of liability. Gatecrasher is more difficult. If 1000 seats are occupied and only 499 tickets were sold, potentially all attendees at the concert, including those who already paid, would be liable for the ticket price. A market-share liability response (under either the all-or-nothing approach or substantive market-share allocation) cannot suffice here because each attendee is individually liable; either the action succeeds against all of them or none. A solution is provided for by the law of evidence. In any civil action, the burden of proof rests on the moving party; the plaintiff. If the evidence meets the standard of proof, the onus shifts to the defendant to disprove those facts or prove the existence of a legitimate defence. The same applies to unavoidable liability. If a plaintiff tenders evidence in a civil case against a party that objectively meets the threshold, the onus shifts onto the defendant to answer that evidence.[72] And that could be achieved by evidence to the effect of 'I bought a ticket'. NSE is flimsy evidence, but it is enough to meet the standard of proof under the strict (but highly artificial) conditions of the proof paradox. Because it lacks Keynesian weight, however, the moment any contrary evidence is introduced, its probative value plummets.

Two things occur from the contrary evidence in Gatecrasher. First, if that evidence is given, and no proof of purchase is produced or no reasonable explanation given for why it was not, that could be a compelling inference against the gatecrasher over and above the NSE. Second, the objective probability is automatically no longer 'naked'; now there are competing considerations to take into account in forming an epistemic belief in the truth. The paradoxical element has been dispelled. Procedures of this type are commonplace, for example, applications for default judgment. The plaintiff commences proceedings based on evidence of a debt. Notification of the proceeding is sent to the defendant. If the defendant chooses not to respond, default judgment is entered without further evaluation or hearing of the evidence. If the defendant does respond, default judgment cannot be entered; the analogy to NSE being the existence of evidence in addition to the objective probabilities.

As such, the objection to NSE in civil fact-finding is misplaced. For the most part, NSE can never actually arise. Even if one were to insist on resolution by way of NSE, the objection is resolvable because the defendant has conceded its right to adduce evidence in response. Defendants are entitled to put the plaintiff to proof by eschewing any evidence on their own behalf.[73] But once

[71] Koehler and Shaviro (n 30) 258–59.
[72] Hodgson, 'Probability' (n 43) 59–60.
[73] Eg *Australian Prudential Regulation Authority v Kelaher* [2019] FCA 1521, [140].

the plaintiff has produced evidence that prima facie meets the standard of proof, it is for the defendant to put on its own case or to challenge the cogency and credibility of the plaintiff's evidence. The defendant has to bear the consequences of its strategic decision not to put on its own case.

If, however, the criminal standard of proof applies, this process fails entirely. One cannot, in the abstract, quantify a reasonable doubt because the existence of a reasonable doubt (numerically expressed or otherwise) is itself subjective.[74] There is no rational point before $p=1$ where a doubt is no longer 'reasonable' because how the fact-finder perceives those probabilities will differ. A probability of .99 still entails a reasonable or 'rational' possibility of the individual being not guilty.[75] A reasonable doubt (unlike, perhaps, the civil standard) is not capable of quantification because it is subjective and has no objective expression that the law will accept. That does not mean that statistical evidence (or perhaps even NSE) could never be sufficient to satisfy the criminal standard. If it is do so, however, it is not exclusively by virtue of the degree of probability, but instead due to its power to inform the necessary belief of the fact-finder, including by reason of the sensitivity of the evidence to the facts that have to be proved.[76] Where the criminal standard applies,[77] fact-finders must form categorical beliefs in that-*p*. Of course, statistical evidence and objective probabilities can contribute to the fact-finder's belief in that-*p*.[78] But that is very different to identifying a numerical standard of 'beyond reasonable doubt'. It makes no sense to couch any discussion of NSE in the context of the criminal standard. NSE, by definition, allows for a competing, rational inference of non-guilt.

B. Certainty

Objections to NSE over the role of uncertainty arose from the rejection of the use of classical probability in fact-finding. Cohen argued that probabilistic fact-finding was believed to be prima facie incompatible with the inductive method.[79] Logically, the existence of past events can only be rationally expressed categorically as either true (1) or false (0); if one is to resolve disputes based on the existence of past events, one cannot say that a past event 'probably occurred'.[80] Either it did

[74] Thomson (n 42) 201; Tribe (n 48) 1341; J Franklin, 'The Objective Bayesian Conceptualisation of Proof and Reference Class Problems' (2011) 33 *Sydney Law Review* 545, 553–54.

[75] cf S Moss, *Probabilistic Knowledge* (Oxford, Oxford University Press, 2018) 204.

[76] See, eg, Di Bello (n 31) 12258.

[77] The criminal standard typically applies to *factum probandum* and 'intermediate facts' from which inferences are to be drawn: *Shepherd v The Queen* (1990) 170 CLR 573, 579.

[78] R Schmalbeck, 'The Trouble with Statistical Evidence' (1986) 49 *Law and Contemporary Problems* 221, 236.

[79] LJ Cohen, 'The Role of Evidential Weight in Criminal Proof' in P Tillers and E Green (eds), *Probability and Inference in the Law of Evidence* (Philadelphia, Kluwer, 1988) 117–22.

[80] See discussion in *Gregg v Scott* [2005] 2 AC 176 (HL) 182 (Lord Nicholls).

or it did not occur. NSE presents a problem because it acknowledges an explicit risk of error.[81] That is, if the probability Blue caused the accident is .51, there is a .49 chance that Blue did not cause the accident. How are fact-finders supposed to make a categorical statement about their belief in the truth when there is an explicitly acknowledged risk of falsehood?

The uncertainty objection has arisen from a mistaken assumption about the process of fact-finding, led in part by some awkwardly phrased jurisprudence. Cohen reveals that part of the rejection of probabilistic methods of legal reasoning comes from an assumption that facts in legal proceedings must be established to a certainty[82] and '[have] a right answer, irrespective of the person uttering the answer'.[83] Ho's requirement that fact-finders believe that-*p* (accepting that-*p* and probably-*p* are distinct) would also suggest that NSE is always insufficient for liability because there is an express probability assigned to not-*p*.[84] NSE is always insufficient on this logic (as in criminal law) because even though a fact-finder may '[believe the event] to be probably true … he does not know and therefore does not believe the proposition to be *in fact* true'.[85] The difference according to Cohen and Ho, is that non-quantitative evidence processed inductively can be categorically believed as no explicit risk of error remains. However informal, a fact-finder can disregard competing explanations and form an unimpeded categorical belief in the truth.[86]

Moss makes a similar claim from moral philosophy. Her thesis is that legal fact-finding in particular requires 'knowledge' in order to epistemically justified.[87] In non-legal contexts it is possible to derive knowledge from 'credences' (probabilistic beliefs) even though they are necessarily attended by uncertainty.[88] However, Moss suggests that knowledge is not capable of being formed in legal fact-finding (whether to the civil or criminal standard) by statistical evidence (for which she uses naked statistical evidence hypotheticals as examples) because she contends that such evidence does not exclude a possibility that the 'defendant is an exception to the statistical generalisation presented by the plaintiff'.[89]

As noted above, some tacit support for this point of view can be drawn from Dixon J's statement in *Briginshaw* that fact-finders should feel an 'actual persuasion of its occurrence or existence'. One could interpret actual persuasion to mean a belief in the truth, and because truth is binary, a probabilistic standard can never rationally support such a belief, making NSE ipso facto insufficient. But that is not

[81] Levanon, 'Statistical Evidence' (n 67) 286–87; Koehler (n 29) 687.
[82] Cohen, 'Subjective Probability' (n 45) 632.
[83] ibid 630.
[84] Ho (n 1) 140.
[85] ibid 140.
[86] ibid 141–42; Cohen, *Probable* (n 14) 271–72.
[87] Moss (n 75) 10.1–10.2.
[88] ibid 5.1.
[89] ibid 211.

what Dixon J meant and nor has the law developed in this way. The civil burden of proof only requires a fact-finder to believe *p* to a 'reasonable satisfaction',[90] which is emphatically a probabilistic standard. 'Certainty' in legal fact-finding is not a product of reasoning but of law.[91] A fact is not proven because it possesses or is found to possess a 'probabilistic' value of 1. 'Legal certainty' is a status the law gives to facts because 'no other conclusive answer can be given'.[92] Requiring 'certain' beliefs would obliterate the distinction between the civil and criminal standards,[93] and fact-finding would be converted into an exercise in futility. The law accepts that absolute 'truth' is unnecessary for fact-finding;[94] what is actually sought is a justifiable reasonable and epistemological approximation of the truth.

C. Individuality

Individuality (Cohen's 'problem of negation')[95] suggests that the law prohibits reliance on NSE because the evidence does not reveal anything that is personal to the individual. In effect, NSE cannot be generalised. The problem is said to be both epistemic and moral. One cannot form a subjective belief from an insufficiently discriminatory objective probability, and finding the individual liable on this evidence would undermine their autonomy because liability attaches to a shared trait over which they have no control. Two theoretical camps have developed over the problem of individualisation: those who believe objective probabilities promote accuracy and should be sufficient (probabilists), and those who object to fact-finding on objective probabilities on epistemic, moral and normative grounds (particularists).

Cohen and Wright, both of whom make similar arguments, best represent the particularist position. Cohen suggests that the link between sitting at the rodeo and gatecrashing is spurious and 'quite irrelevant to the matter at issue because it is only an accident and not the manifestation of some causal link' between attendance and gatecrashing.[96] Such a causal link can only be provided if one could infer that this individual gatecrasher, or Blue's buses, had a particular propensity to do the act. But as NSE relies only on a probability reflected in a single instance event where there is an express disconnect between the variables Blue and accident, no such interpretation can be made.[97] Wright argues that because the proportion of

[90] *Helton* (n 19) 712 (Dixon, Evatt and McTiernan JJ).

[91] Ch 1, section I.D.3.

[92] *Tabet* (n 66) 578 (Kiefel J); *Commonwealth v Amann Aviation* (1991) 174 CLR 64, 124.

[93] The difference between those standards is a 'matter of critical substance' and rigidly enforced: *Rejfek v McElroy* (1965) 112 CLR 517, 521–22.

[94] See (amongst many others) HL Ho, 'Evidence and Truth' in C Dahlman, A Stein and G Tuznet (eds), *Philosophical Foundations of Evidence Law* (Oxford, Oxford University Press, 2021) 14–16.

[95] Cohen, *Probable* (n 14) ch 7.

[96] Cohen, 'Subjective Probability' (n 45) 633.

[97] ibid 634.

buses exists independently of any accident, the evidence cannot be probative to identify which colour of bus caused the accident.[98] There is no causal relationship between the fact to be proved (the colour of the bus involved in the accident) and the evidence used to prove it (market share of bus colour).[99] That might be compared to, for example, a circumstance where an individual identifies and testifies to the presence of a blue bus. Such evidence cannot exist but for a witness' attendance at the scene of the accident and is therefore 'caused' by it.[100]

If Cohen and Wright are correct, and the epistemic value of NSE is 'spurious', then NSE is irrelevant. But the links between Blue and accident, and attendee and gatecrashing are not spurious. Relationships between variables are spurious when there is no logical connection between them. NSE is not so implicated. True, colour does not, in logic (or at least without more evidence), predispose a particular bus towards accidents. But there is a logical connection between Blue and accident by reason of the proof paradox's construct; there are more Blue buses in the area than any other colour. The link is not one of causation (in the sense that because the buses are coloured blue they are responsible for accidents) but simple mathematics and logical probability; frequency, not propensity, justifies the link. As the next section demonstrates, breaking the strict paradigm of the proof paradox fundamentally alters this conclusion. As NSE is premised on a closed circuit such that all possible eventualities are known, it is manifestly untrue to say that the probability of an individual Blue bus causing an accident is spurious.

Ordinarily, the individualisation objection to the use of class-based probabilities is predicated on the uncertainty in using the class-based probability to represent what actually happened to the individual. That is not a problem for NSE. Accounting for all possible events means that it is logically justifiable under a frequentist approach to attribute the class-wide probability directly to the individual member of that class. The number of events is sufficiently large to allow frequentist logic to identify an association.[101] There is no need for any innate causal or propensity relationship between colour and accident to extrapolate from the class probability to the individual. Indeed, Blue Bus and Gatecrasher draw their strength from the random association between the variables. If one takes a jar and fills it with 51 yellow and 49 green marbles randomly distributed throughout the jar, any randomly drawn marble is more likely to be yellow than green. Yellow is not inherently predisposed to be chosen; it is more likely to be chosen because of its increased frequency within the group. If the marbles were not randomly distributed, and yellow was predominant toward the top of the jar, one would need to re-estimate the probability of drawing a yellow marble on first try because now

[98] R Wright, 'Causation, Responsibility, Risk, Probability, Naked Statistics, and Proof: Pruning the Bramble Bush by Clarifying the Concepts' (1988) 73 *Iowa Law Review* 1001, 1053–54.

[99] See further Thomson (n 42) 204.

[100] ibid.

[101] cf AL Caze, 'Frequentism' in A Hajek and C Hitchcock (eds), *The Oxford Handbook of Probability and Philosophy* (Oxford, Oxford University Press, 2016) 343–44.

there is an additional causal explanation for yellow being initially more probable; the frequency of yellow is higher at the top of the jar and therefore a yellow marble is more likely to be chosen initially. The tendency for yellow to be chosen is not a product of a behavioural trait of the drawer (or the marble), but arises from the frequency.

The probability of the accident being caused by a bus belonging to Blue is greater than .5. The standard of proof in civil cases is satisfied if the fact-finder believes the event is more likely than not. One could not believe that Blue is more likely than not if there was any contraindication that the objective probability was inaccurate, such as a discovery that the underlying figures were unreliable. The proof paradox directly excludes any such chance. The objective probability is entirely uncontradicted. It is a canon of logic and of legal reasoning that if a fact is uncontradicted (whether by other evidence or inference) then it should be accepted.[102] In the absence of a reason otherwise, it is logical that subjective probability should follow objective probability.[103] The objective class-based probability (n) and the subjective individual probability (p) must under the conditions of the proof paradox become one. NSE is individualised evidence.

Particularists have sought to get around this problem of the automatic merger of n and p through speculation about hypothetical reference classes. Despite an individual accidentally belonging to a class of gatecrashers, the individual may also belong to other reference classes that would alter that probability. He could be a member of the 'boy scouts' (leading to an inference that boy scouts are less likely than the average person to gatecrash).[104] This logic has been pervasive in the debate around NSE. However, it is fundamentally flawed. The reference class debate in practice usually arises about individuals for whom there is evidence of membership in other possible classes. In the '*Shonubi* cases', there was an extant question of why the reference class 'Nigerian drug smuggler' was a more appropriate reference class for the defendant than 'bridge attendant at the George Washington bridge'.[105] Evidence demonstrated that the defendant actually belonged to both of those classes and for whom probabilities could be (in theory) calculated. But that does not arise in NSE. There is no evidence that the gatecrasher was a boy scout. If there was, the evidence could no longer be called naked.

A more challenging example arises in Blue Bus. The reference class for Blue Bus assumes that the probability for the individual bus can be derived from a

[102] *R v Brennan* [2015] Cr App R 14 (CA) [45], [56], citing *R v Bailey* (1978) 66 Cr App R 31 (CA) 32 (Lord Goddard CJ). This is distinct from the principle that judges need not accept unchallenged facts: *Various claimants v Giambrone* [2015] EWHC 1946 (QB) [17]–[21]. NSE presents a factual scenario where there is no rational possibility of contradiction.

[103] See D Gillies, *Philosophical Theories of Probability* (Oxford, Routledge, 2000) 410–11, referring to C Howson and P Urbach, *Scientific Reasoning: The Bayesian Approach* (Open Court, 1989) 228.

[104] D Meyerson, 'Risks, Rights, Statistics and Compulsory Measures' (2009) 31 *Sydney Law Review* 507, 517; RJ Allen and M Pardo, 'The Problematic Value of Mathematical Models of Evidence' (2007) 36 *Journal of Legal Studies* 107, 109ff.

[105] See discussion in M Colyvan, HM Regan and S Ferson, 'Is it a Crime to Belong to a Reference Class?' (2001) 9 *Journal of Political Philosophy* 168, 172.

particular undefined zone. But buses rarely appear randomly throughout a zone. Buses are usually subject to a timetable with set routes. If so, the probability of a blue or red bus being in a particular area of the zone is clearly not the same as the background probability for all buses within that zone, and so the proof paradox fails at the first hurdle. There is an objection to the individualisation of the background probability to the individual bus because there may yet be a propensity associated with colour for which no probability estimate has been provided. If only Red buses travelled the street where the accident took place, the background probability is clearly wrong. The anti-liability intuition arises in that scenario not because of the nature of the evidence as such, but because it is inapposite to prove the fact in issue required to establish the cause of action, being whether, to the civil standard, the bus was blue or red. Unlike speculation as to whether the defendant was a boy scout, a fact is not being invented to alter the probabilities. The risk in fact is inherent to the evidence that is being adduced given the circumstances of the hypothetical whereby two bus companies are operating, by definition and based on the body of knowledge that a fact-finder brings to a fact-finding process, to a timetable and pre-set routes.

If we assume, by contrast, that the set up to the hypothetical was akin to the marble example given above, that reference class objection falls away. Assume that all pre-set bus routes were cancelled on that day, such that there was no reason why a blue bus was more likely than a red bus to be in the area. We can no longer ascribe a propensity for bus colour to be associated with that region of the zone as colour is again random. If colour is random, the probability of a bus in that area being blue or red returns to the background probability, and the reference class predicated on zone is an apposite predictor of the probability that the bus was more likely than not to be blue.

Legal reasoning does not and cannot permit speculation about possible facts.[106] Even if no new evidence is adduced, one can challenge the credibility of evidence. Inferences can be made from evidence. Evidence that an individual is lying about a state of affairs can be used to prove the opposite state of affairs, even if there is no other evidence supporting that view.[107] But to fabricate the existence of evidence is another matter entirely. One could change the probability of an individual having committed murder on direct evidence if one could invent or speculate about possible witness testimony, fingerprint evidence, DNA evidence or CCTV evidence. Decisions must be made only on the admitted evidence (or the absence of evidence) and reasonably available inference, not wilful speculation.[108]

[106] Eg *Lockyer Investment v Smallacombe* (1994) 50 FCR 358 (FCAFC) 366C–E, 370–71, where Einfield J rejected further speculation into what might have happened but for the misleading representations.

[107] *Shah v Hagemrad* [2018] FCA 91, [95], citing *Steinberg v FCT* (1975) 134 CLR 640.

[108] Albeit where to draw this line is not always clear: see consideration in *Kay's Tutor v Ayrshire and Arran Health Board* 1987 SC (HL), 166–67, concerning Lord Keith's deliberations about how far one may infer effects from statistical evidence to cover epistemic gaps between the reference class and the instant case.

Although inventing membership in reference classes is not permissible, the proof paradoxes do suggest the availability of inferences contrary to the objective probability. Hodgson argues that even if the objective probability in Blue Bus might be sufficient in some cases, this doesn't apply to Gatecrasher. Without evidence of the ticketing process, it is unreasonable to decide against the individual based on the objective probability alone.[109] With respect, Hodgson's argument is correct within a model of judicial proof – there are many available inferences that override the objectively probable but Keynesian weight-deficient evidence. But to take those matters into account destroys the 'naked' paradigm and renders the evidence of .501 probability moot. Now the evidence has to be reassessed in light of the competing inferences. The same applies to Blue Bus. In a model of legal fact-finding it is necessary to take into account the credibility of the figures used to establish the probability. Unless those figures are conceded (as they are in the proof paradox) that assessment affects the fact-finder's belief in truth of the fact, however minutely, and causes the objective probability to no longer apply directly from the group to the individual.

One might contend that the assumption above regarding the cancellation of bus routes on the day violates the conditions of NSE. Instead, assume that no evidence is led about bus timetables at all. That leaves a question for a fact-finder of how to cope with the background generalisation that buses operate according to timetables and no way of knowing how that affects the probabilities of the reference class against the individual probabilities of the accident-causing bus. This raises a quandary. What is the difference between inferring a different probability because of the generalisation that buses operate according to timetables against the absence of the evidence about the personality or memberships of the gatecrasher? There are two answers to this question. The first is that the questions are different. An inference that buses operate according to timetables and routes is part of a commonsense or background generalisation that may be dispelled by evidence. If, for example, the exclusive zone in fact had no timetables or routes, the (unknown) propensity to be in an area falls away and thus so does the individualisation problem. By contrast, there is no commonsense or background generalisation supporting the proposition that all gatecrashers, or at least all of the people who are potentially gatecrashers, are boy scouts. In the absence of such a commonsense or background generalisation, which fact-finders are legitimately entitled to make as part of the fact-finding process that requires them to use their innate knowledge to solve real world problems, one cannot take into account the probabilities of unknown facts for which there is no evidence in support. The second answer is that the law of evidence in fact provides a solution to the failure to adduced evidence. It is an integral part of any piece of litigation that the party asserting a fact has the burden of proving that fact. If the victim in Blue Bus is to rely on the background probability of buses in a particular zone, she will have to satisfy a court that the probabilistic evidence she is leading is capable of doing so. That means she has to prove that the

[109] Hodgson, 'Probability' (n 43) 59.

probability of *n* and *p* are the same. She can only do so if she can establish that the reference class from which the probability is drawn is apposite. Due to the background generalisation about the nature of buses, she will need to prove that there is no reason red buses are not more common in that area than the background probability would suggest. If she does not lead any evidence on that point, a court will be satisfied that in fact the probability of *p* may not be entirely explained by *n*, and the proof paradox fails. If she can prove that there is no causal relationship between colour and location of the incident, then the probability of *n* is an apposite measure of *p*.

Particularists object to fact-finding from NSE due to a larger moral dynamic. Merging objective and subjective probabilities is a mistake without a source of independent verification of that belief. The merger is considered analogous to betting.[110] The objective probability can be taken to represent the likelihood that an individual would bet on the outcome. As objective probabilities are flimsy, a rational actor would not bet on these objective probabilities for fear of cutting across evidence or inferences, currently unknown to the fact-finder, that might influence the fact-finder's decision. Similarly, one might argue that fact-finding from NSE elides the principles in *Briginshaw* and the requirement of actual belief.[111] As belief must be sensitive to the inherent improbability of the fact-in-issue, one could argue that the proof paradoxes cannot account for the need for some facts to be established from evidence with greater warrant.

For the purpose of resolving the proof paradox only, the answer to fact-finding from flimsy evidence lies in the nature of the scenario. In short, these 'problems' have no place in the proof paradox. The proof paradoxes are deliberately free of all countervailing inferences. The moment those walls are breached, objective probabilities of *p* must be revised in light of a myriad of other facts, inferences and presumptions that weigh on the objective probability, obviating the point of the proof paradox in its entirety. As such, in proposing a sensible resolution of the proof paradox, the lack of Keynesian weight presents no true obstacle.

Betting is an inapposite analogy to legal reasoning in these scenarios. Bets are, by definition, actions taken on the basis of probabilities that are ultimately verifiable. If X is bitten by a venomous snake, the ex ante probabilities of 'will X die without treatment' or 'will X survive with treatment' can be approximated from previous empirical research and tested, because those conditions can come to fruition depending on which avenue is taken. Those outcomes lie yet in the future. By contrast, the existence or non-existence of a fact may not be verifiable; legal fact-finding is self-confirmatory. A bet made under those conditions is nonsensical because it could never be settled.[112] It is akin to asking 'will I die from

[110] M Dant, 'Gambling on the Truth: The Use of Purely Statistical Evidence as a Basis for Civil Liability' (1988) 22 *Columbia Journal of Law and Social Problems* 31, 47; Ho (n 1) 142.

[111] *Briginshaw* (n 1) 362.

[112] Cohen, 'Subjective Probability' (n 45) 631, repudiating Kaye's claim that with sufficient resources metaphysical truths could be uncovered; cf D Kaye, 'The Laws of Probability and the Law of the Land' (1979) 47 *University of Chicago Law Review* 34, 45.

this snake bite' when, first, the identity of the snake is not known, and second, when one cannot even be sure that the bite is from a snake – or a bite at all. If one accepts that the objective probability is true and epistemologically meets the civil standard, does this supposed immorality of accepting a non-confirmable bet differ in any way from the ordinary fact-finding process? If a difference between fact-finding from direct evidence and fact-finding from NSE could be shown, then one could argue that NSE should be insufficient for fact-finding. If no such difference exists, and because the probability of the event being true is identifiable, then no prejudice could arise.

With respect, there has never been a satisfactory explanation for why fact-finding from NSE is different from other 'individualised' evidence. Dant argues that there is a distinction between betting on an outcome and believing in an outcome.[113] If one assumes the existence of a jar of randomly distributed blue and red marbles, where 60% are blue and 40% are red, it would be a rational inference in Dant's view to bet that there is a 60% probability that any marble drawn at random would be blue. But that same individual could not form an ex ante belief that the marble is red because 'her bet would be a mere guess as to the actual color of the particular marble'.[114] Dant's view is predicated on 'rational decision making' requiring 'evidentiary support' whereas gambling is only about maximising utility in the long term; the latter being an impermissible basis for legal fact-finding. The problem for this view is that in the context of NSE there is no evidentiary basis to reject the objective probability. The proof paradox forces the evidence to be individualised. This decision is not a mere guess. It is an objective probability for which there is no rational basis for not forming a concomitant subjective belief. The individualisation objection upon which particularists rely doesn't arise in NSE.

Likewise, Levanon's objections to NSE premised on the guarantee of error are similarly contended to be mistaken. The key thesis in this objection is that because NSE, over the long run, guarantees erroneous decisions, and logically individualised evidence does not, fact-finders will be laboured with what Levanon refers to as 'burdensome errors', that is, a belief that the fact-finder does not trust to be true.[115] As such evidence is not capable of eliminating error, especially in the criminal context, fact-finding based on such evidence is 'tragic' by reason of the risk of false convictions uniquely presented by such evidence.[116] There appear to be at least two flaws with Levanon's argument. First, the claim that case-specific evidence can be trusted to be true in the long run seems overly optimistic. Narrowing a reference class (drawn on Levanon's thesis from case-specific evidence) can improve the strength of the generalisation from that reference class to the individual case but cannot provide a guarantee of accuracy. Suggesting otherwise is simply

[113] Dant (n 110) 44.
[114] ibid 45.
[115] Levanon, 'Statistical Evidence' (n 67) 287.
[116] Levanon, *Evidence* (n 68) 127–28 (for similar fact evidence), 135–37 (for NSE meeting Levanon's definition).

turning one's eyes from the possibility of error rather than identifying an epistemic process that actually reduces error. Ignoring the possibility of error is quite different from demonstrating the absence of error. Second, even assuming there was a rational difference between NSE and individualised evidence in the way Levanon suggests (and ignoring the problem of making evidentiary arguments based on probabilities that play out in the long run), the contention that fact-finders should not be required to find facts from evidence they do not 'trust' is misplaced. If the fact-finder has sufficient subjective doubt about the probabilities of the evidence, clearly the fact cannot be found because it falls foul of *Briginshaw*. But, in the closed context of NSE, there is no rational objection to NSE merely because of its flimsiness.

The mistaken nature of this objection is best seen in Ho's account of the difference between betting and fact-finding:

> Fact-finding is unlike betting on the truth; it is not about acting on probabilities. To bet that the defendant did not pay for his entrance is not to assert that he did not pay for his entrance. On the other hand, to find the defendant had gatecrashed is ordinarily to assert that he had gatecrashed. While the statistics may justify the belief that the defendant had probably committed trespass (a partial belief), it does not justify the belief that he had in fact committed trespass (a categorical belief). The latter is necessary for a finding of liability.[117]

As noted above, belief in the truth need not be categorical. Risk arising from direct evidence (that the evidence does not reflect the truth) is identical to the risk from NSE (that the probability does not reflect the truth). Neither source of evidence is ever independently verifiable. In the tightly constrained paradigm of the proof paradox, the problem of individualisation, at least insofar as it is different from or worse for other types of evidence, does not arise.

IV. Objective Probabilities and Statistical Evidence

By reason of their forcibly individualised nature, proof paradoxes have only limited explanatory worth to statistical evidence. Many scholars have complained that the proof paradox is beset by excessive artificiality and could never arise in practice.[118] Although it may be going too far to say that it could never arise, it is nonetheless extremely unlikely. For objective and subjective probabilities to meet requires all other factual disputes to be conceded. The existence of another fact or inference (Z) immediately creates at least four separate probabilistic calculations; the probability of *n*, the probability of Z, the probability adjustment of

[117] Ho (n 1) 142.

[118] Eggleston (n 3) 41; D Kaye, 'Apples and Oranges: Confidence Coefficients and the Burden of Persuasion' (1987) 73 *Cornell Law Review* 54, 55–56; RJ Allen and CK Smiciklas, 'The Law's Aversion to Naked Statistics and Other Mistakes' (2022) 28 *Legal Theory* 179, 197.

n and Z given each other, and the probability of p given n and Z and any necessary adjustment. Under ordinary circumstances, a fact-finder may express some doubt that the injured individual could categorically identify a bus without forming any view on its colour. One might infer that the individual did not see the vehicle in question, but relied on other, less accurate, sensory stimuli. That inference would undermine the flimsy Keynesian weight of the NSE, requiring a revaluation of the probabilities. So, whilst in theory the proof paradox is easily resolved, its significance to fact-finding is limited. Yet, NSE assumes a disproportionately large role in the debates around statistical evidence and has led the arguments of the probabilists and particularists to run at cross-purposes to one another.

Before entering into that debate, it must be noted that the arguments below focus on epistemic and moral-epistemic accounts of objections to NSE. There are, however, a myriad of other objections firmly within the moral and normative categories that are not addressed. These include Moss's arguments on moral encroachment, and Dahlman's incentive approach, amongst many others. They are not addressed in detail in this book because in general terms they do not implicate the law of evidence.

For example, the incentive account of NSE suggests that such evidence should not be the basis for a conviction because allowing such convictions would not 'contribute in a positive way to the incentive structure for lawful behaviour'.[119] The difficulty with such an approach is that it is not clear what the law of evidence could or should do about it. If the suggestion is that the evidence is bad only because some future person may not be appropriately incentivised, there is no identifiable prejudice in adducing that evidence that the law of evidence understands (and those in support of the theory do not claim that incentive structure is a basis for inadmissibility).[120] Parliament could, if it so chose, seek to act on such a view by creating a law substantive rule that individuals should not be convicted on the basis of statistical evidence alone. Such a rule would be difficult to implement in practice and, if it were further limited to NSE, would almost never arise.

Similarly, the application of moral encroachment theories to the NSE debate may be able to raise questions about the underlying premise of certain substantive rules, but says little about how the law of evidence should approach NSE or statistical evidence. Moss defines moral encroachment to mean that that 'epistemic status of an opinion can depend on its moral features'.[121] That is, the extent to which relying on statistical evidence may be morally concerning can depend on the subject matter of the evidence itself. Evidence of the propensities of dogs of a particular species to bite humans is said to be morally less concerning than relying on racial profiling, and that in turn has an effect on the epistemic status of the evidence. The fact-finder should be more concerned about the capacity of evidence of race

[119] Dahlman and Pundik (n 46) 339.
[120] ibid 340.
[121] S Moss, 'IX – Moral Encroachment' (2018) 123 *Proceedings of the Aristotelian Society* 177, 179.

to map the truth than evidence of the propensity of dogs to bite.[122] This in turn is said to undermine the capacity of the fact-finder to form an opinion from that evidence that constitutes knowledge as opposed to belief, in circumstances where the former is necessary for fact-finding.[123] As noted above, that misconceives what is required for fact-finding at law. But what is significant for present purposes is the claim that such evidence should not be capable of generating knowledge even if it permits the formation of a true belief.[124] Even if the evidence is epistemically sound and capable of supporting the underlying rationale of the law of evidence to find truth and allocate error, the risk latent in racial profiling, as opposed to the propensity of dogs to bite, is that *if* it turns out to be false, the profiled person will suffer a special and unacceptable form of harm,[125] over and above any harm associated with a wrong legal outcome.

Although Moss does not claim that such evidence should be inadmissible, it is difficult to rationalise how such a fundamental defect could exist in evidence and yet still allow its admission. If the evidence is admitted there is a risk that racial profiling played some role in the fact-finding exercise. The difficulty is that the kind of prejudice that moral encroachment identifies has no parallel in how prejudice is understood by the law of evidence. Parliament could decide that evidence of racial tendencies is inadmissible in a criminal proceeding by reason of the risk of moral encroachment. After all, the law of evidence does permit certain highly probative evidence to be excluded from the corpus of evidence on policy grounds, such as evidence that is protected by legal professional privilege. Short of such a step, however, there is no reason why judge-made evidence law would create such a rule or find that such evidence is prejudicial because of the societal impact of that evidence in the event that it is wrong. By contrast, evidence of racial tendencies may be inadmissible if they are spurious, or if adducing that evidence could be characterised as prejudicial in the ordinary way. But that is entirely separate from its probabilistic nature.

A. Probabilists: Ignoring the Problem of Generalisation

NSE can be successfully resolved because the probability of each member of the class Blue causing the accident and the probability that an individual blue-coloured bus caused the accident are identical. There is no need to generalise from n to p. The same applies to Gatecrasher. The probability drawn from n gatecrashers is the same for the individual gatecrasher p. Particularists have (erroneously) sought to counteract this argument by speculating as to the existence of hypothetical reference classes within the proof paradox. But one cannot

[122] bid 180–82.
[123] ibid 189.
[124] ibid 198.
[125] ibid 194.

speculate about the existence of hypothetical relevant evidence; it is illogical to hold parties to the standard of proving the non-existence of evidence not tendered in a proceeding.

Probabilists do not account for the more likely situation where the probability of *n* and *p* are not identical. There is no epistemological guarantee that the probability of a class of individuals being liable is the same for any particular individual. Compression prejudice does not arise in NSE; it is reasonable (and accurate) to assume that the probability of *n* equals that of *p*. No contradicting information is rationally available that undermines the objective probability.[126] Whereas statistical evidence is not so confined. *Brennan* expressly acknowledges that in the absence of contradiction the fact ought to be found, but if further or contradictory evidence is available, the existence of the putative fact needs to be construed in light of that additional evidence.[127] The presumption of nakedness that governs NSE does not apply to statistical evidence.

When interpreting statistical evidence within the commonsense method, failing to address the issue of individualisation is fatal to the probabilists' cause. This flaw is clearly seen in Enoch and Fisher's arguments about 'sensitivity'. Enoch and Fisher acknowledge that statistical evidence is not 'sensitive'; to find Blue liable simply because it possesses more buses means that 'whether or not the finding matches the facts seems to be a matter of luck; we do not base our finding on anything that tracks the truth'.[128] Even if Blue did not cause the accident, the probability that Blue did so from the NSE remains the same. But Enoch and Fisher argue sensitivity is unnecessary because 'good' statistical evidence will facilitate accurate fact-finding.[129]

Enoch and Fisher envisage a balancing exercise between accurate fact-finding on one side and epistemological purity (or sensitivity) on the other. But this argument doesn't develop how to assess whether statistical evidence is 'good' or 'reliable'.[130] For statistical evidence to promote accuracy, the probability obtained relating to *p* from *n* has to be 'accurate'. It follows that if the only evidence of the

[126] K Steele and M Colyvan, 'Meta-uncertainty and the Proof Paradoxes' (2023) 180 *Philosophical Studies* 1927, 1937, who, rightly, identify that the reliability underlying the statistical model may also explain the anti-liability feeling inherent to NSE. The problem remains, however, that once reliability is allowed to permeate the confines of NSE, the Keynesian weight of the evidence is destroyed, rendering the probabilistic inference from NSE nugatory.

[127] *Brennan* (n 102) [66]–[68].

[128] Enoch and Fisher (n 21) 575.

[129] ibid 579; see also Enoch, Spectre and Fisher (n 31) 212ff. Pardo criticises the sensitivity account of statistical evidence as being incapable of explaining the different treatment of statistical evidence from individualised evidence: Pardo (n 31) 63. The gravamen of Pardo's claim is that sensitivity and admissibility are not correlated. Some insensitive evidence is admissible, and some sensitive evidence is inadmissible. This mistakes the interaction between admissibility and sensitivity. Insensitive evidence can be epistemically prejudicial by reason of the inferential gap. It may then be inadmissible if the probative value of the evidence is outweighed by that prejudice. Sensitivity – the consequence of the need to generalise the evidence – does distinguish statistical evidence from other evidence that is not sensitive ex ante.

[130] See S Steel, *Proof of Causation in Tort Law* (Cambridge, Cambridge University Press, 2015) 101.

probability of p is the probability of n, some means of confirming that n is a good representation of and generalisable to p is necessary. Because Enoch and Fisher have argued from NSE (where generalisability is given), they have ignored this crucial step in asserting the worth of statistical evidence and concluding that sensitivity need not matter.

In a later article, Enoch and Spectre state that their conclusions about sensitivity are limited to NSE and not to statistical evidence more broadly.[131] If that is right (which is difficult to accept, as many examples they cite in their prior work are not pure NSE cases),[132] then their conclusion that the law should not be concerned by sensitivity with respect to statistical evidence is limited indeed, because NSE, as such, almost never actually exists. Enoch and Spectre claim that *Tyson Foods* (described below), which is about as close to true base rate and pure NSE evidence as one could imagine existing in the real world, is 'irrelevant' to their claims about sensitivity.[133] If so, it would seem unlikely that there is any practical application of their views. Their conclusion about the unimportance of sensitivity can be explained by the individualised nature of NSE, which is not the case for other statistical evidence.

A similar problem of failing to adequately understand the distinction between NSE and statistical evidence arises in Australian jurisprudence. In *State Government Insurance Commission v Laube*, the Full Court of the Supreme Court of South Australia (SASCFC) stated that merely being able to show that most drivers would have been intoxicated and incapable of controlling a vehicle with a blood alcohol level of 0.15% could not 'itself amount to legal proof on balance of probabilities for the proposition [of lack of control would be] true of any individual'.[134] Hodgson criticises this decision and contends that it is incorrect because

> *subject to the requirement of adequate material concerning the particular case*, and, in particular, the calling of appropriate evidence by the party bearing the onus of proof, evidence of the kind given in *Laube* should be enough to enable an inference to be drawn, on the balance of probabilities, if the defendant chooses not to give evidence.[135]

This statement is revealing of the limitations of the NSE debate. In *Laube*, the Court refused to draw the inference for want of material that could individualise the evidence to the defendant. Hodgson suggests that such evidence is useful once it has been individualised. In effect, Hodgson is not making any real criticism of *Laube*; they are *ad idem* on the drawing of inferences from objective probabilities.

[131] Enoch and Spectre (n 32) 183–84.

[132] Enoch and Fisher (n 21) and cases referred to at 561–63. See also Pardo (n 31) fn 67.

[133] Enoch and Spectre (n 32) 183. Cf M Spottswood, 'Paradoxes of Proof" in C Dahlman, A Stein and G Tuznet (eds), *Philosophical Foundations of Evidence Law* (Oxford, Oxford University Press, 2021) 320.

[134] *State Government Insurance Commission v Laube* (1984) 37 SASR 31 (SASCFC) 33 (King CJ).

[135] Hodgson, 'Scales' (n 2) 742 (emphasis added).

The vital point is how to recognise 'adequate material'. Hodgson's reasoning obscures the possibility that the evidence itself may have contained inferences for or against individualisation, as might other evidence already tendered. Ignoring that step perpetuates the same problem inherent to most probabilist theories; they are open to the attack of not sufficiently explaining why the probability of *n* can be individualised to *p*.

Once the basis for generalising from *n* to *p* is established, objective probabilities are quite capable of being sufficient for proof and the formation of an actual belief. In *Essop v Home Office*,[136] the claimants were employees of the UK Home Office who identified as 'Black and Minority Ethnic' (BME) and 'older'. Race and age are 'protected characteristics' meaning that any discriminatory action taken by an employer against those characteristics is unlawful. The Home Office required applicants for promotion to complete the Core Skills Assessment (CSA). A statistical analysis of a sample of the test results (the *n*) revealed that BME and older candidates performed worse on the CSA than white and younger applicants.[137] No evidence showed why the CSA resulted in lower scores amongst these groups.

The claimants failed to establish direct discrimination because there was no direct causal explanation for the 'less favourable treatment' (lower score on the CSA) and the protected characteristic.[138] There was no directly discriminatory 'tendency' revealed by the evidence that could be generalised to the claimants. But the UK Supreme Court (UKSC) held the statistical evidence relevant and potentially dispositive of indirect discrimination because the CSA had a tendency to indirectly discriminate against particular protected characteristics. That is, the evidence was capable of showing a pattern of discrimination through favouring one group over another.[139] The UKSC accommodated for the potentially flimsy nature of such findings by noting that a finding relying on *n* could be rebutted by evidence regarding individual candidates suggesting that some extraneous factor might explain their failure, for example, failing to adequately prepare for the exam, or that the discrimination was justifiable because the test assessed some essential skill required for promotion.[140]

This approach to objective probabilities is common, especially in class actions. It rests on the creation of uniform rebuttable presumptions.[141] In *Tyson Foods v Bouaphakeo*, the Supreme Court of the United States approved the certification

[136] *Essop v Home Office* [2017] WLR 1343 (UKSC).

[137] ibid [7]–[10].

[138] Cf Thomson (n 42) 205. *Essop* (n 136) and *Wal-Mart Stores v Dukes* 564 US 338 (2011) would reject Thomson's view of individualisation. Thomson doesn't explain how the evidence could overcome the absence of information going to intention (as opposed to indirect effect) that her definition appears to assume. At its highest the evidence reveals a tendency to discriminate but does not reveal any reason why that is the case.

[139] For a discussion of direct versus indirect discrimination from statistical evidence, see L Brilmayer and L Kornhauser, 'Quantitative Methods and Legal Decisions' (1978) 46 *University of Chicago Law Review* 116, 123, cf fn 27.

[140] *Essop* (n 136) [32].

[141] See ch 4, section III.B.

of an employment class action for unpaid time based on probabilities derived from a sample of time spent donning and doffing working equipment.[142] Here, *n* (a sample from the class) and *p* (any one member of the class) overlapped so that there was a clear basis, in the absence of countervailing evidence, to generalise the probability from *n* to *p*. Similarly, the 'fraud on the market' theory (also known as the '*Basic* presumption') in US securities class actions supports the existence of reliance on public statements of listed companies by presuming that that holders of securities read and rely on public statements in purchasing those securities in the absence of any 'direct' evidence of such reliance.[143] What underlies these rebuttable presumptions from objective probabilities is a sufficient nexus to at least prima facie generalise the circumstances of *n* to *p* and rationally form a belief in *p* from the objective probabilities. Unlike the proof paradox, these examples do not rely on the automatic merger of *n* to *p* but share enough similar characteristics to support a generalising inference from the objective probability to the individual case.

B. Particularists: An Exaggerated Problem?

If probabilists fail to appreciate the problem of generalisation, particularists exaggerate it. Particularists are right to assert that at least epistemic and moral-epistemic objections arise in consequence of the need to generalise from *n* to *p* in statistical evidence. Many, however, go one step further and argue that one can never use statistical evidence to draw conclusions about individuals. The proof paradox is the source of this argument. For particularists, it is not enough to show that an event is objectively more probable, the fact-finder must also believe it, and belief cannot or ought not be predicated only on objective probabilities. Take away the proof paradox paradigm and this argument seems to become even stronger. Now, the probability of *p* is likely to be different from the probability of *n*, and a further calculation has to be made about just how separate those probabilities are.

Presenting arguments about statistical evidence in light of observations from NSE obscures the differences between them. It is true that for statistical evidence the separation of *n* and *p* presents an additional obstacle. But equally a gain may be had in the nature of the relationship between *n* and *p*. For NSE the relationship between the class and event were 'accidental'. Outside the closed circuit, nothing logically connects Blue with the accident other than frequency. Statistical evidence by contrast obtains its relevance by a potentially causal relationship between the variables predicated on a propensity to act across conditions. Even if colour and accident are not causally linked, that is not necessarily true of carcinogenic toxins and cancer.

[142] *Tyson Foods v Bouaphakeo* 577 US 442, I (2016).
[143] *Erica P John Fund v Halliburton* 573 US 258, 279 (2014).

Failing to appreciate this difference plagues the arguments of particularists. Meyerson suggests that it is epistemologically unjustified and immoral to rely on risk assessments (which are derived from statistical evaluations of the behaviour of groups of similar individuals) about the likelihood of offending because 'any prediction about a particular individual on the basis of statistics about a group to which they happen to belong will be unfounded'.[144] Meyerson's argument has two flaws. The first is to couch any discussion of proof from NSE in the context of the criminal standard. She asserts that the issue of probability has 'nothing to do with the criminal standard of proof'.[145] But as has been shown at section III.A above, it has everything to do with the standard. There will always be a rational explanation for non-guilt from NSE in criminal proceedings. The phrasing of the criminal standard does not permit NSE to be sufficient and any decision based on NSE alone would be improper.

The second problem is her reliance on the particularist accounts of the proof paradox. Meyerson concludes from the Prisoner One hypothetical[146] that although one might be able to infer something about the group of prisoners, one cannot make an inference about any individual because of the lack of 'case-specific' or individualised evidence.[147] The absence of case-specific evidence is said to expose the individual to 'too high a risk of erroneous conviction'.[148] This claim mixes the proof paradox and the problem of generalisation because it is predicated on the potentiality for 'missing evidence' to revise the probability estimates unbeknownst to the fact-finder. That is not a problem NSE need confront because evidence that has not been tendered need not be considered. Her claim that 'for all the court knows, [the individual] is different from the other prisoners, or most of the other prisoners, in a respect which would lead it to downgrade its probability estimate' is beside the point.[149] A court does not know what it doesn't know and it should not act as if there is some salient but missing evidence in the absence of an explanation about the absence.[150] There is no greater risk of wrongful conviction under NSE because the probabilities of n and p are the same. Ergo the risk of error is no higher than the probability identifies (4%).[151]

Meyerson is right to argue, however, that there is no connection in the Prisoner paradox, because the paradox is deliberately designed that way. But the paradox doesn't need that connection to support a rational belief. Meyerson expresses a particular concern about risk assessments.[152] The logic underlying the paradox

[144] Meyerson (n 104) 521.
[145] ibid 512.
[146] Described in ch 6, section II.A.
[147] Meyerson (n 104) 519, citing Stein, *Foundations* (n 44).
[148] Meyerson (n 104) 520.
[149] ibid 516.
[150] Courts can use the absence of evidence to make findings in some circumstances. An unexplained failure to adduce evidence that would be expected may give rise to an inference that the evidence would not have been favourable: *Jones* (n 56) 321.
[151] See Pundik, 'Epistemology' (n 44) 119–20.
[152] Meyerson (n 104) 512ff.

doesn't work for statistical evidence like risk assessments, because *n* and *p* are not the same. There is no need to speculate about membership in reference classes; for statistical evidence about individuals, they will in fact be members of other reference classes that may influence the outcome in either direction.

Similarly, Wright disputes that statistical evidence can be appropriate evidence of causation.[153] He divides evidence into four categories: particularistic; ex post probability; ex ante probability; and NSE. Ex post probabilities are probabilities generated from case-specific evidence that can serve as evidence of causation. Ex ante probabilities (that broadly reflect statistical evidence) cannot serve as evidence of causation because they are 'abstract class-based [probabilities], independent of the particularistic evidence specific to a particular occasion'.[154]

What Meyerson, Stein, Wright and others fail to account for is that mere membership of multiple classes does not automatically cause membership in one such class to be spurious and unreliable. Relying on NSE means that Meyerson has disregarded the chance to connect the individual under assessment to the reference classes used in the assessment process. There may be other means of connecting *n* and *p* in the case of risk assessments. Wright's statement that ex ante probabilities are 'useless' for the attribution of causation in individual cases is premature.[155] It is true that if they remain as ex ante probabilities as he describes, then no individual attribution can be made as the probabilities were not generalised. But ex ante probabilities that exist prior to and independent of a particular event can become part of an ex post probability. It depends on how tightly the individual is interwoven into the group. Thomson suggests that statistical evidence can be individualised if it is 'causally connected' to the putative fact.[156] In fairness, the example she gives of this process is open to challenge. She suggests that statistical evidence of an unbalanced racial composition in a workforce would be causally connected to the claim that the company has discriminatory hiring practices, and therefore a decision about a particular individual was discriminatory. By itself, that does not counteract the particularists' claim. There is still a gap between 'differential hiring practices' (which may or may not be caused unlawfully) and 'a personal hiring decision' that is in fact unlawful.[157] Although the example is flawed, the essential point Thomson makes must be correct. The formation of a subjective belief in the probability of *p* from the probability of *n* is permissible under these circumstances.

[153] Wright, 'Bramble' (n 98) 1050–51.
[154] ibid 1050.
[155] ibid 1054.
[156] Thomson (n 42) 205.
[157] eg *Wal-Mart* (n 138) (employees were not entitled to rely on class-based statistical evidence to prove individual employment decisions); *ALA15 v Minister for Immigration and Border Protection* [2016] FCAFC 30 (past judicial decisions could not be used to establish the probability of a future unlawful decision). cf *Essop* (n 136) (class-based statistical evidence could be used to establish indirect discrimination).

How does one connect *n* and *p* outside of the confines of the proof paradox? Cohen proposed that the causal link between evidence and fact could be achieved on a propensity basis. If the statistical evidence established a propensity of action, it would be a reasonable inference, given certain conditions, for that propensity to continue from the group into the individual case.[158] If the statistical fact was 'probability of death after imbibing a lethal dose of arsenic', it would be a courageous fact-finder who asserted that one could not believe in the (high) probability of death drawn from statistical evidence of mortality rates from arsenic poisoning. Arsenic has a propensity to cause human death, established by 'non-specific' evidence. One need not form an absolutely certain belief in an outcome to believe it to be true and to act upon that belief. Arguments about the general inapplicability of statistical evidence to individual facts fail to recognise that there may be circumstances where such attributions are appropriate. The question is deciding when the conditions for such an inference have been met, described in chapter three.

A similar problem arises for the civil standard. Dant argues that both NSE and epidemiology produce the same epistemic deficits in reasoning and are equally unreliable bases upon which to formulate conclusions of fact.[159] Other evidence in support of the causative proposition, such as medical notes describing the disease progression, are necessary to interpret the statistical evidence. First, the comparison between epidemiology and NSE is inapposite. Causal inferences about individuals from epidemiology must account for the real risk that the probabilities assigned to the particular facts are wrong. NSE has no such problem because the probabilities are artificially constrained. The only question for NSE is whether the fact-finder is prepared to run the risk of error presented by the facts, but at least knowing that the facts themselves are correct. There is no such comfort for fact-finding from statistical evidence.

Second, it cannot be correct that if a contaminant has a propensity to cause a particular illness, the statistical evidence nevertheless 'does not, by itself, provide any means for determining whether a particular plaintiff's disease was caused by chemical exposure'.[160] Establishing a propensity can be akin to asserting an individualisation of the evidence because the fact-finder could accept that whatever conditions caused the relationship between the contaminant and the disease in *n* may have carried over into *p* (if similar conditions existed) by way of that propensity.

Third, Dant (and others)[161] insist that statistical evidence can only ever be corroborative with 'particularistic' evidence 'such as her particular symptoms and when they appear, tissue analyses, medical history, or the circumstances of

[158] Cohen, 'Subjective Probability' (n 45) 633–34.

[159] Dant (n 110) 63; S Green, *Causation in Negligence* (Oxford, Hart, 2015) 117–18.

[160] Dant (n 110) 64. Similar reasoning exists at common law: see *King v Western Sydney LHN* [2013] NSWCA 162, [136].

[161] Tribe (n 48) 1350.

her exposure'.[162] This too cannot be correct. Statistical evidence can be individualised through propensity and can serve as evidence relating to *p* in the absence of additional direct evidence as long as there is sufficient evidence that allows the inferential gap to be bridged. Adducing further non-statistical evidence does not remove the concerns about the potential crushing effect of probabilities, the disregard of other evidence, and the potential prejudice to the accused as being treated as a member of a class because of some trait outside of the accused's control. It fails to appreciate that although particularistic evidence outside of statistical evidence may be helpful in informing inferences about *p*, it doesn't actually reduce the epistemic and moral-epistemic prejudice caused by the need to generalise from statistical evidence. Some assessment of the applicability of the reference class to the individual is needed. Particularist theories do not outline by what means generalisation should take place.

Fourth, particularist theories in response to this problem of generalisation are non-responsive to evidence law. Dant[163] and Allen and Pardo's[164] proposals for the 'inference to the best explanation', and Stein's 'principle of maximal individualisation'[165] regulate how the fact-finder ought to reason with evidence by setting conditions for fact-finding. But, underneath the auspices of commonsense, evidence law does not regulate fact-finding in this way. A judicial officer, acting as gatekeeper, cannot say to a jury that 'you must not find this statistical evidence to be true for the accused unless you identify at least five sources of particular evidence in support'. The same considerations apply to a judge-alone trial. A judge may have regard to reasoning processes, but unless a rule of law was established mandating that statistical evidence be reasoned from in a particular way, judges are free (and it would not be erroneous) to adopt an inductive, commonsense approach to statistical evidence. Any other position would intrude on the exclusive function of the fact-finder to determine the 'truth'. Evidence law regulates fact-finding by excluding or warning against the reliability of evidence, or by asserting ex ante or ex post that no reasonable fact-finder could have relied on it to form a belief. How to deal with objections from statistical evidence, and the generalisation objection in particular, has not been adequately accounted for in evidence law. NSE exacerbates rather than solves this problem.

[162] Dant (n 110) 64.

[163] ibid 53–58, 68.

[164] MS Pardo and RJ Allen, 'Juridical Proof and the Best Explanation' (2008) 27 *Law & Philosophy* 223, 227ff. For a contrary view of the inference to the best explanation model, see Steel (n 130) 78–80.

[165] Stein, *Foundations* (n 44) 100ff ('First, fact-finders must receive and consider all case-specific evidence pertaining to the case. Second, fact-finders must not make any finding against a litigant, unless the argument generating this finding and the evidence upon which this argument rests were exposed to and survived maximal individualized examination'). Stein argues that the principal of maximal individualisation is a feature of evidence law reflected by procedural rules governing requirements for cross-examination: at 101. But what it actually regulates is the point at which this evidence justifies a particular conclusion. Unless Stein is suggesting that maximal individualisation is a canon of rationality, such a rule does not exist.

Conclusion

Fact-finding from objective probabilities has been the subject of a great deal of debate. Much of that debate, however, has been based on a false equivalence between NSE and statistical evidence. The conditions that control NSE allow one to identify that, strictly speaking, there is no real legal impediment to fact-finding on purely objective probabilities in civil cases. But outside of those controlled conditions, the usefulness of NSE is largely eroded. NSE can support an argument that when an event is probabilistically likely to occur in the absence of any other countervailing probabilities, the standard of proof should be satisfied. Relying on the finality of probabilities is a weakness in the usefulness of NSE, as it entirely ignores the need to generalise almost all statistical evidence to the individual case, and then to find, subjectively, what the probabilities of the occurrence in the individual are. Instead, proof by statistical evidence should be seen as a problem of how to sufficiently account for the difference between the probability of n to the probability of p. The next chapter considers how courts and scholarship have responded to evidence of mathematical techniques that are used to find the probability of p from that of n outside of the inductive model.

8

Statistical Analysis of Evidence

Proof paradoxes are designed so that the probability of the reference class (n) necessarily also represents the probability of p. Outside that limited universe, the probability of p is to be derived from all evidence (including statistical evidence) and inferences in the proceeding. The last stage of the statistical inference syllogism is to infer the probability of p from n and all other information by 'weighing' that information to form a subjective and rational belief in the existence of p. How this belief is formed is not typically regulated by evidence law as long as it is rational. The process is 'inductive' insofar as each stage of the syllogism is uncertain,[1] and is otherwise governed by 'commonsense judgement' leading to a fact-finder reaching 'a level of actual persuasion on the whole of the evidence'.[2] Commonsense is the product of the application of the 'experience' and 'judgment' and 'knowledge of the ways of the world'.[3] This accords with how the law believes human beings reason in the natural world; not by reference to numerical probabilities but by making connections between phenomena using their experience.[4]

I. Statistical Inference

Statistical evidence presents a challenge to this commonsense process of fact-finding because numerical probabilities are perceived to be atypical forms of evidence in commonsense reasoning.[5] The law rejects fact-finding predicated on mathematical approaches and output based on numerical probabilities.[6] How then does

[1] P Roberts, *Roberts & Zuckerman's Criminal Evidence*, 3rd edn (Oxford, Oxford University Press, 2022) 155–57; L Cohen, *The Probable and the Provable* (Oxford, Clarendon Press 1977); *Fernandez v Tubemakers of Australia* [1975] 2 NSWLR 190 (NSWCA) 199A–D.

[2] *R v Galli* (2001) 127 A Crim R 493, [55].

[3] *R v Olugboja* [1982] QB 320 (CA) 327E (quoting a direction to a jury). See further *Shepherd v The Queen* (1988) 85 ALR 387 (NSWCCA) 392; *Burger King v Hungry Jack's* (2001) 69 NSWLR 558 (NSWCA) [591]; *R v T* [2011] Cr App R 9 (CA), [105] (referring to 'experience and judgment').

[4] JJ Koehler, 'The Psychology of Numbers in the Courtroom: How to Make DNA-Match Statistics Seem Impressive or Insufficient' (2001) 74 *South California Law Review* 1275, 1299–30; D Hodgson, 'Probability: the Logic of the Law – a Response' (1995) 15 *OJLS* 51, 56.

[5] See Cohen, *Probable* (n 1) ch 15.

[6] This is an aggregate of two principles: first, per *Davies v Taylor* [1974] AC 207 (HL) and *Briginshaw v Briginshaw* (1938) 60 CLR 336, that the law does not make findings of fact predicated on numerical probabilities only. This is premised on the widely held belief in the common law that '[d]egrees of probability and degrees of proof with which juries are concerned are rarely capable of expression in

a fact-finder construe, according to commonsense, the impact of the numerical probability of *n* to the probability of the truth of *p* so as to properly understand the role of *n*, as a 'strand in the cable, with other relevant facts', in proving *p*?[7] There are two 'grand' schools of thought within statistical inference literature as to how best to account for this potential conflict.[8]

First, frequentism, stipulates that probabilities can only be derived from phenomena that are manifest in base rates tested over the long run.[9] A frequentist only offers the probability of *n*; the frequentist does not purport to offer the probability of *p*, save for noting that in general terms, *n* appears to generalise to *p*.[10] So, within the commonsense model, the probability of *n* may be given to the fact-finder, who can then either accept that the probability of *n* and *p* are equal, or use the probability of *n* to form an independent view of the probability of *p*. For the most part, lawyers adopt a frequentist approach to the presentation of statistical inference by experts. An expert should not transgress the fact-finder's function of determining the probability of *p*.[11] Experts are supposed to give evidence about matters that fall within their specialised field and are outside the common knowledge of laypersons.[12] Once that knowledge has been imparted, it is for the fact-finder to determine how it assists them in deciding 'what happened' to *p* (or, what will happen or what would have happened when dealing with hypothetical facts).[13]

Even so, one pertinent question for the expert will be how the probability of *n* should inform the fact-finder's degree of belief in *p*. Under a frequentist model, the expert would only be able to provide general (or framework) guidance on the degree of fit between the reference class and the instance case. Where available, this could take the form of actuarial tools aided by the use of scores generated from populations (whether of people, animals, objects or phenomena) that can be compared to the individual. For example, measures of 'Breslow thickness' describe the thickness of a melanoma tumour so as to determine the probability of metastasis. This may be used to inform (but not conclusively) the probability of metastases in any individual case given the Breslow thickness of the patient's

mathematical terms': *Shepherd* (n 3) 392 (Roden J). Second, that the law does not reason with probabilities using formal methods. The latter principle is the subject of this chapter.

[7] *Seltsam v McGuiness* (2000) 49 NSWLR 262 (NSWCA) [91], [101] (Spigelman CJ).

[8] For a summary of the frequentist and Bayesian accounts, see J Sprenger, 'Bayesianism vs Frequentism in Statistical Inference' in A Hajek and C Hitchcock (eds), *The Oxford Handbook of Probability and Philosophy* (Oxford, Oxford University Press, 2016).

[9] GT Harris and ME Rice, 'Bayes and Base Rates: What Is an Informative Prior for Actuarial Violence Risk Assessment?' (2013) 31 *Behavioural Sciences and the Law* 103, 104–05.

[10] ibid 105. In discussing an actuarial tool designed to predict violent recidivism, the authors comment that a frequentist approach 'would not have conceived of an individual offender's probability of subsequent violent recidivism; rather, we conceived of a large group of offenders … and speak in frequentist terms about the proportion who had met the operational definition of violent recidivism in follow-up studies'.

[11] *Makita v Sprowles* (2001) 52 NSWLR 705 (NSWCA) [71]ff.

[12] *Honeysett v The Queen* (2014) 253 CLR 122, [23].

[13] This is sometimes referred to as the ultimate issue rule: *Holtman v Sampson* [1985] 2 QdR 472, 474.

tumour at a point in time.[14] These can provide fairly coherent probabilities for the probability of metastasis of the plaintiff's tumour (p) based on the probability of metastasis derived from the reference class. In many instances, however, such measures are not available. An expert may be asked to opine, based on their experience, where they believe p fits within the reference class, and the likely outcomes. Although the law no longer prohibits experts giving evidence of the ultimate issue,[15] the responsibility for calculating the probability of p given n that is necessary to determine the fact rests with the fact-finder. For that task, fact-finders will need to rely on their own commonsense, exercised rationally, to process the probabilities and the evidence of the fit of those probabilities to the fact-in-issue without further guidance. This leaves open a risk that the fact-finder will reason with the numerical probabilities in a prejudicial manner by misconstruing the proper weight of the evidence. It also means that how evidence is weighted is left to an individual's (idiosyncratic) 'experience' and 'judgment'. Such reasoning is often hidden from view and has been likened to a 'black box'.[16]

The status quo accepts these risks and does not otherwise require or permit any further processing of the probabilities. But there is, in theory, another option. For over 60 years, practitioners and scholars of the law of evidence have debated how best to ameliorate this risk.[17] The most controversial idea has been the suggestion that fact-finders utilise formal (mathematical) methods of ascertaining probative value from evidence, referred to in this chapter as the 'statistical analysis of

[14] See *Coote v Kelly* [2013] NSWCA 357, [63].

[15] Whereas at common law evidence of the 'ultimate issue' was inadmissible, Evidence Act 1995 (NSW) s 80 now permits expert evidence to opine on the ultimate issue without being inadmissible. Practically, the ultimate issue rule for expert evidence is nonsensical. When a risk assessment for sentencing purposes is undertaken, an expert is expressly opining on the risk that p is likely to re-offend given n as that is the entire function of the assessment. The extent of any transgression on the ultimate issue will be influenced by the subject matter about which the evidence is to be given. Logically, expert evidence is at its most useful when it is able to identify all the various factors that might impact on the probability of p and give some guidance as to how p might be impacted. cf R Kune and G Kune, 'Proof of Cancer Causation and Expert Evidence: Bringing Science to the Law and the Law to Science' (2003) 11 *Journal of Law and Medicine* 112, 119, suggesting that '[i]t is unhelpful for an expert witness to say that he or she is satisfied on the balance of probabilities or beyond reasonable doubt that a particular exposure caused a cancer. This is, indeed, a question for the tribunal. Moreover, what the expert means by "balance of probabilities" or "beyond reasonable doubt" may be quite different from the legal concept.' That view is insufficiently nuanced. At the very least, experts will be called on to identify those features, in their view, that are likely to guide whether the phenomenon is generalisable to the individual. It may be a question for the tribunal, but with the aid of the expert on that very subject.

[16] B Robertson, G Vignaux and C Berger, 'Extending the Confusion About Bayes' (2011) 74 *MLR* 444, 454.

[17] Whilst this debate is ongoing, the central pillar on which it turns was a debate between M Finkelstein and W Fairley, 'A Bayesian Approach to Identification Evidence' (1970) 83 *Harvard Law Review* 489 and L Tribe, 'Trial by Mathematics: Precision and Ritual in the Legal Process' (1971) 84 *Harvard Law Review* 1329, where it is generally accepted amongst lawyers that Tribe's view prevailed: R Eggleston, 'Similar Facts and Bayes Theorem' (1991) 31 *Jurimetrics* 275, 278 fns 9–11; RO Lempert, 'Modeling Relevance' (1977) 75 *Michigan Law Review* 1021, 1021. For a different view, see N Fenton, M Neil and D Berger, 'Bayes and the Law' (2016) 3 *Annual Review of Statistics and its Application* 51, 64 (describing Tribe's argument as being 'demolished'). Whereas victory is in the eye of the beholder, here at least, courts have not taken up the invitation to use Bayesian logic in fact-finding.

evidence'. In law, the debate around the statistical analysis of evidence has focused on the second school of statistical inference, Bayesian reasoning.

Bayes Theorem

> tells us how to update our knowledge by incorporating new evidence. We start with some knowledge about the hypothesis, expressed as odds in favour of it. These are known as the prior odds. The prior odds (our assignment without the evidence) must be multiplied by the likelihood ratio of the new piece of evidence to give the posterior odds. The posterior odds are what we want to know – the odds in favour of the hypothesis after taking into account the new piece of evidence.[18]

Bayesian analysis is a mathematical and logical method of understanding how subsequent evidence influences the probability of a given hypothesis.[19] Unlike frequentists, Bayesians seek to calculate the precise probability of *p* given *n* and the variables influencing *n*. Bayesian methods are expressly not objective, insofar as the probability of *p* is divorced from the present circumstances.[20] Probabilities for Bayesians should reflect the degree of belief of the fact-finder in the probabilities of what occurred or could occur given the evidence relevant to *p*. On one view, performing these calculations takes the reasoning process out of the black box of commonsense and exposes it to critique, thereby ameliorating or at least exposing the kinds of error commonly associated with the inductive model.[21]

II. The Rule in *Adams*

Courts will generally permit the use of Bayesian methods where they are relied on by an expert using robust statistical evidence in the formation of their opinions.[22] There is a strident view that evidence of Bayes should not be given to fact-finders to conduct their own formal calculations of the probability of *p*. In *R v Adams*, the Court of Appeal ruled that evidence in the form of instructions to a jury on how to apply Bayes to the facts in the case was not admissible.[23] First, the Court suggested that this evidence 'trespass[ed] on an area peculiarly and exclusively within the province of the jury, namely the way in which they evaluate the relationship between one piece of evidence and another'.[24]

[18] B Robertson, G Vignaux and C Berger, *Interpreting Evidence* (Hoboken, Wiley, 2016) 15.

[19] Sprenger (n 8) 382.

[20] eg AI Goldman, 'Quasi-Objective Bayesianism and Legal Evidence' (2002) 42 *Jurimetrics* 237, 239.

[21] See D Hodgson, 'A Lawyer Looks at Bayes' Theorem' (2002) 76 *Australian Law Journal* 109, 112.

[22] *T* (n 3) [80]–[86], [90]. For a critical commentary of the reliability requirement, see Robertson, Vignaux and Berger (n 16) 447 noting that the 'structure of the argument is dictated by logic not by the nature of the data'. See also *Latcha v The Queen* (1998) 104 A Crim R 390 (NTCCA) 396ff, setting out procedural criteria for the admissibility of 'DNA and statistical evidence'.

[23] *R v Adams* [1996] 2 Cr App R 467.

[24] *Adams* (n 23) 481; DH Kaye and JJ Koehler, 'The Misquantification of Probative Value' (2003) 27 *Law and Human Behavior* 645, 648.

Second, Rose LJ asserted that:

> the theorem's methodology requires … that items of evidence be assessed separately according to their bearing on the accused's guilt, before being combined in the overall formula. That in our view is *far too rigid an approach* to evidence of the type that a jury characteristically has to assess, where the cogency of (for instance) identification evidence may have to be assessed, at least in part, in the light of the strength of the chain of evidence in which it forms part … *Jurors evaluate evidence and reach a conclusion not by means of a formula, mathematical or otherwise, but by the joint application of their individual common sense and knowledge of the world to the evidence before them.*[25]

Australian civil[26] and criminal law has adopted the *Adams* approach.[27] In *R v GK*, the NSW Court of Criminal Appeal (NSWCCA) endorsed the general principle that experts giving evidence are entitled to rely on Bayesian approaches in forming their opinion.[28] Such evidence could not then be adduced to a jury as a method to facilitate their analysis of the totality of the evidence,[29] albeit the probabilities relied on by the expert would be the product of Bayesian logic.[30] *GK* does not otherwise expand on why Bayesian methods should not be admitted.

Justice Hodgson, writing extra-judicially, appears to have extended the reasoning of the Court of Appeal in *Adams* to include fact-finding by judicial officers. His explanation of the prohibition of formal methods is more instructive:

> decision-making generally involves a global assessment of a whole complex array of matters which cannot be given individual numerical expression. Such a decision depends more on commonsense, experience of the world and beliefs as to how people generally behave (folk psychology), than on mathematical computations; *and concentration on mathematical probabilities could prejudice this commonsense process.*[31]

Hodgson's views appear to have been taken up by the judiciary. Kathleen Folbigg was convicted of the murder of her four children in 2003. In 2023, a second inquiry into those convictions was held. In closing submissions before the inquiry, it was put by a barrister appearing for Ms Folbigg's husband that the odds of calculating the deaths of four children in one family could be calculated by reference to Bayes Theorem. Putting to one side the correctness of that submission, the Tribunal observed:

> I'm familiar with Bayes Theorem. Rather than applying Bayes Theorem I would prefer to apply the principle governing the ascertainment of guilt in criminal cases.[32]

[25] *Adams* (n 23) 481 (emphasis added).

[26] *Norris v Blake* (1997) 41 NSWLR 49 (NSWCA) 69–71, referring extensively to D Hodgson, 'The Scales of Justice: Probability and Proof in Legal Fact-Finding' (1995) 69 *Australian Law Journal* 731.

[27] A Ligertwood, 'Can DNA Evidence Alone Convict an Accused?' (2011) 33 *Sydney Law Review* 487, 501–02.

[28] *R v GK* (2001) 53 NSWLR 317, [21]–[22].

[29] ibid.

[30] Robertson, Vignaux and Berger (n 16) 446, 452–54.

[31] Hodgson, 'Scales' (n 26) 736 (emphasis added).

[32] Inquiry into Convictions of Kathleen Megan Folbigg, Transcript (26 April 2023) 833.

This comment presupposes that Bayesian reasoning is incompatible with how guilt is to be ascertained. The Tribunal did not expand on the reasons for why it formed this view. To date, scholars and jurists alike identify the complexity of applying a Bayesian approach to legal fact-finding as being a chief reason against its use. Potentially hundreds of individual pieces of evidence would need to be individually considered, including how those individual probabilities interrelate and interact with one another.[33] Whilst it may be conceded that ordinary reasoning is much like Bayes Theorem, such that knowledge is updated with new evidence, it is quite another to suggest that this everyday process involves the application of quantified probabilities to each piece of new evidence and the computation of an overall probability by way of a mathematical formula.[34] Quite obviously, for most people and fact-finders in the legal process, it does not.[35] Likewise, the requirement to set prior probabilities, whether derived from base rate evidence, or purely based on the belief of the fact-finder absent any evidence, has troubled both statistical inference scholarship and the law.

Assume for present purposes, that the prior probability could be set by reference to empirically derived base rates from past research. This arguably represents the best-case scenario for generating prior probabilities. It would be rare indeed that only one base rate exists. In most cases, there will be a variety of different base rates to choose from, even assuming one logical reference class.[36] The fact-finder or researcher may not be able to identify why those base rates are different, or how that difference relates to p. How is a fact-finder to decide which to use, and why? Further, when there are different applicable reference classes with different or even conflicting base rates (the reference class problem), this also raises questions about the legitimacy of the choice of the fact-finder in choosing one over the other.[37] That is especially so for formal reasoning, because, first, Bayes cannot account for the degree of fit of the reference class to the individual and adjust the probability accordingly,[38] and, second, the probability ultimately chosen for any particular

[33] Tribe (n 17) 1361ff.

[34] Hodgson, 'Probability' (n 4) 51, 66ff.

[35] Hodgson, 'Scales' (n 26) 737:

> 'Judges do not generally follow a mathematical or computational system of fact-finding. A better model for most judicial fact-finding might be called a recognition model, rather like a decision as to whether a person now in one's presence is a particular person with whom one was acquainted many years ago but has not seen since. In arriving at this decision in a doubtful case, one will pay close attention to the component features and characteristics – eyes, nose, mouth, facial shape, hair, height, manner, etc – having regard to the changes likely to have resulted from the passage of years. *However, one does not assess numerical probabilities concerning each of these characteristics (for example, that this is X's nose, etc) and compute from that an overall probability of identity.* Rather, one will make an overall judgment, in which the contributions of the component characteristics cannot clearly be separated out. This is a process of inference, to which quantitative rules make no contribution. (emphasis added)

[36] eg *Seltsam* (n 7).

[37] R Allen and M Pardo, 'The Problematic Value of Mathematical Models of Evidence' (2007) 36 *Journal of Legal Studies* 107, 113–14; Tribe (n 17) 1058–59.

[38] L Brilmayer, 'Second-Order Evidence and Bayesian Logic' in P Tillers and E Green (eds), *Probability and Inference in the Law of Evidence: The Uses and Limits of Bayesianism* (Springer 1988) 156.

fact (whether from empirical research or self-generated) can radically change the outcome of the Bayesian analysis in ways that may be unintended and differ with the fact-finder's subject belief.[39]

On the other hand, those who support a Bayesian approach to fact-finding find the legal approach difficult to rationalise. In *Adams*, the expert who gave evidence before the jury of Bayes noted that the 'only logically consistent way' to combine the probabilistically expressed DNA evidence and the non-statistical factors was by way of Bayesian computations.[40] Further, where statistical evidence has already been introduced in support of the probability of *p*, it does seem somewhat arbitrary to say that the process of fact-finding may be prejudiced by reasoning mathematically when some form of mathematical reasoning is necessarily taking place.[41]

It is beyond the scope of this work to fully do justice to the various arguments for or against the statistical analysis of evidence. Instead, it makes the simple point that the position taken by *Adams* and the contrary positions in much of the literature represent the extremes of possible views. *Adams* suggests that Bayesian reasoning can never be undertaken by a fact-finder and that evidence of Bayes would be ex ante prejudicial. That seems to be a substantial overreach in the interpretation of prejudice. Where courts have accepted that experts may rely on Bayes it seems odd that a fact-finder could not then consider the basis on which those conclusions from Bayes were reached. Evidence of Bayes should at least be admissible, and Bayesian reasoning deployable, in the event of a dispute over whether an expert has properly performed their own analysis underlying their opinion.[42]

The mere fact that Bayesian approaches may rely on the generation of numerically expressed subjective probabilities (whether from base rate evidence or only reflective of a fact-finder's subjective impression) doesn't appear to be any more prejudicial to the outcome of a dispute than relying on heuristically derived estimates of probability that remain unquantified. As Hodgson identifies,

> even if, as is often the case, the educated guesses concerning prior odds and likelihood ratios are on no sounder ground than a judgment as to the overall result, the process of applying Bayes' Theorem will at least disclose whether or not there is consistency between all one's educated guesses and one's judgment.[43]

That conflicting base rates and reference classes may exist is a problem, but it is a problem for fact-finding generally. On a frequentist account, the fact-finder would be told of the existence of differing probabilities from different studies. How is the fact-finder meant to reason with those different possibilities under

[39] Tribe (n 17) 1358–59.

[40] *Adams* (n 23) 472. See also Fenton, Neil and Berger (n 17); J Koehler and D Shaviro, 'Veridical Verdicts: Increasing Verdict Accuracy Through the Use of Overtly Probabilistic Evidence and Methods' (1990) 75 *Cornell Law Review* 247, 258.

[41] A Ligertwood, 'Avoiding Bayes in DNA cases' (2003) 77 *Australian Law Journal* 317, 322.

[42] cf Robertson, Vignaux and Berger, 'Extending' (n 16).

[43] Hodgson, 'Lawyer' (n 21) 112. See also Eggleston (n 17) 286; AP Dawid, 'Probability and Statistics in the Law' (2005) *Proceedings of the Tenth International Workshop on Artificial Intelligence and Statistics* 89, 3.4.

the commonsense approach? In *Hotson v Fitzgerald*, the trial judge dealt with two different base rate probabilities by, apparently, averaging them.[44] Subsequent scholarship criticised this approach as 'unscientific'.[45] But it is not clear what else could have been done with two conflicting probabilities. Likewise, there is robust experimental psychological literature that suggests the order by which evidence is presented can influence the ultimate finding when ordinary fact-finding methods are applied.[46] Problems associated with the setting of priors are common to both frequentist and Bayesian approaches.[47] This is not to say that one or other should always be preferred. But it is hard to justify why a Bayesian approach is ex ante prejudicial.

It should be recognised, however, that the practicalities of applying Bayes in a fact-finding setting are very limited. Hodgson (in a somewhat more strident rejection of a Bayesian approach than his later work) noted that practicality of applying a Bayesian approach in the context of real world fact-finding was 'absurd'.[48] Notwithstanding some empirical evidence suggesting that Bayes can be taught to lay decision-makers with relative accuracy,[49] Bayes is complex and clearly capable of producing legal error. Requiring a fact-finder to identify the express probability relating to every item of evidence, and every inference from that evidence, would very likely be an unworkable task in most situations. There are protracted disputes even within statistical inference literature about usefulness and appropriateness of Bayesian approaches.[50] In light of those disputes, it would be strange for the law to accept that it must utilise a Bayesian approach in all cases when fact-finding from statistical evidence. Professor Donnelley's statement in *Adams*, broadly echoed in the wider literature about Bayes, that Bayes is the 'only logical' means of combining different forms of evidence[51] may be correct for disciplines that rely on Bayes (about which this book does not comment), but cannot extend to legal fact-finding.

This is not to suggest that Bayes has no role. Hodgson and Eggleston, for example, both suggest that Bayes could have a role in 'checking' how fact-finders

[44] *Hotson v Fitzgerald* [1985] 3 All ER 167 (QB) and see commentary in G Turton, *Evidential Uncertainty in Causation in Negligence* (Oxford, Hart, 2016) 104.

[45] Turton (n 44) 104.

[46] eg A Feeney, JD Coley and A Crisp, 'The Relevance Framework for Category-Based Induction: Evidence from Garden-Path Arguments' (2010) 36 *Journal of Experimental Psychology* 906, 916 (describing the garden-path phenomenon).

[47] For a helpful summary of proposed resolutions to the setting of priors in Bayesian analyses for criminal fact-finding, see N Fenton and others, 'The Opportunity Prior: A Proof-based Prior for Criminal Cases' (2019) 18 *Law, Probability and Risk* 237.

[48] Hodgson, 'Probability' (n 4) 55.

[49] DJ Mazur, 'A History of Evidence in Medical Decisions: From the Diagnostic Sign to Bayesian Inference' (2012) 32 *Medical Decision Making* 227; D Schum, *The Evidential Foundations of Probabilistic Reasoning* (Evanston, Northwestern University Press, 2001) 51.

[50] cf the different views expressed by Harris and Rice (n 9) 119–20 and TD Lyon, EC Ahern and N Scurich, 'Interviewing Children Versus Tossing Coins: Accurately Assessing the Diagnosticity of Children's Disclosures of Abuse' (2012) 21 *Journal of Child Sexual Abuse* 19, 38.

[51] See further Ligertwood, 'Avoiding' (n 41) 322; Koehler and Shaviro (n 40) 258.

have reasoned with probabilities.[52] Presently, however, the law is fundamentally frequentist. It allows the presentation of probabilities of *n*, and otherwise leaves fact-finders to their own commonsense devices in how to arrive at the probability of *p* given *n*, without the assistance of any mathematical or logical formulae. That should not mean that Bayes is ipso facto prejudicial. That is a judgement that needs to be made depending on the evidence that is admitted, and the purpose for which Bayes is introduced.

[52] Eggleston (n 17) 277, 286; Hodgson, 'Lawyer' (n 21) 112.

Conclusion

Statistics pose a difficult challenge for the law of evidence. One may accept that statistics provide very good evidence of causal propositions. The challenge lies in how decision-makers are to assess whether those statistics are 'good' for adjudicative fact-finding. Teaching decision-makers in the legal process more about statistics might be a prima facie helpful way of demystifying some of the more arcane and complex aspects. But that solution is unlikely to be practicable in the near future and nor does it address how decision-makers would understand the statistics in the context of the discipline or area of study in which they were created. This book argues that experts should be required to explain the statistical evidence upon which they rely by reference to three categories: the robustness of the statistical evidence in the proof of general factual causation; the generalisability of the statistical evidence to the instant case; and the ability of the statistical evidence to, in whole or in part, inform on the existence of facts-in-issue about *p*.

Statistical inferences start from the most basic proposition: 'X caused Y in *n*' (that is, variable X caused effect Y in the sample *n*). This stage of the inference concerns general factual causation. Can the statistical evidence reliably demonstrate the existence of an association (and perhaps a causal association) in a state of nature that a fact-finder can believe exercising their commonsense? Whilst Australian law does not expressly recognise general factual causation as an element in most causes of action, it nevertheless remains an essential part of the statistical syllogism connecting phenomena observed in reference classes to individual litigants. This book has argued that Australia's approach to general factual causation, at least as it is articulated in the authorities, is unsatisfactory. Statistics are usually introduced into legal proceedings by way and in support of expert opinion. Rules regulating such opinions operate to shield the statistical evidence from adequate interrogation. In circumstances where courts continue to denigrate expert evidence for a lack of independence and inadequate bases, it seems counterintuitive to allow a situation whereby the underlying basis for that opinion remains unexamined.

This book has proposed that statistical evidence should be analysed for its robustness as a function of its admissibility. Effect size, confidence therein and methodology form the basis of such review. Whilst courts are not expert statisticians, by ensuring that these factors are conditions of admissibility, experts will be required to address them in their opinions. The standard of review of these factors should be limited to whether, in the mind of the gatekeeper, the evidence has the capacity to support the fact-in-issue. Setting up a framework for admissibility will also assist fact-finders (either directly for judge-alone trials or by jury directions) in understanding how to weigh statistical evidence and the opinion relying on it.

Litigation between private citizens rarely turns exclusively on causal relationships in populations. For the sample (*n*) to be relevant to a determination about the individual (*p*) there must be some observable basis for a connection between *n* and *p*. Only then can the association observed in *n* be inferred to inform the probability of the existence of a similar association in *p*. Much of the angst expressed in scholarship is focused on this leap across the inferential gap to generalise conclusions from *n* to *p*. This book has sought to outline how courts should approach the generalisation objection in three stages.

The first stage is to recognise that the objection to inferring from statistical evidence to individuals is an epistemic objection contiguous with the inferential gap. Generalisations are an essential feature of all evidence. An epistemic theory predicated on finding a difference between evidence relying on generalisations or not is impossible. Instead, the law should be concerned with regulating evidence of objectionable generalisations and individualisations. Both the nature of the inferential gap and the existence of other considerations play a role in the degree of any dissonance felt in inferring the probability of *p* from *n*. That does not detract, however, from the central goal of identifying the inferential gap as the primary source of dissonance in fact-finding from statistical evidence.

Second, the epistemic objection arising from the gap between *n* and *p* logically mirrors the gap observed in evidence of 'similar facts'. Similar fact evidence has also proven challenging to decision-makers in litigation. This work argues that an analogy between similar facts and statistical evidence shows the pathway by which *n* is relevant to *p*; by a function of the magnitude and similarity of the association in *n*, the similarity of *n* to *p*, and the magnitude of *p*. Viewed in that light, the basis for the epistemic objection is clear and a taxonomy for how to categorise the different layers of that objection is created. What is also revealed is how courts have obfuscated their approach to statistical evidence by overemphasising the degree of difference between the statistical evidence and the present facts in ascertaining the relevance of statistical evidence to facts-in-issue.

Third, the analogy to similar facts also provides a means for scrutinising the admissibility of relevant statistical evidence. Statistical evidence may, like similar fact evidence, be prejudicial to the fact-finding process where it poses an unjustified risk of error in construing the probative value of that evidence. This book argues that such prejudice is epistemic and arises from at least four related conditions: whether the statistical evidence has an appropriate basis, poses a risk of compressing the probabilities relating to *n* and *p*, may have its probative value irrationally inflated, or confuse a fact-finder by presenting incredible probabilistic coincidences. Whereas prejudice can also be described as 'moral', moral prejudice for statistical evidence is the expression of the consequence of epistemic prejudice on the fact-finder's reasoning process.

Once statistical evidence has been found relevant and admissible, the debates turn to whether, by itself, statistical evidence can be sufficient in the proof of *p*. This book has argued that consonant with how facts are proved at law, so-called 'objective probabilities' observed in *n* can be sufficient for the proof of *p* where the objective probabilities are subjectively believed. Proof paradoxes provide an interesting account of objective probabilities for philosophers but are shown to be an unwelcome distraction for how decision-makers should reason with probabilities derived from statistical evidence.

Once the objective probabilities of *n* to *p* are marshalled, evidence law tends to end its involvement in the fact-finding process. Fact-finders are then tasked with determining whether, on all the evidence in the proceeding, they believe, to the required standard of proof, the fact claimed about *p*. Fact-finders form this belief based on their commonsense and experience of the world and not by reference to quantified probabilities per se. This frequentist approach to fact-finding can be contrasted to a Bayesian approach, whereby the fact-finder seeks to calculate the probability of *p* given all the evidence in the proceeding, whether statistical or not. To date, the common law has forbidden such an approach. This book contends that whereas the applicability of Bayes Theorem to fact-finding is likely to be limited, that does not mean that in every case, evidence of Bayes is 'prejudicial'. As with all fact-finding, the approach to be taken by the courts should be predicated on the question 'does or could this evidence assist the fact-finder in constructing a reasonable approximation of the truth'. If the answer is yes, the evidence should be admitted.

Statistics and law speak different languages. Both, however, have the same goal in mind; to better understand what is likely to have been or to be the truth. It is beyond the scope of this work to 'solve' the problems posed by statistical evidence in the law of evidence. There is no panacea to protect the law from criticism for its reliance on statistical evidence. The law can, however, try to do better. In 1897, Justice Holmes predicted that the '[person] of the future is the [person] of statistics and the master of economics'.[1] That prediction has come to fruition. Statistical evidence is increasing in importance and frequency in legal proceedings. In the absence of a consistent and considered approach to statistical evidence, the largely avoidable criticisms directed to the law will, rightly, continue.

[1] O Holmes, 'The Path of the Law' (1897) 10 *Harvard Law Review* 457, 469.

BIBLIOGRAPHY

Books

Adam, C, *Forensic Evidence in Court* (Hoboken, Wiley-Blackwell, 2016).

Anderson, T, Schum, D and Twining, W, *Analysis of Evidence*, 2nd edn (Cambridge, Cambridge University Press, 2005).

Beaton-Wells, C, *Proof of Antitrust Markets in Australia* (Alexandria, Federation Press, 2003).

Beecher-Monas, E, *Evaluating Scientific Evidence* (Cambridge, Cambridge University Press, 2007).

Blackstone, W, *Commentaries on the Laws of England* (Oxford, Clarendon, 1765–1769).

Cohen, L, *An Introduction to the Philosophy of Induction and Probability* (Oxford, Oxford University Press, 1989).

Cohen, L, *The Implications of Induction* (Yorkshire, Methuen, 1970).

Cohen, L, *The Probable and the Provable* (Oxford, Clarendon Press, 1977).

Cowen, Z and Carter, P, *Essays on the Law of Evidence* (Oxford, Oxford University Press, 1956).

Dennis, I, *The Law of Evidence*, 6th edn (London, Sweet & Maxwell, 2017).

Eggleston, R, *Evidence, Proof and Probability*, 2nd edn (London, Weidenfeld and Nicolson 1983).

Finkelstein, M, *Basic Concepts of Probability and Statistics in the Law* (New York, Springer, 2009).

Freckelton, I, *Expert Evidence*, 7th edn (Sydney, Thomson Reuters, 2023).

Freckelton, I, *Scholarly Misconduct: Law, Regulation, and Practice* (Oxford, Oxford University Press, 2016).

Freckelton I, *The Trial of the Expert* (Oxford, Oxford University Press, 1987).

Freckelton I and others, *Expert Evidence and Criminal Jury Trials* (Oxford, Oxford University Press, 2016).

Gillies, D, *Philosophical Theories of Probability* (Oxford, Routledge, 2000).

Green, S, *Causation in Negligence* (Oxford, Hart, 2015).

Haack, S, *Evidence Matters* (Cambridge, Cambridge University Press, 2014).

Hart, H, *Essays on Bentham: Jurisprudence and Political Philosophy* (Oxford, Oxford University Press, 1982).

Hart, H and Honore, T, *Causation in the Law*, 2nd edn (Oxford, Oxford University Press, 1985).

Heydon, J, *Cross on Evidence*, 11th edn (Chatsworth, LexisNexis, 2017); 14th edn (Chatsworth, LexisNexis, 2023).

Ho, H, *A Philosophy of Evidence Law* (Oxford, Oxford University Press, 2008).

Hodge, M, *Phipson on Evidence*, 20th edn (London, Sweet & Maxwell, 2021).

Howson, C and Urbach, P, *Scientific Reasoning: The Bayesian Approach* (Open Court, 1989).

Keynes, J, *A Treatise of Probability* (1921).

Levanon, L, *Evidence, Respect and Truth: Knowledge and Justice in Legal Trials* (Oxford, Hart, 2022).

Miller, R, *Miller's Australian Competition and Consumer Law*, 45th edn (Sydney, Lawbook, 2023).

Monahan, J and Walker, L, *Social Science in Law*, 9th edn (New York, Foundation Press, 2017).

Moss, S, *Probabilistic Knowledge* (Oxford, Oxford University Press, 2018).

Nance, D, *The Burdens of Proof* (Cambridge, Cambridge University Press, 2016).

Redmayne, M, *Character in the Criminal Trial* (Oxford, Oxford University Press, 2015).

Roberts, P, *Roberts & Zuckerman's Criminal Evidence*, 3rd edn (Oxford, Oxford University Press, 2022).

Robertson, B, Vignaux, G and Berger, C, *Interpreting Evidence* (Hoboken, Wiley, 2016).

Rothman, K, Greenland, S and Lash, T, *Modern Epidemiology*, 3rd edn (Philadelphia, Wolters Kluwer Health, 2013).

Schauer, F, *Profiles, Probabilities and Stereotypes* (Cambridge Mass, Harvard University Press, 2003).
Schum, D, *The Evidential Foundations of Probabilistic Reasoning* (Evanston, Northwestern University Press, 2001).
Starkie, T, *Law of Evidence* (1876).
Steel, S, *Proof of Causation in Tort Law* (Cambridge, Cambridge University Press, 2015).
Stein, A, *Foundations of Evidence Law* (Oxford, Oxford University Press, 2005).
Thayer, J, *A Preliminary Treatise on Evidence at the Common Law* (1898).
Turton, G, *Evidential Uncertainty in Causation in Negligence* (Oxford, Hart 2016).
Vigen, T, *Spurious Correlations* (Sydney, Hachette, 2015).
Walton, D, *Legal Argumentation and Evidence* (Pennsylvania, Penn State University Press, 2002).
Yowell, P, *Constitutional Rights and Constitutional Design: Moral and Empirical Reasoning in Judicial Review* (Oxford, Hart, 2018).

Book Sections

Befurt, R, MacMenamin, N and Mohammad, AP, 'Use of Conjoint Analysis in Litigation' in Gersen, JE and Steckel, JH (eds), *The Cambridge Handbook of Marketing and the Law* (Cambridge, Cambridge University Press, 2023).
Brilmayer, L, 'Second-Order Evidence and Bayesian Logic' in Tillers, P and Green, E (eds), *Probability and Inference in the Law of Evidence: The Uses and Limits of Bayesianism* (New York, Springer, 1988).
Cohen, L, 'The Role of Evidential Weight in Criminal Proof' in Tillers, P and Green, E (eds), *Probability and Inference in the Law of Evidence* (Philadelphia, Kluwer, 1988).
Dahlman, C and Pundik, A, 'The Problem with Naked Statistical Evidence' in Dahlman, C, Stein, A and Tuznet, G (eds), *Philosophical Foundations of Evidence Law* (Oxford, Oxford University Press, 2021).
Derksen, T and Meijsing, M, 'The Fabrication of Facts: The Lure of the Incredible Coincidence' in Kaptein, H, Prakken, H and Verheij, B (eds), *Legal Evidence and Proof: Statistics, Stories, Logic* (Hampshire, Ashgate, 2009).
Edmond, G, 'Re-assessing Reliability' in Roberts, P and Stockdale, M (eds), *Forensic Science Evidence and Expert Witness Testimony* (Cheltenham, Elgar, 2018).
Edmond, G and Mercer, D, 'Rebels Without a Cause?: Judges, Medical and Scientific Evidence and the Uses of Causation' in Freckelton, I and Mendelson, D (eds), *Causation in Law and Medicine* (Routledge 2002).
Galavotti, M, 'The Origins of Probabilistic Epistemology' in Hajek, A and Hitchcock, C (eds), *The Oxford Handbook of Probability and Philosophy* (Oxford, Oxford University Press, 2016).
Gillies, D, 'The Propensity Interpretation' in Hajek, A and Hitchcock, C (eds), *The Oxford Handbook of Probability and Philosophy* (Oxford, Oxford University Press, 2016).
Haack, S, 'Correlation and Causation' in Martin-Casals, M and Papayannis, D (eds), *Uncertain Causation in Tort Law* (Cambridge, Cambridge University Press, 2015).
Hamer, D, '"Tendency Evidence" and "Coincidence Evidence" in the Criminal Trial: What's the Difference?' in Roberts, A and Gans, J (eds), *Critical Perspectives on the Uniform Evidence Law* (Sydney, Federation Press, 2017).
Hersch, J, 'Breast Implants: Regulation, Litigation, and Science' in Viscusi, W (ed), *Regulation Through Litigation* (2002).
Huang, V, Weatherall, K and Webster, E, 'The Use of Survey Evidence in Australian Trade Mark and Passing Off Cases' in Kenyon, A, Richardson, M and Ng-Loy, WL (eds), *The Law of Reputation and Brands in the Asia Pacific* (Cambridge, Cambridge University Press, 2012).
La Caze, A, 'Frequentism' in Hajek, A and Hitchcock, C (eds), *The Oxford Handbook of Probability and Philosophy* (Oxford, Oxford University Press, 2016).
Magnusson, E, 'Statistical Proof of Causation' in Freckelton, I and Mendelson, D (eds), *Causation in Law and Medicine* (Oxford, Routledge, 2002).

Pardo, MS and Allen, RJ, 'Generalizations and Reference Classes' in Dahlman, C, Stein, A and Tuznet, G (eds), *Philosophical Foundations of Evidence Law* (Oxford, Oxford University Press, 2021).
Plante, C and Anderson, C, 'Media Violence, Aggression, and Antisocial Behaviour: Is the Link Causal?' in Sturmey, P (ed), *The Wiley Handbook of Aggression and Violence* (Hoboken, Wiley, 2017).
Puppe, I and Wright, R, 'Causation in the Law: Philosophy, Doctrine and Practice' in Infantino, M and Zervogianni, E (eds), *Causation in European Tort Law* (Cambridge, Cambridge University Press, 2017).
Spottswood, M, 'Paradoxes of Proof' in Dahlman, C, Stein, A and Tuznet, G (eds), *Philosophical Foundations of Evidence Law* (Oxford, Oxford University Press, 2021).
Sprenger, J, 'Bayesianism vs Frequentism in Statistical Inference' in Hajek, A and Hitchcock, C (eds), *The Oxford Handbook of Probability and Philosophy* (Oxford, Oxford University Press, 2016).
Stapleton, J, 'Reflections on Common Sense Causation in Australia' in Degeling, S, Edelman, J and Goudkamp, J (eds), *Torts in Commercial Law* (Thomson Reuters 2011).
Tversky, A and Kahneman, D, 'Causal Schemas in Judgments Under Uncertainty' in Kahneman, D, Slovic, P and Tversky, A (eds), *Judgment under Uncertainty: Heuristics and Biases* (Cambridge, Cambridge University Press, 1982).
Wright, R, 'Proving Causation: Probability versus Belief' in Goldberg R (ed), *Perspectives on Causation* (Hart 2011).
Zabell, S, 'Symmetry Arguments in Probability' in Hajek, A and Hitchcock, C (eds), *The Oxford Handbook of Probability and Philosophy* (Oxford, Oxford University Press, 2016).

Government Documents

AHRC, *An Age of Uncertainty: Inquiry into the Treatment of Individuals Suspected of People Smuggling Offences who Say that They are Children* (2012).
Aitken, C, Roberts, P and Jackson, G, *Fundamentals of Probability and Statistical Evidence in Criminal Proceedings* (Royal Statistical Society 2010).
Australian Law Reform Commission, *The Protection of Human Genetic Information in Australia* (Report 96, 2003).
Australian Law Reform Commission, *Uniform Evidence Law* (Report 102, 2005).
Federal Judicial Center, *Reference Manual on Scientific Evidence* 3rd edn (Washington DC, National Academies Press, 2011).
Inquiry into Convictions of Kathleen Megan Folbigg, Transcript (26 April 2023).
Ipp, D, Cane, P, Sheldon, D and Macintosh, I, *Review of the Law of Negligence: Final Report* (Commonwealth of Australia 2002).
National Research Council, *The Evaluation of Forensic DNA Evidence* (Washington DC, National Academy Press 1996).
US Judicial Conference, *Handbook of Recommended Procedures for the Trial of Protracted Cases: Report of the Judicial Conference Study Group on Procedure in Protracted Litigation* (1960).

Journal Articles

Acorn, A, 'Similar Fact Evidence and the Principle of Inductive Reasoning: Makin Sense' (1991) 11 *OJLS* 63.
Allen, RJ, 'Common Sense, Rationality and the Legal Process' (2001) 22 *Cardozo Law Review* 1417.
Allen, RJ and Pardo, M, 'The Problematic Value of Mathematical Models of Evidence' (2007) 36 *The Journal of Legal Studies* 107.
Allen, RJ and Smiciklas, CK, 'The Law's Aversion to Naked Statistics and Other Mistakes' (2022) 28 *Legal Theory* 179.

Andretta, J and others, 'Applying Statistics to the Gatekeeping of Expert Evidence: Introducing the Structured Statistical Judgment' (2019) 37 *Behavioral Sciences & the Law* 133.

Bagaric, M and Amarasekara, K, 'The Prejudice Against Similar Fact Evidence' (2001) 5 *Journal of Evidence and Proof* 71.

Beecher-Monas, E, 'Lost in Translation: Statistical Inference in Court' (2014) 46 *Arizona State Law Journal* 1057.

Bennett, H and Broe, GA, 'The Civil Standard of Proof and the "Test" in Briginshaw: Is There a Neurobiological Basis to Being "Comfortably Satisfied"?' (2012) 86 *Australian Law Journal* 258.

Bernstein, D, 'Junk Science in the United States and the Commonwealth' (1996) 21 *Yale Journal of International Law* 123.

Bernstein, D, 'The Misbegotten Judicial Resistance to the Daubert Revolution' (2013) 89 *Notre Dame Law Review* 27.

Bradford Hill, A, 'The Environment and Disease: Association or Causation?' (1965) 58 *Proceedings of Royal Society of Medicine* 295.

Brewer, S, 'Scientific Expert Testimony and Intellectual Due Process' (1998) 107 *Yale Law Journal* 1535.

Brilmayer, L and Kornhauser, L, 'Quantitative Methods and Legal Decisions' (1978) 46 *University of Chicago Law Review* 116.

Broadbent, A, 'Epidemiological Evidence in Proof of Specific Causation' (2011) 17 *Law Times Reports* 237.

Choo, A, 'Evidence, (In)efficiency, and Freedom of Proof: A Perspective from England and Wales' (2015) 66 *University Alabama Law Review* 493.

Cohen, L, 'Subjective Probability and the Paradox of the Gatecrasher' [1981] *Arizona State Law Journal* 627.

Colyvan, M, Regan, H and Ferson, S, 'Is it a Crime to Belong to a Reference Class?' (2001) 9 *Journal of Political Philosophy* 168.

Coroneos, C and others, 'US FDA Breast Implant Postapproval Studies' (2019) 269 *Annals of Surgery* 30.

Cossins, A, 'The Legacy of the Makin Case 120 Years on: Legal Fictions, Circular Reasoning and Some Solutions' (2013) 35 *Sydney Law Review* 731.

Dant, M, 'Gambling on the Truth: The Use of Purely Statistical Evidence as a Basis for Civil Liability' (1988) 22 *Columbia Journal of Law & Social Problems* 31.

Davis, D and Follette, W, 'Toward an Empirical Approach to Evidentiary Ruling' (2003) 27 *Law and Human Behaviour* 661.

Dawid, A, 'The Difficulty about Conjunction' (1987) 36 *Statistician* 91.

Dawid, A, 'Probability and Statistics in the Law' (2005) *Proceedings of the Tenth International Workshop on Artificial Intelligence and Statistics* 89.

Dawid, A, Faigman, D and Feinberg, S, 'Fitting Science Into Legal Contexts: Assessing Effects of Causes or Causes of Effects?' (2014) 43 *Sociological Methods Research* 359.

Di Bello, M, 'When Statistical Evidence is not Specific Enough' (2021) 199 *Synthese* 12251.

Donnelly, P and Balding, D, 'The Prosecutor's Fallacy and DNA Evidence' (1994) CrimLR 711.

Dore M, 'A Commentary on the use of Epidemiological Evidence in Demonstrating Cause-in-Fact' (1983) 7 *Harvard Environmental Law Review* 429.

Edelman, J, 'Unnecessary Causation' (2015) 89 *Australian Law Journal* 20.

Edmond, G, 'Against Oracular Pronouncement: A Reply to Heydon' (2015) 36 *Adelaide Law Review* 173.

Edmond, G, 'Icarus and the Evidence Act: Section 137, Probative Value and taking Forensic Science Evidence "at its highest"' (2017) 41 *Adelaide Law Review* 106.

Edmond, G, 'What Lawyers Should Know about the Forensic "Sciences"' (2015) 36 *Adelaide Law Review* 33.

Edmond G and Mercer D, 'Keeping "Junk" History, Philosophy and Sociology of Science out of the Courtroom' (1997) 20 *University of New South Wales Law Journal* 48.

Eggleston, R, 'Similar Facts and Bayes Theorem' (1991) 31 *Jurimetrics* 275.

Elwood, P and others, 'A Randomized Controlled Trial of Acetyl Salicylic Acid in the Secondary Prevention of Mortality from Myocardial Infarction' (1974) 1 *British Medical Journal* 436.
Enoch, D and Fisher, T, 'Sense and "Sensitivity": Epistemic and Instrumental Approaches to Statistical Evidence' (2015) 67 *Stanford Law Review* 557.
Enoch, D and Spectre, L, 'Sensitivity, Safety, and the Law: A Reply to Pardo' (2019) 25 *Legal Theory* 178.
Enoch, D, Spectre, L and Fisher, T, 'Statistical Evidence, Sensitivity, and the Legal Value of Knowledge' (2012) 40 *Philosophy & Public Affairs* 197.
Faigman, D, Monahan, J and Slobogin, C, 'Group to Individual (G2i) Inference in Scientific Expert Testimony' (2014) 81 *University of Chicago Law Review* 417.
Feeney, A, Coley, J and Crisp, A, 'The Relevance Framework for Category-Based Induction: Evidence From Garden-Path Arguments' (2010) 36 *Journal of Experimental Psychology* 906.
Fenton, N and others, 'The Opportunity Prior: A Proof-based Prior for Criminal Cases' (2019) 18 *Law, Probability and Risk* 237.
Fenton, N and Neil, M, 'Avoiding Probabilistic Reasoning Fallacies in Legal Practice using Bayesian Networks' (2011) 36 *Australian Journal Legal Philosophy* 114.
Fenton, N, Neil, M and Berger, D, 'Bayes and the Law' (2016) 3 *Annual Review of Statistics and its Application* 51.
Finkelstein, M and Fairley, W, 'A Bayesian Approach to Identification Evidence' (1970) 83 *Harvard Law Review* 489.
Franklin, J, 'The Objective Bayesian Conceptualisation of Proof and Reference Class Problems' (2011) 33 *Sydney Law Review* 545.
Gageler, S, 'Evidence and Truth' (2017) 13 *The Judicial Review* 249.
Gardiner, G and Zaharatos, B, 'The Safe, the Sensitive, and the Severely Tested: A Unified Account' (2022) 200 *Synthese* 1.
Gill, R, Groeneboom, P and de Jong, P, 'Elementary Statistics on Trial (the case of Lucia de Berk)' (2018) 31 *Chance* 9.
Gold, S, 'Causation in Toxic Torts: Burdens of Proof, Standards of Persuasion, and Statistical Evidence' (1986) 96 *Yale Law Journal* 376.
Goldberg, R, 'Epidemiological Uncertainty, Causation, and Drug Product Liability' (2014) 59 *McGill Law Journal* 777.
Goldman, A, 'Quasi-Objective Bayesianism and Legal Evidence' (2002) 42 *Jurimetrics* 237.
Goode, M, 'Some Observations on Evidence of DNA Frequency' (2002) 23 *Adelaide Law Review* 45.
Green, M and Sanders, J, 'In Defense of Sufficiency' (2014) 23 *Widener Law Journal* 663.
Greiner, D and Matthews, A, 'Randomized Control Trials in the US Legal Profession' (2016) 12 *Annual Review Law and Social Sciences* 295.
Guthrie, C, Rachlinksi, JJ and Wistrich, AJ, 'Inside the Judicial Mind' (2001) 86 *Cornell Law Review* 777.
Haack, S, 'Warrant, Causation, and the Atomisim of Evidence Law' (2008) 5 *Episteme* 253.
Haidich, A, 'Meta-analysis in Medical Research' (2010) 14 *Hippokratia* 29.
Hamer, D, 'The Legal Structure of Propensity Evidence' (2016) 20 *International Journal of Evidence & Proof* 136.
Hamer, D, 'Similar Fact Reasoning in Phillips: Artificial, Disjointed and Pernicious' (2007) 30 *University of New South Wales Law Journal* 609.
Hamer, D, 'Structure and Strength of the Propensity Inference- Singularity, Linkage and the Other Evidence' (2003) 29 *Monash Law Review* 137.
Harris, G and Rice, M, 'Bayes and Base Rates: What Is an Informative Prior for Actuarial Violence Risk Assessment?' (2013) 31 *Behavioural Sciences and the Law* 103.
Heydon, J, 'Evidence of Forensic Scientific Opinion and the Rules for Admissibility' (2015) 36 *Adelaide Law Review* 101.
Heydon, J, 'Is the Weight of Evidence Material to its Admissibility?' (2014) 26 *Current Issues in Criminal Justice* 219.
Ho, H, 'An Introduction to Similar Fact Evidence' (1998) 19 *Singapore Law Review* 166.

Ho, H, 'Similar Facts in Civil Cases' (2006) 26 *OJLS* 131.
Hodgson D, 'A Lawyer looks at Bayes' Theorem' (2002) 76 *Australian Law Journal* 109.
Hodgson, D, 'Probability: the Logic of the Law – a Response' (1995) 15 *OJLS* 51.
Hodgson, D, 'The Scales of Justice: Probability and Proof in Legal Fact-Finding' (1995) 69 *Australian Law Journal* 731.
Hoffmann, L, 'Similar Facts After Boardman' (1975) 91 *LQR* 193.
Holmes, O, 'The Path of the Law' (1897) 10 *Harvard Law Review* 457.
Hooper, L, Cecil, JS and Willging, T, 'Assessing Causation in Breast Implant Litigation: The Role of Science Panels' (2001) 64 *Law and Contemporary Problems* 139.
Jaffe, L, 'Of Probativity and Probability: Statistics, Scientific Evidence, and the Calculus of Chance at Trial' (1985) 46 *University of Pittsburgh Law Review* 925.
James, G, 'Relevancy, Probability and the Law' (1941) 29 *California Law Review* 689.
Johnson King, ZA, 'Sensitivity, safety and admissibility' (2022) 200 *Synthese* 1.
Kaye, D, 'Apples and Oranges: Confidence Coefficients and the Burden of Persuasion' (1987) 73 *Cornell Law Review* 54.
Kaye, D, 'The Laws of Probability and the Law of the Land' (1979) 47 *University of Chicago Law* 34.
Kaye, D and Koehler, J, 'The Misquantification of Probative Value' (2003) 27 *Law and Human Behavior* 645.
Koehler, J, 'The Probity/Policy Distinction in the Statistical Evidence Debate' (1991) 66 *Tulsa Law Review* 141.
Koehler, J, 'The Psychology of Numbers in the Courtroom: How to Make DNA-Match Statistics Seem Impressive or Insufficient' (2001) 74 *South California Law Review* 1275.
Koehler, J, 'When do Courts Think Base Rate Statistics are Relevant' (2002) 42 *Jurimetrics* 373.
Koehler, J and Shaviro, D, 'Veridical Verdicts: Increasing Verdict Accuracy Through the Use of Overtly Probabilistic Evidence and Methods' (1990) 75 *Cornell Law Review* 247.
Kotsglou, KN, 'The Specific Evidence Rule: Reference Classes–Individuals–Personal Autonomy' (2023) 4 *Quaestio facti - International Journal on Evidential Legal Reasoning* 1.
Kumar, M, 'Admissibility of Expert Evidence: Proving the Basis for an Expert's Opinion' (2011) 33 *Sydney Law Review* 427.
Kune, R and Kune, G, 'Proof of Cancer Causation and Expert Evidence: Bringing Science to the Law and the Law to Science' (2003) 11 *Journal of Law and Medicine* 112.
Lempert, R, 'Modeling Relevance' (1977) 75 *Michigan Law Review* 1021.
Lennings N, 'Assessing Significant Probative Value for the Purposes of Admitting Coincidence Evidence: *DSJ v R; NS v R*' (2013) 17 *International Journal of Evidence & Proof* 202.
Levanon, L, 'Statistical Evidence, Assertions and Responsibility' (2019) 82 *MLR* 269.
Ligertwood, A, 'Avoiding Bayes in DNA Cases' (2003) 77 *Australian Law Journal* 317.
Ligertwood, A, 'Can DNA Evidence Alone Convict an Accused?' (2011) 33 *Sydney Law Review* 487.
Ligertwood, A, 'What Lawyers Should and Can do Now that They Know about the Forensic Sciences' (2015) 36 *Adelaide Law Review* 153.
Livingstone, M, 'Have we Fired the "Hired Gun"?' (2008) 18 *Journal of Judicial Administration* 39.
Lyon, T, Ahern, E and Scurich, N, 'Interviewing Children Versus Tossing Coins: Accurately Assessing the Diagnosticity of Children's Disclosures of Abuse' (2012) 21 *Journal of Child Sexual Abuse* 19.
Maxwell, C, 'Preventing Miscarriages of Justice: The Reliability of Forensic Evidence and the Role of the Trial Judge as Gatekeeper' (2019) 93 *Australian Law Journal* 642.
Mazur, D, 'A History of Evidence in Medical Decisions: From the Diagnostic Sign to Bayesian Inference' (2012) 32 *Medical Decision Making* 227.
McIvor, C, 'Debunking some Judicial Myths about Epidemiology and its Relevance to UK Tort Law' (2013) 21 *Medical Law Reports* 553.
McShane, B and others, 'Abandon Statistical Significance' (2019) 73 *The American Statistician* 235.
Meyerson, D, 'Risks, Rights, Statistics and Compulsory Measures' (2009) 31 *Sydney Law Review* 507.
Mirfield, P, 'Bad Character Evidence – Again' (2023) 82 *CLJ* 395.
Mirfield, P, 'Similar Facts – Makin Out?' (1987) 46 *CLJ* 83.

Monahan, J and Walker, L, 'Social Science Research in Law: A New Paradigm' (1988) 43 *American Psychologist* 465.
Moss, S, 'IX – Moral Encroachment' (2018) 123 *Proceedings of the Aristotelian Society* 177.
Munday, R, 'Case Management, Similar Fact Evidence in Civil Cases, and a Divided Law of Evidence' (2006) 10 *International Journal of Evidence & Proof* 81.
Murad, M and others, 'New Evidence Pyramid' (2016) 21 *Evidence Based Medicine* 125.
Nair, R, 'Weighing Similar Fact and Avoiding Prejudice' (1996) 112 *LQR* 262.
Nance, D, 'The Weights of Evidence' (2008) 5 *Episteme* 267.
Nesson, C, 'The Evidence or the Event? On Judicial Proof and the Acceptability of Verdicts' (1985) 98 *Harvard Law Review* 1357.
Odgers, S and Richardson, J, 'Keeping Bad Science Out of the Courtroom' (1995) 18 *University of New South Wales Law Journal* 108.
Oosthuizen, J and Cross, M, 'Establishing Cause, What Does That Mean from an Epidemiological and Legal Perspective' (2018) 35 *Environmental and Planning Law Journal* 426.
Palmer, A, 'The Scope of the Similar Fact Rule' (1994) 16 *Adelaide Law Review* 161.
Pardo, M, 'The Nature and Purpose of Evidence Theory' (2013) 66 *Vanderbilt Law Review* 547.
Pardo, M, 'Safety vs Sensitivity: Possible Worlds and the Law' (2018) 24 *Legal Theory* 50.
Pardo, M and Allen, R, 'Juridical Proof and the Best Explanation' (2008) 27 *Law & Philosophy* 223.
Pattenden, R, 'Expert Opinion Evidence based on Hearsay' (1982) *Criminal Law Review* 85.
Pattenden, R, 'Similar Fact Evidence and Proof of Identity' (1996) 112 *LQR* 446.
Picinali, F, 'Generalisations, Causal Relationships and Moral Responsibility' (2016) 20 *International Journal of Evidence & Proof* 121.
Popper, K, 'The Propensity Interpretation of Probability' (1959) 10 *British Journal for the Philosophy of Science* 25.
Posner, R, 'An Economic Approach to the Law of Evidence' (1999) 51 *Stanford Law Review* 1477.
Pundik, A, 'Against Racial Profiling' (2017) 67 *University of Toronto Law Journal* 175.
Pundik, A, 'Epistemology and the Law of Evidence: Four Doubts about Alex Stein's Foundations of Evidence Law' (2006) 25 *Civil Justice Quarterly* 504.
Pundik, A, 'The Epistemology of Statistical Evidence' (2011) 15 *International Journal of Evidence & Proof* 117.
Pundik, A, 'Freedom and Generalisation' (2016) 37 *OJLS* 189.
Pundik, A, 'Statistical Evidence and Individual Litigants: a Reconsideration of Wasserman's Arguments from Autonomy' (2008) 12 *International Journal of Evidence & Proof* 303.
Redmayne, M, 'Exploring the Proof Paradoxes' (2008) 14 *Legal Theory* 281.
Redmayne, M, 'Recognising Propensity' (2011) 3 *Criminal Law Review* 177.
Redmayne, M, 'The Relevance of Bad Character' (2002) 61 *CLJ* 684.
Redmayne, M, 'Standards of Proof in Civil Litigation' (1999) 62 *MLR* 167.
Roberts, P, 'Theorising Evidence Law' (2023) 43 *OJLS* 629.
Robertson, B and Vignaux, G, 'Inferring Beyond Reasonable Doubt' (1991) 11 *OJLS* 431.
Robertson, B and Vignaux, G, 'Probability – The Logic of the Law' (1993) 13 *OJLS* 457.
Robertson, B, Vignaux, G and Berger, C, 'Extending the Confusion About Bayes' (2011) 74 *MLR* 444.
Schmalbeck, R, 'The Trouble with Statistical Evidence' (1986) 49 *Law and Contemporary Problems* 221.
Shaviro, D, 'Statistical-Probability Evidence and the Appearance of Justice' (1989) 103 *Harvard Law Review* 530.
Smith, H, 'Components of Proof in Legal Proceedings' (1942) 51 *Yale Law Journal* 537.
Stapleton, J, 'Choosing what we mean by Causation in the Law' (2008) 73 *Missouri Law Review* 433.
Steele, K and Colyvan, M, 'Meta-uncertainty and the Proof Paradoxes' (2023) 180 *Philosophical Studies* 1927.
Stein, A, 'The New Doctrinalism: Implications for Evidence Theory' (2015) 163 *University of Pennsylvania Law Review* 2085.
Stone, J, 'The Rule of Exclusion of Similar Fact Evidence: England' (1932) 46 *Harvard Law Review* 954.
Stow, F, 'Evidence of Similar Facts' (1922) 38 *LQR* 63.

Thomson, J, 'Liability and Individualised Evidence' (1986) 49 *Law and Contemporary Problems* 199.

Tillers, P, 'If Wishes were Horses: Discursive Comments on Attempts to Prevent Individuals from being Unfairly Burdened by their Reference Classes' (2005) 4 *Law, Probability and Risk* 33.

Tillers, P, 'Introduction: Three Contributions to Three Important Problems in Evidence Scholarship' (1997) 18 *Cardozo Law Review* 1875.

Tribe, L, 'Trial by Mathematics: Precision and Ritual in the Legal Process' (1971) 84 *Harvard Law Review* 1329.

Twining, W, 'The Boston Symposium: A comment' (1986) *Boston University Law Review* 391.

Twining, W, 'Narrative and Generalization: Argumentation about Questions of Fact' (1999) 40 *South Texas Law Review* 351.

Verheij, B, 'To Catch a Thief With and Without Numbers: Arguments, Scenarios and Probabilities in Evidential Reasoning' (2014) 13 *Law, Probability and Risk* 307.

Ward, T, 'Explaining and trusting expert evidence: What is a "sufficiently reliable scientific basis"?' (2020) 24 *International Journal of Evidence & Proof* 233.

Wasserman, D, 'The Morality of Statistical Proof and the Risk of Mistaken Liability' (1991) 13 *Cardozo Law Review* 935.

Wells, G, 'Naked Statistical Evidence of Liability: Is Subjective Probability Enough?' (1992) 62 *Journal of Personality and Social Psychology* 739.

Williams, C, 'Burdens and Standards in Civil Litigation' (2003) 25 *Sydney Law Review* 165.

Wright, R, 'Causation in Tort Law' (1985) 73 *California Law Review* 1735.

Wright, R, 'Causation, Responsibility, Risk, Probability, Naked Statistics, and Proof: Pruning the Bramble Bush by Clarifying the Concepts' (1988) 73 *Iowa Law Review* 1001.

Zuckerman, A, 'Similar Fact Evidence – The Unobservable Rule' (1987) 103 *LQR* 187.

INDEX

www.ingramcontent.com/pod-product-compliance
Ingram Content Group UK Ltd.
Pitfield, Milton Keynes, MK11 3LW, UK
UKHW020801290926
15470UKWH00003B/880

9 781509 957330